CAPITALISM: SHOULD YOU BUY IT?

CAPITALISM: SHOULD YOU BUY IT?

An Invitation to Political Economy

CHARLES DERBER

AND

YALE R. MAGRASS

Paradigm Publishers

Boulder • London

Copyright © 2014 Paradigm Publishers

Published in the United States by Paradigm Publishers, 5589 Arapahoe Avenue, Boulder, CO 80303 USA.

Paradigm Publishers is the trade name of Birkenkamp & Company, LLC, Dean Birkenkamp, President and Publisher.

Library of Congress Cataloging-in-Publication Data

Derber, Charles.
  Capitalism : should you buy it? an invitation to political economy / Charles Derber and Yale Magrass.
    pages cm
  Includes bibliographical references and index.
  ISBN 978-1-61205-689-0 (pbk. : alk. paper)
  ISBN 978-1-61205-674-6 (consumer e-book)
  1. Capitalism. 2. Economics. I. Magrass, Yale R. II. Title.
  HB501.D428 2013
  330.12'2--dc23

                                                                        2013031115

Printed and bound in the United States of America on acid-free paper that meets the standards of the American National Standard for Permanence of Paper for Printed Library Materials.

18 17 16 15 14 1 2 3 4 5

Contents

PART I

Why Political Economy?

Introduction to Part I

In Part I, we introduce and define *political economy* and discuss why we feel it is so important. Great thinkers such as Adam Smith, Max Weber, and Karl Marx introduced political economy to understand the rise of capitalism, which led to one of the greatest transformations in history. Because of capitalism, life has arguably changed in the past two hundred years more than in all of the rest of human history. The early political economists created the way of thinking that would allow modern scholars and citizens to understand this revolutionary system and deal with its enormous implications, including whether it must be embraced, reformed, or overthrown.

But since the early 1900s, political economy, as a discipline, has been subjected to great intellectual and political struggles, eroding its centrality and vitality. Power elites within capitalism as well as pressures within academic social sciences both contributed to this decline. The erosion of political economy deprives intellectuals and citizens today of the main tradition for understanding the modern capitalist world, just in its period of greatest crisis.

In our view, there is hardly a more important intellectual agenda than renewing an understanding of political economy, for without it, citizens lose the tools for coping with the great challenges humanity faces today.

Our aim in Part I is threefold:

1. to define political economy as a framework for thinking, distinguish it from economics, and explain why we view it as crucial
2. to examine the forces that have weakened the appeal of political economy and its approach, using brief case studies from the fields of economics and other social sciences
3. to set forth our own view of the sociological imagination as a tradition for renewing political economy not only in sociology but in all social sciences and in the politics of modern societies

CHAPTER 1

Economics Lost

Why We Need Political Economy

Money makes the world go around,
Of that we can be sure.[1]

Before there was economics, there was political economy. Today, there are two separate disciplines: economics and political science. In most universities, they are housed in different academic departments. The implication is that they represent two distinct realms and operate independently of each other.

In our view, the separation of economics from political science has crippled both fields and represents an assault on political economy itself. It is a key part of the story of what political economy is, why it is important, and how it can thrive in the modern world.

Economics is a crucially important field, but only as an integral part of the broader enterprise that we call political economy (PE). Even before economists segregated themselves from political scientists and sociologists, thereby pulling away from political economy, economics became known as "the dismal science," a phrase coined by historian Thomas Carlyle in the mid-nineteenth century. In its current form, economics is even more dismal—which has put its usefulness to society in some jeopardy.

By separating from politics and other social sciences, economics has become detached from the real world. It has become a world of equations on blackboards, beautiful but floating in a heavenly sphere of its own creation. Our economics students, who learn equations and abstract market theories, tell us they learn from their economics classes little about what is going on in the real world, including the real economy. Perhaps the greatest economist of the twentieth century, John Maynard Keynes, said much the same thing and would be sympathetic to their critique: "Too large a proportion of recent 'mathematical' economics are mere concoctions, as imprecise as the initial assumptions they rest on, which allow the author to lose sight of the complexities and interdependencies of the real world in a maze of pretentious and unhelpful symbols."[2]

Economics, as it evolved in the twentieth century and became more focused on form than substance, claimed to be an objective, value-free science. In order to hold the mantle of science, it tried to reduce all of economics to a series of equations and formulas. For the most part, it imitated an antiquated model of physics, before relativity and quantum mechanics became the dominant paradigms. As Larry Summers, former treasury secretary and Harvard president, put it, calling for the public to have faith in economists' expertise, "Start with the idea that you can't repeal the laws of economics. Even if they are inconvenient,"[3] but Nobel Prize–winning economist Paul Samuelson responded, "Economics has never been a science."[4]

In our view, embracing the discipline of political economy, by rejecting the separation of economics from politics and society, that is, from the real world, rescues us from the pathologies of an artificially segregated economics, that is, from farce, false science, and detachment from the world. Understanding political economy offers the possibility of understanding the real economy. And it can contribute something useful to solving the deep socioeconomic and environmental crises now engulfing the United States and much of the world.

The economy does what it does because of the decisions people make, usually people with—or aspiring to—political power. It can only be understood if we look at who has power. Indeed, most economic policy is a result of "class struggle," the balance of forces between people with power and those whom they rule or who are trying to challenge them. *Economics* became a popular term when powerful people in corporations, government, and universities wanted to create the impression that the economy is something that follows laws not subject to politics, laws that rest in nature, almost like the laws of physics. The great political economist, John Kenneth Galbraith, argued his own economics profession was making itself irrelevant with this approach:

> The decisive weakness in neoclassical and neo-Keynesian economics is not the error in the assumptions by which it elides the problem of power. The capacity for erroneous belief is very great, especially where it coincides with convenience. Rather, in eliding power—in making economics a nonpolitical subject—neoclassical theory destroys its relation to the real world. In that world, power is decisive in what happens. And the problems of that world are increasing both in number and in the depth of their social affliction. In consequence, neoclassical and neo-Keynesian economics is relegating its players to the social sidelines where they either call no plays or use the wrong ones.[5]

Galbraith made clear that we must ask if the capitalist economy—the principal focus of the political economy approach—is really rooted in nature or if it was something created at a particular moment in history. He is making the argument for reintegrating economics into political economy, raising the key questions about capitalism central to both inquiries. Is the capitalist economy grounded in something universal, valid everywhere, or a reflection of a specific culture and set of values that advances the interests of one class of people at the expense of everyone else? Is it something that people automatically gravitate to, whenever they are allowed, or is it something that some people impose on others? How does the type of economy a society has affect its style of government and its cultural values? And vice versa?

Economics treats economies—and specifically the capitalist economy that it focuses on today—as an abstract force with a life of its own and universal laws, independent of the people who created it and their society. The study of political economy moves away from this flawed premise and asks how capitalism came into being and whom it serves.

Economics often regards politics, culture, the environment, and the larger society as "externalities," which can be abstracted out of the picture. But is it really possible to understand the economy without looking at those other factors? Do they not all profoundly affect each other? And if the economy and the rules of the economic game are created by people, who are these people and why do they create the rules they do? In the absence of economics taking up these questions, it is often our great novelists who step into the void, such as Kurt Vonnegut:

> Thus did a handful of rapacious citizens come to control all that was worth controlling in America. Thus was the savage and stupid and entirely inappropriate and unnecessary and humorless American class system created. Honest, industrious, peaceful citizens were classed as bloodsuckers, if they asked to be paid a living wage. And they saw that praise was reserved henceforth for those who devised means of getting paid enormously for committing crimes against which no laws had been passed. Thus the American dream turned belly up, turned green, bobbed to the scummy surface of cupidity unlimited, filled with gas, went bang in the noonday sun.[6]

Vonnegut's cry would not be heard alongside the blackboard economics in our universities' Departments of Economics. It appears subjective and outside the economists' scientific domain. But political economy takes up Vonnegut's concern and makes it a central object of study, as we show throughout this book.

Economists who have abandoned the political economy approach, though, claim that as objective experts, it is their duty to analyze, not prescribe or moralize. It secures their academic position as scientists but it leaves to political economy the urgent questions we need to ask about the economy. We need to ask if it is always good to increase wealth for the sake of increasing wealth. Is it not also important how that wealth is distributed? Does it make some people richer and more powerful, while hurting everyone else? How are wealth, growth, value, and price to be defined and measured? Should our criteria not include these: Who benefits and who does not? How do they deplete or build resources? Do they preserve or erode the environment? Do they enhance or undermine democracy and the quality of life? Do they bring people together or drive them apart? An economics segregated from political science, sociology, history, and ethics cannot answer these questions, leaving a huge void that political economy seeks to fill.

What Is Political Economy?

Political economy was the term most people studying the economy—including such famous nineteenth-century theorists as Adam Smith, David Ricardo, John Stuart Mill, Karl Marx, and Max Weber—used before economics assumed its modern quasi-scientific form. It also was a popular phrase in the 1960s, 1970s, and perhaps 1980s. It was adopted by people who came to wonder if economic, political, and military policies could be separated. It also asked if the governments of so-called democracies, like the United States, are really intended to serve the very rich, the 1 percent, instead of the rest of us, the 99 percent. Clearly, those issues have not gone away, so we offer this book as an invitation to revive and join the political economy tradition.

Defining *political economy* is not easy, and many still view it as another name for economics before it matured and became scientific. The *American Heritage Dictionary* defines political economy as "the early science of economics through the 19th century."[7] Likewise, the *Collins English Dictionary* defines political economy as "the name given formerly to economics."[8]

In other words, "economics" has replaced "political economy." And in a sense it did. In Adam Smith's University of Glasgow, when Smith taught there, the Department of Political Economy's name was changed to the Department of Economics, a very early shift. It is misleading because Smith was a moral philosopher, historian, sociologist, political scientist, and economist—a political economist in the best sense of the term. In 1848, John Stuart Mill wrote the *Principles of Political Economy*, showing, despite some economistic assumptions about markets, that you cannot segregate economics from politics or society and hope to understand the real world.[9]

But by the late nineteenth century, when capitalism entrenched itself as the West's idealized economy, economics, led by the influential British economist Alfred Marshall and his followers, began its assault to replace political economy as the science of wealth management. Universities began funding professional economists, who would treat economics as a science and capitalism as operating by natural laws. In 1890, Marshall wrote the textbook *Principles of Economics*, creating a mathematical science of economics, segregating the whole field from politics and society.[10] Around the same time, William Stanley Jevons, one of the early mathematical economists, argued that *economics* should become "the recognized name of a science."[11] This declaration that economics was bound by unchangeable scientific laws would remove academic authority from the potentially subversive ideas that Marx, Weber, and other political economists of the day posed to capitalism and to the identity of economists as scientists. Economics was tacitly kicking political economy out the door, relegating it to the prescientific and precapitalist era.

But political economy, while subordinated, never disappeared, even among economists themselves, including many luminaries such as Galbraith and Nobel Prize–winning economist and *New York Times* columnist, Paul Krugman, who could not embrace the pure "economism" of their own profession. And even the early Robber Barons of the 1890s Gilded Age, who helped found modern universities and were the big beneficiaries of the new economics, recognized that it was absurd to separate politics and economics. One of the most influential Robber Baron capitalists, Mark Hanna, when asked what was important in politics, responded, "The first is money and I can't remember what the second one is."[12]

Political economy was first taught in the United States in the College of William and Mary, with Smith's *Wealth of Nations* as the main textbook in 1784. Despite the hegemony of economics, students can still find some universities with Departments or Programs of Political Economy. Some of the core questions of political economy have been taken up by economists who rejected the limiting definitions of their professions. Other key issues have been exported and sent piecemeal to other segregated disciplines, including especially sociology and political science.

To move forward, we need to define the field of inquiry, and in doing so we return to the assumptions that guided its original great and highly diverse political thinkers, including both Adam Smith and Karl Marx. Political economy is not wedded to a particular political ideology, and can be Right, Left, or anywhere in between. But it recognizes there can be no stripping of the study of the economy from the study of politics and society.

In contrast to economics, the study of political economy is based on the following premises. We present these assumptions to highlight the differences between economics and political economy—and to point to the way that sociologists or political scientists or even some renegade economists might contribute to a counter-assault against the hegemony of economics. As in economics, there are serious debates within political economy but we see five core premises. Not everyone engaged in political economy agrees on each of these five premises. For each of these assumptions, there will be a range of positions, with some people agreeing more with the political economy paradigm, as defined here, and others embracing more "economics-ized" or economistic thinking.

The Political Economy Code

1. Human nature is not seen as fixed or biologically uniform in all societies, as it is viewed in economics, but shaped by society, culture, and the political and economic system itself. If there are innate properties within human nature, they are different and more malleable than many economists assume.
2. The market is not seen as a part of nature or created by natural law, as seen in economics, but as a creation of people, particularly those exercising power in the economy and in the political arena.
3. Rather than being self-regulating according to natural laws, as defined by economics, social and political intervention is necessary for the economic system to work properly.
4. The "naturalization" of people and the economy—the economics view that personal behavior and economic laws are determined by nature—is rejected, replaced by the view that individual and institutional conduct are largely determined by political power and social values.
5. The economy, or any other social institution, cannot be studied in an objective value-free way. Rather, the way people study the economy and the policy recommendations they make inherently reflect their values and vision of what constitutes the good society.

Economics treats the economy, particularly the capitalist economy, as an insular and perfect machine—a *deus ex machina*—abstracted from and independent of the rest of society while political economy sees the economy as intertwined with and both shaped and shaping the larger political and social order. Political economy essentially views the economy as a part of and shaped by society and its power arrangements, a commonsense view that has been largely obliterated by economics itself.

Having made these arguments, we need to highlight again that political economy traditions do not fully agree on these points, and that even within particular political economy traditions, there are significant disagreements. Each political economy tradition today has large sectors that are heavily economistic, that is, while they recognize that political and moral values impact their philosophy, they treat their analysis of market laws as equivalent to the laws of physics and independent of the social context. Thus, all political economy traditions are flawed deeply today, a reason we argue for the need for a new political economy school, one that recognizes the embeddedness of the economy in society. Such a new approach to political economy should be spearheaded academically by social scientists, as discussed in Chapter 2, and politically by engaged citizens seeking to better the world and save society itself.

The struggle among the paradigms and between economics and political economy is one of the great issues of twenty-first-century intellectual and political life. In this book, we align ourselves with both the historical and contemporary proponents of political economy, hoping to revive the theoretical ideas and public debates that were silenced by economics but are at the heart of a robust political economy and the prospects of social survival. We view the hegemony of economics as a serious challenge to intellectual life and social change, with the renewal of political economy as vital to social theory and social justice, and essential to the future existence of society itself.

Adopting the perspective of political economy gives us a tool to challenge the claims of scientific expertise made by economic planners, who mask their value judgments, as well the economic and political interests they represent, as objective truths that are beyond question. There is a risk that if the current economic, political, social, and cultural arrangements persist, supporting the class who now rules, inequality will continue to fester, the quality of life for most people will continue to degenerate, discontent will brew, wars will become likely, resources will become depleted, and the environment may face a catastrophe from which it—and society—will never recover. Novelist Alice Walker has put the risks of our current capitalist society very simply: "Well, capitalism is a big problem, because with capitalism you're just going to keep buying and selling things until there's nothing else to buy and sell, which means gobbling up the planet."[13]

Indeed, the renewal of political economy may be crucial to solving the great existential threats created by capitalism now facing humanity, determining the question of whether any civilized society can survive: climate change, wars of mass destruction, and the collapse of a precarious global economy generating mass poverty and inequality. The rise of economics is not just an academic dispute; it represents the assertion of a hegemonic mode of thinking that is intended to both legitimate the current capitalist order and discredit social forces seeking to overturn that order. This book situates political economy within struggles crucial to the university but, even more important, crucial to the titanic battles shaping the political and economic system and the very prospects of survival of any civil society.

The rise of existential threats to society makes this book, for us, something far more than simply an academic exercise. The hegemony of economics—and its legitimation of capitalism as we know it in the United States—excludes the most important question that intellectuals must raise today: whether US capitalism is fundamentally sociopathic, giving rise to a "sociopathic society" that is fundamentally self-destructive and gives rise to "sociocide"—or the extinction of civil society itself.[14] This is, in the twenty-first century, by far the most important intellectual and moral issue—and it is one that economics does not recognize and cannot analyze. Political economy, though, is the natural intellectual home, along with reconstructed, interdisciplinary Departments of Sociology, Political Science, and Economics, for addressing the question of capitalist sociopathy and the end of society.

CHAPTER 2

Social Sciences Found?

Political Economy and the Sociological Imagination

This chapter has a hero. His name is C. Wright Mills. He was a lanky, plain-spoken Texan who became one of the great twentieth-century sociologists. He had a swashbuckling personality. He rode a motorcycle. He developed ideas so controversial for his time that his own Department of Sociology at Columbia University prevented him from teaching undergraduates. In 2009, *Columbia University Magazine* said of Mills, "Much like John Kennedy,... Mills's reputation benefited from an early exit."[1] (They both died in their mid-forties.) Why is he our hero here? You'll have to read this chapter to find out. But here's a hint. It was Mills who crafted a way of thinking—the "sociological imagination"—that we think can guide the way toward a twenty-first-century political economy.

As economists abandon political economy (PE), sociologists, or more accurately anyone with the sociological imagination, can help save it: political scientists, historians, policy makers, activists, artists, journalists, and natural scientists.

As we explain what the sociological imagination is and why we see it as essential to reviving political economy, we don't want to imply it is the exclusive property of sociologists. Some sociologists have it; some don't. The best sociologists have it, but so do the best economists, political scientists, and anthropologists. The sociological imagination is a way of thinking about society that should inform all social sciences. And political economy requires the integration of the now separate fields of sociology, politics, and economics.

In this chapter, we use sociology as our example, but we believe that both the sociological imagination and political economy are and must be inter-disciplinary. The argument here is not just an argument for a certain kind of sociology. It is a view that all the social sciences—economics, political science, anthropology, sociology, and others—must be reconstructed through an interdisciplinary, critical, and holistic imagination to help create the political economy we need.

One note to our readers. In this chapter, we dig into some history and theory that may seem sometimes abstract. But we must do this both to show how political economy developed and to introduce those who have tried to subvert or destroy it. We dwell as part of this history on Mills, to show how we think political economy can survive and thrive through his idea of the sociological imagination. Only then can we move to the very personal and politically explosive issues that are the flesh and blood of political economy and that you will find in the rest of the book.

Political Economy and Sociology

Political economy and sociology were born married to each other, and both reflected the sociological imagination, although that term was not used until much later. Their mutual purpose—also the mission of the sociological imagination—was to understand and morally assess how capitalism emerged and changed the world.

As political economy and sociology were born, the rising capitalist order was turning the world upside down. Influential thinkers, such as political economy founder Adam Smith and sociology founder Emile Durkheim, largely supported the new capitalist system. Karl Marx, a founder of both fields, passionately denounced it. Founding sociologist Max Weber took a more dispassionate and ambiguous view. But they all shared the view that capitalism—its historical, economic, political, and moral elements—defined their field of study, however they might name it.

In Chapter 1, we showed that academic economists have turned to the blackboard, where they create elegant mathematical models, which have little to do with the real world of capitalism. They explain neither the economy nor the larger society—and have divorced economics from political economy. These are economists abandoning the sociological imagination, which calls for all social sciences, including economics, to apply an interdisciplinary and critical framework for understanding capitalism. Fortunately, there are other economists, whom we quote extensively in this book, who use the sociological imagination and reject blackboard economics.

In this chapter, we show that a long and related struggle for the soul of sociology is under way. On one side are those hungry for a continuing "marriage" between sociology and political economy, inspired by the sociological imagination and focused on the analysis of capitalism. On the other side are "blackboard sociologists," the sociological "divorcers," who argue that sociology must separate and focus on narrower social themes that are scientific, value-free specialties. They claim that sociologists cannot claim expertise on the economy or politics, nor should they practice a value-oriented critique of capitalism. The divorcers are sociologists but have abandoned the sociological imagination and the practice of political economy. We believe in the marriage.

Here is what political economists study, or at least should study: *work, money, wealth, inequality, ownership, individualism, community, stratification, class, race, gender, power, globalization, freedom, democracy, war, social justice*—all in a capitalist world.

How can sociology abandon such economic and political issues, which have long been central to its mission? It can't—without giving up the passions and ideas that led to the founding of the discipline in the first place. But it is a process that has been building, sadly, for many decades.

In 1971, the great sociologist Alvin Gouldner, in his *The Coming Crisis of Western Sociology*, analyzed a sociological unraveling that was destroying the heart of the field.[2] Gouldner saw the breakdown of sociology into professionalized and insular subspecialties, each claiming expertise in its own narrow area. The study of macroeconomics and politics was being left behind—creating a divorce between sociology and political economy. And with this divorce, Gouldner saw a tragic loss of sociology's critical edge as it mimicked the methods and value-free stance of "objective" science and embraced a "functionalism"—reigning supreme from the 1940s to the early 1960s in the United States—that legitimated the existing society.[3]

He aligned himself with C. Wright Mills. A decade earlier, Mills wrote *The Sociological Imagination*. Mills's book was about a crisis in sociology that was driving sociologists away from the grand concerns of political economy and sociology's original liberating promise.[4] If Mills were an economist, he would have written a similar book about economics, and if he were a political scientist, he would have written a comparable book in that field.

Even more than Gouldner, Mills was horrified by the changes in sociology that, in the name of science and academic respectability, were narrowing and, in his view, destroying sociology and the study of our political economy. He wrote *The Sociological Imagination* to preserve the marriage and fight the divorcers—and we shall argue that it is a call for all social science disciplines to integrate economics, politics, sociology, and cultural studies in the critical analysis of capitalism and capitalist society. It is a call for a revival of political economy.

The Marriage

The story of the marriage (the impulse to create political economy) must be told before looking at the impetus to divorce (the drive to destroy political economy). It is a story about why political economy is so controversial and crucial for society and why it matters to our lives.

Two of the great founders of sociology were Karl Marx and Max Weber, both German political economists. Marx, who wrote *Capital*, and Weber, who wrote *Economy and Society*, both believed that the economic system could only be understood historically as part of the development of society and politics.[5] Neither Marx nor Weber separated sociology from political economy (nor from political science or history or anthropology). Their central concern was looking at the economy and political and cultural systems within the historical context of society itself. While they did not share the same view of capitalism and had different values, they both saw sociology as centrally defined by the imperative to understand the capitalist system.

For both of them, sociology *was* political economy. We might add they also believed the same of political science and economics. From their point of view, students today wouldn't major in one of these fields; an educated student and citizen would have to concentrate on all of them folded into the real major: political economy.

Neither Marx nor Weber could contemplate serious sociological work that separated the economy from society and broke the original promise of political economy. In Chapter 2 of *Economy and Society*, his manifesto for sociology, Weber argued that economic behavior was a type of social or sociological behavior, specifically, social action and exchange dealing with the production of "utilities"—advantages or profits.[6] In his book, *General Economic History*, as well as *Economy and Society*, Weber developed a general theory of capitalism, which a leading sociological theorist, Randall Collins, describes as one of the great sociological theories of capitalism—and arguably the best example of the political economy of the capitalist system ever written:

> Weber's model continues to offer a more sophisticated basis for a theory of capitalism than any of the rival theories of today. I put forward this formalization of Weber's mature theory not merely as an appreciation of one of the classic works of the past, but to make clear the high-water mark of sociological theory about capitalism. Weber's last theory is not the last word on the subject of the rise of capitalism, but if we are to surpass it, is the high point from which we ought to build.[7]

Collins makes clear that, for Weber, sociology is so inherently intertwined with the study of the history, economy, and politics of capitalism—that is, with political economy—that the divorcers would undermine Weber's entire conception of the field that he helped invent.

Marx saw economies as based on "social relations" of production, and social relations were defined by the control and power of different groups over economic resources, which necessarily integrates themes of political power into any analysis of the economy and society. He suggested that domination of the economy leads to domination of almost all other aspects of society, particularly culture and the state. Within capitalism, virtually all institutions are created to preserve the wealth and power of the property-owning class. In one of his most famous paragraphs, Marx sears into the brain the connections among three things: the capitalist economy, issues of social relations and class power, and the zeitgeist of the entire society:

> The bourgeoisie [the capitalist class] cannot exist without constantly revolutionizing the instruments of production, and thereby the relations of production, and with them the whole relations of society.... Constant revolutionizing of production, uninterrupted disturbance of all social conditions.... All fixed, fast-frozen relations, with their train of ancient and venerable prejudices and opinions are swept away.... All that is solid melts into air, all that is holy is profaned, and man is at last compelled to face with sober senses his real conditions of life and his relations with his kind.[8]

Even more than Weber, Marx devoted his entire career to the analysis of capitalism: it was the central focus of both the sociology and the political economy that he was helping create, and both fields fused or "married"—along with economics and political science—to analyze the capitalist system. The most important founders of sociology thus would have been thunderstruck at the idea of creating a specialized technical discipline of sociology separate from political economy or from the analysis of capitalism. Nor did they intend that these two modes of inquiry would focus on different basic questions. The primary concern was to understand the connection of society and economy and politics, whether one called it sociology or political economy (or economics or political science). Marx saw himself as a political revolutionary and had no interests in worrying about the "property" of academic disciplines. Weber was more concerned with academic domains and embraced value-neutral social science, a concept Marx dismissed. Their mutual hallmark, though, was looking through a critical lens wide enough to encompass the history, present, and future of the capitalist system itself.

Marx and Weber had very different values, but the work of both provides a mandate for sociologists to be historical and center their efforts on the relation of economy, politics, and the larger culture. Both viewed capitalism as a central concern, which could only be studied from the broadest possible context.

The Sociological Imagination

With Weber's and Marx's inspiration, a "political economy sociology"—that is, a call to revive political economy—was advocated in the mid-twentieth-century United States by C. Wright Mills. When Mills began his work, positivist thinking was becoming dominant in American sociology, narrowing it and turning it into data-driven "science," one that largely accepted American capitalism and society as it was and turned its attention to academic subspecialties lacking the vision and even the vocabulary to conceptualize or assess the larger political economy. Mills spent his career fighting these "divorcer" forces, reinventing the marriage of sociology and political economy with his vision of "The Sociological Imagination." Mills's book of that title helped kindle a new critical sociology and political economy in the 1960s and 1970s. Mills described his vision—an authentic vision of both sociology and political economy:

> For that imagination is the capacity to shift from one perspective to another—from the political to the psychological; from examination of a single family to comparative assessment of the national budgets of the world; from the theological school to the military establishment; from considerations of an oil industry to studies of contemporary poetry. It is the capacity to range from the most impersonal and remote transformations to the most intimate features of the human self—and to see the relations between the two.[9]

Mills can be very succinct about his big idea: "The sociological imagination enables us to grasp history and biography and the relations between the two within society. That is its task and its promise."[10]

When Mills decried the lack of the "sociological imagination," he was making a case to restore political economy and end its divorce from sociology. He was making the same basic argument against the divorcers in economics, political science, and other academic social sciences. Mills did not have much patience with the modern university's departmental divisions of economics, politics, and sociology, for he thought they all focused on different aspects of the overall social structure. That structure was itself an intersection of macrosociety and personal biography, an idea at the heart of political economy. He argued it was crucial to realize "personal troubles" are often "public issues," that the problems people face in everyday life are often reflections of historical developments in corporations, government, and the military, a consequence of living in a society orchestrated in the service of a "power elite" whose existence was central to society but had been rendered invisible.

The real world was not as it seemed. Mills exploded on the scene in the 1950s by challenging the triumphalism of an all-powerful and self-satisfied America in the post–World War II era. America had won the war, produced half the world's wealth, and embodied democracy, or so the public in their new suburban homes and white-collar office towers thought. And sociologists of the era (as well as the economists and political scientists) did not much question those assumptions.

Mills argued it was sociology's responsibility—indeed the responsibility of all social scientists and all citizens—to embody reason and illuminate truth, in this case speak truth to power, a pithy way of describing political economy. The truth was that America was not a democracy but a hierarchical system of "organized irresponsibility." A "power elite" had taken over, that was "in command of the major hierarchies and organization of modern society. They rule the big corporations. They run the machinery of the state and claim its prerogatives. They direct the military establishment.... They occupy the strategic command posts of the social structure, in which are now centered the effective means of the power and the wealth and the celebrity which they enjoy."[11]

Mills argued that the men in the power elite, those of "the higher circles," were not "representative men; their high position is not a result of moral virtue; their fabulous success is not firmly connected with meritorious ability.... They are not men held in responsible check by a plurality of voluntary associations which connect debating publics with the pinnacles of decisions."[12] In other words, the leaders did not emerge from a democratic process but have been "selected and formed" by the "means of power and the sources of wealth."

The result is not pretty, especially for a country reveling in triumphalism: "America appears now before the world a naked and arbitrary power, as, in the name of realism, its men of decision enforce their often crackpot definitions upon world reality.... Commanders of power unequaled in human history, they have succeeded within the American system of organized irresponsibility."[13]

This had the feeling of "it just can't be true" in the 1950s, in an America reveling in exceptionalism. It was heresy. But this was just Mills's point: that it was sociology's role—and that of other social sciences committed to a meaningful intellectual life—to strip away the veil and show the emperor when he had no clothes. But sociology, like economics and political science, was going the other direction.

Mills saw the social sciences, especially sociology, becoming dominated by "grand theory" and "abstract empiricism," essentially forms of pseudoscience or positivist science creating a blackboard sociology parallel to blackboard economics, telling us little about the real world. The "grand theorists," like Harvard professor Talcott Parsons and Mills's colleague at Columbia Robert Merton, spoke at a level so general that it was almost meaningless and gained authority through barely understandable esoteric jargon. Mills suggested if they used simpler language, people would recognize how commonsensical or even trivial was much of what they said, and they would lose their veneer of expertise. The grand theorists did not reveal the power elite or the system of "organized irresponsibility"; they obscured it and made it invisible. Abstract empiricists, for their part, do not conceptualize problems based on their intrinsic interest or their relevance for shedding light on a broader picture, such as the power elite. Rather for the sake of establishing their scientific credentials, they seek to "operationalize" reality, reduce it to a series of measurable phenomena, which may not have any meaning. If a problem cannot be quantified—such as Mills's concept of "organized irresponsibility"—they will dismiss it from consideration.

Mills is a pivotal figure since his critique of social science laid the groundwork to return the discipline to its original value-oriented critical study of capitalism.

We have formulated a "code" that describes simply the main premises of *The Sociological Imagination*:

The Sociological Imagination Code

1. Personal troubles are often reflections of public issues. The problems people face in everyday life can be caused by social forces beyond their immediate control.
2. Biography and history intersect. People's lives are shaped by the time, place, and culture in which they live. To understand your own life, you must understand the society in which you live.
3. Listen to Marx: "Men [and women] make history, but not of circumstances of their own choosing." We are not simply products of society; we are also its creators.
4. To create the society we want to live in, we must act with others, who are often victims of the same force, and share our interests, values, and concerns. As Gandhi said, "Be the change you want to see."
5. The main force standing in the way of most people gaining control of their lives is the "power elite"—corporate capitalist elites, military chiefs, and their political handmaidens—who, if no one stops them, will orchestrate society in their own interests, at the expense of everyone else.

6. In particular, the power elite runs corporations and the state, including the military, to serve them, but they try to create the illusion that these institutions benefit everyone.
7. Without the "sociological imagination" people are likely to see the society created by the power elite as the "best of all possible worlds"—something fixed, given, and unchangeable, which serves everyone, the 99 percent as well as the 1 percent.
8. Without the sociological imagination, social scientists are likely to become professional technocratic agents of the power elite.
9. Inaction is action, leaving society as it is to persist and the problems it creates to fester. There is no such thing as a neutral, value-free stance. You must choose one side or the other. As historian Howard Zinn said, "You can't be neutral on a moving train."

The sociological imagination—as boiled down in this code—is the sociological face of political economy. It is equally applicable to economics, political science, and other social sciences—each of which needs the same imagination within an interdisciplinary enterprise of political economy—to do useful intellectual work. Sociologists and all social scientists need to unite to practice a sociological imagination and political economy with Mills's core principles: the need to be a critical thinker; the impossibility of being value-free; the urge to challenge the power elite; the imperative of uniting historical, economic, political, and sociological thinking; the necessity of thinking systemically; the linking of macro and micro; the sociopathic and self-destructive nature of the existing capitalist order; the need for intellectuals to ally with the disenfranchised everywhere to create a better world.

The reductionist, compliant, positivist tendencies Mills was challenging in *The Sociological Imagination* were not unique to sociology. They can be found in economics, political science, history, and psychology. With his *Sociological Imagination*, Mills was making an argument for remarrying sociology and all the other social sciences with political economy, precisely as Marx and Weber had done at the founding.

Mills helped inspire a new generation of political economy sociologists in the 1960s and beyond. In the 1960s, a whole new generation was hungry for the critical, even revolutionary way of thinking that Mills's political economy had inspired. When the 1960s died down, the social sciences began to go back to the 1950s divorce model, as we show below. But advocates of "the marriage" persist, even to the present day. The roster of "PE sociologists" in the late twentieth and early twenty-first centuries spans almost every field of social science, the humanities, and even the natural sciences and reflects some of the luminaries of the contemporary intellectual community, as well as many everyday practitioners.

The sociological imagination—and political economy sociology as conceived here—is brilliantly manifested in the work of an eccentric interdisciplinary mix of sociologists, economists, political scientists, historians, journalists, novelists, and activists. It is not simply the property or creation of another academic department in the university. It is inherently interdisciplinary, breaking the boundaries enshrined in the current academic structure.

Is there a special role for sociology? Perhaps. Among all the academic disciplines, sociologists are most familiar with the idea of the sociological imagination. Because of Marx and Mills, sociology has a foundation in interdisciplinary work as well as a critical mode of value-driven inquiry. The divorcers in the field are trying to narrow it and turn it into "scientific" specialties, but those believing in the marriage have a strong basis for helping lead the struggle within the university and society for a new interdisciplinary model of intellectual inquiry and for a twenty-first-century political economy.

Today, the dominant social sciences may lie not with those living and teaching the marriage but those who have long sought a divorce. There is a story here too that must be told, crucial to this book, for the divorcers are leading an intellectual assault on the very existence of the field of political economy. The divorcers have gained enormous power because they have helped to protect the capitalist system itself as well as the interests of academic professionals seeking to establish their own secure careers in the name of science. If the divorcers succeed, political economy will fade and disappear.

The Divorce

It began early in the nineteenth century with the great philosophers and sociologists Auguste Comte and Herbert Spencer. Comte gave grand importance to sociology. Sociology, he proclaimed, was "the Queen of the sciences."

But Comte, perhaps the great father of the divorcers, rejected entirely a value-oriented critical sociological approach and substituted his view of science. He advocated a "positivist" academic and scientific discipline—no different from physics or the new mathematical economics. It should be defined by objectivity, value-neutrality, empirical rigor, and scientific respectability. It did not aim to challenge capitalism or society but rather to explain the functions of the existing order.[14]

Emile Durkheim, often considered with Marx and Weber to be the third great founder of sociology, was bit by the bug of positivist philosophy. Durkheim was a great interdisciplinary intellectual, a systemic thinker about the division of labor and the great issues of community, culture, and religion. But, influenced by the positivistic methodologies advanced by Comte coming to the fore of the universities in his era, Durkheim worked to create a more technical, empirical, and scientific model of sociology that established social laws akin to those envisioned by nineteenth-century physics—and that helped legitimate capitalism itself. Durkheim wrote, "Our main goal is to extend scientific rationalism to human conduct. . . . What has been called our positivism is but a consequence of this rationalism."[15]

Durkheim wanted to establish a separate scientific realm for sociology, which would distinguish it from all other disciplines. He invented "functionalism" and treated society as an organism, which exists outside, indeed above, the individuals who comprise it. The well-being of the individual was secondary to the preservation of existing society and the need for social order. Thus despite its claim to objectivity, Durkheimian thinking clearly allies with ruling elites. Although Durkheim saw himself primarily as a sociologist, he also helped found clinical psychology, social work, and criminology, which see their task as helping clients "adjust" to a society that they cannot challenge. Functionalism functions as a tool for managing the 99 percent in the service of the 1 percent. Durkheim saw himself as founding a profession of technical experts, who make policy recommendations based on objective science. They would end up setting the agenda for managing society for the alleged benefit of everyone, but the real beneficiaries would be the power elite.

Durkheim and his followers wanted to create "scientific social sciences," modeled after a nineteenth-century image of physics, which postulates an objective world that exists independently of the observer. Physics abandoned this view of the world when it adopted relativity and quantum mechanics. Nonetheless, this objective claim allowed these social scientists to adopt the mantle of "experts" who discover universal truths. Anyone who challenged the alleged knowledge that they produced in the service of the state and the elite could be dismissed as biased, ignorant laypeople, in need of guidance from professional authorities. They treated capitalism as grounded in the laws of science and not subject to questioning.

Following Durkheim, many schools of modern sociology, especially in the American academy, tended to break the indivisible tie between analysis of society from the study of history, politics, and economics. Many dominant academic schools of sociology in the United States—exemplified by the structural-functional paradigm advanced in the mid-twentieth century by leading sociologists such as Talcott Parsons and Kingsley Davis—narrowed it to an ahistorical and positivist discipline, and they became the focus of Mills's blazing attack, as already described. But within several more decades, the divorcers were, to a large degree, back in command, abandoning the authentic sociology embedded in political economy.

This has been the story not only in sociology but in economics, political science, and other social sciences. Wrapped in the mantle of science and professionalism, the divorcers have staked out a strong position in the university and society. The question is whether the marriers throughout the social sciences can unite and wage a successful revolution in the twenty-first century.

Who Wins? Marriers versus Divorcers in Capitalist Society

What determines the outcome of the contest between marriers and divorcers? The fate of political economy, indeed the larger society, perhaps the biosphere, rests on the answer.

The divorcers have been emerging ascendant for pretty clear reasons. To use a phrase made famous by the great PE thinker, John Kenneth Galbraith, the marriers operate to question and examine power at all levels, satisfying this dictum, central to political economy: "In all life one should comfort the afflicted, but verily, also, one should afflict the comfortable, and especially when they are comfortably, contentedly, even happily wrong."[16] This threatens the powerful. But the divorcers have an approach that leads to the opposite mandate: *Comfort the comfortable and afflict the afflicted.*

The divorcers in sociology and all social sciences have long been ascendant because they do not zealously change the powers that be; instead they tend to legitimate them. They thus have strong backing and funding from the powerful: the economic and political elites of the country as well as the professional elites in the university.

The rising capitalist system itself had a fundamental interest in eliminating the holistic social analysis that was capable of envisaging capitalism as a system and subjecting it to rational analysis and critique. Marx—and the movements that took his ideas seriously—represented the symbol of how destructive that might prove to the capitalist system.

Capitalist elites are centrally concerned with ideology, ideas, and beliefs, particularly about capitalism itself. They have thus always been deeply involved in shaping the "intellectual apparatus," and particularly the university. John D. Rockefeller founded the University of Chicago, which would become the greatest contemporary intellectual bastion of capitalist economics as well as one of the centers of functionalist sociology. These Chicago-led approaches in all social sciences treated capitalism as grounded in the laws of science.

These scientific divorcers, especially in sociology but also in economics, political science, and all social sciences, came back from the threat posed by Mills in the 1960s with heavy ammunition, fortified by the rise of the Right under Ronald Reagan, both as governor of California, when he brutally attacked California's public universities, and, later, as president. Reagan and his supporters vigorously assaulted academics who were focused on the analysis and critique of capitalism, picturing them as unpatriotic. Conservatives essentially considered them to be traitors after 9/11. These conservative ideologues have relentlessly attacked education, the university, especially the liberal arts, above all the social sciences, for undermining patriotism, questioning fundamental American values and ideology, not conducting research in the service of the state and dominant corporations, not preparing students to accept their place within those institutions, and infecting students with independence, creativity, and critical thinking.

They fear that the sociological imagination might inspire another generation who sang, around the time C. Wright Mills wrote, of their unwillingness to accept the power elite's authority.

> Oh I am just a student, sir, and only want to learn
> But it's hard to read through the risin' smoke of the books that
> you like to burn
> So I'd like to make a promise and I'd like to make a vow
> That when I've got something to say, sir, I'm gonna say it now.[17]

As governor of California at the time of the student protests, Reagan proclaimed, "If it's to be a bloodbath, let it be now. Appeasement is not the answer."[18]

These Reaganesque attacks had real implications for job security and funding of professors—and the research budgets of whole disciplines. After the Reagan revolution, beginning nationally in the early 1980s, schools, universities, and leaders of academic disciplines decided that in order to survive they had to become more bureaucratized and produce education and scholarship that were acceptable to the powerful and the political and intellectual specialists in service to the powerful. Mills had already seen premonitions of this trend in the 1950s, another conservative era, and made it a central focus in the sociological imagination. To feel good about what they were doing, many academics embraced what Mills called "the bureaucratized ethos"—shaped by the power elite—in the name of becoming more "professional." Many social scientists came to believe their survival depended upon serving agencies of social control, rather than challenging those authorities' evolving purpose, subordinating all of society to the interests of the corporation and the state.

Within the social sciences, legitimacy, funding reputation, and career often depend on establishing a specialized niche. This leads to seeing society not as an integrated system, but rather as a series of separate institutions and spheres, another point much emphasized by Mills in *The Sociological Imagination*.[19] The question—how do the demands of a ruling capitalist class affect government, culture, individual psychology, law, and the quality of life—seldom gets asked. Indeed, the capitalist class has a strong interest in producing technicians who will develop techniques for managing each institution in the service of the corporate elite and state bureaucrats. They certainly do not want to develop a perspective that suggests the root cause of many, if not most, problems is the capitalist system itself. There is a tendency for capitalism to become an unseen background, almost like air, whose existence and impact are unquestioned and ignored.

As the university became institutes for professional experts in service of elite power, they tended to shun "public intellectuals," people who raise new provocative ideas, which stimulate debate among a wide community, including students and lay people. This began in the late nineteenth century with the assault on political economy and has intensified over the twentieth and early twenty-first century. At some universities, people who focus too much on teaching or whose writings are too "popular" are often denied tenure or even expelled from graduate school. In social science graduate schools, students are encouraged to use esoteric technical jargon, use passive voice, and avoid the word "I." If they write in passive voice, they give the appearance that the paper, indeed the facts, write themselves, that any two objective scholars would write the same paper. Convoluted sentence structure can be preferred to clear writing. They need to learn this style because it is what the research journals usually accept. This gives an air of authority, of "expertise," special objective knowledge that ordinary people cannot question.

Marx and Weber were certainly public intellectuals. You can hear them groan at the rise of academically insular and positivist disciplines—separating sociology, economics, and political science from each other, to say nothing of the humanities—and moving away from a laser focus on the capitalist system. The morally charged intersection of economy and society—and of politics and history too—was at the heart of their work.

Despite all their successes, the divorcers have not fully carried the day in sociology—or in economics or political science. As discussed earlier, the critical founding visions of Marx and Weber, the fact that the economy and political system are inherent parts of the larger society, the inspiration provided by Mills in defining the sociological imagination, the critical sociologists and other social scientists of the 1960s and 1970s, and the current generation of interdisciplinary and value-driven scholars—whether in sociology, cultural studies, economics, or political science—have left open the possibility that the marriage not only of sociology and PE, but of a critical holistic interdisciplinary social science with political economy can emerge and thrive.

In this book, we are calling for a revival of political economy that is also a call for a renewal of the sociological imagination. The disciplines of political economy and sociology, along with history, economics, and political science need to find common ground and marry, in the sense of collectively offering a new critical focus on a capitalist order that is becoming ever more unsustainable and unjust.

Part II

The Three Paradigms

Introduction to Part II

In this part, we examine the three dominant schools, or paradigms, within political economy: neoclassicism, Keynesianism, and neo-Marxism. All of them are also paradigms within economics, but we shall analyze them as broad social philosophies and moral codes that translate into policies, which profoundly affect the lives of most people. The paradigms tend to hold fundamentally different values and make different assumptions about how the world actually operates, as well as approach burning social issues with different policies. Within each school of political economy, however, there are also substantial disagreements among the followers, and we shall highlight these divisions among contemporary proponents of each paradigm. Within each of the three political economy paradigms, fierce battles rage between believers seeking to "economics-ize" the tradition and other proponents who try to maintain the more holistic perspective—emphasizing that economics falsely seeks to define a model of the economy that functions independently of society, culture, and politics. We argue that the main distinction between economics and political economy (PE)—whether practiced by academic economists or other thinkers and advocates—is that political economy does not try to study the economy by removing it from other social forces.

Why do certain paradigms develop and gain power in certain historical eras? This is a second great issue we take up in this part, by looking closely at the history of each political economy school, showing how much these paradigms are tied to political developments. We argue that a paradigm's popularity and power are typically a reflection of who controls the state. University departments widely adopted Keynesianism beginning with Franklin Roosevelt's New Deal when the Great Depression generated skepticism that the capitalist economy could thrive without government intervention. It continued to dominate after World War II and through the Great Society until the 1970s. Neo-Marxism was never a mainstream paradigm in the United States. However, in the late Keynesian period, largely in reaction to the Vietnam War, it was treated seriously and admitted into academic and policy discussion in many US universities. Neoclassicism had a resurgence with the inauguration of Ronald Reagan, who was committed to undoing the New Deal. From the 1980s on, Keynesians found themselves on the periphery of departments they had once dominated and neo-Marxists found themselves dismissed, expunged, and beyond the pale. We show that power begets knowledge and knowledge legitimates power.

CHAPTER 3

The Neoclassical Paradigm

On October 23, 2008, Alan Greenspan, the head of the Federal Reserve Bank, was testifying to Congress about the Wall Street meltdown. It was high drama. After being hammered by Representative Henry Waxman, a Democrat from California, for failing to regulate derivatives and to protect the public against toxic bundled mortgage loans, Greenspan finally confessed that "those of us who have looked to the self-interest of lending institutions to protect shareholder's equity—myself especially—are in a state of shocked disbelief."[1] Greenspan, the high priest of the neoclassical paradigm, was apparently questioning his disbelief in regulation and his own "free market" faith. He confessed, "I have found a flaw. I don't know how significant or permanent it is. But I have been very distressed by that fact."[2]

Waxman responded, "In other words, you found that your view of the world, your ideology, was not right, it was not working."[3] Greenspan responded memorably, "Absolutely, precisely.... You know, that's precisely the reason I was shocked, because I have been going for 40 years or more with very considerable evidence that it was working exceptionally well."[4]

Greenspan's questioning of his basic faith in his free market philosophy was a bombshell. It was something like the pope raising questions in the divinity of Jesus.

This ricocheted throughout the culture. *Time* magazine called Greenspan one of the twenty-five people most responsible for the Wall Street meltdown. Public opinion polls suggested a loss of credibility in "free market" economists such as Greenspan and, more important, a crumbling faith in Wall Street and the stock markets.[5]

The public was right to begin to doubt the faith. The neoclassical paradigm, symbolized by Greenspan—an icon in both the worlds of neoclassical economists and high finance—had become the reigning economic religion of America since at least the election of President Ronald Reagan. To challenge the neoclassical paradigm—even though most Americans might not recognize the term—was almost like challenging America itself.

This was not always the case. When the markets crashed in 1929, the free market religion expressed by the neoclassical paradigm also crashed. The nation elected a new president, Franklin Delano Roosevelt, who turned to the Keynesian paradigm to create his New Deal, essentially abandoning neoclassicism and changing the national economic religion, leading big business to call him "a traitor to his class." Following the election of Roosevelt in 1932, the Keynesian paradigm dominated for almost half a century, until the 1970s, when the US economy began to run into headwinds of competition from Germany and Japan. When the United States got buried in the "stagflation" crises of the late 1970s and early 1980s, with interest rates exceeding 20 percent in a stagnant economy, neoclassicism made a full-scale comeback, ushered in with great rhetorical fanfare by President Reagan's election in 1980.[6] Reagan repeatedly attacked government and thus New Deal Keynesian thinking:

Government is not the solution to our problem; government is the problem.

Governments tend not to solve problems, only rearrange them.

The most terrifying words in the English language are I'm from the government and I'm here to help.

The current tax code is a daily mugging.

I consider all proposals for government action with an open mind before I say "no."[7]

Reagan used traditional antigovernment rhetoric to help replace a Keynesian America with a neoclassical one. Neoclassicism remained the ruling religion from Reagan until the 2008 Great Recession and then reasserted itself in just a few short years. It has proved the most durable economic worldview in America. In fact, we can trace the neoclassical paradigm all the way back to Adam Smith, who wrote his famous founding tract, *The Wealth of Nations*, in 1776, the year Americans asserted their new national creed.[8] And we can understand much of US history as the worldview of leading economic thinkers and captains of industry who embraced the neoclassical faith. The story of America, from the perspective of political economy, is, to a large degree, the story of the neoclassical paradigm itself.

We shall return to the long and fascinating history of neoclassicism but first we need to understand its basic principles. For most Americans, it can be stated simply as the doctrine of "free market" economics and of American capitalism. In truth, neoclassicism offers more the rhetoric than the reality of America. But it is certainly the case that the neoclassical paradigm treats the market as sacred, the foundation of the US economy and the guarantor of prosperity and freedom everywhere.

The neoclassical paradigm can be summarized as a fifteen-point "code" that outlines its basic philosophical, economic, and moral principles. The neoclassical code reflects a social worldview, heavily shaped by politics and the interests of the most powerful elites in the United States. However, it presents itself not as a manifesto for any class or group, but rather as a set of principles that reflect natural law and can be embraced profitably by all rational societies. Those principles are set forth here.

The Neoclassical Code

1. Human nature is inherently selfish but rational.
2. Rational individuals weigh pleasure against pain and benefit against cost. They try to maximize pleasure and benefit or personal utility, while minimizing pain and cost.
3. The rational pursuit of self-interest is institutionalized in the market. A market is a voluntary exchange among rational individuals seeking to maximize their own utility, pleasure, and benefits.
4. Capitalism, a system of private property and free markets, makes freedom possible. The core of liberty is the right to acquire property and rise to your maximum potential through participation in the market.
5. The market is the most efficient way of organizing economic behavior. It leads to optimal equilibriums, understood as stable outcomes in which supply meets demand at the lowest cost and with the least waste.
6. Competition disperses power and ensures that markets are free rather than coercive; nobody can control—there is no power structure—in a properly organized market.
7. The market allows individuals to compete with each other and operates through an "invisible hand." Left to its own, it will select deserving winners, who, through their selfishness—or self-interested behavior—will create the greatest possible wealth to the benefit of society as a whole.
8. The laws of the market are as ingrained in nature as the laws of physics. Interfering with them will make things worse.
9. The market knows best. It is wiser than government economic planners or anyone else who did not prove themselves by succeeding in business.

10. When the market operates without interference, people deserve their fate. The poor and other losers are lazy or incompetent. Trying to help them through welfare or government social services can make their situations worse.

11. The market goes through natural cycles of growth and contraction. It is self-correcting and will grow on its own in the long run. Intervening—through government regulation, subsidies, or taxation—will make things worse.

12. Government is coercive while the market is voluntary. This is why free societies minimize government and maximize markets.

13. All wealth and jobs come from private businesses. The government cannot create wealth.

14. Taxes and big government simply transfer wealth from the productive to the unproductive. Money in the hands of private business will "trickle down" and produce jobs and prosperity for everyone.

15. Government has a small number of legitimate functions, including defending the safety of the population and the institutions of private property and contracts that make the market possible. Using the government to influence the quantity of money in circulation may be legitimate. Any other government intervention leads to tyranny.

The essence of the neoclassical paradigm is to equate "free markets" with freedom and define "free market exchange" as rational and in the social interest. It makes it impossible to separate free markets from freedom. This is a powerful linguistic appeal, and it has mass resonance in the US population. Politically, it has been the intellectual creed of modern economic conservatism embraced in different forms by the Republican Party, the Tea Party, and many leading academic economists, notably those identifying with the University of Chicago School, where many of its most famous proponents, such as Milton Friedman, taught.[9] And Friedman seared the equation of the "free market" with freedom into his millions of readers: "The only way that has ever been discovered to have a lot of people cooperate together voluntarily is through the free market. And that's why it's so essential to preserving individual freedom."[10] Friedman also wrote, "Underlying most arguments against the free market is a lack of belief in freedom itself."[11]

Part of the neoclassical appeal is the simple beauty of its imagery of the market. The market is efficient, rational, and the golden goose delivering prosperity. Best of all, it is self-perpetuating, self-governing, and self-correcting. It is the perfect machine that humankind has dreamed of but never quite achieved until Adam Smith affirmed its reality in his portrayal of the rising Western capitalist system.[12]

Who runs this perfect machine? Well, that is part of the beauty. According to the theory, nobody is in charge. As *New York Times* journalist, Tom Friedman, has put it to those who want to call and yell at those in charge of global markets, "Well, guess what ... there's no one on the other end of the phone! I know that's hard to accept. It's like telling people there's no God. We all want to believe that someone is in charge and responsible."[13]

The neoclassical doctrine is clear. No individual or small group has the power to direct the markets, which respond only to the free choices of millions of consumers, producers, investors, and workers.[14]

In fact, the charm of the image is that the market largely eliminates power, leaving only free individuals to exercise true self-government. There is no possibility, advocates of the neoclassical paradigm say, of power concentration in a properly functioning market economy. There is no dictator or tyrannical government in the competitive free market system that neoclassicists propose. If you believe in freedom and democracy—in self-regulation—the free market is for you.[15]

The neoclassical paradigm demonstrates this through mathematical equations. The supply and demand curves that college students learn in Economics 101 show that the supply will ultimately adjust to meet demand (and vice versa) such that, in the end, there will be no waste. The correct price—the point where supply and demand meet—ensures that producers will make just the number of goods demanded by consumers, a marvel of rationality dictated by no government or individual but by the beautiful internal logic of the market itself.[16]

The equilibrium idealized by neoclassical theories—where markets take us in every sector and for every product—is a golden mean in several senses. It maximizes the utility of all the players: producers and consumers, investors and workers. It also reduces costs, waste, and surplus, producing the most goods at the lowest price. Moreover, it does so by assuming only that each individual pursue his or her own self-interest to maximize personal utility or pleasure. There is no utopianism here, only the realist assumption that individuals will act to benefit themselves. As Adam Smith put it, "It is not from the benevolence of the butcher, the brewer, or the baker that we expect our dinner, but from their regard to their self-interest. We address ourselves, not to their humanity, but to their self-love."[17]

Showing that the pursuit of individual self-interest is, paradoxically, the golden route to achieving the best outcome for society is the trump card of the neoclassical paradigm—and the touchstone of modern conservatism and the Republican Party. Adam Smith famously called this "the invisible hand" of the market. Each individual thinks only of himself or herself, but in pursuing that self-interested dream unwittingly helps to maximize the benefit of all. As Adam Smith framed the idea, the individual who "intends his own gain" is "led by an invisible hand to promote an end which was no part of his original intention. Nor is it always the worse for the society that it was no part of it. By pursuing his own interest he frequently promotes that of the society more effectually than when he really intends to promote it. I have never known much good done by those who affected to trade for the public good."[18]

As Milton Friedman put it, "Adam Smith's flash of genius was his recognition that the prices that emerged from voluntary transactions between buyers and sellers—for short, in a free market—could coordinate the activity of millions of people, each seeking his own interest, in such a way as to make everyone better off."[19]

By putting such a magnificent principle into practice—and demonstrating through mathematical certainty that the invisible hand will maximize both individual and societal interests—the neoclassical paradigm puts forth an extraordinarily seductive case. All other economic systems postulate some tension between individual self-interest and social well-being. The free market system of the neoclassicists frees us from that tension, allowing us to pursue our dreams and, however selfish they may be, assuring us that the ultimate outcome will be best for society.

Yet another argument—that of the market's capacity for virtually perfect self-correction—adds to the allure of neoclassical thinking and the market itself. Neoclassicists acknowledge that there are ups and downs—business cycles—in the market economy. That is obvious. The less obvious point is that the properly structured free market—free from government intrusion or interference beyond monetary policy, discussed below—always finds a way to solve cyclical downturns on its own. Downturns are temporary, reflecting inevitable short-term disruptions in information or transparency that the market itself will correct. In severe cases such as the Great Depression, though, as Milton Friedman acknowledged, it is sometimes necessary to use the government to expand the supply of money, to prevent liquidity and credit crises, although many of today's conservative or antigovernment neoclassicists disagree with Friedman on this. But even Friedman, who seems "liberal" or relatively more supportive of limited government than many contemporary neoclassicists, believed that central banks often misuse their authority, exacerbating crises and decreasing money supplies in ways that can cause far more harm than good, as Friedman argued was the case in the early 1930s.[20] Under most circumstances, there is no need to bring in the government, particularly to increase spending through fiscal rather than monetary policy. Government interference will help create the very crisis that markets are designed to avoid.[21] Most often, as in the Great Depression, neoclassicists, such as Friedman, blame government for creating and prolonging a crisis, which markets alone will not cause: "The Great Depression, like most other periods of severe unemployment, was produced by government mismanagement rather than by any inherent instability of the private economy."[22] This is to say that there can be no true long-term crisis in the market economy, when organized correctly and left to its own devices. Other theories postulate inevitable deep recessions, depressions, or even collapse, without intervention by government or other forces. The neoclassicists, as Alan Greenspan showed perfectly, have a simple response to Keynesians or neo-Marxists who devote so much time to analyzing crises: Nonsense, don't waste your time. Crises, so much the source of anguish in other schools of thought, are really just like common colds, not toxic flu cases. Like the common cold, the cyclical downturn—that brings uncomfortable aches and sneezing—will disappear on its own if the patient acts rationally and doesn't call in doctors who are unnecessary and will probably do more harm than good.

Again, the image is beautiful, approximating the very real attraction of holistic medicine. The body has its own defenses and anti-immune devices to fight off disease and protect the patient. Give those natural biological defenses a chance, and they will fight off most disease. So, too, even those economic disruptions that seem frightening will resolve themselves through the economic auto-immune mechanisms of the market, if we resist the temptation to apply strong but toxic medicine, such as major government stimulus programs or other forms of government fiscal intervention and regulation, an argument advanced today forcefully by "small government" Republicans seeking to cut government spending to the bone and eliminate stimulus programs.[23] This became the mantra of Mitt Romney in his 2012 race against President Obama: small government is the medicine for rekindling individual responsibility and "getting our economy back": "We believe in individual initiative, personal responsibility, opportunity, freedom, small government, the Constitution. These principles, these American principles are key to getting our economy back to being successful and leading the world."[24]

The argument for self-correction is similar to the adjustment of supply and demand already discussed. If, for example, temporary disruptions lead to significant unemployment, a reduced demand for labor, then the market will solve this by one of a few simple forms of "auto-immunity." Supply (in this case, of workers) will always create its own demand. If workers really want to work, the price of labor will fall until it is low enough that it becomes attractive for companies to hire again. Workers will reenter the labor force at these low wages, and if they are productive, their wages will rise as goods they produce become attractive to consumers, who will demand more. If workers refuse to enter at low wages, it means they really don't want to work, choosing perhaps, a holiday. Then, fewer workers reflect the free and true choice of the worker, not any failure in the market to offer the supply of jobs demanded. University of Chicago neoclassical economist Casey Mulligan made this argument explicitly: "Employees face financial incentives that encourage them not to work.... Decreased employment is explained more by reduction in the supply of labor (the willingness of people to work) and less by the demand for work (the number of people employers need to hire)."[25]

If government intervenes to force wages up or to create jobs, it is distorting the natural outcomes of the market. Rather than correcting a crisis, it will intensify it, interfering with the natural adjustment of the supply of jobs with the demand for them. It is precisely this sort of government interference that helped create the protracted crisis of the Great Depression and the long-term high unemployment rates during the Obama years. Neoclassicists say that both FDR and Obama turned the common economic cold into the Great Economic Flu, by intervening with government stimulus, regulation, and subsidies preventing self-recovery by the market. Republicans made this argument about Democratic support of the Fannie Mae and Freddie Mac loan programs to encourage housing ownership among the poor—as well as critiquing Obama for extending the Great Recession by spending on stimulus and jobs. The role of the neoclassical paradigm is to guide presidents and other policy makers to avoid giving their patient—the economy—the poison pills administered by FDR, Obama, and other possibly well-meaning but misinformed liberals. The road to economic hell is paved with the good intentions of liberal government.[26] Milton Friedman wrote, "Concentrated Power (i.e., government) is not rendered innocuous by the good intentions of those who create it."[27] Friedman then explicitly indicted the Keynesians who, as we see in the next chapter, viewed government—and the New Deal approach—as the solution to most of our economic and social problems: "Keynes was wrong on just about everything, and his followers are wrong on absolutely everything."[28] And Friedman, as noted above, argued that government intervention usually caused or worsened the problems it intended to fix: "If you put the Federal government in charge of the Sahara Desert, in five years there'd be a shortage of sand."[29]

This all helps explain the neoclassical emphasis—both at home and globally—on shrinking government, privatizing resources, and spreading the market far and wide. Because the market is almost perfect, it should be extended into every sector of life. Gary Becker, the University of Chicago Nobel economist, argued that all social institutions, including the family, operate according to the laws of neoclassical markets and are subject to market analysis and principles, leading to the image that the family itself is less a haven from the heartless world than a mini-model of a free market capitalist system.[30]

While this may seem extreme, neoclassicists have been successful in arguing for privatizing areas such as education, health care, prisons, and even military services. This has opened the door to corporate hospitals and for-profit universities, profitable privately owned prisons and military corporations performing combat as well as other military services.[31] As we show later, it also has provided the rationale for corporate globalization. Through global institutions such as the World Trade Organization, the neoclassical paradigm has been used as the rationale to force governments around the world to sell off their public banks, media, and other government-owned enterprises to global corporations and private owners, a transformation of unparalleled magnitude.[32]

The most dramatic and important shift at home and abroad in this respect is in the attitude toward natural resources and the environment. Neoclassicists, while recognizing a minimal need for regulation to protect the planet from toxic poisons, view the market as the best instrument for determining the use of environmental resources—including land, water, and air—just as with all other resources. Neoclassicists thus argue for privatizing nature and for allowing the environment itself to be an integral part of the market system, with water, land, and even air up for sale and private ownership. This has enormous implications for how people meet basic social needs and for environmental sustainability and has helped create the crisis of climate change that we discuss later.[33]

The neoclassical paradigm has helped manufacture the contemporary debate about the role of government in the US economy, the dominating philosophical and policy issue in US politics. Republicans make their stand around small government and private markets, using the deficit issue to attack public spending and investment. The debate is actually highly distorted, since neoclassical Republicans are champions of huge military spending and vast corporate welfare, breaking with their own arguments of small government when the profits of the biggest corporate players are at stake.[34] Nonetheless, the neoclassical paradigm has provided the most potent weapon for modern conservatives and the Republican Party to attack the residues of the New Deal and the government stimulus and regulatory initiatives of President Obama, which are relatively modest. Even Democrats in the Obama and Clinton presidencies hewed to free market rhetoric, with Obama saying, "Contrary to the claims of some of my critics and some of the editorial pages, I am an ardent believer in the free market."[35]

In this respect, the neoclassical paradigm has triumphed in both parties since Reagan's election in 1980, an internal "regime change" that ended the New Deal and created a new neoclassical corporate regime.[36]

Nonetheless, we should not overstate or caricature the neoclassical argument with the hyperbole of lobbyists such as super-lobbyist and anti-tax activist, Grover Norquist, famous for saying that "I don't want to abolish government. I simply want to shrink it to the size where I can drag it to the bathroom and drown it in the bathtub."[37]

Leading neoclassical thinkers such as Milton Friedman are very clear that government has a minimal but essential set of functions. The first is protection of the country, so that the economy can function without being destroyed from outside.[38] Neoclassicists thus often support vast military spending, a crucial form of government intervention but one that can be viewed by neoclassicists as entirely consistent with their "small government" philosophy.

Just as important, Friedman and most other neoclassicists realize that markets cannot function without legal contracts and social norms that governments create. The voluntary exchange that markets represent can only take place with enforceable contracts, established in the law and defended through the judicial system. The primary function of law, in fact, is to construct the necessary infrastructure that makes markets possible. And law is, of course, the creation of government, while government itself, Friedman emphasized, must serve to enforce the rules that make the market possible. Friedman wrote in regard to essential but strictly limited government: "We need an umpire ... to mediate differences among us on the meaning of the rules, and to enforce compliance with the rules on the part of those few who would otherwise not play the game."[39]

This reflects a tension in two images of neoclassical thinkers. One is that market exchange is part of nature, and thus operates before and independent of government. This is the "naturalized" view of the market. But many of the same thinkers realize that, in an advanced society, market exchange requires laws, courts, and a large system of complex contracts. The "naturalization" of the market sits, philosophically, uncomfortably with the need for massive government involvement allowing the market to operate. Most neoclassicists deal with this tension by saying that the role of the government is simply to set up the preconditions under which a free market can function, providing the safe conditions, much as the national defense of the nation does, for the market then to operate freely and in a self-governing manner.

Some neoclassicists, including Milton Friedman, as noted earlier, also see a more intrusive proper role for government, typically described as monetary policy. Friedman, the modern pioneer of the Chicago School and the neoclassical paradigm, believed that government had to help stabilize business cycles by setting up "a framework" for the monetary system and a reluctant regulation of the money supply and interest rates, exercising extreme caution not to allow this use of government to expand or proliferate.[40] Not all neoclassicists accept this view, believing that the money supply—and the price of money—should be determined naturally by the market like all other resources exchanged on the market. Thus while Friedman accepts the existence (with very limited powers) of a central bank such as the Federal Reserve, other neoclassicists—represented by Tea Party economic thinkers such as Senator Rand Paul and his father, Representative Ron Paul—would like to eliminate it.

These tensions within the neoclassical paradigm do not undermine it. All schools of thought have internal contradictions and large differences exist within all political economy paradigms on important issues. The differences have not prevented the neoclassical tradition from gaining a ruling position in both academia and Washington and have not undermined its effectiveness in justifying the existing US market system.

Yet there are many deep flaws within the neoclassical paradigm, which we describe in later chapters. The most important is that it does not correspond to the realities of the US system that it claims to explain and defend. The United States is, in fact, a system with highly developed concentrations of economic power, monopolistic or oligopolistic corporations rather than small competitive firms of Adam Smith's day, devastating economic crises, and massive, often essential, government involvement in all aspects of the economy.[41] The theory is elegant and appealing, but so distant from the reality on the ground as to call into question the entire paradigm itself. It was that huge disparity that led Alan Greenspan to express his "shock" and begin questioning his own deepest neoclassical assumptions when the 2008 Wall Street meltdown became the very deep crisis that he and his fellow neoclassical economists viewed as impossible.

Given this detachment from reality, how has the neoclassical paradigm survived as a dominant economic religion in the United States, almost from the beginning? This reflects the reality that political economy thought—like all forms of thought—is constructed by people in specific institutional positions, often with great power, who are expressing their own values and interests. The neoclassical paradigm offered US capitalists one of their most powerful forms of intellectual and moral self-defense, cloaked in a beautiful theory of mathematical certitude. In the end, the neoclassical paradigm has survived because US capitalist elites embrace it, giving them a free hand to do whatever they want.

A trip down memory lane can help illuminate this dynamic and show how a theory always reflects the interests of the theorists who create it as well as the underlying need for the ruling economic system and classes to find a theory to justify the existing social order. The neoclassical paradigm is extraordinarily important—whatever you think of the merits of its intellectual argument—because it has played such an important role in justifying the US capitalist model and helping to bring so much of the population to embrace it.

Almost everyone sees Adam Smith, a Scottish moral philosopher and political economist of the eighteenth century, as the founder of the neoclassical paradigm. Smith's great book, *Wealth of Nations*, set forth the core economic and moral virtues of self-regulating market capitalism.[42] Smith invented the idea of the invisible hand that justified the principle of the new capitalist order taking hold in Great Britain. Merchants, industrialists, and entrepreneurs who followed their own self-interest—as selfish as it might seem—were actually the heroes of the new system that would bring prosperity, freedom, and social well-being to the entire world. In his own classic work, *The Worldly Philosophers*, economist Robert Heilbroner summed up Adam Smith's neoclassical manifesto in *Wealth of Nations*: "Don't try to do good.... Let good emerge as the byproduct of selfishness."[43]

In justifying what appeared to be the ruthless selfishness of a rising capitalism, Smith might appear to be the original architect of what would become the American Dream: focus on yourself, and both you and society will prosper. But Smith recognized that societies required feelings of moral solidarity and the existence of robust communities to support the new capitalism. In his earlier book on moral sentiments, Smith devoted enormous energy to showing how altruism and regard for others were both possible and necessary. He also recognized that not just government but corporate monopolies could pose a danger to the market competition that allowed the invisible hand to work.[44] This side of Smith is usually forgotten by modern neoclassical economists, who take from Smith only the benefits of selfishness and forget the social and moral preconditions—including limiting corporate power, sustaining competition, and maintaining strong communities—that Smith assumed as a given of his times.

Nonetheless, Smith vigorously upheld the idea of free market capitalism as a self-governing system that would bring more freedom, prosperity, and social harmony than any prior system. The popularity of his theory, much celebrated during his lifetime, reflected its convenient fit with the great transformation of the era. Capitalism was finishing off the remnants of feudalism and seeking to spread markets and competition, often in the face of state-driven mercantilism or government aid and protection. Smith gave them the economic logic and moral seal of approval that they needed.[45]

In the century following Smith, other famous economists played the same role, legitimating, with early neoclassical ideas, essential elements of the rising nineteenth-century capitalist system. These included prominent British figures such as David Ricardo, a financier and wealthy stock-trader as well as economist, who defended the expansion of capitalist trade in the British Empire as a system of "comparative advantage"—the theory for which he is best remembered—in which both poor and rich nations benefit.[46]

Ricardo also played an important role in the debate about welfare that emerged in 1830s England. Capitalism had thrown hundreds of thousands off the land, who migrated to cities such as London and ended up, as described memorably in the novels of Charles Dickens, as miserable beggars on the street. Like neoclassicists today, Ricardo opposed social welfare, organized through the "Poor Laws," to this new army of the poor. He believed that any government relief was an incentive for laziness and rewarded sloth, which he viewed as the natural condition of the working class, while taking funds from the rest of the economy that could raise wages and profits of productive members of society.[47]

Edwin Chadwick, another early advocate of "free market" principles and architect of brutal workhouses where many poor were given miserable shelter for slave-like enforced labor, made a similar argument against welfare, stigmatizing the poor as lazy and undeserving. As secretary of the 1832 Royal Commission investigating the "Poor Law," which was legislation to provide some measure of social protection, Chadwick signed on to this statement: "Every penny bestowed, that tends to render the condition of the pauper more eligible than that of the independent labourer, is a bounty on indolence and vice."[48]

Ricardo's and Chadwick's hard views toward the poor—blaming them for their condition rather than criticizing the harsh new market forces—should sound familiar. It is the early expression of today's neoclassical punitive attitudes toward the poor and the welfare system, and a key feature of contemporary conservative and Republican doctrine. The neoclassical idea is that markets offer opportunity for those with talent and hard work, and reward the deserving. The poor, then, are undeserving, and any government help is stealing from the worthy to give to the unworthy, in the process undermining the natural forces of the market and making everyone worse off.

Two major figures—one before Ricardo and one after—built a more rigorous foundation of contemporary neoclassical doctrine. Auguste Comte, a major philosopher and social theorist, argued that social sciences, whether economics or sociology or anthropology, were sciences like physics. The equations of the rising class of academic economists and sociologists were universal laws, like gravity. Comte viewed neoclassical laws of the market in precisely this light, making them as immune from question as the laws of physics, and thus making any questioning of the free market a questioning of scientific truth. Comte argued that the new academic social science disciplines must use the scientific methodology and "positivism," an empirical, quantitative, and "value-free" approach that he believed inherent in natural science. This meant rejecting out of hand any historical, political, or critical analysis of power and capitalism, as later developed by Weber and Marx, and instead turning toward a more technical and "objective" social science, one that offered no inherent challenge to the existing order.[49]

While Comte offered the methodology that would ground neoclassical sociology and economics, it was the great British economist Alfred Marshall who put the flesh on the bones of Comte's "science." Economists today generally view Marshall as the first great modern economist, who put the discipline on scientific footing, although Marshall was also a moral philosopher, like Smith, and did not discount the role of politics and culture in economic outcomes. Marshall became a distinguished professor of political economy in Cambridge University and transformed the field.

Marshall brought together all the core elements of neoclassical political economy, in a theory that systematized earlier ideas about marginal utility supply and demand, and the market as a feedback system creating optimal equilibrium, creating perfect prices guaranteeing the cheapest costs and lowest waste. His magnum opus was *Principles of Economics*, published originally in 1881. It became the standard textbook of academic economics through much of the twentieth century.[50] Both the methods and theory of neoclassical political economy—and of academic economics even today—can be traced back to Marshall.[51]

The views of Comte and Marshall traveled from Europe to the United States, just when the Gilded Age tycoons, such as J. P. Morgan, John D. Rockefeller, and Andrew Carnegie, were building the new US corporate capitalist system. Rockefeller founded the University of Chicago, which would become the bastion of neoclassical political economy. Carnegie was an author as well as the man who built the US steel industry and argued in his book, the *Gospel of Wealth*, that industrialists like himself both created wealth and then redistributed it to the community through philanthropic ventures such as the Carnegie Foundation and the many libraries and universities Carnegie helped fund.[52] Carnegie was not a formally trained political economist, but his writings incorporated the perspective of neoclassical political economy that defined the "job creators" as also the builders of civil society and social justice. Carnegie felt no compunction about calling in private security forces to shoot striking workers, making the neoclassical argument that unions subverted the free market for labor, but then claimed—in another variant of the invisible hand argument—that the market winners would give back to the losers through charity.

In the United States, the neoclassical paradigm imported from Smith and Marshall reigned in the United States through the Gilded Age and the Roaring Twenties, offering the elegant intellectual and moral justification of these business-dominated corporate capitalist eras. But with the crash of 1929 and the Great Depression, neoclassical arguments collapsed and the paradigm gave way to New Deal Keynesians, who offered a remedy for the market crisis that the neoclassical paradigm had called impossible.

As we show in the next chapter, the Keynesian paradigm reigned for fifty years, until New Deal economics came up against the headwinds of adverse economic and political circumstances in the 1970s. Even before the new crisis related to the Vietnam War, global competition, and stagflation brought Keynesianism down, a new generation of neoclassical political economists—the Chicago School—had already begun to reconstruct the basis of a new neoclassical PE, closely associated with Milton Friedman, that would gain ascendancy under President Reagan.

We should note that earlier economists and cultural figures had already begun to fight the new battle against both Keynesianism and Marxism. One was Frederick Hayek, an Austrian economist and philosopher who had long done battle with his friend John Maynard Keynes. Hayek looked at the massive government intervention orchestrated by Keynes as the beginning of the end: the road toward the death knell of freedom and the foundation of future tyrannies not so different from either German Nazism or Soviet communism.

In his book, *The Road to Serfdom*, Hayek produced a popular masterpiece, one that gained particular resonance in the United States. Many market economists and right-wing activists were horrified by the progressive activism of the 1960s and the government activism of President Lyndon Johnson's Great Society. Hayek saw government planning, as it developed in the New Deal and Great Society, as a form of "central planning" or "collectivism" that subverted the "individualism" at the heart of freedom in Western civilization. Any collectivist planning inevitably "leads to dictatorship."[53] Influential conservative and neoclassical thinkers and politicians, from Milton Friedman to Ronald Reagan and Margaret Thatcher, hailed Hayek as the prophet of a new market society, which they believed to be the only guarantee against tyranny.[54]

Hayek was appointed Professor of Social Thought at the University of Chicago and won the Nobel Prize in Economics in 1974. In *Road to Serfdom*, he created a manifesto for the freedom of the market as the only defense of freedom itself. Both Keynesianism and Marxism created concentrations of government power destined to lead to autocracy and dictatorship, wiping out individual liberty. Collectivism led to socialism or communism on the Left and fascism on the Right—Hayek saw them as equivalent expressions of collectivist visions.[55] The only salvation was a return to the economic liberty of the market that protected the freedom of the individual as consumer, worker, and investor or entrepreneur against coercive government control leading to totalitarianism. Big government, European social democracy, and the New Deal threatened to turn all governments' growing wards and dependents—most of the population—into modern "serfs." Hayek wrote of New Dealers and Social Democrats: "It is one of the saddest spectacles of our time to see a great democratic movement support a policy which must lead to the destruction of democracy and which meanwhile can benefit only a minority of the masses who support it. Yet it is this support from the Left of the tendencies toward monopoly (of big government) which make them so irresistible and the prospects of the future so dark."[56]

Hayek's work became part of a growing right-wing cultural and economic movement to oppose the 1960s Keynesian liberalism of President Johnson and the neo-Marxist movements on the streets protesting the Vietnam War and the capitalist order itself. Business elites were rocked by the 1960s revolution and determined to put an end to it. They founded a variety of well-funded big business associations, such as the Business Roundtable, and helped fund a new network of right-wing think tanks and activist groups coalescing around economic liberty and the defense of "free market" capitalism. They aimed to demonize and destroy the "new Left" and organized relentlessly to bring in a new political leader, first Barry Goldwater and then Ronald Reagan, who would do the job.[57]

One of the most important figures in this conservative neoclassical revivalism was, ironically, a Hollywood script writer and novelist, Ayn Rand. In her epic bestsellers, *The Fountainhead* and *Atlas Shrugged*, Rand created a new cultural hero: the business entrepreneur and corporate executive.[58] They represented the iconic spirit of freedom and enterprise that had made America great, and Rand's work argued that the very survival of America rested on defeating the "parasites"—or "looters and moochers"—who in the 1960s had seemed to become heroes themselves.

In the 1960s and 1970s, Rand argued that big business was the most persecuted and oppressed institution in America: "The American businessmen, as a class, have demonstrated the greatest productive genius and the most spectacular achievements ever recorded in the economic history of mankind. What reward did they receive from our culture and its intellectuals? The position of a hated, persecuted minority. The position of a scapegoat for the evil of the bureaucrats."[59]

In the same vein, Rand wrote, "If you care about justice to minority groups, remember that businessmen are a small minority—a very small minority compared to the total of uncivilized hordes on earth. Remember how much you owe to this community and what disgraceful persecution it is enduring."[60]

Rand almost single-handedly resurrected popular appetites for heroic business leaders and a new age of corporate expansion that could ward off the growing tyranny of parasites—the poor, minorities, and radical student agitators—aligned with government bureaucrats and social service workers to undermine America and turn it into a totalitarian state.[61]

Neoclassical economists saw a new opening, capitalizing on the enormous popularity of Rand's books and galvanized by the political movements they helped inspire. They saw in Rand the popularizer of their own scientific economic theories. One economist, especially intrigued, became part of Rand's inner circle and helped her draft her works; he was none other than Alan Greenspan.

But it was Milton Friedman, as discussed earlier, who became the founder of the new neoclassical paradigm that reigns today. Friedman is widely regarded as the leader of the "Chicago Boys," the economists at the University of Chicago seen as the fountainhead of the new neoclassical paradigm. Friedman wrote several popular economics books, such as *Free to Choose* and *Capitalism and Freedom*, that became huge bestsellers themselves and helped to bring neoclassical ideas to the public and the New Right conservative movement.[62]

Friedman reinforced and updated Adam Smith's basic ideas, including the core moral proposition that free markets were essential to ensure a free society. Friedman defined markets as voluntary exchanges while government was, by definition, coercive. He believed that government was necessary to establish preconditions for the market to work—such as ensuring national security, property and contract law, and courts to enforce market rules. He also believed in the importance of monetary policy, as noted earlier, to help manage inflation and stabilize business cycles. But he argued that the great threat to liberty was the institutionalized right to coerce and that by extracting economic life from control by government, the market takes away this coercive threat, permitting economic forces to check rather than reinforce political power.[63]

Friedman was a brilliant mathematical technician, and advanced the positivist method that Auguste Comte and Alfred Marshall had pioneered. Like other academic neoclassical economists of the modern era, he turned Smith's view of the invisible hand into a mathematical argument. And he similarly, with his colleagues, framed equations around marginal utility, supply and demand, and cost that demonstrated the validity of a century of neoclassical thinking about why markets create rational allocation, efficient pricing, and maximal benefit to individuals, corporations, and society.

But as a political economist, his larger contribution was to lead the counterattack against the New Deal Keynesianism that had reigned for fifty years and the neo-Marxist Left that had erupted in the 1960s. The corporate and New Right agenda needed an academic and philosophical framing for the theory of political economy. Friedman offered the technical economics along with the moral and political arguments that resurrected not just the neoclassical paradigm but a conservative movement dedicated to fighting the tyranny of big government and collectivism. In this way, he took Hayek's *Road to Serfdom*, and helped the Right redefine social or job programs by the government as dangerous steps on the road to totalitarianism, while also underscoring Ayn Rand's morality of corporations and entrepreneurs as the true American heroes.

Friedman explicitly indicted the Keynesians who, as we see in Chapter 4, viewed government—and the New Deal approach—as the solution to most of our economic and social problems. Friedman should be seen as the most important intellectual architect of the conservative political economy that has dominated America since Ronald Reagan. The militancy of the Tea Party, the orthodoxy of the twenty-first-century Republican Party, the fervency of modern libertarianism—and the prizing of the individual over community, of the market over the state, of profit over people, of globalization over localism, of private ownership over the commons—are all part of Friedman's legacy. No other political economist has had quite the influence of Friedman over the last forty years.

Why did he have such influence? His ideas, like those of Smith, celebrated the changes favored by the men of power and the dominant capitalist corporations of his era. Friedman resurrected the ideas that animated and morally sanctified the super-capitalist Reagan revolution and finally ended the New Deal and the Leftism of the 1960s. He helped create the orthodoxy of the "end of history," such that, as Tom Friedman put it colorfully, there now remains only one choice: the "free market vanilla" of US capitalism. Tom Friedman writes that capitalism is so efficient and superior in generating wealth that, "ideologically speaking, there is no more mint chocolate chip, there is no more strawberry swirl, and no more lemon-lime. Today, there's only free market vanilla and North Korea."[64]

The great question is whether the 2008 financial meltdown, like the Great Depression of the 1930s, will put an end to the reign of the neoclassical paradigm. Keynesians, neo-Marxists, and new brands of ecological economists are waiting in the wings, offering solutions not only to the 2008 Great Recession but to the corporate globalization, bloody wars, and catastrophic climate change that neoclassical thinkers have failed to address. In chapters to come, we will see whether new crises and theories will discredit the neoclassical paradigm and help give birth to a political economy paradigm that speaks truth to power.

CHAPTER 4

The Keynesian Paradigm

Mr. Speaker, the President of the United States!

February 13, 2013: Most members of both chambers of Congress, the cabinet, the Supreme Court, the Joint Chiefs of Staff, invited dignitaries, and private citizens gather to hear President Obama deliver his "State of the Union Address," where he will outline his agenda as he begins his second term. As he speaks, on the Democratic side of aisle, there are often cheers and enthusiastic applause, but on the Republican side, there is tepid applause or sometimes silence. For the most part in his first term, Obama had criticized the neoclassical assumptions of the post-Reagan era, but he felt constrained to operate within that paradigm, with a few exceptions such as the Affordable Care Act (Obamacare). Now there are hints that he is about to use the bully pulpit to go beyond it.

Where beyond? To our subject of this chapter: the Keynesian paradigm.

Obama is clear that he supports capitalism, like all Keynesians, just in a very different way than the neoclassicists: "It is our unfinished task to make sure that this government works on behalf of the many, and not just the few; that it encourages free enterprise, rewards individual initiative, and opens the doors of opportunity.... The American people don't expect government to solve every problem." He continued, in a robust Keynesian spirit:

> We can't ask senior citizens and working families to shoulder the entire burden of deficit reduction while asking nothing more from the wealthiest and most powerful.... I put forward an American Jobs Act that independent economists said would create more than one million new jobs.... Every dollar we invested to map the human genome returned $140 to our economy.... I'm announcing the launch of three more of these manufacturing hubs, where businesses will partner with the Departments of Defense and Energy to turn regions left behind by globalization into global centers of high-tech jobs.... I also want to work with this Congress to encourage

the research and technology that helps natural gas burn even cleaner and protects our air and water.... Ask any CEO where they'd rather locate and hire: a country with deteriorating roads and bridges, or one with high-speed rail and internet; high-tech schools and self-healing power grids.... Tonight, I propose a "Fix-It-First" program to put people to work as soon as possible on our most urgent repairs, like the nearly 70,000 structurally deficient bridges across the country.

Supporters of the neoclassical paradigm within the Republican Party refused to even consider much of Obama's proposal. Senator Marco Rubio of Florida delivered his party's rebuttal:

This opportunity—to make it to the middle class or beyond no matter where you start out in life—it isn't bestowed on us from Washington. It comes from a vibrant free economy where people can risk their own money to open a business.... [President Obama's] solution to virtually every problem we face is for Washington to tax more, borrow more and spend more.... More government isn't going to inspire new ideas, new businesses and new private sector jobs....

Although billionaires like the Koch brothers fund right-wing movements, like the Tea Party, that push for neoclassicist policies, some leading capitalists support Obama and question neoclassicist assumptions. The second wealthiest American, Warren Buffet, says he should pay more taxes. "More than a quarter of these ultrawealthy paid less than 15 percent of their take in combined federal income and payroll taxes. Half of this crew paid less than 20 percent. And—brace yourself—a few actually paid nothing.... I would suggest 30 percent of taxable income between $1 million and $10 million, and 35 percent on amounts above that."[1]

Much earlier, in the 1930s, Boston department store owner Edward Filene declared, "I consider this tax paying the best bargain of my life. Why shouldn't the American people take half my money from now? I took *all* of it from them."[2] Notice above that Rubio said Obama's plan would not create *private sector* jobs; he did not say it would not create jobs. Rubio, an outspoken neoclassicist, was not counting government jobs. The neoclassical claim that government cannot produce wealth is pure myth. Private auto companies would sell zero cars if the government did not build roads. Speaking as a neoclassicist, Mitt Romney, Obama's 2012 Republican opponent, attempted to show that government inhibits productivity, but here were his examples: "We once built the interstate highway system and the Hoover Dam. Today, we can't even build a pipeline."[3] He neglected to mention that the interstate highway system and the Hoover Dam were federally sponsored public works projects.

Right after America's conception, the government subsidized businesses as they jointly built America's industrial infrastructure. The state dug canals, including the Erie Canal. The federal government handed over huge tracts of land to the private railroad companies. Andrew Carnegie, John D. Rockefeller, and other Robber Barons, the founders of the great industrial corporations, relied on government troops to break unions, stop strikes, and protect their private property from their own workers.

Clearly, there is something wrong with the neoclassical viewpoint. And Keynesians, whom we discuss in this chapter, have lots to say about it.

Saving Capitalism with Government: Keynesian Fundamentals

Contrary to neoclassical claims, capitalists need government—a huge amount of it—to support, protect, and constrain them. As we hinted in Chapter 3 and we shall discuss here in more detail, unbridled neoclassicism brought the capitalist system to crash in the Great Depression. To save the day, economist John Maynard Keynes proposed a new paradigm, which for the next forty years or so became the dominant one in the United States, his native Britain, and most of the capitalist world.

We have developed a code to describe the basic story of the Keynesian paradigm:

The Keynesian Code

1. Human nature is irrational, often driven by greed or "animal spirits."
2. *Irrational* means that individuals in the market will often act to harm their own interests and the economy as a whole.
3. The economy is composed of individuals and sectors that not only need to compete but also need to work together in harmony like an orchestra.
4. The government represents the interests of society as a whole. It should act as a conductor.
5. To maintain harmony and stability, the government, as a conductor, must sometimes direct capital or wealth toward one sector of the economy and, at other times, toward another. Its most important role is to create or stimulate enough demand in the economy—to overcome downturns and maintain full employment.
6. Its other vital role is to regulate the irrational behavior of individuals and of powerful institutional sectors such as finance, which is

particularly prone to greed and speculation, leading to systematic bubbles and meltdowns.

7. The market needs to be protected from itself. Left to its own devices, it will go through cycles when it may prosper but then disastrously crash, either because of insufficient demand or financial speculation and greed.

8. No part of the economy, even the very rich, can flourish if there is extreme poverty. Programs are needed to protect those who cannot protect themselves.

9. Businesses can only profit when most of the population has enough money to consume. Government programs may be needed to guarantee employment and a relatively high standard of living.

10. When the government modestly goes in debt, the economy is only borrowing from itself. It is not a problem, especially if the state limits borrowing from other countries. Excessive debt, however, is dangerous and destabilizing.

11. Well-planned government spending can stimulate growth, investment, and employment. It has a "multiplier effect." A dollar of government spending can create well over a dollar in wealth.

12. Very high growth, employment, and consumption can overheat and destabilize the economy. To prevent a more serious crisis, economic planners may have to occasionally intervene and slow the economy down.

13. Ultimately, what is good for one is good for all. As John F. Kennedy said, "A rising tide raises all ships."

Let us look more closely, first, at the Keynesian core principles, which can be illustrated by contrasting them with the basic ideas of neoclassicism discussed in the last chapter. Then, we shall show how these Keynesian principles became guiding beacons behind FDR's New Deal strategy to save capitalism in the Great Depression, and have been, to a lesser degree, guiding the Obama strategy to revive capitalism after the 2008 Great Recession. We shall see that Keynesianism has presented itself as the only true purveyor of the economic medicine that can save capitalism from its greatest crises—catastrophic downturns that neoclassicists view as self-correcting or even impossible to imagine.

Under the neoclassical doctrine, the fundamental unit of analysis is the rational individual in competition with other individuals. (In certain contexts, corporations are people and neoclassicists treat them as such.) Keynes proposed, instead, to treat the economy as a single unified system. Neoclassicists think individuals are rational and look out for their self-interest, which appears selfish, but there is an "invisible hand," which guarantees they will produce the best possible outcome for society as a whole. On the other hand, Keynes believed that individuals are irrational and will often act against their own interests and do things destructive to the common good. Keynes rejected the invisible hand. There is no automatic mechanism that makes the market self-correcting or ensures that selfish behavior will be good for society. What is rational for the individual may be irrational for the economy as a whole.

Keynes agreed with neoclassicists that the market fluctuates, goes up and down, but disagreed with their prognosis that markets would always self-correct. He thought the results of laissez-faire could be disastrous. While neoclassicists think the market can manage itself better than any human, Keynes believed it could self-destruct unless the government regulated it. People and corporations must be restrained from their own greed. Ordinary citizens must be protected from the chicaneries of the rich; otherwise the rich could bring the whole system down. Keynes suggested that business leaders should be tamed almost like animals. "Business [leaders] have a different set of delusions and need ... handling.... Treat them ... as animals ... [that] have been badly brought up and not trained as you wish."[4]

Can you imagine how Milton Friedman would respond to that?

Keynesians also disagree seriously and profoundly with neoclassicists about issues of power, making it a major theme in political economy. Neoclassicists, as we showed in Chapter 3, deny any human control of the market. All—rich and poor alike—are equal before the market. Market competition disperses power, ensuring a "free market" without anybody making decisions for anyone else. On the other hand, Keynes sees serious built-in inequalities of power. People with wealth will try to manipulate the economy for their own advantage, but power is not concentrated in only one group. Corporations, the government, and workers, through unions, hold each other in check to some degree and prevent anyone from dominating in perpetuity. While neoclassicists are confident no one could control or undermine the entire capitalist system, Keynes did not think it was guaranteed. However, with proper surveillance, the economy could be protected and wealthy elites would not take over and permanently benefit at the expense of the many. As we shall see in the next chapter, Marxists have no such faith that anything will prevent the rich and powerful from maintaining and using their advantage.

Unlike neoclassicists who think anything produced will be consumed, Keynes believed one of the most serious causes of crises is lack of demand, either because too few want to buy or can afford to. This happens often at the beginning of a crisis, when everybody gets nervous and seeks to pay down debt or save for a rainy day, a collective "deleveraging," which can make sense for the individual but crashes the system. Keynes called this the "Paradox of

Thrift"—and we saw it in action as the 2008 Great Recession broke out, as well as earlier in the Great Depression, where Keynes first developed his ideas.

Neoclassicists see thrift as a major economic virtue but Keynes saw a more complex picture. Thrift, especially in downturns, may interfere in a serious way with productivity and enterprise, the real source of wealth. Keynes wrote,

> It is Enterprise which builds and improves the world's possessions.... Thrift may exist without Enterprise, but as soon as Thrift gets ahead of Enterprise, it positively discourages the recovery of Enterprise and sets up a vicious circle by its adverse effects on profits. If Enterprise is afoot, wealth accumulates, whatever may be happening to Thrift; and if Enterprise is asleep, wealth decays whatever Thrift may be doing.[5]

In his biggest and boldest break with neoclassical ideas, Keynes rejected the idea that "the government that governs least, governs best." Quite the opposite is true. The government is the only institution capable of representing the common interests of society as a whole and the capitalist class as a whole. It must regulate and protect people and institutions from their own irrationality. If no one else can or will consume, the government should.

Wealth is valuable only if it circulates, a key way in which government must play a major role. Money stuffed in mattresses and factory inventory rotting in warehouses does no one any good. Corporations can only make a profit if people can buy their products. Keynes proposed a "trickle up" theory, which requires intervention by government. Give to the poor and money will float to the rich while benefiting all. For the sake of the rich in a depression, resources must be directed toward the rest of the population and the government must spend to create jobs and stimulate growth. When people are employed and buying, which in Keynes's view often requires major government stimulus or direct job creation, trade or commerce flourishes. "The fact that many workpeople who are now unemployed would be receiving wages instead of unemployment pay would mean an increase in effective purchasing power which would give a general stimulus to trade. Moreover, the greater trade activity would make for further trade activity; for the forces of prosperity, like those of a trade depression, work with a cumulative effect."[6]

Although Keynes had clear preferences for what he thought government should spend on, he would accept the government spending on anything.

> If the Treasury were to fill old bottles with banknotes, bury them at suitable depths in disused coalmines which are then filled up to the surface with town rubbish, and leave it to private enterprise on well-tried principles of laissez-faire [neoclassicism] to dig the notes up again (the right to do so being obtained, of course, by tendering for leases of the note-bearing

territory), there need be no more unemployment and, with the help of the repercussions, the real income of the community, and its capital wealth also, would probably become a good deal greater than it actually is. It would, indeed, be more sensible to build houses and the like; but if there are political and practical difficulties in the way of this, the above would be better than nothing.[7]

Neoclassicists believe government deficits are the devil incarnate. To Keynes, government deficits, especially in recessions or depressions, are not a problem—they are essential. Trying to balance the budget—the most important goal in the United States according to the neoclassicists—can be extremely self-destructive. "The contrary policy of endeavouring to balance the Budget by imposition, restriction, and precautions will surely fail, because it will have the effect of diminishing the national spending power, and hence the national income."[8]

Since the state is the embodiment of the entire society, when it borrows, unless it borrows from other countries, the economy is only borrowing from itself. Keynes thought there is a "multiplier effect," where government spending could stimulate consumption. With increased demand, industry would have an incentive to produce more and employ more people, who in turn would buy more. State consumption is really an investment. Each dollar the government spends can create more than a dollar in wealth. If the government borrows properly and encourages growth, it can pay for this year's loan with next year's income. President Obama was referring to the multiplier effect when he declared, "Every dollar we invested to map the human genome returned $140 to our economy."

For Keynesians, stabilizing the economy during downturns means stimulate but don't "overheat." There is the old saying: the higher they rise, the harder they fall. Capitalism may require wages high enough so people can consume, but not so high that they interfere with profit. Excessive prosperity might make people feel overly entitled. If not enough people are desperate for jobs, workers might feel free to demand higher wages and better working conditions. The state must act like the maestro of an orchestra, sometimes directing resources to the poor, sometimes toward the rich, depending upon where resources are needed to maintain a harmonious capitalism. Keynes claimed to believe an economy should use all its resources, including human resources. Poverty should be prevented, and economic and social planners should strive for full employment. However, in the United States, full employment is defined as 4 to 6 percent unemployed, not 0 percent. To protect the interests of bosses, economic planners might consider an economy approaching full employment overheated and deliberately induce a "recession" or mini-depression, which will throw people on the street.

Keynes in History: The Rise and Fall of the Keynesian Vision

Keynesianism Is Born: From World War I through World War II

Keynesianism, like all political economy (PE) paradigms, develops in response to historical crises and transformations. Keynes, himself, was a central player in Western and world political economy from World War I until the end of World War II. Looking at the history of this era shows how and why Keynesian ideas developed and became a source of major controversy as capitalism sought to weather world wars and the Great Depression. In political economy, history is always the great window into ideas.

Keynes burst on the scene in war-time, as he linked war and capitalist economics. His prophetic assessment of the economics and politics of World War I and its tragic legacy made him a global guru. World War I held a record for carnage, killing more people than all previous wars combined. However, for American capitalists, it was a bonanza. It transformed the United States from the world's biggest debtor to the world's biggest creditor. While it destroyed the industrial infrastructure of almost all of Europe, it left America stronger than ever. "By 1920, the United States national income was greater than the combined incomes of Britain, France, Germany, Japan, Canada, and seventeen smaller countries."[9]

When the war ended, Keynes attended the peace conference, but was appalled by the resulting Treaty of Versailles. He was convinced that seeds of economic collapse and another world war were being planted by the decision to blame the war on Germany and make it pay the cost of its adversaries' recovery through reparations, while stripping the Germans of their industrial base and their access to raw materials. He expected that the victims would not quietly accept their fate but turn to movements, which threatened civilization itself.

> The fundamental problem of a Europe starving and disintegrating ... was the one question in which it was impossible to arouse their [World War I's victors] interest.... Reparation was their main excursion into the economic field, and they settled it as a problem ... from every point of view except that of the economic future of the States whose destinies they were handling.... The danger confronting us, therefore, is the rapid depression of the standard of life of the European populations to a point which may mean actual starvation.... Men will not always die quietly. For starvation, which brings to some lethargy and a helpless despair, drives other temperaments to the nervous instability of hysteria and mad despair. And these in their distress may overturn the remnants of organization and submerge civilization.[10]

Ironically, when the crisis Keynes predicted happened, he would be the person to propose the remedy.

By the late 1920s, Europe was showing signs of recovery from the war, although that proved to be an illusion. What made European reconstruction possible was American loans and investments. Germany was able to pay its reparations, which financed rebuilding Britain, France, and its other opponents through American aid. Any retraction in the American economy would bring down Europe and the rest of the world with it, a sign of early "globalization" that became important in Keynesian ideas and policy.

During the war, America built an industrial infrastructure—a precursor of military Keynesianism (or government spending on arms)—so large that when peace came, the civilian economy could not sustain it, even though the factories, which had expanded to build armaments, converted to domestic consumer goods. Markets had to be found for American products, but Europe and the rest of the world were now too poor to buy America's stuff. Largely to help them buy American goods, the United States lent money to Europe.

Another problem was that American workers were not paid a wage high enough to purchase the very things they made—a historical irrationality that we see again vividly and tragically today—and it became central in Keynes's thinking. From 1923 to 1929, factory output per worker grew 43 percent, corporate profits rose 62 percent, and corporate dividends climbed 65 percent but workers' wages only increased by 8 percent, while the income of the richest 1 percent of the populations was enhanced by 75 percent.[11] That should sound familiar. The Roaring Twenties, like today, had a polarized economy with a growing gap between the very rich and everyone else. But the very rich can only eat so much or buy so many radios. They will save much more and leave many products without customers, *the beginning of the demand crisis that would shape Keynes's entire theory.*

The 1920s solution to the dilemma was to create a credit economy—something that was important as a precondition for the rise of Keynesian economics. People went in debt to buy new inventions like cars and radios on the installment plan, whether or not they could afford them. During that time, 60 percent of automobiles and 80 percent of radios were purchased through the installment plan. Even before the war, Henry Ford tried to set wages high enough so his workers could buy Ford's Model T, a minimum wage of $5 a day (about $104 in 2012 dollars) in 1916.[12] He was hoping to create standards for the entire economy, but as rich and powerful as Ford was, he was only one capitalist. He was not in a position to establish national economic policy. As Keynes would later point out, only the government could do that.

When the United States entered World War I, President Wilson tried to coordinate the entire economy for the war effort. He even nationalized railroads, telegraphs, and gun manufacturer Smith and Wesson.[13] In reaction, there was a call for a "return to normalcy" when the war ended. Although Wilson may have abandoned neoclassicist policies and initiated a form of military Keynesianism, the old policies were restored under his Republican successors who followed Jefferson's neoclassical advice: the government that governs least, governs best. The armed forces were reduced from 5,000,000 troops to about 250,000.[14] The highest tax rate was cut from 77 percent to 24 percent.[15] Neoclassical President Coolidge believed it was his duty to permit business to run itself, essentially run the country, and stay out of the way as much as he could, as he made clear:

The business of America is business.[16]

The man who builds a factory builds a temple, that the man who works there worships, and to each is due, not scorn and blame, but reverence and praise.[17]

Civilization and profit go hand in hand.[18]

Collecting more taxes than is absolutely necessary is legalized robbery.[19]

Perhaps one of the most important accomplishments of my administration has been minding my own business.[20]

And Coolidge certainly did little to help the worker, although he did plenty to help big business, eliminating any regulations that might restrain greed. Under Coolidge, the Federal Trade Commission and the Interstate Commerce Commission were mandated to regulate business as minimally as possible. Coolidge "twice vetoed farm relief bills, and killed a plan to produce cheap Federal electric power on the Tennessee River."[21] With lax regulation, people typically bought stocks on credit or margin with the investor putting as little as 10 percent down. It seems the prosperity of the 1920s was a bubble destined to burst, which it did in the great crash of October 1929.

The Great Depression followed, devastating the whole world. As President Roosevelt was trying to find a solution, Keynes published *The General Theory of Employment, Interest, and Money*.[22] The book is technical and a difficult read, but it is a major philosophical and economic treatise, reflecting Keynes's effort to understand and solve the Great Depression.

In *The General Theory of Employment, Interest, and Money*, Keynes laid the foundations of a new paradigm, abandoned many of the assumptions of neoclassicism, and helped guide FDR in the creation of the New Deal. It would involve a major break from "free market" neoclassicism and laissez-faire capitalism, but Keynes remained firmly committed to Roosevelt's goal:

saving capitalism from itself. As a side note, Keynes personally showed his interest in capitalism; he was an investor who died with a personal fortune of about £500,000[23] (about $16.5 million in 2009 money), and he always renounced socialism and communism. He asked,

> How can I accept the Communist doctrine, which sets up as its bible, above and beyond criticism, an obsolete textbook which I know not only to be scientifically erroneous but without interest or application to the modern world? How can I adopt a creed which, preferring the mud to the fish, exalts the boorish proletariat above the bourgeoisie and the intelligentsia, who with all their faults, are the quality of life and surely carry the seeds of all human achievement? Even if we need a religion, how can we find it in the turbid rubbish of the red bookshop?[24]

Roosevelt's New Deal, an effort to save capitalism, was guided by and implemented most of the key principles of the new Keynesian paradigm. First, it increased regulation to protect the market from its own irrationality. The Security and Exchange Commission was created to prevent excessive destructive stock market speculation. The Federal Deposit Insurance Corporation built confidence in the economy by assuring savers their money was protected, even if their bank failed. The Glass-Steagall Act separated commercial and investment banking, in order to prevent banks from engaging in dangerous speculation with depositor's money. To build support for capitalism and make the nonrich feel optimistic about their economic future, Roosevelt introduced job-creation programs such as the Civilian Conservation Corps and the Work Projects Administration, bringing millions back to work through government expenditure. Roosevelt also created Social Security and unemployment insurance, which reduced fear of poverty during retirement or lack of work.

By 1938, Roosevelt was convinced that Keynesian principles, whether or not he used the term, offered the path to restore prosperity, bring stability, and assure the survival of both democracy and capitalism.

> Your money in the bank is safe; farmers are no longer in deep distress and have greater purchasing power; dangers of security speculation have been minimized; national income is almost 50% higher than it was in 1932; and government has an established and accepted responsibility for relief. But I know that many of you have lost your jobs or have seen your friends or members of your families lose their jobs, and I do not propose that the Government shall pretend not to see these things.... But I conceive the first duty of government is to protect the economic welfare of all the people in all sections and in all groups. Again production had outrun the ability

to buy.... All the energies of government and business must be directed to increasing the national income, to putting more people into private jobs, to giving security and a feeling of security to all people in all walks of life.... How and where can and should the Government help to start an (upward spiral) economic upturn?... I asked for certain appropriations which are intended to keep the Government expenditures for work relief and similar purposes.... Not only our future economic soundness but the very soundness of our democratic institutions depends on the determination of our Government to give employment to idle men. The people of America are in agreement in defending their liberties at any cost, and the first line of that defense lies in the protection of economic security. Your Government, seeking to protect democracy, must prove that Government is stronger than the forces of business depression.... We are a rich Nation; we can afford to pay for security and prosperity without having to sacrifice our liberties into the bargain.... From our earliest days we have had a tradition of substantial government help to our system of private enterprise.... The Federal debt, whether it be twenty-five billions or forty billions, can only be paid if the Nation obtains a vastly increased citizen income. I repeat that if this citizen income can be raised to eighty billion dollars a year the national Government and the overwhelming majority of state and local governments will be definitely "out of the red."[25]

Like Keynes, Roosevelt viewed capitalism as a fundamentally sound system that needs periodic maintenance and repairs to guarantee its optimal performance. Roosevelt's outlook on the depression of the 1930s—which he came to believe could be managed quite easily by the government if Congress permitted it—was not that different from the diagnosis Nobel Prize–winning Keynesian economist Paul Krugman proposed to explain the economic crisis of 2008.

Suppose your husband has, for whatever reason, refused to maintain the family car's electrical system. Now the car won't start, but he refuses even to consider replacing the battery, in part because that would mean admitting he was wrong before, and he insists instead that the family must learn to walk and take buses. Clearly, you have a problem as far as you are concerned. But it's a problem with your husband, not the family car, which should be easily fixed.[26]

This is a very different assessment from the one given by Marxists, who consider capitalism to be a lemon from the moment it left the assembly line.

For Krugman, Keynes, and Roosevelt the battery that will keep capitalism running is consumer demand. When people are removed from the labor force, consumption can decline and that can create or perpetuate an agonizing recession or depression. If healthy capitalism needs to sustain high consumption levels, why not give people jobs, government payments, or welfare directly? Keynes supported this but FDR ran into strong political hurdles. From a capitalist perspective, government payments make it harder for employers to find workers for low-paying, boring, tedious jobs. If you can support yourself without a bad job, why bother? Accordingly, capitalists would want direct welfare to pay less than the worst jobs and be so unpleasant that hardly anyone would choose it voluntarily. The New Deal did enact a direct welfare program, AFDC (Aid for Families with Dependent Children), but few would want to live under its conditions. It forced recipients to essentially surrender control of their private life to state-supported social workers.[27] A social worker could enter the apartment of an unwed mother and demand that she account for an extra pair of pants. The other way for the government to maintain people's ability to consume is to employ them directly, something that would be expensive but that became a pillar of Keynesian thinking. The government must pay them more than if they were not working, and most jobs require expensive infrastructure to support them. There are no factory workers without factories, road crews without roads, teachers without schools, and doctors and plumbers without equipment.

Building infrastructure was a major government policy that Keynes approved of—as essential to rebuilding employment and saving both the economy and larger society. He saw it as more productive than burying dollars in bottles. Under the New Deal, there were extensive public works projects. These included building dams, roads, schools, hospitals, civic buildings, and bridges such as the Triborough, Golden Gate, and San Francisco Bay. Special effort was made to employ idle artists, writers, and actors through such means as publicly supported theaters. The Civilian Conservation Corps established camps for unemployed youth, who planted trees, made reservoirs and fish ponds, built dams, dug diversion ditches, raised bridges and fire towers, fought tree diseases, restored historic battlefields, cleared beaches and camping grounds, and protected and improved parks, forests, watersheds, and recreational areas.[28]

However, capitalists have real reasons to worry about Keynesian ideas of government employment. What if government jobs pay so well or are so fulfilling that they compete with working for private business? The neoclassicist claim that the government is a wasteful parasite that can never create wealth has no basis in reality. The real danger to capitalists is that state enterprise might be so effective that it is preferable to private corporations. One particularly dramatic example is the Tennessee Valley Authority (TVA). The Tennessee River frequently flooded. In the valley, average income was barely half the national level, half the families were on relief, and barely 2 percent of the farms had electricity. Despite this, if the river was properly dammed, not only would floods be prevented but cheap electricity could be generated. In the 1920s, there was a bill to have the federal government undertake this project, but neoclassical President Coolidge vetoed it. When Roosevelt approved TVA, it went into direct competition with Commonwealth and Southern, the largest private electrical utility in the area. Commonwealth and Southern's CEO, Wendell Willkie, was so outraged at the threat from TVA that he ran against Roosevelt for president as the 1940 Republican nominee.

Although some capitalists like Joseph Kennedy and Edward Filene embraced Roosevelt's Keynesian policies, others formed the ultraconservative Liberty League to defeat it or at least limit it. These include the DuPont brothers, Alfred Sloan, William Knudsen and Jouett Shouse of General Motors, Nathan Miller of US Steel, Ernest Weir of National Steel, Sewell Avery of Montgomery Ward, and Howard Pew of Sun Oil.[29] Roosevelt was also constrained by the southern congressional caucus within his own Democratic Party, who feared generous welfare programs would undermine the southern racial hierarchy. To appease them and keep blacks dependent, welfare benefits were kept under the control of the states, and southern agribusiness was exempt from minimum wage rates and other regulations that applied to northern industries.[30]

Movies at the time often portrayed bankers and other business people as self-serving neoclassicists. Gatewood, the banker in John Ford's 1939 classic western *Stagecoach*, felt entitled to rule and was shocked when the government disagreed.

> I don't know what the government is coming to. Instead of protecting business, it pokes its nose into business! Why they're even talking about having bank examiners. As if we bankers don't know how to run our own banks! ... America for the Americans! The government must not interfere with business! Reduce taxes! Our national debt is something shocking. Over a billion dollars a year! What this country needs is a businessman for president![31]

A criticism often made about Obama might apply to Roosevelt—and it is the constant limitation that capitalist class interests impose on Keynesian policies, a problem that is one of the great limitations of the Keynesian paradigm itself. Obama's Troubled Asset Relief Program (TARP) stimulus, opposed by conservatives, was too small to end the Great Recession of 2008. Total New Deal spending, also attacked relentlessly by the right wing, was insufficient for ending the Great Depression. From 1933 to 1939, Roosevelt spent $41 billion (about $670 billion in 2012 money), mostly on social services and public works. That is almost as much as the total the federal government spent from its formation in 1789 to 1932—$45 billion, which includes the Civil War and World War I.[32] In 1939, US gross domestic product (GDP) reached $92.2 billion, well above its 1933 nadir, $56.4 billion, but still below 1929, $103.6 billion. By 1945, the federal deficit reached $259 billion (about $3.3 trillion in 2012 money) but GDP achieved $223 billion[33] and unemployment was near zero. It was World War II, not Roosevelt's New Deal, that ended the Great Depression—with World War II spending being a form of large-scale military Keynesianism. However you interpret it, though, it was government spending—just as Keynes had prescribed—that finally pulled the nation out of its greatest economic downturn.

Keynes would have preferred spending on infrastructure and social services, but missiles will do—and can be put underground like dollars in bottles. There is one difference: dollars in bottles cannot blow up the planet. Unlike Keynes, much of the corporate elite would rather the government spend on guns than butter. In war, government does not compete with private industries but instead gives them contracts to build tanks, ships, and bombs. Money spent on weapons can "trickle down." It acts as a Keynesian stimulus and increases employment, which increases consumption, which increases production of civilian consumer goods, which increases ...

During World War II, the United States expanded its industrial apparatus, even more than World War I, but immediately after World War II, GDP fell 12.7 percent.[34] The Great Depression was showing signs of a relapse. Some economists argue the depression never ended; the American economy has been sustained by armaments spending ever since. While this was not Keynes's preference, Keynesian policies in the United States have been focused on guns as much as butter, if not more, since military spending did not threaten corporate interests and often subsidized or protected their profits.

When World War I ended, the United States dismantled most of the military it built for the war. After World War II, the United States began to disarm but soon changed its mind. It appointed itself the world police force, whose corporations could gain from perpetual military contracts, as well as the army protecting foreign investments and markets and securing access to third world resources and cheap labor. Rather than reducing its armed forces, America would now become a permanent garrison state. To prevent competition, it discouraged Europe and Japan from maintaining all but minimal militaries. The Soviet Union, the ally who had borne the overwhelming cost of defeating Hitler in World War II, was declared an eternal enemy as brutal as Nazi Germany. To win support among the nonrich for the ensuing cold war, there would be almost no cutbacks in social services. Combining guns and butter requires massive government spending, but that is not a problem from a Keynesian point of view: it is, in fact, important Keynesian medicine needed to treat capitalist economies and bring them out of their recurrent recessions.

1945 to 1980: When Keynesians Ruled America

The Keynesian paradigm had helped take America out of the Great Depression. For the next generation, it would become the dominant public philosophy of the nation. Keynesians view this as a golden age, but we see that it is far more complex and contradictory, raising questions about the virtues of the Keynesian paradigm in capitalist societies.

For the next several decades, Roosevelt's "butter" Keynesianism of the New Deal and his "guns" Keynesianism of World War II became institutionalized as his successors carried them on. Keynesian policies sustained the economy in the aftermath of World War II. With the end of the war came not only the danger of the GDP collapsing but massive unemployment among returning veterans, who as "heroes" felt especially entitled. The stigma of unemployment was minimized through the GI Bill.[35] It was a Keynesian program, if ever there was, setting aside billions of dollars to help returning veterans readapt to civilian life. As the veterans formed families, they could buy homes through federally subsidized mortgages. The GI Bill effectively subsidized not only veterans, but also banks and the construction industry. Home owners might be heavily in debt, but they would identify themselves as part of the propertied class. When they did get jobs, their mortgages would restrain them from doing anything that might put their income at risk. Home ownership helps stabilize capitalism. It builds conservativism among people who might otherwise be disruptive.

The bill—one of the most popular Keynesian initiatives enacted in the United States since it helped build an American middle class—actually encouraged GIs to postpone returning to work and see being outside the labor force as a privilege, thinking they were building skills for better jobs. Before 1940, barely 5 percent of the population attended colleges but through grants offered by the GI Bill, almost half of World War II veterans received higher education. The GI Bill did not increase the number of jobs requiring advanced specialized training like doctors, lawyers, and scientists. Instead, college graduates took jobs for which previously a high school diploma was sufficient: sales manager, nurse, even cop. Even with these jobs, they would believe they achieved the "American Dream" and now identify themselves as educated, middle class, and professional.

To get the veterans, some now with degrees, to buy into the newly formed suburbs with their newly formed families, infrastructure was intentionally dismantled. Keynesian spending can be deliberately destructive as well as constructive, something Keynesians don't usually discuss. Through "urban renewal" projects, viable inner-city neighborhoods and downtowns were eliminated.[36] Downtown department stores were replaced by monotonous strip malls, which ringed the metropolitan areas. Government money was used to destroy central city public transportation. The streetcar became a relic of the past.[37] Completing purchases begun in the 1920s, Standard Oil and General Motors jointly bought the Los Angeles Transit system, then one of the finest in the world, and closed it down.[38] They then pressured the California legislature to build freeways. Life in LA became almost impossible without a car. As similar patterns occurred around the country, President Eisenhower undertook a Keynesian public works project to build a network of multilane interstate highways, which crisscrossed the nation.[39]

Keynesianism says government spending to stimulate the economy, particularly in downturns, is always good, but the impact of urban renewal and the highway system suggests otherwise. Urban renewal transformed inner cities into enclaves of poverty. The highway system fostered the growth of suburbs and dependency upon private cars, which destroyed communities and led to increased air pollution and global warming. We don't even have to include military Keynesianism. It appears misguided civilian domestic Keynesian policies can undermine infrastructure and communities, precipitating economic, social, and environmental decline. A federal plan to build an "inner built" highway through the core of greater Boston met with neighborhood opposition and was abandoned:

> When the feds get it right, cities flourish. And when they get it wrong, the consequences can last for decades.... That ramp to nowhere in Charlestown, the mess in Jackson Square, and the gash running through lower Roxbury all speak to bad transportation decisions in Washington. The three are remnants of the Inner Belt and the Southwest Expressway— 1960s-era federal highway projects that were pitched as urban revitalization projects, but which were ultimately scrapped, in the face of a sustained public uprising, as wasteful and destructive.... It was supposed to connect to the Inner Belt, which was to have plowed through Roxbury to the Fenway, through the middle of Central Square in Cambridge, and over to the Somerville-Charlestown line.... Opponents eventually convinced state and federal leaders that the highways would have choked the life out of Boston, but not before the bulldozers began running through Roxbury and Somerville. To make way for the Inner Belt, Somerville cleared several acres along its eastern edge. The Boston Redevelopment Authority took and demolished scores of homes and businesses from lower Roxbury to Jackson Square. Five decades after they were first cleared, it's still a

struggle to redevelop vacant patches that were supposed to have been paved over.[40]

The 1940s–1960s were truly a Keynesian era. The standard introductory economics textbook of the period was written by the eminent Keynesian, Paul Samuelson, the first American to win the Nobel Prize for economics. The textbook blames the Depression on neoclassical orthodoxies and credits Keynesianism with creating the prosperity of the post–World War II era. In contrast to neoclassicism, the book asserts that the question of how the government can stimulate the economy is a legitimate concern for economics. "Economics also deals with political decisions each citizen must face: Will the government add to my taxes to help unemployed minors, or are there other things it can do to help mitigate the problem of unemployment? Should I vote to build a new school and road now, or vote to put this aside until business slackens and cement prices come down and jobs are needed?"[41] Even more influential than Samuelson in spreading Keynesian ideas to the general public in mid- and late-twentieth-century America was John Kenneth Galbraith. In his *Affluent Society* and *New Industrial State*, he charged that neoclassical economics developed when scarcity was the norm and the main problem was how to increase production, but by the 1950s, overall affluence had been achieved, at least in advanced industrial countries.[42] However, this created new problems: how to distribute the affluence so its bounty is shared and how to use resources to enhance the quality of life rather than to seek profit by producing things that are useless and wasteful, if not destructive. Galbraith denounced the decline of public services and social welfare. But as a Keynesian, Galbraith never questioned capitalism and called for industry, government, and labor to act as countervailing powers and prevent each other from going against the public interest. He believed that economy had become regulated and coordinated. However, he feared this was done by corporations at least as much as by the government. Accordingly, ordinary citizens could not assume they were the beneficiaries as their wants and needs might be manipulated to serve the powerful rather than themselves.

> In the wake of what is now called the Keynesian Revolution, the state undertakes to regulate the total income available for the purchase of goods and services in the economy. It seeks to ensure sufficient purchasing power to buy whatever the current labor force can produce.... This assaults the most majestic of all economic assumptions, namely that man, in his economic activities, is subject to the authority of the market. Instead we have an economic system which, whatever its formal ideological billing, is, in substantial part, a planned economy. The initiative in deciding what is to be produced comes not from the sovereign consumer who, through the

market, issues the instructions that bend the productive mechanism to his ultimate will. Rather it comes from the great producing organization which reaches forward to control the markets that it is presumed to serve and, beyond, to bend the customer to its needs.[43]

True to Galbraith's critique, American industries deliberately made inferior products that would profitably sell. That actually is consistent with the Keynesian principle: it matters less what people buy than that they buy. Cars were marketed by making people's sense of status depend upon having this year's look. If people drive last year's car, their neighbor will think they are poor or "not with it." They may have become poor to look rich, but that increased profit for the auto companies. By the 1950s, Ford and GM adopted "planned obsolescence."[44] They decided it was self-defeating to make well-built cars and focused on appearance, not quality. The sooner cars fell apart, the sooner people would replace them. Technological innovation was actually squelched. American auto companies held patterns for engines, more efficient and less ecologically destructive than the internal combustion. However, these alternatives would compete with existing technology and developing them would require paying to retool plants that were yielding adequate profit, at least for the time being. The patterns were locked in vaults to prevent other people, companies, and countries from using them. Oil companies gave solar and other green energy technologies similar treatment.[45]

The Neoclassical Restoration: Vietnam and Military Keynesianism, Globalization and the Reagan Revolution

The Golden Age of Keynesianism ended in the 1970s. In this final section of the chapter, we explain why Keynesianism declined and how neoclassical thinking came, once again, to dominate America. This reversal helps to explain not only the power of capitalist forces restricting Keynesian policies but inherent limits of the Keynesian paradigm itself, especially as it unfolded in the US context.

In the 1950s and 1960s, with little competition from abroad, American auto, oil, and steel companies could afford to pay their employees enough to buy houses, cars, and televisions and perhaps send their kids to college. The corporations were adopting a role that Keynesianism says is the authority of the state. Wages were set to maintain consumption and social stability, not necessarily on the value of what the worker produced. Government military Keynesian policies helped the corporations do that. Their profits, which trickled down as workers' wages, were underwritten by federal weapons contracts. Armaments became America's staple product, the foundation of the rest of the economy.[46] It supported aerospace, chemicals, energy, mining, communications, and transportation. For many corporations, the Department of Defense was their largest customer, even outweighing the private consumer. Keynesian public works projects, ones that offered butter as well as guns, were sponsored under the Pentagon. Military money built the interstate highways, and federal loans to college students were called National Defense Loans. After World War II, when the United States was the world's economic engine, military research sparked most innovation including transistors, computer circuits, and plastics. US industry so dominated the world, however, that US corporations felt little motive to apply these innovations to civilian consumer goods and infrastructure.[47]

Keynesians may prefer that the government spend on weapons than not spend at all, but weapons are not just waste; they are destructive. The more weapons you have, the more likely you are to use them. As the world's self-appointed policeman, it was almost inevitable that the United States would find itself at war. World War II may have created the image of the United States as beyond challenge, but the Vietnam War showed its vulnerability. There is a long list of reasons why Vietnam was a disaster; for one, it showed the beginning of American economic decline and the destructiveness of military Keynesianism. While World War II was still going on, Samuelson warned of the limits of military Keynesianism.

> Every month, every day, every hour the federal government is pumping millions and billions of dollars into the blood stream of the American economy.... We have reached the present high levels of output and employment only by means of $100 billion of government expenditures, of which $50 billion represents deficits.... Any simple statistical calculation will show that the automobile, aircraft, shipbuilding and electronics industries combined, comprising the fields with the rosiest postwar prospects, cannot possibly maintain their present level of employment, or one-half, or one-third of it.[48]

With his Great Society and War on Poverty, President Johnson wanted to be the ultimate butter Keynesian.

> Because it is right, because it is wise, and because, for the first time in our history, it is possible to conquer poverty, I submit ... the Economic Opportunity Act of 1964.... It strikes at the causes, not just the consequences of poverty.... A new national Work-Training Program operated by the Department of Labor will provide work and training for 200,000 American men and women between the ages of 16 and 21.... A new national Work-Study Program operated by the Department of Health,

Education, and Welfare will provide federal funds for part-time jobs for 140,000 young Americans.[49]

However, Vietnam forced Johnson to instead become a guns Keynesian.

> Our reward will come in the life of freedom, peace, and hope that our children will enjoy through ages ahead.... The actions that we have taken since the beginning of the year: to reequip the South Vietnamese forces, to meet price increases and the cost of activating and deploying reserve forces.... The tentative estimate of those additional expenditures is $2.5 billion in this fiscal year, and $2.6 billion in the next fiscal year.
>
> These projected increases in expenditures for our national security will bring into sharper focus the Nation's need for immediate action: action to protect the prosperity of the American people and to protect the strength and the stability of our American dollar.... I have emphasized the need to set strict priorities in our spending. I have stressed that failure to act and to act promptly and decisively would raise very strong doubts throughout the world about America's willingness to keep its financial house in order.[50]

Afraid to raise taxes to finance an unpopular war, he printed more money. The result was rampant inflation, which continued throughout the 1970s. When Nixon was president, Galbraith proposed federally imposed wage and price controls. Although no fan of Galbraith, Nixon attempted it but it proved ineffective. Nixon's heart may have been in neoclassicism, but he announced, "We are all Keynesians now."[51]

Keynesians say a country can and should go into debt during long downturns, but they tend to ignore what happens when public investments are poured into the military at the expense of civilian economic, social, and physical needs. In these circumstances, when civilian foundations erode, debt repayment becomes problematic. To borrow, you need collateral. For a country, social and physical infrastructure is the main collateral. If you focus almost entirely on armaments and sacrifice your infrastructure, you lose your collateral. While America dismantled its infrastructure and allowed its domestic consumer goods industries to lie fallow, Europe and Japan took the discoveries from American military research to improve their televisions, tape players, and cameras. Forced to rebuild their industries, which had been destroyed in World War II, they adopted the latest technologies. With their people too poor to afford American cars, which were big, ostentatious, inefficient, and short-lived, they built small, durable, more ecological ones. While foreigners didn't purchase American cars, by the late 1960s, Americans regularly bought foreign goods.

By the early 1970s, Europe and Japan had recovered from World War II. Their people no longer felt poor, desperate, and in awe of the United States. They had stronger unions, improved social services, and better public transportation than America. Rather than destroy their inner cities, they rebuilt them.[52] By sacrificing civilian infrastructure to military domination—essentially shifting toward military Keynesianism almost entirely during Vietnam and after—the United States had squandered its advantage. While US corporations hardly used weapons technology to improve the quality of civilian consumer goods, Toyota, Sony, Fuji, Volkswagen, LG, and later, Samsung and Hyundai most certainly did. America's borrowing to buy guns may have bought several decades of prosperity, but by the 1970s, the loan was being recalled. Keynesianism may embrace state spending and deficits, which build an economy, but some debts may undermine it. In the long run, militarism is counterproductive—and military Keynesianism, the form most acceptable in the United States, shows how Keynesianism can go desperately wrong.

With their profits declining, American industrial corporations became less willing to offer the high wages and secure employment to which their workers had become accustomed. One advantage of having the United States act as the world's police force is that it supports puppet governments who make their countries available to American corporate investments. When President Salvador Allende of Chile tried to nationalize mines owned by US corporations Kennecott and Anaconda Copper, the Central Intelligence Agency had him overthrown and replaced by General Augusto Pinochet.[53] Third world dictators opened their countries for factories with low wages, few regulations, low environmental standards, and minimal worker protections. US corporations could say to their employees, "If you won't work on our terms, we can just close the factory and move to other countries. You'll be out on the street and we'll keep making money." Formerly thriving metropolises like Detroit were reduced to rows of boarded-up factories, offices, and houses.

Keynesianism may have brought the United States out of the Great Depression, but America chose guns over butter. By the late 1970s, with rampant inflation, especially soaring petroleum prices, dismantled infrastructure, exported jobs and industries, and serious international rivals, US capitalism was once again in crisis, although not a crisis as severe as the Great Depression. Keynesianism's support for militarism, deficits, and tolerance for the destruction of infrastructure helped create a new crisis. By the time President Jimmy Carter left office, the Keynesian paradigm appeared to have run its course and capitalism needed a new paradigm. The paradigm that was adopted in reaction to contradictions within Keynesianism was not new. It was a restoration of neoclassicism—under President Ronald Reagan. Coincidentally, as Reagan assumed the White House, Keynesianism fell out of favor among academic economists.

They triumphantly announced the death of Keynesian economics without having actually managed to provide a workable alternative. [Nobel Prize–winner] Robert Lucas, famously, declared in 1980—approvingly!—that participants in seminars would start to "whisper and giggle" whenever anyone presented Keynesian ideas. Keynes, anyone who invoked Keynes was banned from many classrooms and professional journals.[54]

This restoration carried all the contradiction of neoclassicism that led fifty years earlier to the Great Depression and additional problems. Reagan melded neoclassicism and Keynesianism and arguably kept the worst of each. Rather than solving the problems of the 1970s, Reagan made them worse. He freed corporations from federal regulations that protect workers' health and safety and the environment. He also cut taxes for the very rich. As a result, corporations used their newfound windfalls to close more American factories and move to countries where wages were lower and regulations were even more lax. Although as a neoclassicist Reagan spoke of the need for a balanced budget and minimal government, he massively increased military spending as he lowered corporate taxes, essentially implementing massive military Keynesianism. The result was deficits that spiraled out of control. One of his heirs, Vice President Richard Cheney, inadvertently implied Reagan vindicated Keynesianism, saying, "Reagan proved deficits don't matter."[55] This is a neoclassicist spouting Keynesian ideology. Keynesians found themselves saying the deficit had gone out of control. Reagan's Democratic opponent in 1984, Walter Mondale, a Keynesian liberal, indicated he would have to raise taxes. Lloyd Bentsen, 1988 Democratic Vice Presidential nominee and another Keynesian liberal, offered this critique:

You know, if you let me write $200 billion [about $382 billion in 2012 dollars] worth of hot checks every year, I could give you an illusion of prosperity, too. This is an administration that has more than doubled the national debt, and they've done that in less than eight years. They have taken this country from the No. 1 lender nation in the world to the No. 1 debtor nation in the world. And the interest on that debt next year, on this Reagan-Bush debt of our nation, is going to be $640 [about $1,223 in 2012 dollars] for every man, woman, and child in America because of this kind of a credit-card mentality. So we go out and we try to sell our securities every week, and hope that the foreigners will buy them. And they do buy them. But every time they do, we lose some of our economic independence for the future. Now they've turned around and they've bought 10 percent of the manufacturing base of this country. They bought 20 percent of the banks. They own 6 percent of the commercial real estate in Los Angeles. They are buying America on the cheap.[56]

The United States was the world's largest debtor before World War I. In that period, it was a healthy debt used to finance rapidly expanding industries like steel, oil, and cars. On the other hand, America's debt in the 1980s and beyond was undertaken by a country in the process of dismantling its infrastructure, one trying to cling to a standard of living that was no longer feasible. The largest holder of US debt is China, a nominally communist country, whom the United States had formerly regarded as a backward enemy. As of 2011, China has lent Americans $1.16 trillion[57] to enjoy a lifestyle that eludes its own people. China, among other countries, now manufactures what America no longer produces. For a while the American people were able to maintain the illusion of prosperity by borrowing on credit cards or through home equity loans. The corporate rich shifted their attention from manufacturing to finances for finances' sake. Instead of productive assets, investors bought mutual funds and derivatives, which bought shares of funds, which bought shares of funds, which ... bought stocks, bonds, and real estate. The total value of mutual funds exceeded the New York Stock Exchange. By the 2000s, the economy was starting to resemble its 1920s ancestor. Neoclassicism made them both bubbles destined to burst.

This time the collapse came in 2008. It has been called the Great Recession. Paul Krugman, perhaps America's leading surviving Keynesian, says that *recession* is a euphemism and America, indeed the world, is in a depression.[58] As a Keynesian, Krugman is committed to capitalism and believes the right policy can save it. He does not entertain the Marxist prognosis that perhaps there will be a crisis from which there can be no recovery. If Keynesianism ended the depression of the 1930s, surely it will end the recession/depression of the 2010s. As a Keynesian committed to major stimulus to move capitalism out of Depression, Krugman is vehemently against the "austerity" programs, the reduction in government services that neoclassicists offer as a solution to the Great Recession and adopted in European countries, which historically had much stronger Keynesian and socialist policies than the United States.

> The Obama stimulus ... was temporary and fairly small compared with the size of the US economy.... It took effect in an economy whipsawed by the biggest financial crisis in three generations. How much of what took place in 2009–2011, good or bad, can be attributed to the stimulus? Nobody really knows.
>
> The turn to austerity after 2010 was drastic, that the usual cautions lost most of their force.... The answer is that the results were disastrous.... Three years after the turn to austerity, then, both the hopes and the fears of the austerians appear to have been misplaced. Austerity did not lead to a surge in confidence; deficits did not lead to crisis....

I'd argue that Keynes was overwhelmingly right in his approach, but there's no question that it's an approach many people find deeply unsatisfying … slashing government deficits in the face of mass unemployment may deepen a depression, but it increases the certainty of bondholders that they'll be repaid in full.[59]

Krugman offers a powerful Keynesian critique of today's neoclassical restoration. He rightfully looks at the responses to the economic crisis of the George W. Bush and Obama administrations and finds them inadequate: stimulus packages whose main beneficiaries are banks and other corporations; austerity programs, including calls to reduce the deficit with accompanying cuts in social services and entitlements like Social Security and Medicare; lowering the expectations of the average citizen. He correctly sees austerity as a device to transfer wealth from the poor and middle class to the wealthy. Krugman does not go as far as Cheney and declare that "deficits don't matter," but he believes there are times when they are desirable—and necessary to save the economy. Like other Keynesians, he believes deficits should be restrained in the long term. It is wise to use deficits to mitigate an economic downturn, as in the years following the 2008 meltdown, and try to pay them off during prosperity. A recession or depression is the wrong time for austerity. The austerity programs in Europe have made their economic crises worse. When infrastructure is deteriorating, spend to rebuild it. There is much to do: support public transportation and create clean energy. Prescribe Keynesian medicine again, in a massive dose!

However, there are major differences between the 1930s and the 2010s. As weak as the American economy may have been in the 1930s, the United States was still the unqualified world leader and the world's largest creditor. It did not have to account to any other country as it set its economic policy. US industry and infrastructure may have lied fallow but it was not dismantled. Infrastructure is a county's collateral for borrowing and too much of it may have been exported or destroyed, from the 1970s on, to make the United States a good credit risk. Already, America's bond rating has been reduced from AAA to AA+. Its infrastructure may be too far gone to rebuild. Late Apple CEO Steve Jobs saw the situation as bordering on irreversible: the jobs aren't coming back.[60] He openly preferred to invest in China rather than America. Journalist Arianna Huffington laments that America is becoming a third world country,[61] with its declining infrastructure and collapsing middle class.

The resources and money to rebuild America's infrastructure may simply no longer exist. Now with America so heavily in debt to other countries, especially China, it may not have the freedom to spend and do as it chooses. Creditors can dictate, or at least profoundly influence, American policies in their interests, not the interests of the American people. If the United States tried to rebuild its infrastructure and reemploy its people through Keynesian public works projects, it is not clear it could raise sufficient money. Even if reconstruction were possible, neoclassicists within the Republican Party and the very rich would likely block it. Is the United States entering an irreversible decline or could Keynesianism offer a solution like it did in the 1930s? Is Keynesianism itself, especially Keynesianism blended with neoclassicism, responsible for the recent crisis? In the next chapter, we shall discuss Marx's prediction that eventually capitalism will face a crisis from which there will be no solution. Could this be that crisis? If it is, the collapse does not have to be imminent, but the prosperity of the 1940s, 1950s, and 1960s is something present and future generations may never know. Is Marxism—or an entirely new paradigm—a better choice than Keynesianism? One thing we say with confidence: social Keynesianism is problematic; military Keynesianism is disastrous.

CHAPTER 5

The Neo-Marxist Paradigm

It's the 2011 Occupy Movement:

People—working people, students, activists from the 1960s and 1970s, unemployed, homeless—pitch tents to sleep, love, cook, read, discuss, plan, protest, and live.

They form a circle near the stage. Unemployed ex-computer programmer asks: Why did I lose my job? Is it my fault? What did I do wrong? The 1 percent tells us this is the land of opportunity and if I don't make it, I ain't got nobody to blame but myself. Is this true?

Student asks: Why may I not live as well as my parents? Why am I so heavily in debt to prepare for a job that may not exist?

Somebody goes up on stage. Someone speaks on the stage and everyone listening repeats: Unemployed, unfulfilled, alienated; school or work gives no satisfaction. It's not your fault, not your problem. It's the system, the capitalist society, the capitalist economy. It's got to be changed!

The Occupy movement is a recent manifestation of an old pattern: people rallying together in social movements to address their "personal troubles," which sociologist C. Wright Mills tells us are often "public issues." Since capitalism's inception, there have been poverty and misery and the fear of failing, even among people getting by and doing well. There has been a widespread sense of alienation and lack of fulfillment, meaning, and satisfaction, a lack of control over your own life, even if your stomach is full. People are pitted against each other in a competitive struggle, a rat race. The Occupy movement emerged in response to an economic downturn, which began in 2007, but there have been other crises before: 1929, 1907, 1893, 1873, 1837. It appears capitalism is subject to periodic downturns that it may not be able to solve.

This was certainly the perspective of Karl Marx, the founder of the third major paradigm of political economy. He thought that capitalism was destined to face endless Occupy-type revolts, bred by the DNA of the capitalist system. Marx wrote that capitalist crises would keep coming and get worse and worse:

"Great catastrophes and crises develop—and these cannot in any way be got rid of by the pitiful claptrap that produces exchange against products.... The existence of the market guarantees catastrophic crises that market exchange itself inevitably produces. And what it produces it cannot undo."[1]

While the other two paradigms, neoclassical and Keynesian, see capitalism as resolving its problems and bringing long-term prosperity and well-being, the neo-Marxist paradigm raises entirely new questions: Can capitalism self-destruct? Will it self-destruct? Or perhaps, should it self-destruct? Would the world be a better place without capitalism?

Karl Marx and Friedrich Engels took up these questions as the co-creators of the paradigm that we call neo-Marxist. They lived when capitalism was relatively new but thought they might see its demise in their lifetime. Although both grew up comfortable, they identified themselves as the spokesmen for the poor. Engels described "satanic mills" in Manchester, England, around the 1840s.[2] He should have known; his family owned factories. On seeing his own father's factory, Engels wrote Marx, "A few days in my old man's factory have sufficed to bring me face to face with this beastliness, which I had rather overlooked.... It is impossible to carry on communist propaganda on a large scale and at the same time engage in huckstering and industry."[3] For Engels the conditions were just too terrible to continue in his father's business. The early factories were frigid cold in winter and stifling hot in summer. Diseases like tuberculosis, cholera, diphtheria, and typhoid were rampant. By the 1850s, life expectancy fell to about twenty-five for the poor in Liverpool and Manchester.[4]

Karl Marx, usually considered the senior partner, was never as wealthy as Engels. In fact, Engels partly supported him. His background was in philosophy and his early writings focused on how capitalism produces alienation, undermines human potential,[5] and reduces human interaction to market exchanges, in which everything, including human labor, is regarded as a commodity, something to buy and sell.[6]

Marx considered himself a scientist, but was hardly a value-free positivist. Instead he believed people see and act from a perspective largely determined by their position in society (social class). Marx embodied the scholar-activist ideal, that is, the scientist who seeks truth but feels a responsibility to use it to make a better world.

Marx and Engels were convinced capitalism was an inherently exploitative system that would bring untold wealth and power to a small elite, the bourgeoisie (or capitalist class), who control almost all institutions, including the government, banks, factories, schools, and media. To survive, the majority must forfeit their freedom and creativity and become essentially "wage slaves." The gap between the rulers and the oppressed would grow. Marx and Engels expected the exploited would develop "class consciousness" and turn against their rulers. There would be periodic crises that could grow in intensity and possibly bring capitalism to collapse. As Marx put it, "It is enough to mention the commercial crises … put on trial, each time more threateningly, the existence of the entire bourgeois society."[7]

Marx expected capitalism's demise to be something to celebrate; it would bring socialism, a far more democratic and egalitarian, less exploitative and alienating society.[8] But he wrote far more about capitalism than what would follow it, so we know less about what Marx imagined or hoped a post-capitalist society would bring.

Marx was above all else a theorist of capitalism. He got much wrong, but he was amazingly accurate in many of his predictions. The Marxist paradigm, while demonized in most of the United States, is indispensable to anyone seeking to understand and change our own twenty-first-century capitalist world.

The grand reach, complexities, and ambiguities in Marx's and Engels's writing allowed them to be interpreted in many different ways. Following sociologist Alvin Gouldner,[9] we can group the followers of Marx and Engels into two schools: structural/scientific and critical. They have such different understandings of Marx's and Engels's goals, expectations, visions of the good society, how to create social change, and the meaning of science that we shall treat them as two closely linked but different paradigms that require separate codes.

The Structural/Scientific Marxist Code

1. Capitalist society is divided into classes with inherently irreconcilable interests and entrenched power inequities. It is ruled by the capitalist class, or bourgeoisie, who exploit all other classes and expropriate their labor and productivity.
2. Capitalist markets are irrational, subordinating the use value of products and services to exchange values. The result is excess production and consumption of socially destructive commodities.
3. The laws of capitalism require the bourgeoisie to compete against each other. Competition results in winners and losers. The capitalist class will grow smaller and smaller, but its surviving members will become richer and more powerful.
4. The irreconcilable conflict between the ruling class and the subordinate classes, especially the working class or proletarian class, makes capitalism an inherently unstable system, facing periodic crises, and doomed to eventual collapse.
5. The primary role of the state is to ensure the continued rule of the capitalist class.
6. Capitalist democracy is an illusion, since the capitalist class controls government and exercises dominant power in capitalist society.

7. With the support of the state, the bourgeoisie will sacrifice the well-being of the rest of society, indeed their fellow capitalists, for their own profit and power.
8. There will be times of growth when life for the subordinate classes will improve. However, there also will be periods of decline with much of the population suffering a reduced standard of living.
9. Every once in a while, a downturn will result in a severe crisis. Eventually, there will be a crisis from which capitalism will not recover.
10. Inevitably, the subordinate classes will find the growing disparity between themselves and the capitalists intolerable. They will develop "class consciousness" and turn against capitalism.
11. History has laws like physics. The laws of history guarantee the victory of the working class.
12. The victorious proletarian will create socialism, almost a utopia, a far more equitable, just, and satisfying society than capitalism.
13. The actions or ideas of individuals will not alter the course of history. However, people must side with the inevitably victorious proletarian class and work to overthrow capitalism and create socialism.

Structural Marxists view themselves as scientists discovering the iron, inexorable laws of capitalism. These laws describe a society structurally divided into a capitalist class owning productive property (that is, factories, investments, banks) and a class lacking such property, the working class. The structure of this class division is inevitable and inevitably polarized. Marx wrote that society was destined to break into two vast antagonistic classes, workers and capitalist bosses, who would wage everlasting war against each other.[10] It is a system by which the ruling class extracts labor and wealth from the working class, an exploitative and abusive system that cannot be ameliorated through reform. Class warfare is in the DNA of capitalist society, and the contradictions built into the system lead to its own self-destruction. Such contradictions included the "wage paradox." Each capitalist makes more profit by paying his workers less but when all capitalists do this at once, stagnation and depression are inevitable. Over time, the class warfare intensifies and capitalists, relying on monopoly, state control, and globalization, will reduce wages ever more drastically, pushing most of the population into a state of poverty, unable to buy. According to Marx, "In these crises there breaks out an epidemic that in all earlier epochs would have seemed an absurdity—the epidemic of over-production.... Capitalists must accumulate while the mass of producers [workers] must be restricted in their consumption of subsistence.... The last cause of all real crises always remains the poverty and restricted consumption of the masses."[11]

Capitalists will try to solve the overproduction crisis and stagnation by turning to credit schemes, debt, and financial speculation. Neo-Marxists view this as the driving force behind the 2008 Great Recession as well as the 1930s Great Depression. Drawing on the neo-Marxist great economists, Paul Baran, Paul Sweezy, and Harry Magdoff, contemporary neo-Marxist sociologist John Bellamy Foster and political economist Fred Magdoff claim:

> Our argument in a nutshell is that both the financial explosion in recent decades and the financial implosion now taking place [in the 2008 Great Recession] are to be explained mainly in reference to stagnation tendencies within the underlying economy.... The root problem ... was to be found in a real economy experiencing slower growth, giving rise to financial explosion as capital sought to "leverage" its way out of the problem by expanding debt and gaining speculative profits.[12]

Foster and Magdoff, fleshing out the structural Marxist analysis, argue that the 2008 crash reflects the inevitable deepening of the overproduction and stagnation crises endemic to capitalism, something that both neoclassicists and Keynesians have largely ignored or dismissed:

> Mainstream economists have paid scant attention to the stagnation tendency in the mature economies.... A capitalist economy in order to continue to grow must constantly find new sources of demand for the growing surplus that it generates. There comes a time, however, in the historical evolution of the economy when much of the investment-seeking surplus is unable to find new profitable investment outlets. The reasons for this are complex, having to do with (1) the maturation of economies ... (2) the absence for long periods of any new technology that generates epoch-making stimulation ... (even the widespread use of computers and the Internet has not had the stimulating effect on the economy of earlier transformative technologies) (3) growing inequality of income and wealth, which limits consumption demand at the bottom of the economy and (4) a process of monopolization (oligopolization), leading to an attenuation of price competition—usually considered to be the main force accounting for the flexibility and dynamism of the system.[13]

Neo-Marxists argue that capitalists seek to cope with the iron law of stagnation by "financializing" the economy, where less and less is created by actually producing the things that enhance the quality of life. Financialization includes shifting capital into global financial services, expanding risky debt, and developing new types of mortgages, such as derivatives and credit default swaps. These types of novel Wall Street instruments created the housing bubble, which, among other crises, resulted in the economy crashing in 2008.

Structural Marxists argue that nothing can stop new crises that become more and more severe. In its drive for maximum profit, capitalism eventually and inevitably undermines the conditions for creating any profit at all. Capitalism would crash in momentous crises of overproduction, stagnation, and speculation, and eventually collapse altogether. Marx, who developed the foundation of the structural Marxist perspective and stagnation theme 150 years ago, wrote there was only one ultimate conclusion: "What the bourgeoisie produces, above all, are its own gravediggers. Its fall and the victory of the proletariat are equally inevitable."[14]

This is an inevitability in the structural Marxist view, determined, as Marx frequently wrote, by the laws of capitalism itself. But actual people have to act to bring about the revolutions. Structural Marxists foresee the dispossessed workers mobilizing on the streets and eventually "occupying" the factories and government command centers, as the capitalist world collapses around them. That final "Occupying movement" would be the beginning of the end of capitalism, which would yield to a new system controlled by the disenfranchised classes.

Structural Marxists share a few views with neoclassicists. They agree that the driving engines of capitalism are competition and profit, but foresee a very different historical scenario and conclusion. They reject the invisible hand. Competition is an inherently self-destructive dynamic. It produces winners and losers, which pits capitalists in a struggle against each other to wipe each other out. The result will be that the capitalist class will grow smaller and smaller, but the survivors—who increasingly would be monopoly corporations with little competition—will be richer and richer. Capitalism is cannibalistic. There is no option of standing still; you either expand and take a larger share of the market or you contract and possibly get eliminated. In the process, competitive capitalism becomes monopoly capitalism, a scenario that neoclassicists believe is false. In contrast to Marxists, they argue that monopolists will always be challenged by new and more innovative challengers who will restore true competition. Neo-Marxists in turn, such as Sweezy, Magdoff, and Bellamy Foster, see neoclassicists in a dream world, failing to acknowledge the obvious: that capitalism is increasingly a marriage of monopoly companies and the government, driving out competitors as well as immiserating the population.

Profit requires getting back more than you put in. Consequently employers pay their workers, who are the source of all value, less than the worth of what the laborers produce. Competition between capitalists creates a drive for ever-greater profit, forcing corporations to exploit their employees all the more, the inexorable class warfare at the heart of structural Marxism. Over time, workers' wages will fall, the ultimate force underlying recurrent crises. In Marx's time, bosses often demanded more hours for less pay, with results that Marx describes poignantly:

> Mary Anne Walkley, 20 years of age, employed in a highly respectable dressmaking establishment, exploited by a lady with the pleasant name of Elise.... This girl worked, on an average, 16.5 hours, during season often 30 hours without a break, whilst her failing labour-power was revived by occasional supplies of sherry, port or coffee.... Mary Anne Walkley had worked without intermission for 26.5 hours, with 60 other girls, 30 in one room, that only afforded 1/3 of the cubic feet of air required for them.... And this was one of the best millinery establishments in London. Mary Anne Walkley fell ill on the Friday, died on Sunday.... The doctor, Mr. Keys, called too late to the death-bed, duly bore witness before the coroner's jury that "Mary Anne Walkley had died from long hours of work in an overcrowded workroom, and a too small and badly ventilated bedroom."[15]

Ms. Walkley, Marx notes, was described in a conservative London newspaper, the *Morning Star*, as one of "our white slaves, who are toiled into the grave, for the most part silently pine and die."[16]

Later, the assembly line and a process of "scientific management" called "Taylorism" became the standard way to intensify exploitation and extract more productivity from workers, while giving them less in exchange. Like a cog in a machine, each laborer was forced to repeat the same action, like screwing on one part of the car wheel as someone else, further down the line, screwed on another. No worker could feel he made any creative contribution to the final product; all decisions were outside his control. He was an employee, a tool of production, who was to have no opinion, authority, or production, almost a living robot, a cost of production, whose only purpose was to contribute to his boss's profit. If he failed to do so or was too costly, he was as dispensable as an obsolete machine. Marx notes that even Adam Smith recognized this process turns ordinary workers into beasts of burden, stripped of humanity: "The man [says Smith as noted by Marx] whose whole life is spent in performing a few simple operations ... has no occasion to assert his understanding.... He generally becomes as stupid and ignorant as it is possible for a human creature to become."[17]

Marx points out that this is precisely how capitalist manufacturers organize work: "It is developed in manufacture which cuts down the labourer into a detail labourer.... To subdivide a man is to execute him.... The subdivision of labour is the assassination of a people."[18]

The other way for capitalists to make more profit is to replace workers with machines, but Marx's "labor theory of value" asserts technology cannot create wealth. While you can squeeze a living human to produce more wealth, a machine cannot make more than it was built to create. The more money capitalists invest in technology, the less additional profit it will yield. As surviving capitalists destroy their rivals, they will have few clients to do business with and sell their products. Simultaneously workers, facing declining wages or losing their jobs altogether, will be unable to buy. As a result, the rate of profit will fall and the remaining capitalists will lose their incentive to invest, which will cause the rate of profit to fall all the more. This will result in the periodic and terminal crises we have already described. Marx agreed with the neoclassicists that a crisis may drive wages down to the point where it is profitable to invest again and capitalism will recover. However, unlike the neoclassicists, Marx expected the recoveries to be unstable and subsequent crises to grow progressively worse. There will be fewer surviving capitalists, the working class will face greater poverty, and eventually, there will be a crisis from which there will be no recovery. Capitalism will collapse. As Marx put it, capitalism is like "the sorcerer, who is no longer able to control the powers of the nether world whom he has called up by his spells."[19] The impoverished class-conscious working class will not tolerate these demonic spells and will ultimately rise up and create socialism.

The revolution will be global. Another factor making capitalism unstable is that the search for more markets, cheaper labor, and raw material drives business elites to go beyond national borders. As rivals from different countries confront each other in competition to control the same territory, wars become more likely.

There is a contradiction within structural/scientific Marxism that is not easy to resolve. On the one hand, a structural/scientific Marxist proclaims that all is predetermined; the decisions and actions of individuals do not matter; the victory of the proletarian and the creation of socialism are inevitable. Since they are inevitable, anyone who opposes them is a reactionary, standing in the way of history. The only choice you have is whether to be on the winning side or be cast aside in the dustbin of history. What the majority will choose is clear. If one person makes the wrong choice, enough will choose the right side to ensure the proletarian's victory. On the other hand, if personal choices do not matter, why should an individual act at all?

For the first generation or so after Marx and Engels died, the structural/scientific paradigm dominated. An extreme authoritarian form of structural Marxism—in our view, a tragic distortion of Marx's basic philosophy and values—was adopted in most countries where Marxism became the ruling ideology. Vladimir Lenin, the leader of the Russian revolution and founder of the Soviet Union, shared the structural Marxist conviction that history followed predetermined laws, which ensured the inevitable victory of the proletariat, or working class. A vanguard party, trained in Marxist science, understood the interests of the working class better than the people themselves. To create socialism, the people must, at least temporarily, establish a "dictatorship of the proletariat."[20] In a "backward" country, like Russia, the need to develop the economy overrode the desire for democracy and the concern for individual rights. To guarantee the success of socialism and realize long-term class interests, everyone must submit to the will of the Communist Party. Those who did not submit were enemies of the people, who forfeited all rights. Lenin implied that members of the proletariat would retain democratic rights, but not their opponents: "Dictatorship does not necessarily mean the abolition of democracy for the class that exercises the dictatorship over other classes; but it does mean the abolition of democracy (or very material restriction, which is also a form of abolition) of democracy for the class over which, or against which, the dictatorship is exercised."[21]

Structural/scientific Marxism does not automatically lend itself to this kind of authoritarianism; most contemporary neo-Marxists, those who embrace both structural and critical Marxism, have a very strong commitment to economic democracy and view Leninism as a travesty or frightening parody of Marxism. But Leninism is one possible extrapolation of the structural Marxist vision, one often embraced by self-defined Marxist regimes despite its departure from Marx's own most basic aspirations for overcoming despotism and alienation.

Some Marxists of Lenin's generation, like Rosa Luxemburg,[22] feared that his "dictatorship of the proletarian" would never lead to a socialist democracy, which maximized human freedom. She warned it would create a new source of oppression:

> Lenin's thesis is that the party Central Committee should have ... the right to impose ... its own ready-made rules of party conduct. It should have the right to rule without appeal on such questions as the dissolution and reconstitution of local organizations.... The Central Committee would be the only thinking element in the party.... Social Democracy is not merely the replacement of the authority of bourgeois rulers with the authority of a socialist central committee. The working class will acquire the sense of the new discipline, the freely assumed self-discipline of the Social Democracy, not as a result of the discipline imposed on it by the capitalist state, but by extirpating, to the last root, its old habits of obedience and servility.[23]

On observing Lenin's regime, anarchist Emma Goldman declared, "If I can't dance, I don't want your revolution!"[24] In 1917, when Lenin initiated his revolution, many of Marx's early writings, including the *Economic and Philosophic Manuscripts of 1844*,[25] where he spoke of alienation and the human need for creativity and meaning, had been lost. Here, he critiqued capitalism as "forced labor," something that seems unlikely to be overcome in a Leninist dictatorship.

> In his work, therefore, he does not affirm himself but denies himself, does not feel content but unhappy, does not develop freely his physical and mental energy but mortifies his body and ruins his mind. The worker therefore only feels himself outside his work, and in his work feels outside himself. He feels at home when he is not working, and when he is working he does not feel at home. His labor is therefore not voluntary, but coerced; it is forced labor. It is therefore not the satisfaction of a need; it is merely a means to satisfy needs external to it.[26]

These manuscripts were rediscovered in the 1920s and seemed to support people who worried that Lenin's revolution perverted Marx's vision. For some, the Russian Revolution represented Marxism's triumph; for others, it put Marxism in crisis. Would a socialist revolution produce a dream or a nightmare? *What is to be done*[27] to bring true freedom, democracy, and equality, to allow people to realize their full potential? Critical Marxists doubted if following scientifically determined laws was the solution.

Critical Marxism emerged in the aftermath of World War I, which saw government after government collapse throughout Europe. If ever there was an opportune time for socialist revolutions, it was then. Lenin's revolution was followed by aborted revolutions in Germany, Hungary, Austria, and Italy. Rosa Luxemburg herself was killed by a rival socialist faction. Fearing that communist uprisings would spread, the United States and Britain supported the White Russian army, who tried to overthrow Lenin. It was a time to rethink Marxist assumptions: Why throughout Europe and in America, did the working class rally behind the elite in a war that could only bring them death and misery? Why when the people finally rose up, did the revolutions fail? Why in some cases, like Germany, did they self-destruct? Why, in Russia, where the revolution did succeed, did it produce something, in many ways, more oppressive than capitalism?

These questions helped lead to the rise of the Critical Marxist school, in our view a way of thinking most closely linked to Marx's basic values and worthy of serious study and practice today.

The Critical Marxist Code

1. Nothing is inevitable. History does not have objective scientific laws comparable to the positivist understanding of physics.

2. "Men (and women) make history, but not of circumstances of their own choosing." Individuals are simultaneously the products and creators of society. History gives us a range of choices, but the choices we make determine the future course of history.

3. Capitalist society is divided into classes with inherently irreconcilable interests. It is ruled by the capitalist class or bourgeoisie, who exploit all other classes and expropriate their labor and productivity.

4. Capitalist markets are irrational, creating a fetishism of commodities and subordinating the use value of products and services to exchange values. The result is excess production and consumption of alienating and socially destructive commodities.

5. Capitalism is an unstable system, subject to periodic crises, and likely to collapse.

6. The primary role of the state is to ensure the continued rule of the capitalist class.

7. Capitalist democracy is an illusion, since the capitalist class controls the state and exercises dominant power in capitalist society.

8. With the support of the state, the bourgeoisie will sacrifice the well-being of the rest of society, indeed their fellow capitalists, for their own profit and power.

9. Capitalism subjects much of the population to poverty and misery and most of the rest to an alienating unfulfilling life where they feel isolated, lacking a sense of community and support.

10. There will be times of growth when life for the subordinate classes will improve. However, there also will be periods of decline with much of the population suffering a reduced standard of living.

11. In class struggle, everyone must decide whether to side with the bourgeoisie or the exploited classes. There is no such thing as a neutral, value-free stance. Inaction is action: leaving society as it is to persist, and the problems it creates to fester. As Howard Zinn said, "You can't be neutral on a moving train."

12. There is no guarantee who will win the class struggle or that the society that replaces capitalism will be a utopia or a barbaric dystopia. Indeed, there is no guarantee the planet will survive.

Structural/scientific Marxists assert there are forces that constrain individual action. People are products of the society in which they grow up, belong to a particular class within that society, are forced to react to historical events, and are restrained by their class interests. Critical Marxists agree with this but believe that individuals are not only products of history; they are also its creators. The decisions people made in the past determine the options people have now, and the choices we make today create all subsequent history. People are indeed constrained by society, but have a wide range, perhaps an infinite range, of ways to react to the conditions in which they find themselves. Critical Marxists suggest we must act together to create the society we want to live in, although few anticipated seizing power themselves.

Critical Marxism pays a great deal of attention to "structure"—the class divisions, concentration of wealth, and use of state power by the capitalist class. But it believes that structure can evolve and be transformed in multiple ways within capitalism. It sees that capitalists often devise strategies to attract the working class, to overcome many of its contradictions, and to pay workers for long periods at wages higher than Marx believed possible. They do not accept the idea that the revolution is imminent or inevitable, although they see the same exploitative processes described by the structural Marxists as a relentless force driving immiseration in the population.

Critical Marxists emphasize "agency" as much as "structure." Agency is the ability of people to shape a capitalist world and change its economic and social forms, despite the power of capitalist elites. Agency also implies capacity to think "outside the box" of even one's own class position. Gouldner noted that structural Marxists appear to deny agency: "[structural] Marxism did indeed say that capitalist society was subject to blind and necessary [scientific] laws to which persons were inescapably subject."[28] This implies no free agency, by people, whose thoughts and actions are locked in and determined by the unbending structural laws of capitalism and their own class position.

But in describing critical Marxism, Gouldner wrote, "It treats persons as free agents who will not only do what they must, but who can respond to appeals and be won over even against their own class interests."[29] Gouldner noted that not only are there many workers who embrace capitalist values but, as Marx noted, there are even capitalists who exercise their own free agency and reject their own capitalist system: "A small section of the ruling class cuts itself adrift and joins the revolutionary class."[30] This is the critical Marx rather than the structural Marx speaking, highlighting the free agency of human beings despite the overwhelming power of the structural forces shaping their existence. Those following the critical Marx (or critical Marxism) thus focus more attention on the "agents" of change: the workers, racial minorities, women, the unemployed, and ethnic groups. They highlight history—the study of history is, in fact, central to neo-Marxists and differentiates them from neoclassicists and many Keynesians. They focus on how agents within the society change and are changed by the powerful structures that capitalists have created. The makers of ideology—including the schools, the media, and the intelligentsia—also become central to critical Marxism, because they influence the "agents" and help to determine how social movements and dispossessed groups see and act in the world.

Unlike structural/scientific Marxism, critical Marxism never seized state power or ran a government bureaucracy. Nonetheless, in eras such as the 1960s, it inspired students, intellectuals, and activists, particularly in the West. It led many to reassess whether capitalism can provide democracy and a fulfilling lifestyle for the vast majority; whether they should trust the state, the corporation, and the military; and whether there was a need to endlessly compete in a rat race and amass commodities for their own sake. It encouraged experimentation in art and lifestyles and supported rejecting mainstream society and forming "countercultures." With its call for creativity and free thinking, it did not breed the discipline, loyalty to party leadership, or willingness to follow a predetermined "party line" that many structural/scientific Marxists believed would be necessary to successfully stage a revolution or run a bureaucracy, once in power.

Although many participants in the 2011 Occupy movement may not have been familiar with critical Marxism, they seemed to gravitate to many of its assumptions. Some observers predicted the Occupy movement would fail because it lacked leadership and a unifying ideology and objective. However, powerful leaders could undermine a movement whose purpose is to bring everyone together to participate and think for themselves. Some Occupiers and critical Marxists adopted the anarchist spirit and feared that anyone who wanted power could not be trusted with it. Winning may not have been the goal for many critical Marxists. Rather, they hoped to raise new perspectives and widen debate, so that the charge that capitalist society is irreparably flawed would be seriously heard. Many embraced a slogan from the French student uprising of 1968: "Be realistic; demand the impossible."[31]

Marxism in America: The Hidden History of the US Marxist Paradigm

Most Americans believe Marxism has played no role in the United States, except at the very fringes. They see it as an alien way of thinking, associated with dictatorship rather than democracy, and mostly related to poor and third world countries or to European socialism. But just a brief history shows that while Marxism began in Europe, and created both European socialism and right-wing, horrifying, European counterrevolutions such as Leninism and Stalinism, it has helped shape American thinking and important US social movements—from the abolitionists and nineteenth-century workers' movements all the way up to Occupy.

Marxism did, of course, originate in Europe and played an important role in European politics before it became significant in the United States. The

Leninist revolution brought a self-defined structural/scientific Marxism to Russia, one, as already noted, that was a distorted parody of Marxist thinking. In the aftermath of the Russian Revolution and World War I, brutal regimes in Europe, notably fascism, seized power, winning struggles against Marxist European parties, particularly in Italy and Germany.

Trying to understand why so large a segment of the population gravitated toward fascism helped stimulate the growth of critical Marxism in Europe. Fascism attracted many people whom Marxists would have expected to turn to socialism. Antonio Gramsci wrote from an Italian prison because of his opposition to fascism.[32] He concluded that structural/scientific Marxism too readily assumed that people act on their rational economic class. Marxists must look more at culture, ideology, and national identity to understand how the capitalist class and the state maintain "hegemony" (domination) to breed loyalty and even get young soldiers to proudly march to their death in defense of regimes that oppress them.

In Germany, the Great Depression, discussed in previous chapters, almost brought socialism; instead, it brought Nazism, a version of fascism that may have been the most brutal regime in the history of the world. Determining how and why this happened brought a new European resurgence of critical Marxist scholars, some of whom banded together to form the Frankfurt School.[33] Several concluded, like Gramsci, that Marxism must take psychology more seriously and tried to synthesize Marx and Freud. One of them was Herbert Marcuse, who in his later life, after he immigrated to the United States, became a hero to students, activists, and members of the counterculture in the 1960s and 1970s. He felt capitalism, fascism, and Soviet Marxism have more in common than would be obvious on the surface. They all place technical efficiency ahead of human needs. In his most famous book, *One-Dimensional Man*,[34] he argued they strip the vast majority, including the working class, of their creative potential and revolutionary fervor by making their survival dependent on seeing the world through the eyes of the elite. Advanced capitalism, in particular, binds the working class to compete and consume with little sense of why they are doing it.

Marcuse was a major force in bringing Marxist thinking to America, mainly in the 1960s when he became the intellectual guru of student activists, but in earlier eras as well. He described how modern societies—whether democratic-capitalist, fascist, or communist—provide just enough comfort so people comply, accept their situation, and do not challenge their rulers.

A comfortable, smooth, reasonable, democratic unfreedom prevails in advanced industrial civilization, a token of technical progress. Indeed, what could be more rational than the suppression of individuality in the mechanization of socially necessary but painful performances; the concentration of individual enterprises in more effective, more productive corporations; the regulation of free competition among unequally equipped economic subjects; the curtailment of prerogatives and national sovereignties which impede the international organization of resources.... The distinguishing feature of advanced industrial society is its effective suffocation of those needs which demand liberation—liberation also from that which is tolerable and rewarding and comfortable.[35]

American Marxism from World War I to the 1950s

European thinkers such as Marcuse bring us now to the surprisingly long and important role of Marxism in the United States—a kind of hidden history. World War I did not provoke a revolution or fascism in the United States, but it did lead to increased repression of civil liberties and the beginnings of a significant American Marxism. Marxists helped lead the American labor movement, particularly Eugene Debs,[36] who was jailed several times for organizing strikes, and then for opposing World War I, a cause in which he believed the working citizen was expected to sacrifice himself, while reinforcing the wealth and power of the capitalist. Here is an excerpt from the speech that got Debs arrested:

> The poor, ignorant serfs had been taught to revere their masters; to believe that when their masters declared war upon one another, it was their patriotic duty to fall upon one another and to cut one another's throats for the profit and glory of the lords and barons who held them in contempt.... The working class who fight all the battles, the working class who make the supreme sacrifices, the working class who freely shed their blood and furnish the corpses, have never yet had a voice in either declaring war or making peace. It is the ruling class that invariably does both. They alone declare war and they alone make peace. Yours not to reason why; Yours but to do and die.... You need at this time especially to know that you are fit for something better than slavery and cannon fodder. You need to know that you were not created to work and produce and impoverish yourself to enrich an idle exploiter. You need to know that you have a mind to improve, a soul to develop.[37]

Although Marx, Engels, and Lenin were hardly pacifists, for decades, many American Marxists have come to the forefront in opposition to militarism, a trend that continued through the wars in Vietnam, Iraq, and Afghanistan. Debs probably knew little about critical Marxism; it was structural/scientific Marxism that gave him and other labor organizers the confidence to strike, act, and agitate. In 1920, while in jail, Debs received 919,799 or 3.4 percent of the vote for president of the United States.[38] Debs was hardly alone. The fear that the Russian Revolution or even the antiwar movement could prove infectious provoked Attorney General Mitchell Palmer to round up Marxists and sympathizers. As a result, 249 immigrants, including Emma Goldman, were deported.[39]

In the short run, Palmer's raids succeeded. The labor movement declined and American Marxism retreated. However, the Great Depression brought a revival. The Great Depression was the biggest economic crisis capitalism had yet faced. Unlike Keynesians who felt capitalism can and should be revitalized, many Marxists speculated it was evidence of the system's imminent collapse. They felt emboldened. It was a time to act, a time for "praxis," the Marxist term for the unification of theory and practice. By 1934, there were 1,856 strikes with almost one and a half million participants. That year there was a general strike, begun by longshoremen in San Francisco, along with major uprisings in Toledo and Minneapolis. Later in the decade, there were mass sit-down strikes at Goodyear Rubber and Tire, Alcoa Aluminum, and General Motors. The American Communist Party, the Socialist Workers Parties, and other Marxist factions helped organize the unions and urged workers to strike.[40] Most Marxists involved were structural/scientific; critical Marxism was yet to gain a large American following. Wanting to integrate themselves into the American mainstream, the Communist Party adopted a "popular front" strategy, through which they would try to work with other groups. Many became active in the Democratic Party. There were politicians, like Minnesota governor Floyd Olsen, who said he would abandon capitalism if it could not resolve the Great Depression.[41] Indirectly, Marxism may have influenced New Deal policies. The threat of a socialist uprising made Keynesianism more attractive. One of Roosevelt's strongest supporters, Boston department store owner Edward Filene, for example, was convinced that without guarantees of higher wages, better working conditions, and stricter regulation of business, the working class would turn against capitalism. Capitalism's survival would require changing some of its basic assumptions and giving workers a sense of economic freedom. In Filene's words,

> The economic freedom that will come from high wages, lower prices and shorter hours greatly reduces and ultimately eliminates the social and industrial unrest [that] threatens like a latent mutiny our entire industrial order.[42]

> There is socialism, for instance, in which all industries and all business would come under the direction of political bureaus, or communism with its complete uprooting of all that Americans have generally come to revere.[43]

Some Marxists actually joined the Roosevelt administration. Among them was Marxist theorist and Harvard economist, Paul Sweezy, who in a federally funded project, demonstrated that most of the two hundred largest industrial corporations were controlled by eight families and banks.[44]

In contrast to its treatment during World War I, Marxism acquired a certain respectability in World War II, largely because the United States was forced to ally with the Soviet Union. This ended along with the war, when official US government policy replaced Nazi Germany with the Soviet Union as the primary enemy. The dawn of the cold war, forty years of tension between the United States and Russia, which encouraged each side to build nuclear arsenals capable of destroying the biosphere eighty times over, brought the McCarthy era. This was an effort to expunge anyone suspected of socialist sympathies from the government, the universities, the arts, and the professions.[45] Unions actively participated. "United Auto Workers (UAW) President Walter Reuther, a former member of the Socialist Party of America, launched an extended campaign to oust Communists and their allies from his union."[46] In Hollywood, the purges were led by Screen Actor's Guild president, Ronald Reagan.[47] Rather than being catalysts for agitation, the unions entered a détente with the corporations and the state. Most mainstream union leaders embraced the cold war. In exchange for guarantees of high wages, unions would assist in managing the working class, if "working class" was the right term, because so many identified themselves as "middle class." This was a catastrophe for American Marxists, brought on not only by capitalist and labor repression but also partly by themselves in their misguided embrace of Soviet communism.

The immediate post–World War II decades brought the United States a prosperity, never before seen in the history of the world, in apparent contradiction to all of Marx's predictions. As pointed out in Chapter 4, an unprecedented percentage of the population could own houses, cars, televisions, and acquire a college education. Class conflict abated. There was a new harmony and patriotism. It seemed God had blessed America—the "American Dream" was available to everyone. Not only had Marxism been repressed, it became irrelevant. Marx's predictions appeared to be proven wrong and his vision seemed to create, not utopias, but nightmares like the Soviet Union. There was a new consensus. Ex-socialist Daniel Bell proclaimed "The End of Ideology."[48] Even ex-Marxists recognized that Soviet communism proved American capitalism was preferable. The difference between Marx's promise and the way it really was applied was too deep. Because Europeans had struggled against fascism in their own countries, unlike Americans, the European Left was more reluctant to abandon Marx than their American counterparts. According to Bell, the Marxist "excitement evaporated" in the wake of "the Moscow Trials" (the mass murderous purges by Stalin) and the Nazi-Soviet Pact.[49]

While the Soviet realities did lead many Marxists ultimately to abandon communism, new generations after World War II quickly embraced a more democratically oriented critique of American capitalism. Anyone looking beneath the surface could see that the post–World War II consensus of the 1950s—the celebration of America as a capitalist paradise—was hardly universally shared. One of the few respected socialists at the time, Michael Harrington, observed an "other America"[50] in the South, Appalachia, and northern inner-city black ghettoes. "Tens of millions of Americans are, at this very moment, maimed in body and spirit, existing at levels beneath those necessary for human decency.... They are without adequate housing and education and medical care.... This poverty twists and deforms the spirit. The American poor are pessimistic and defeated, and they are victimized by mental suffering to a degree unknown in Suburbia."[51]

By the late 1950s, blacks with white allies began to demand civil rights and broke the illusion of harmony. Many of these blacks moved toward Marxist thinking and helped revive neo-Marxism in the United States. W. E. B. Du Bois, the first black Harvard PhD, founder of the National Association for the Advancement of Colored People (NAACP) and one of the early leaders of the civil rights movement, identified himself as a Marxist and believed Marxism was essential for understanding why capitalists give a few benefits to white workers, which they deny to blacks and thus use racism to turn the working class against itself.

> Black and white work together in many cases, and influence each other's rate of wages. They have similar complaints against capitalists, save that the grievances of the Negro worker are more fundamental and indefensible, ranging as they do, since the day of Karl Marx, from chattel slavery, to the worst paid, sweated, mobbed and cheated labor any civilized land.... It is white labor that deprives the Negro of his right to vote, denies him education, denies affiliation with trade unions, expels him from decent housing and neighborhoods.... There is not at present the slighted indication that a Marxian revolution based on a united class-conscious proletariat is anywhere on the American horizon. Rather race antagonism and labor group rivalry is still undisturbed.[52]

The new American Marxists thus understood that race was a major factor keeping white workers from turning against capitalism. Accordingly, American neo-Marxists considered racism among the most important issues they had to address. Among themselves, they debated questions about how Marxists in America could help build a movement among both white and black workers, often moving back and forth between supporting anticapitalist movements and civil rights movements that at least temporarily did not challenge capitalism directly.

Another early black labor leader who helped advance neo-Marxism in America was A. Philip Randolph, who joined Debs in resisting World War I, believing blacks should not fight white wars when they are being lynched. He founded the socialist magazine *The Messenger*, formed the Brotherhood of Sleeping Car Porters, and then helped organize the 1963 March on Washington where Martin Luther King gave his "I Have a Dream" speech.[53] Governor Ronald Reagan lobbied UCLA to fire black professor Angela Davis, a student of Herbert Marcuse and Communist Party USA candidate for vice president of the United States, despite having enrollments of over two thousand in her classes.[54] In her most famous book *Women, Race and Class* she argued that the struggle against racial and gender discrimination cannot be separated from the need to end capitalist class inequality.

> Working women, therefore, have a special and vital interest in the struggle for socialism. Moreover, under capitalism, campaigns for jobs on an equal basis with men, combined with movements for institutions such as subsidized public health care, contain an explosive revolutionary potential. This strategy calls into question the validity of monopoly capitalism and must ultimately point in the direction of socialism.[55]

Clearly, in the 1950s, the notion that poverty, misery, inequality, alienation, and dissent ended with World War II was a myth. If you wanted to see real poverty, go to Appalachia or the slums of Newark or LA or Chicago. Or go to the third world colonies, or allegedly independent former colonies, of Western capitalist empires. Marx had argued that capitalism must be viewed as a unified world system, which forever tries to expand markets, ignores national boundaries, and goes wherever labor and raw materials are cheapest, a point we discuss in Chapter 9 on globalization. Capitalist profit comes not only from exploiting the labor of people in the home country but immiserating the population of intentionally underdeveloped areas. Competition to control the third world causes wars, including world wars. Lenin elaborated on this idea in *Imperialism: The Highest Stage of Capitalism*.[56] It continues to be developed by more recent neo-Marxist sociologists like Immanuel Wallerstein who argue the history of capitalism must be viewed as an ever-expanding world system.[57] If jobs and resources can be exported to the periphery of an empire, the citizens of the core country can be made anxious that they too can fall into poverty and become all the easier to exploit.[58]

The 1960s: Civil Rights, Vietnam, and the Neo-Marxist Revival

Moving on from the 1950s, the link between racism in the United States, misery and war in the third world, and alienation among the white middle class stimulated the birth of student Left protests of the 1960s and 1970s. While a study showing why Harvard students did not engage in protests was at press, hundreds of students gathered in Harvard Square in opposition to the Vietnam War.[59] The student Left of the period resembled Occupy as a broad movement, valuing spontaneity and lacking a definitive shared ideology, agenda, or hierarchy. However, if one organization represented the student Left, it was Students for a Democratic Society (SDS). SDS began as the Student League for Industrial Democracy (SLID), an anti-Leninist socialist organization. In the 1950s SLID's general secretary was James Farmer, a black man of socialist leanings who also founded the Congress of Racial Equality (CORE). Through CORE, whites—many of them also beginning to question capitalism and call for socialism—became involved in the "Freedom Rides," where whites and blacks would sit beside each other on buses, expecting to be arrested in the segregated South.

The civil rights movement was one force bringing white students to believe they could no longer seek a comfortable place within corporate capitalism and move to the suburbs with a white picket fence and 2.3 children. Another factor was the Vietnam War. A consensus emerged that the war was not a mere mistake stemming from a fundamentally sound policy carried out too zealously, but rather a manifestation of an American society controlled by a small corporate elite who orchestrated foreign and domestic policy to ensure their continued wealth and power. Poverty, racial discrimination, militarism, and imperialism—aggressive foreign policy through which the United States seeks to dominate other countries—were all seen as symptoms of the same core cause: *American capitalism itself.*

After SLID reconstituted itself as SDS, students started referring to themselves as a "New Left," to distinguish themselves from the "Old Left," by which they meant mostly Leninist structural/scientific Marxists whom they perceived as authoritarian, manipulative, secretive, and undemocratic. They also disassociated themselves from Keynesian liberals whom they came to see as members, or at least allies, of the corporate elite, attempting to contain protest in ways that do not threaten the rich and powerful. In particular, liberals bore most of the responsibility for the Vietnam War. Some within the New Left, like Yippie (Youth International Party) Jerry Rubin,[60] felt that they should shun theory altogether because it interferes with spontaneity: don't think, act. This may have led a tiny number to commit pointless random violence, like robbing banks and murdering police—acts which may have helped discredit the cause and drive members away. However, the sense that they were part of a larger movement may have brought many others to read, reflect, and discuss all the more. They absorbed Marxist texts and despite the slogan "Don't trust anyone over thirty,"[61] sought sympathetic professors. Many were attracted to calls for creativity and independent thinking, offered by critical Marxism, especially Marcuse,[62] who said revolutionary consciousness was more likely to be found in the third world and among students, youth, and people of color than among the traditional industrial working class. The debates also attracted some people to structural/scientific Marxism like French theorist Nicos Poulantzas and philosopher Louis Althusser, who rejected Marx's early works—where he spoke of alienation, the reduction of interpersonal relations to a commodity, and the need for personal fulfill-ment—as pre-Marxist unscientific humanism. Although critical Marxism's spontaneity did attract many people to the New Left, there were also others who gravitated toward Leninist parties, which emphasized discipline and centralized leadership. Among them were Progressive Labor, the Spartacus League, the Weathermen, and the Black Panthers.

As the New Left revived interest in Marxism, students studied Marxist economists who said that changing conditions required reconsidering Marx-ist orthodoxy. Paul Sweezy collaborated with Paul Baran to write *Monopoly Capital*[63] where they proposed that the concentration of wealth in the hands of a few corporations, as Marx predicted, had taken place. However, it did not bring about capitalism's collapse; nonetheless, it changed the rules of the economy. The monopolies did not need to figure out how to produce more but how to find customers for what they made. The "one-dimensional men" Marcuse spoke about could serve the largest corporations. Their self-worth could be tied to their possessions and they could be encouraged to buy! buy! buy! The state could be used to consume what the private citizen did not.

Like C. Wright Mills, Baran and Sweezy felt that social scientists had been reduced to narrow overspecialized technocrats, blinding themselves to the big picture and unable to see the real problems. They thought Marxism might provide an antidote:

> Only a few years ago, during what C. Wright Mills aptly called the Great American Celebration, social scientists were assuring us that everything was fine. The opposite is true—that idle men and idle machines coexist with deprivation at home and starvation abroad, that poverty grows in step with affluence, that enormous amounts of resources are wasted in frivolous and often harmful ways, that the United States has become the symbol and defender of reaction all over the world.... If [social scientists] have failed to throw light on the great issues of our time, the reason is not opportunism, but the inherent limitations of their outlook and methodologies.... Fol-lowing this road, social science has become more and more compartmen-talized, with its practitioners turning into ever narrower specialists—but knowing and indeed able to understand less and less about the specialties of others.... The same cannot be said of the Marxian social sciences.[64]

Intellectuals such as Marcuse, Sweezy, and Michael Harrington helped build a socialist and Marxist revival throughout the 1960s. A huge swath of youth moved from Kennedy and liberal Keynesianism toward a Marxist-style critique of the capitalist system. Keynesian government spending had prevented collapse during the Great Depression, but in the 1960s, it produced a bubble in which things were made that were not needed—some of these, like nuclear weapons, would be better as pure waste than being used for their intended purpose. Vietnam and US militarism turned many students toward a rejection of American capitalism itself.

The horrors of the cold war—and US cold war hysteria—built further anticapitalist sensibilities among US students in the 1960s. When America found itself with the bomb at the end of World War II, the temptation to intimidate Russia by dropping it on Japan was just too great. Although the Soviet Union and the United States never went directly to war with each other, cold war anticommunism was used to justify building ever more weapons. Capitalism and communism would confront each other through proxy wars in the third world periphery, including Cuba, where human survival seemed in peril. All these horrors led young people to see serious systemic problems in the United States as well as the Soviet Union. And then came Vietnam, the ultimate anticapitalist spark for students facing the prospect of fighting and dying in a tropical jungle to save what many saw as capitalist profits and power.

The emergence of the civil rights movement was consistent with orthodox Marxist expectations; an oppressed group was not willing to accept its subordinate position. However, the growth of an increasingly anticapitalist student movement might seem a little surprising. It developed among relatively privileged people at a time, for middle-class students at least, of prosperity. But critical Marxism suggests looking for motives beyond economic advancement; consider alienation and the need for meaning and purpose. Students were asking themselves: Did they want to inherit the world their parents were bequeathing them? Were they "growing up absurd"?[65] Did they want to become the "white collar workers"[66] or the "men in gray flannel suits,"[67] who commute daily from their big house in the suburbs to their downtown office in a competitive rat race to make money and power for the sake of making money and power? Did they really want money and power that come from the exploitation and impoverishment of two-thirds of the world's population, building weapons capable of destroying the biosphere and provoking wars to guarantee their country remains prosperous and dominant? Were not community, free expression, creativity, leisure, and support more important? Mario Savio, spokesperson for one of the first major student protests of the 1960s, the Berkeley Free Speech Movement, explained students' underlying grievances:

> The bosses build schools for the children of their workers. They build schools to further their own interests. Accordingly, the schools have become

training camps—and proving grounds—rather than places where people acquire education. They become factories to produce technicians rather than places to live student lives. And this perversion develops great resentment on the part of the students. Resentment against being subjected to standard production techniques of speedup and regimentation; against a tendency to quantify education—virtually a contradiction in terms. Education is measured in units, in numbers of lectures attended, in numbers of pages devoted to papers, number of pages read. This mirrors the gross and vulgar quantification in the society at large—the real world—where everything must be reduced to a lowest common denominator, the dollar bill. In our campus play-world we use play money, course units.... Who takes undergraduate courses in the history of the labor movement, for example? Certainly no one at the University of California. Likewise, American Negro history is a rarity and is still more rarely taken seriously.[68]

Savio viewed students essentially the way Marx viewed workers. Actually, he saw students as even worse off. The faculty were the workers; the students the raw material. But like workers, they faced an exploitation so intense that the only response was to reject and rebel.

The faculty are a bunch of employees, and we're the raw material! But we're a bunch of raw material[s] that don't mean to have any process upon us, don't mean to be made into any product, don't mean to end up being bought by some clients of the University, be they the government, be they industry, be they organized labor, be they anyone! We're human beings! ... There is a time when the operation of the machine becomes so odious, makes you so sick at heart, that you can't take part; you can't even passively take part, and you've got to put your bodies upon the gears and upon the wheels, upon the levers, upon all the apparatus, and you've got to make it stop. And you've got to indicate to the people who run it, to the people who own it, that unless you're free, the machine will be prevented from working at all![69]

Most students who protested initially joined the movement not because they read Marxist, particularly critical Marxist, texts. Instead, as they became attracted to alternatives to mainstream lifestyles, critical Marxist writings gave them a framework to explore why the society they were questioning was organized the way it was and why they faced alienation, boredom, tedium, and meaninglessness if they did not act to transform it.

As the New Left developed into a mass movement, spreading the Marxist spirit of revolt in unexpected ways, there were teach-ins on college campuses around the country, support for draft resistance, and antiwar marches that attracted tens of thousands of participants in such cities as New York,

Chicago, Boston, San Francisco, and Los Angeles, and nationwide gatherings converging on Washington, DC. Students demonstrated against the university itself, opposing the Reserve Officer Training Corps (ROTC), war-related research, on-campus recruiters for the military, and corporations producing weapons, like Dow Chemical. Many students became convinced that universities do not produce objective, value-neutral knowledge but train professionals and conduct research in service to the ruling corporate elite. A small number of critical neo-Marxist professors like Noam Chomsky[70] and Howard Zinn[71] encouraged that critique and helped catalyze major campus protests. In April 1968, the Columbia chapter of SDS took over several buildings, effectively shutting the university down. When the university administration called the police, activity did not return to normal but instead erupted into a campus-wide student strike. The Columbia demonstration was followed by similar strikes and building takeovers on hundreds of campuses over the next several years. In 1970, a national student strike simultaneously shut down hundreds of campuses. All of this reflected a resurrection of protest against the system that nobody, even many neo-Marxists, had thought possible a decade earlier.

Whether they joined formal organizations or called themselves Marxists, youth, in the hundreds of thousands, came to identify themselves with the radical New Left. Both students and nonstudents came to question the fundamental values of the society they were about to inherit. The antiwar movement even won sympathy among soldiers and high-ranking representatives of the government, corporations, universities, and media and may have even influenced President Johnson not to seek another term. Largely to appease student discontent, the voting age was lowered to eighteen, the draft was abolished, and many universities granted students more authority and voice in governing campus affairs. Fear of provoking a radical movement may have motivated presidents Johnson and Richard Nixon to gradually withdraw from Vietnam. This did not prevent the student movement from evolving beyond a critique of racial discrimination and the Vietnam War toward a broader critique of the capitalist system itself. By the late 1960s, SDS had developed many variants of Marxist activists who called for a more general struggle against capitalism. Some went off campus to organize in unions or poor communities to stir up a popular base for revolution.

Contrary to orthodox Marxist predictions, the New Left grew in response not to an economic crisis but a political crisis. As the escalation of the Vietnam War began, the economy was experiencing unprecedented prosperity, largely as a result of military Keynesianism. Prosperity may have actually helped the movement grow because young people may have felt they had the luxury to "drop out" for a while since they could "drop back in" and get a professional job if and when they chose. The movement had little appeal to the industrial working class, which classical Marxism would expect to be its base. For the most part, they were hostile and saw it as an assault on their patriotism and culture. In May 1970, a group of construction workers, chanting "All the way, U.S.A." and "Love it or leave it," attacked student demonstrators outside Wall Street, injuring about seventy.[72] As the war dragged on, polls indicated that larger and larger percentages of the population saw it as a tactical mistake,[73] but they still found the New Left offensive. George McGovern, the 1972 Democratic nominee for president, was a Keynesian liberal, hardly a Marxist, but he strongly opposed the war. He only carried one state, Massachusetts. Most leaders of the national labor unions did not support him.

As we discussed in Chapter 4, Vietnam undermined the affluence and the consensus that World War II brought the United States. It actually brought the country a sense of malaise, even among those who supported the war, perhaps even more so among the supporters, because they felt their country had been insulted. It seemed that the country was waking up from the "American Dream." It was no longer in sight for everyone. With declining profits, the corporations broke their détente with the unions, closed factories, and fired workers. Factory jobs that allowed American auto and steel workers to sustain a comfortable middle-class lifestyle were exported to low-paying third world countries. If high-paying industrial jobs in US Steel and General Motors were replaced at all, they were replaced by low-paying sales and service jobs at Wal-Mart and McDonald's. Even middle-class educated professionals were affected, as computer programming was transferred to India. As we noted in the last chapter, leading capitalists, themselves, suggested these changes are permanent. Late Apple CEO Steve Jobs told President Obama, "Those jobs aren't coming back."[74] The "deindustrialization of America"[75] raises a question: Is "industrial, proletarian working class" still the best way to describe most employees of the capitalist class? President Obama continually refers to the victims of deindustrialization as "middle class," but that may be a euphemism. The transformation and impoverishment of much of labor and the working class have been a major focus for contemporary Marxist sociologists like Harry Braverman,[76] Stanley Aronowitz,[77] and American Sociological Association presidents Michael Burawoy[78] and Erik Olin Wright.[79]

The Reagan Revolution and the Repression of the Marxists

For a while, the widespread prosperity of the immediate post–World War II decades seemed to refute Marx's claim that capitalism would bring increasing poverty. However, the reversal that began in the late 1970s suggests the good years could have been a temporary glitch. The immiseration Marx predicted may have been delayed, but, in the view of many neo-Marxists, has been continually ongoing since the aftermath of Vietnam.

Orthodox Marxists would expect a declining economy to reinforce leftist opposition. That happened in the 1930s, but not in the 1970s. Some Marxists applaud letting conditions deteriorate on the assumption that they must get worse before they will get better or as Mao Tse-tung, the founder of the People's Republic of China, put it, "To make an omelet, you must break eggs."[80] However, a crisis can end in a victory for the Right as well as the Left. The crisis of the 1970s ended in the Reagan counterrevolution and restoration of neoclassical economics as the mainstream. Keynesian liberalism came to be considered the Left fringe, and Marxism, as in the McCarthy era, was pushed beyond the pale. The Reagan purges were more subtle and, in some ways, more effective than the McCarthy purges. People were not arrested or deported; there were no formal blacklists. However, to be relevant and heard, Marxists and other leftists felt pressured to tone their language down, present themselves as patriotic, stop denouncing American policy as the domination of the planet, and quit treating capitalism as an inherently exploitative system whose demise would serve humanity.

As of this writing, over thirty years after Reagan's election, the neoclassicist restoration continues. The gap between the richest 1 percent and everyone else has mushroomed. In the largest corporations, the average CEO made 24 times the average worker's wage in 1965;[81] by 2011, that ratio ballooned to 343.[82] In 1983, the wealthiest 1 percent held 125 times more net worth than the median family. By 2010, it held 288 times.[83] Just as neoclassicism caused the Great Depression, the cumulative effect of over thirty-five years of neoclassicist policies produced the largest recession since then, with net average family wealth falling 40 percent from 2007 to 2010.[84] For the capitalist class, the recession has ended. The Dow Jones Industrial Average has risen from 7,000 in 2009 to over 15,000 in 2013.[85] However, it has been deemed a "jobless recovery." "When the economy recovers, jobs in the middle won't."[86] The growing gap Marx predicted between the capitalist class and everyone else, whether or not they are best called working class, is happening. However, that does not mean the collapse of capitalism is imminent or likely to happen anytime soon. Nor is there any way to predict if anticapitalist, prosocialist consciousness will become widespread.

The Occupy activists of 2011 hint that a revival of movements like those of the 1960s and 1970s is possible. While Occupy seems to have been successfully suppressed, history suggests it could well reemerge in another guise. Unlike the generation of the Vietnam era, the current generation has reason to seriously worry if the jobs, lifestyle, and security, which their parents had, will be available to them. A shrinking economic pie could intensify competition to make sure I get my slice. It could create passive resignation or build the sociological imagination and bring people to act collectively. If there is to be a *new* New Left, Marxism may be vital, more for the questions it raises than the answers it provides. Even if many of its specific details are flawed and many of its predictions miss the mark, Marxism offers a framework for understanding the interconnections among economics, politics, and culture. It exposes many myths and warns against trusting the mass media, the corporations, politicians, many professors, or so-called experts. Pay attention to social class, look at power relations, and ask if institutions and policies are really designed to serve you or keep you in your place. Ask who is your real ally and your adversary. Try to envision the world you want to live in, and as non-Marxist revolutionary Gandhi advised, "Be the change you want to see in the world."[87] As neo-Marxist veterans of the 1960s and 1970s, we offer this suggestion: Don't accept a revolution without dancing.

PART III

Political Economy and Contemporary Issues

Introduction to Part III

In Part II, we reviewed the assumptions underlying our three main paradigms of political economy, as well as traced each school's development and influence throughout modern history. As we have seen, each has a very different explanation for why people live as they do and a fundamentally different vision of the ideal society. In this part, we compare how the paradigms address specific and vital societal and public policy issues, which are likely to confront us for the foreseeable future. These are the great issues of our times, and the importance of political economy is that it shapes how we think and act on them.

What are these issues—and what questions must be answered? Here are a few we address in this part.

Inequality: Is economic inequality a natural state essential for human progress or a source of misery and oppression?

Democracy: Do capitalism and democracy need each other, or do they conflict with each other?

Individualism versus Community: Must individuals compete against each other, or will their needs be better met by recognizing their interdependency?

Globalization: Is globalization a process that will bring a better life to the entire world or one that will destroy local communities, culture, and identity, only to profit a small elite in the West at the expense of the vast majority of the planet?

Environment and Climate Change: Will capitalism build an environment that will ensure the health, happiness, and prosperity of all of humanity, or will an unrestrained capitalism destroy the biosphere?

Education: Under capitalism, does education serve as the "great equalizer" and bring people to realize their full potential, or does it serve as a "great divider" and transform the vast majority into a tool for profit, benefiting a small minority?

Race and Gender: Is capitalism the path to eradicate racial and gender oppression, or does it impoverish and oppress the majority of women and people of color, even as it allows a growing number to thrive? Does capitalism foster racial and sexual equality or lock people into racially and sexually stereotyped roles?

Chapter 6

Inequality

The Occupy movement made the 1 percent and the 99 percent household terms. The 1 percent are the richest Americans, mostly millionaires and billionaires. In 2009, they owned about 42 percent of the stocks, bonds, and other financial assets in the United States. In the past several decades their income and wealth multiplied at astonishing levels. Between 1979 and 2007, the top 1 percent took in about 60 percent of all income gains in the United States. The bottom 50 percent of the population now owns only 2.5 percent of all US total wealth and less than 1 percent of the nation's financial assets.[1] The 99 percent—all those who are not super-rich—went nowhere in recent decades. They have economically stalled or fallen downward, many from the middle and working classes into poverty.

We have become a society of a few big winners and a huge number of losers.

The inequality gap is so big that even many in the 1 percent are protesting. One Occupy activist showed up with a sign reading,

> I have an amount of money that is much more than I need. I am the 1%. My taxes are at a historical low and the influence of money on our government is at a historical high. These are not good things! … I am personally advocating for the repair of our broken system. I am part of Occupy Boston. My money gives me no special influence here. That's the way it should be.[2]

One of the richest members of the 1 percent, Warren Buffett, the second wealthiest US multibillionaire, expressed his own concerns about extreme inequality today when he said it was wrong that he paid less tax than his secretary. He concluded, "There's class warfare, all right, but it's my class, the rich class, that's making war, and we're winning."[3]

As far back as the Roman Republic, wise men sounded the alarm about the dangers of extreme inequality. Plutarch, a Roman philosopher who lived in the first century before Christ, wrote, "An imbalance between rich and poor is the oldest and most fatal ailment in all republics."[4] And Jesus himself famously said, "And I tell you again, it is easier for a camel to go through the eye of a needle than for a rich man to enter the kingdom of God."[5] But not all religious leaders condemn either wealth or inequality. In the Calvinist theology that Dutch and English settlers brought to America, worldly success was a mark of divine Grace. God had Himself created inequality. Calvin wrote that people "are not created on equal terms, but some are preordained to eternal life; others to eternal damnation."[6]

Those who made money believed that God had blessed them and that they were virtuous; their fortunes were a sign that they would go to heaven. The poor were marked as unworthy, destined not to get through the pearly gates. In his famous tract, *The Protestant Ethic and the Spirit of Capitalism*, the great sociologist Max Weber argued that this religious view laid the foundation of capitalism and allowed capitalists to legitimate the inequality and wealth that capitalists inevitably create.[7]

Today, we have the extreme inequality protested by Occupy: a fabulously wealthy elite, a falling middle class, and a growing underclass of the poor, hungry, homeless, or jobless. For many Americans, the Calvinist view remains the lens for understanding the vast inequality among these groups, which divide the worthy and unworthy. For others, only the rigged rules of our corporate economy created by the power elites can explain the huge chasm between the plutocratic rich and immiserated poor.

Much is at stake over which view is correct. The insecurity of the middle class and the growth of an enormous underclass are a social, economic, and moral crisis. How are we to understand why such a wealthy nation as the United States has such vast inequality and overwhelming social problems—with some of the highest rates of poverty, hunger, homelessness, incarceration, joblessness, and inequality in the developed world? Why has the "land of equality" become one of the most stratified and unequal advanced societies? Each of our three schools of political economy offers its own theory.

Neoclassicists

In the 2012 elections, Republican candidate Mitt Romney famously remarked that 47 percent of the people would never vote for him because they were "dependents" who felt entitled to be supported by government handouts and didn't want to work. Romney's vice-presidential running mate, Wisconsin Republican, Congressman Paul Ryan, made similar arguments for many years, dividing Americans into "makers" and "takers." In 2010, Ryan said that a majority of Americans were takers:

Right now about 60 percent of the American people get more benefits in dollar value from the federal government than they pay back in taxes.... So we're going to a majority of takers versus makers in America and that will be tough to come back from that. They'll be dependent on the government for their livelihoods [rather] than themselves.[8]

Romney and Ryan, who represent the economic orthodoxy of both Wall Street and the Republican Party, were offering a contemporary Calvinist view of inequality, the poor, and the social problems engulfing the nation. It is the heart of neoclassical theory, cooked into its concept of the market and the long history of its moral philosophy.

Adam Smith, the father of neoclassical thinking and great moral advocate of markets, wrote that since capitalism created great wealth, inequality was inevitable: "Wherever there is great property, there is great inequality."[9] Smith went on to say, "For one very rich man there must be at least five hundred poor, and the affluence of the few supposes the indigence of the many. The affluence of the rich excites the indignation of the poor, who are often both driven by want, and prompted by envy, to invade his possessions."[10] Yet, while seeing inequality and poverty as inevitable, Smith was concerned about the moral implications: "The disposition to admire, and almost to worship, the rich and the powerful, and to despise, or, at least, to neglect persons of poor and mean condition is the great and most universal cause of the corruption of our moral sentiments."

Today's neoclassicists generally do not share Smith's concern. Markets may generate inequality and poverty, but the system overall is the most virtuous and efficient possible. Those who get rich are getting the fair and just rewards due the most talented and hardworking. This means that the "envy" of the poor cannot be morally justified. The rewarding of the "makers" rather than the "takers" is what makes capitalist markets rational and morally admirable, making clear that, as Weber suggested, neoclassical thought is a form of economic Calvinism.[11]

Two sociologists, Kingsley Davis and Wilbert Moore, in 1945—part of the "structural-functional" school of sociology made famous by Talcott Parsons and Robert Merton—wrote one of the most influential and enduring neoclassical arguments for inequality. In "Some Principles of Stratification," they argue it is a "functional necessity" to pay deserving people—those doing complex, high-skill, or creative work—far more than others, since it is the only incentive to ensure those crucial jobs get filled. That is why doctors, lawyers, and talented entrepreneurs are highly paid while fast-food workers or ditch-diggers are not. Higher income for some is the efficient market at work, ensuring that the supply of workers at each skill level is adjusted to the demand, thereby ensuring overall economic and social well-being.[12]

Structural-functionalists joined the neoclassicists in saying that the capitalist market creates an absolutely essential and morally just inequality. The market—rational and meritocratic—always selects and rewards those who deliver the goods.

Who are these market winners?

Ayn Rand, author of *The Fountainhead* and *Atlas Shrugged*, a heroine of today's conservative economic movement and a frequent collaborator with prominent neoclassical economists, such as Alan Greenspan, divided societies into "producers," or the "creative minority" (what today we would call the 1 percent), and a majority of "parasites." Rand was unapologetic about her view that while most people are "mental parasites" a small number of exceptionally creative people deserve everything because they alone allow everyone in the society to advance: "It is the members of this exceptional minority who lift the whole of a free society to the level of their own achievement, while rising further and further."[13]

Only the producers are the great creators, the innovators, and talented inventors blessed with the intelligence, motivation, and moral virtue to produce what the market requires. If capital-holders did not invest and disproportionately reward these exceptional "creatives," they would go bankrupt, unable to compete with the investors who were more rational and placed their bets on those with merit. And the entire society would suffer and decline.[14]

In *Atlas Shrugged*, Rand argued that the very wealthy "exceptional minority" is actually underpaid by the market, since the market does not fully recognize their contributions. They not only invent the concepts and ideas that drive whole industries, but their inventions are the only things that make possible everyone else's jobs and incomes:

> the [creative] man who creates a new invention receives but a small percentage of his value in terms of material payment, no matter what fortune he makes, no matter what millions he earns. But the man who works as a janitor in the factory producing that invention receives an enormous payment in proportion to the mental effort that his job requires of him. And the same is true of all men on all levels of ambition and ability. The man at the top of the intellectual pyramid contributes the most to all those below him, but gets nothing except his material payment, receiving no intellectual bonus from others to add to the value of his time.[15]

In other words, capitalism produces too much equality; inequality should actually be substantially higher.

The parasites are the masses of "takers" who become dependent and take government handouts because they lack the creative intelligence, moral fiber, and drive to work hard that attracts capital and moves markets toward profitable new products. These are the losers by their own design, those who lack the will, motivation, and talent to succeed by their own efforts. They lack the virtue and the personal responsibility demanded by the market, and they are a drag on society. There was an element of sociopathy in Rand's discussions of the moochers and looters, captured in her simple quote, endlessly repeated in her novels and essays in different variants: "Parasites should perish."

Rand was an atheist, but her language makes clear the underlying Calvinist neoclassical argument: the market losers are eternally damned. Rand also hints at a variant of eugenics in neoclassical thinking that was popular in the 1920s when she began to write: that the poor and other market losers are useless and not worthy of social support. Markets are not sentimental; they seek out productive people and reward them on grounds of merit and efficiency, while discarding those who are parasites. They do not deserve government help—or perhaps even private charity. Rand is blunt:

> It is morally obscene to regard wealth as an anonymous tribal [collective] product and to talk about "redistributing" it. The view that wealth is the result of some undifferentiated, collective process, that we all did something, and it's impossible to tell who did what, therefore some sort of equalitarian "distribution" is necessary—might have been appropriate in a primordial jungle with a savage horde moving boulders by crude physical labor (though even there someone had to initiate and organize the moving). To hold that view in an industrial society—where individual achievements are a matter of public record—is so crass an evasion that even to give it the benefit of the doubt is an obscenity.[16]

Rand argues that the "tribal" or collectivist impulse is leading to overpaying and coddling the poor, along with underpaying the rich. A fairer society would produce greater inequality and more poverty.

While Rand and other earlier neoclassicists hinted the "dependents" or "takers" had genetic or divine flaws, many neoclassicists today say the "parasites" are not necessarily born unworthy, lazy, or stupid. The problem is that big government social welfare programs have given them an incentive to not perform up to their potential. If they can get food stamps, housing subsidies, and welfare checks, they are being turned into "dependents" by the big government of bleeding-heart liberals. Instead of helping them, liberals who support these programs are actually punishing the poor. Paul Ryan, who ran for vice president on the Republican ticket in 2012, calls social welfare programs a "hammock" that lulls people into lives of "dependency and complacency." And in 2011 he said that welfare was actually an "injustice to the poor," because it made them lazy "takers" unwilling to work.[17]

The "takers" need the spark that will inspire them to raise themselves by their bootstraps. The whip takes the form of fear of poverty, fear of homelessness, or dread of starvation. For lazy people or free-riders, giving them even the most minimal charity is the worst favor you can give them. "Victimization," says Ryan, "is not dignifying." Social welfare or service programs may assuage the conscience of the bleeding heart, but it is a selfish act, encouraging parasitical nature and dependency. The only solution to poverty and extreme inequality is to abolish welfare programs, which is "in [the poor's] best interests."[18]

There are several serious flaws to the neoclassical argument that inequality reflects personal differences between "productives" and "parasites," one of the most obvious being that the poor today tend to work long hours. Around 70 percent of the poor in America work at least half-time and many want more hours—some finding them but still earning less than a living wage. It is hard to characterize people working two jobs for more than forty hours a week as lazy and "takers"—and then to blame them for poverty and inequality. Similarly, when unemployment is at the very high levels it has been since the 2008 meltdown, it is difficult to blame it on the jobless, many of whom are desperately seeking work.

It's worth noting, given the neoclassical language around "parasites" and "takers," that almost anybody can be defined as "productive" or "lazy," with the term reflecting more the power of the person doing the labeling than the person being labeled. Productivity, laziness, and parasitism are ideologically defined categories. By definition in capitalist societies, what the rich and powerful do is productive. It is a matter of who has the ideological power to define what they do as productive. Flying around the world to attend banquets at business conferences is hard work. Working sixty hours a week as a McDonald's fry girl is laziness. If you think about it, standing on a corner holding a cup and begging for change for hours and hours is a lot of work. The ideological definition of who is productive or lazy undercuts much of the neoclassical terminology and persuasiveness.

The underlying problem for neoclassicists is their belief in the virtual perfection of the market. Any problem must be a personal fault if the structure of the economic system is perfect. If people want and demand work, the supply of jobs will increase if the price of labor, that is wages, falls low enough. Employers will hire if the wage is right and workers truly want work. Neoclassicists rest on the case that workers are simply demanding excessive wages, encouraged by their unions or high minimum-wage laws, or are too lazy to work at fair wages, choosing instead to take a holiday from any work.

Yet the evidence of deep problems in the economic and political system—particularly when such a high percentage of hardworking people are unable to make ends meet or find even low-paying jobs—makes the argument implausible. Wages have already fallen to very low levels in high-unemployment service sectors. The neoclassical market theory saying that supply (in this case of jobs) will always meet demand has clearly gone astray. Moreover, focusing on "parasites" and "takers" when even low-wage jobs are unavailable—and social welfare has been sliced by austerity—is unpersuasive. And when, at the same time, fabulously wealthy corporations and their executives are being given massive bailouts, subsidies, tax breaks, and other "corporate welfare," the neoclassical argument that inequality rises from differences in natural talent falls entirely apart.

Keynesians

The Great Depression made it nearly impossible to blame poverty, unemployment, and inequality on parasites or takers. That would have meant defaming the character of too many Americans, although conservatives certainly continued to blame the victims. With unemployment at 33 percent, and people doing everything under the sun to find work—usually without success—it became less persuasive to fault the people out of work themselves. As Robert Lekachman, a historian of the Depression and chronicler of Keynes, wrote, "The Great Depression had made it plain that even the prudent man could not protect himself against indigent old age, lengthy unemployment and other vicissitudes of an unstable economy."[19]

The same problem exists today, in the Great Recession—another crisis of joblessness and poverty too widespread to indict the mass of the population on their character. Keynesians today, as in the Great Depression, thus turn neoclassical thinking on its head. Inequality and poverty are systemic rather than personal: the deepest imperfections of a deeply imperfect market system. Nobelist Keynesian economist Joseph Stiglitz has emerged as the most important Keynesian critic of today's inequality. His critique is devastating on economic, political, and moral grounds, hinting that the problem is systemic and deeply entrenched in the US capitalist model:

Our skyrocketing inequality—so contrary to our meritocratic ideal of America as a place where anyone with hard work and talent can "make it"—means that those who are born to parents of limited means are likely never to live up to their potential. Children in other rich countries like Canada, France, Germany and Sweden have a better chance of doing better than their parents did than American kids have. More than a fifth of our children live in poverty—the second worst of all the advanced economies, putting us behind countries like Bulgaria, Latvia and Greece.[20]

Stiglitz described succinctly the magnitude of the problem:

> Most Americans' most important asset is their home, and as home prices
> have plummeted, so has household wealth—especially since so many had
> borrowed so much on their homes. Large numbers are left with negative
> net worth, and median household wealth fell nearly 40 percent, to $77,300
> in 2010 from $126,400 in 2007, and has rebounded only slightly. Since
> the Great Recession, most of the increase in the nation's wealth has gone
> to the very top.[21]

Stiglitz summarized the Keynesian view that this systemic disorder is a potentially lethal blow to the recovery of US prosperity and the American Dream:

> Inequality leads to lower growth and less efficiency. Lack of opportunity
> means that its most valuable asset—its people—is not being fully used.
> Many at the bottom, or even in the middle, are not living up to their poten-
> tial, because the rich, needing few public services and worried that a strong
> government might redistribute income, use their political influence to cut
> taxes and curtail government spending. This leads to underinvestment in
> infrastructure, education and technology, impeding the engines of growth....
> Most importantly, America's inequality is undermining its values and identity.
> With inequality reaching such extremes, it is not surprising that its effects are
> manifest in every public decision, from the conduct of monetary policy to bud-
> getary allocations. America has become a country not "with justice for all," but
> rather with favoritism for the rich and justice for those who can afford it—so
> evident in the foreclosure crisis, in which the big banks believed that they were
> too big not only to fail, but also to be held accountable.[22]

Paul Krugman, the other contemporary Nobel Keynesian, put the problem
more succinctly: "Banana Republic, here we come!"

Some Keynesians argue that inequality and poverty built up over several
decades since the Reagan revolution are the real cause of the 2008 financial
meltdown. The most influential Keynesian who made this argument is
Robert Reich: "The fundamental problem is that Americans no longer have
the purchasing power to buy what the US economy is capable of producing.
The reason is that a larger and larger portion of total income is going to
the top."[23] In his bestseller, *Aftershock*, Reich makes clear that the problem
is not parasites but employers who don't pay their hardworking employees
a "fair share":

> Unless America's middle class receives a fair share, it cannot consume
> nearly what the nation is capable of producing, at least without going deeply

into debt. And debt on this scale is unsustainable, as we have seen. The inevitable result is slower economic growth and an economy increasingly susceptible to great booms and terrible busts.[24]

Reich is arguing that inequality and poverty—bred by the unfairness of the employer class—caused the Great Recession, which in turn caused yet more inequality and poverty. A vicious spiral is built into capitalism itself, breeding vast social problems that cannot be blamed on the personal qualities of the victims.

Keynesians have a two-stage perspective on inequality and poverty. In "normal" capitalism, we can expect the growth of both inequality and poverty as an inherent part of the market mechanism, especially in the United States where there is an institutionalized propensity to underinvest in public goods, such as education, and to pay workers low wages. Keynesians believed they had tools to mitigate if not eradicate joblessness and poverty in "normal" or booming eras, such as the 1950s and 1960s. But at a certain stage, exacerbated by casino-style financial profiteering seen in the 1920s and, much later, in the 1980s Reagan revolution, the problems get so deep that they help trigger depressions. These create a second form of extreme inequality and poverty, which Keynesians see as neither economically nor morally bearable. The cycle seems embedded like DNA in the functioning of capitalism itself.

Yet, starting with Keynes himself, despite the tragedy of "normal" inequality and poverty, and then the horror of the Depression, the solution is not to destroy capitalism but to save it. The depth of the problem and its tragic consequences for millions can be corrected, often easily within a capitalist system. As contemporary Keynesian Paul Krugman has put it, the car is not broken, nor the engine; there is only the need for a tune-up by a skilled Keynesian technician.[25]

The Keynesian paradox is that crises so deep can be solved so easily.

Look first at the stage of crisis, since at this writing we are still in it. Here, Keynesians have their simplest and most persuasive case: the problems of inequality and poverty are unambiguously systemic, engulfing such a huge majority of a hardworking US population that the problem can't be explained simply by calling them moochers or looters. The Depression was such a clear failure of the deregulated, laissez-faire capitalist system—the one built by the 1890s Robber Barons and resurrected by Calvin Coolidge and Herbert Hoover in the financially reckless 1920s—that it forced all but the most die-hard conservatives to move beyond blaming people and to consider problems built into the economic and political order. Neoclassicists had asserted a crisis such as the Great Depression was impossible. When it happened, it shook faith in the entire neoclassical paradigm, and required the majority of both citizens and economists to move toward a critique of unregulated capitalism and neoclassical ideas of a meritocratic and self-correcting market. The New Deal was a "regime change at home," shifting the dominant ideas of the nation.[26]

Neoclassicism did not die out. There were many neoclassicists during the Great Depression and the Keynesian Age. At first they organized against Roosevelt through the Liberty League, a populist right-wing group. And they persisted, looking for someone to bring them back to power. They tried Robert Taft, then Barry Goldwater, until Ronald Reagan was finally able to do it, backed by a movement resurrecting the theories about takers and makers.

But neoclassicists lost public credibility in the Depression, for fairly clear reasons. Mass unemployment, and the accompanying deep inequality and poverty, could not plausibly be a sign of the mass working population being lazy or parasitical. Just a decade earlier, in the Roaring Twenties, the same people had worked hard to create mass prosperity. As Keynes recognized, the problem was the inability of business after the 1929 crash to create the jobs that millions wanted. And people's desperation to work suggested neither moocherism nor looterism among the workers but rather problems created by rapacious capitalists. As Keynesian Robert Lekachman wrote, "Since the great industrialists and financiers had been delighted to take credit for the prosperity of the 1920s, what could be fairer than to debit them with the failures of the ensuing decades."[27]

Keynes still had to confront the reigning neoclassical argument that the supply of jobs would always rise to meet the demand for work if wages were allowed to fall and workers really wanted to work. Keynes rejected Say's law, the cherished neoclassical belief that supply always created its own demand, meaning that involuntary employment was impossible since the supply of labor would inevitably create demand for it. It was evident to Keynes in the Depression that the neoclassical faith in the market's ability to match supply and demand—and thus always self-correct temporary disruptions in the labor market—was terribly wrong. The labor market was not self-correcting. Business would not invest and create the jobs workers demanded for two reasons: the impoverished population had insufficient money to buy what business produced, and people after the 1929 crash would collectively withhold spending in order to save for the gloomy days ahead and pay down their debt. Until there was a new demand for goods, investment would dry up and unemployment would keep going up, leading to more people in poverty, hungry, or homeless.[28]

For Keynesians, then, the problems of poverty, joblessness, and inequality—manifested especially severely during crises—have little to do with Calvinist ideas of the blessed (hardworking and talented) and the damned (lazy and stupid). Rather, they reflect the inevitable failure of an unregulated, laissez-faire, badly managed capitalism. When too many people who anticipate long-term recession or depression save or hoard their money, this may be rational for each saver but is disastrous for the economy as a whole, creating a "paradox of thrift," leading to a demand side crisis needing an immediate fix. To fix joblessness, poverty, and inequality, you don't have to reform parasites or save those damned by God. Rather, you have to fix the capitalist machine that just badly needs a tune-up using the right Keynesian tools.[29]

And the tools are simple, including regulation, progressive taxes, globalization reforms protecting workers and restricting capital flight, and investment in the education and health of the 99 percent.[30] The government must engage during crises in massive stimulus, creating jobs and education for the masses at the bottom. Public spending must take up the slack in demand created by people who are hoarding money or are low paid or out of work—and create living-wage jobs for all. The neoclassical solution is austerity but the Keynesian solution is the opposite—spending almost like a drunken sailor at the depths of an economic downturn while also regulating like a sober and enlightened watchman. Keynesians such as Paul Krugman have documented persuasive evidence supporting stimulus over austerity in crises. In dealing with the 2008 Great Recession, nearly all the countries adopting or forced into austerity—Greece, Portugal, Ireland, and Great Britain—went back into recession by 2012 and suffered massive joblessness, poverty, and homelessness. In the United States, where President Obama was able to advance a modest stimulus in his first term, the economy began to recover. The recovery has been slow, but the stimulus was way too small.[31]

Keynesians realize that the biggest obstacle to the solution is political rather than economic. Unlike neoclassicists, they take power seriously and recognize that corporate capitalism creates huge concentrations of power and wealth that will resist the use of the Keynesian tool box. Stiglitz drummed the political sources of inequality home over and over again:

> There are all kinds of excuses for inequality. Some say it's beyond our control, pointing to market forces like globalization, trade liberalization, the technological revolution, the "rise of the rest." Others assert that doing anything about it would make us all worse off, by stifling our already sputtering economic engine. These are self-serving, ignorant falsehoods.
>
> Market forces don't exist in a vacuum—we shape them. Other countries, like fast-growing Brazil, have shaped them in ways that have lowered inequality while creating more opportunity and higher growth. Countries far poorer than ours have decided that all young people should have access to food, education and health care so they can fulfill their aspirations.[32]

Stiglitz, like Krugman and Reich, argues that only politicians, armed with Keynesian tools, can solve the problem. At the start of Obama's second term, he wrote,

As Mr. Obama's second term begins, we must all face the fact that our country cannot quickly, meaningfully recover without policies that directly address inequality. What's needed is a comprehensive response that should include, at least, significant investments in education, a more progressive tax system and a tax on financial speculation.[33]

But Obama has not acted, with corporate money and political lobbies blocking nearly everything. That is why the most sophisticated Keynesian political analysts have long argued, as J. K. Galbraith did through most of the second half of the twentieth century, for the countervailing power of unions, government, and mobilized citizens to get the necessary tune-up done.[34]

Galbraith's work, with its focus on power and his essential role as a political sociologist, helped explain the chronic problems of inequality and poverty that stain capitalism not just in great crises but during periods of prosperity. Depressions make these problems worse, but inequality and poverty are always part of capitalism, especially the US model. Galbraith spent much of his career in the mid-twentieth century, when the economy was booming. Yet he devoted much of his Keynesian genius to coping with the question of why even in its booms, capitalism generates so much inequality and poverty.[35]

Galbraith had a simple answer. Capitalists invest in private goods for their own profits. They get rich not because of a neutral market but because they control investment and allocate rewards in their own interests, as Galbraith sardonically noted here: "The salary of the chief executive of a large corporation is not a market award for achievement. It is frequently in the nature of a warm personal gesture by the individual to himself."[36]

They disinvest in public goods that serve the well-being of the larger society. Like Keynes, Galbraith never believed in Adam Smith's invisible hand; rather, he argued that private investments for profit would deplete investment in workers and community for the common good. Galbraith was blunt: "The sense of responsibility in the financial community for the community as a whole is not small. It is nearly nil."[37]

Galbraith's major work was documenting—during US capitalism's "normal" and even booming years of the 1950s—the failure to carry out the major public investment that would ensure social well-being and equal opportunity. The "affluent society" would produce invisible poverty. And at the heart of this was the failure to invest in people and the schools that would ensure them a critical mind, technical skills, and a democratic and empowered civil and political life.[38]

President Lyndon Johnson, schooled under FDR's New Deal, heard Galbraith's message. He called for a Great Society based on a War on Poverty. LBJ's vision was a Keynesian dream—and one that we have not heard from presidents since Reagan's regime change. LBJ was enthusiastic in his famous 1964 "War on Poverty" speech:

Because it is right, because it is wise, and because, for the first time in our history, it is possible to conquer poverty, I submit, for the consideration of the Congress and the country, the Economic Opportunity Act of 1964.

The Act does not merely expand old programs or improve what is already being done.

It charts a new course.

It strikes at the causes, not just the consequences of poverty.

It can be a milestone in our one-hundred-eighty-year search for a better life for our people.

This Act provides five basic opportunities.

It will give almost half a million underprivileged young Americans the opportunity to develop skills, continue education, and find useful work.

It will give every American community the opportunity to develop a comprehensive plan to fight its own poverty—and help them to carry out their plans.

It will give dedicated Americans the opportunity to enlist as volunteers in the war against poverty.

It will give many workers and farmers the opportunity to break through particular barriers which bar their escape from poverty.

It will give the entire nation the opportunity for a concerted attack on poverty through the establishment, under my direction, of the Office of Economic Opportunity, a national headquarters for the war against poverty.[39]

Tragically, Johnson's choice to go to war in Vietnam overwhelmed and destroyed his War on Poverty, depleting and wasting the funds that could have conquered poverty and joblessness. But this failure did not disprove Keynesianism; it heightened the appetites for it among liberals, at least until the Reagan regime change. Then, even liberals retreated from Johnson's expansive Keynesian vision.

Nonetheless, Galbraith's work on inequality and poverty in the midst of plenty—central to the US Keynesian critique—persists today, continuing among critical intellectuals throughout the Reagan boom years and expanding its audience after the 2008 meltdown. As noted earlier, Keynesians Joseph Stiglitz and Robert Reich have long focused on inequality—national and global—in the decades since President Reagan's election. And these years, while often marked by rapid growth, were a slow-motion unfolding catastrophe for the US working population.

Like Galbraith, Reich wrote of a 1980s and 1990s era in which a booming capitalism was drastically underinvesting in workers and communities. Globalization empowered corporations to break unions, threaten communities and politicians, and fuel a right-wing attack on funding public needs, especially education and social welfare. For Reich, in the new high-tech, postindustrial global era, expanding education and worker skill is the overarching imperative: the Keynesian antidote—almost a magic wand—to solving the crises of inequality, middle-class decline, and poverty. Only Keynesian policies of massive investment in education and human capital could keep the United States competitive and save not only the 99 percent but the entire US economy.

Reich's focus on education and worker skill is surely important, but it misses the crucial fact that even the educated American is disposable or "surplus" in the globalized, high-tech economy. He fails to dwell on the rising capitalist political strategy to disinvest in America, and abandon even much of its educated workforce, since there are cheaper and more profitable opportunities abroad. Giant global corporations had the political clout to turn the "surplus American" into a grim reality for both the unskilled and skilled US worker.[40]

The great problem for Keynesians is their political optimism. While they recognize the power of the 1 percent in capitalism, and that the rich tend to control government in capitalist countries, they are confident that it can be overcome by the 99 percent. History suggests that Keynesians are slow to see the full dimensions of capitalist power relations. Money power has trumped people power through most eras of US capitalism, and the government itself has been controlled in most eras by big corporations and the wealthy. This was true in the Robber Baron Gilded Age, in the Roaring Twenties, and in the Reagan revolution that continues to shape political discourse and policy today.

This means that stimulus will never be as big as necessary—except perhaps during huge wars such as World War II. And government regulators will be like foxes guarding the henhouse. With new decisions, such as the 2010 *Citizens United* Supreme Court ruling, allowing billionaires to pour as much money as they want into political campaigns and issue advertising, the 1 percent's control of government is likely to stymie Keynesian solutions more than ever. This is bad news for the Democratic Party and even worse for economists who view Keynesianism as the solution to our extreme inequality and spreading plague of surplus people, poverty, hunger, and homelessness.

Neo-Marxists

Neo-Marxists see the 99 percent sinking, no matter what the Keynesians do. They see the Keynesian failure as both economic and political. For neo-Marxists, Keynesians simply have failed to see that fixing capitalism and solving its social crises are not like fixing a car needing a tune-up. It's like trying to repair a car that was programmed from the beginning to crash and burn.

Marx saw extreme inequality emerging 150 years ago in the capitalism of his era: "Society as a whole is more and more splitting up into two great hostile camps, into two great classes facing each other: the Bourgeoisie and Proletariat."[41] Marx was essentially one of the first great theorists of the Occupy movement. He saw the bourgeoisie becoming the 1 percent and the proletariat swelling into the 99 percent.

Neo-Marxists, following Marx himself, see unemployment, poverty, hunger, and homelessness as baked into the social divisions that define the capitalist system. Over time, as downturns become more severe and prolonged, the condition of the 99 percent becomes unbearable. Poverty, job insecurity, low wages, and fear of falling become a way of life, documented by socialist writer Barbara Ehrenreich, in her huge bestseller, *Nickel and Dimed.*[42]

This reflects the basic class division within capitalism between those with property and those without. Early nineteenth-century competitive capitalism supported a lot of people with small amounts of productive property, mainly farmers. But as capitalism develops, it moves into a monopoly phase, where farmers and small businesses of all kinds are put out of business by giant corporations. Marx wrote how virtually the entire middle classes find themselves destined to sink into a massive but despairing and increasingly insecure and low-paid working class, the proletariat who are chronically nickel and dimed:

> The lower strata of the middle class—the small trades-people, shopkeepers and retired tradesmen generally, the handicraftsmen and peasants—all these sink gradually into the proletariat, partly because their diminutive capital does not suffice for the scale on which Modern Industry is carried on, and is swamped in the competition with the large capitalists, partly because their specialized skill is rendered worthless by new methods of production. Thus the proletariat is recruited from all classes of the population.[43]

Marx was foretelling that mom-and-pop stores can't compete with Wal-Mart, and Mom and Pop will sink into the working class or the unemployed. The global companies and their executives become the 1 percent and operate in a way that increasingly leaves most of the 99 percent without property or prospects. In the nineteenth century, the United States had a "competitive capitalism," with thousands of small enterprises driving the economy. But in their influential work, *Monopoly Capital*, Paul Sweezy and Paul Baran argue that competitive capitalism yields in the twentieth century to a monopoly capitalist model dominated by giant corporations that control the market and the state, while driving out most competitors: "Monopoly capitalism is a system made up of giant corporations. . . . Under competitive capitalism the individual enterprise is a 'price taker' while under monopoly capitalism the big corporation is a 'price maker.'"[44]

Baran and Sweezy argue that big corporations, while still competing with each other, also collaborate to reduce risk and gain more control of the state and workers, all in the pursuit of money. The essence of capitalism, neo-Marxists say, is the capitalist class's ruthless pursuit of profit. Neoclassicists believe this pursuit of profit will benefit almost all (except the most parasitical) in the long run. But neo-Marxists argue the opposite: maximizing profit requires exploiting most of the working population—the 99 percent—and driving them into the working poor or the "reserve army of the unemployed," where poverty is king. As Marx wrote,

> The modern labourer ... instead of rising with the progress of industry, sinks deeper and deeper below the conditions of existence of his own class. He becomes a pauper, and pauperism develops more rapidly than population and wealth. And here it becomes evident that the bourgeoisie is unfit any longer to be the ruling class of society, and to impose its conditions of existence upon society as an over-riding law. . . .[45]

Marx is arguing that monopoly capitalism is a sociopathic society, as it polarizes and drives the masses into unacceptable struggles for existence. Marx here makes his most important sociological argument: that capitalism is sociopathic and cannot sustain society itself because the ruling corporate class reduces all else to an instrument of its own gain.[46] The capitalist engine requires this exploitation because of the inherent conflict of interest between capitalists and workers. Workers are a cost of production to capitalists, and profit-maximization requires extracting as much labor as possible from workers at the lowest price or wage. As we have already shown, neo-Marxists see no escape within capitalism from the capitalist need to drive down costs of labor, stripping as much skill as possible from workers to pay them less. Even high-skill workers, threatened with outsourcing and without unions, see wages fall, and often must work extra hours without pay. It all leads inevitably to paying workers less than the value of what they produce—ultimately barely enough to get by and, as Marx notes, leaving them unable to buy the fruits of their own labor: "The mass of producers are absolutely excluded from the purchase of their own products."[47]

A crucial way to cut labor costs is to build up the "reserve army"—or expand the pool of surplus people. When the supply of workers far outstrips the demand, workers will be desperate and will accept almost any wage, no matter how low. Technology also plays a role since machinery and robots can replace workers and are preferable, because they don't ask for vacations, benefits, or unions. As robots replace workers, unemployment grows and wages are pushed down further, creating more poverty among those both working and unemployed. Finally, globalization allows capitalists to outsource jobs and increase the number of surplus people—or "reserve army" at home—while paying the remaining workers less. Marx explained,

> The whole form of the movement of modern industry depends, therefore, upon the constant transformation of a part of the labouring population into unemployed or half-employed hands ... an ever growing reserve army of unemployed develops. The condemnation of one part of the working-class to enforced idleness by the over-work of the other part, and the converse, becomes a means of enriching the individual capitalist and accelerates at the same time the production of the industrial reserve army.[48]

In another work, *The Surplus American*, we argue that the process in the United States has moved beyond Marx's expectations. Since capitalists can now access a global labor market with far lower wages and regulations than in the United States, they are disinvesting in the entire US infrastructure, while outsourcing jobs of every skill level to poor nations around the world. US corporations thereby accumulate huge profits, ironically subsidized by the US government, while more and more Americans are driven into the "reserve army" and become surplus. Remaining Americans, terrified of becoming surplus, accept low wages and benefits. The gap between the corporate elites and the mass of surplus Americans helps drive inequality to new and frightening levels.[49]

The wheels of exploitation are greased by the inevitable capitalist capture of government and the politicians. Marx argued that government within capitalism is always the servant of the capitalist class: "The bourgeoisie has at last, since the establishment of Modern Industry and of the world-market, conquered for itself, in the modern representative State, exclusive political sway."[50]

The capitalist state creates the necessary laws and economic policies that enable the exploitation driving the 99 percent into low-wage hell, ensuring severe class-based inequality within capitalist systems. As discussed in our chapter on democracy, Marx's theory is borne out in work by contemporary political sociologists and political scientists, such as G. William Domhoff and Thomas Ferguson, who examine the relation between business and the state and document how the state locks in business priorities and policies creating growing gaps between the wealthy and everyone else. As Domhoff meticulously documents in his analysis of the power elite, politicians work hand in glove with the business elites to promote industrial and tax policies that increase the wealth of the 1 percent at the expense of the 99 percent.[51] They create labor laws that weaken unions and prevent workers from exercising control over the workplace, thereby increasing profits at the expense of wages. They cut big holes in the social safety net, while investing public money in corporate welfare. As Ferguson shows, leading political parties are competing blocs of financial investors, not of voters or ordinary citizens.[52] There is really no party of labor, particularly in the US capitalist model, only two parties of business competing in the "political marketplace": Bush and Bush-lite. There are meaningful differences but in the end both parties will ally with business to increase corporate wealth and reduce everyone else's wealth, although the Bush-liters in the Democratic Party will take a softer approach and sometimes align with the workers rather than their corporate patrons.[53]

As most neo-Marxists see it today, the political influence of the 1 percent—the very wealthy—has deeply exacerbated the inequality problem since the New Deal era. Chuck Collins, a leading neo-Marxist authority on inequality, argued in his 2012 book on "extreme inequality," *99 to 1*, that the current massive polarization of wealth has been created not by the natural operation of the market, but by intensified political rule-rigging exercised by the 1 percent, newly empowered since the Reagan revolution to "use a wide variety of tools—political contributions, charitable giving, media ownership and control over think tanks and advocacy groups to tip the scales in their favor."[54]

Political influence through contributions and lobbying has become extremely concentrated, with Collins noting that those who gave more than $2,400 to candidates in 2010 represented .05 percent of the population, 146,715 people out of a population of 312 million.[55] It's not surprising they are the only ones heard up on Capitol Hill, as they "channel millions directly to candidates, legislative issues, political parties and a myriad of influence channels such as political action committees (PACs) and 501c4 corporations."[56]

Collins noted that the most politically active and successful are those in the very top sliver of the 1 percent, the biggest financial firms on Wall Street, which he calls the "Wall Street Inequality Machine":

> Wall Street financial firms exercise tremendous financial power, but also, by virtue of the enormous sums of money and profits generated by this sector, they exert significant political power through campaign contributions, lobbying clout, and the funding of research and advocacy that advance their interests. The financial, insurance and real estate (FIRE) sectors are the largest contributors to political campaigns and employ thousands of lobbyists, several for each member of Congress.[57]

Collins described the Koch Brothers as classic twenty-first-century 1 percent rule-riggers, utilizing their multibillion-dollar oil wealth to create an empire of political rule-rigging:

Perhaps the best case study of using wealth and power to perpetuate wealth and power is the Koch brothers. David and Charles Koch, two brothers who inherited an oil business, are worth an estimated $25 billion each. They use every tool possible to advance their interests—which include blocking climate change legislation, cutting their taxes and weakening government regulation.[58]

The Koch Brothers, who at this writing in 2013 were seeking to buy eight major newspapers including the *Los Angeles Times*, exemplify Collins's concern that extreme inequality—manufactured by and for the very wealthiest of the 1 percent—is "destroying everything that we value." Democracy, fairness, community, and the American Dream of mobility are all casualties of extreme inequality, which is the sociopathic spear of corporate capitalism driven by the capitalist class into the heart of society itself. It will bring down, in the end, even the wealthiest, such as the Koch brothers, who cannot insulate their global oil companies or themselves from the ravages of climate change and destabilizing social divisions.

Collins, who was born into a wealthy family, notes that not all of the wealthy are politically engaged, and that some who are, such as Bill Gates Sr. and Warren Buffet, are seeking to reduce inequality by raising taxes at the top and promoting social values. Nonetheless, the overall thrust of his years studying "extreme inequality" reinforces the neo-Marxist view that concentration of wealth begets more concentration of wealth, through political processes at the core of the corporate capitalist system.

Can this go on and on? Collins sees hope that it can end, offering many proposals—both reformist and revolutionary—for stopping the rule-riggers and reversing the "death spiral" of extreme inequality. Collins joins many other neo-Marxists in calling for radical limits on corporate campaign contributions and lobbying, ending corporate tax loopholes like those brought to the attention of the country by the congressional hearings in 2013 on Apple's scandalous foreign tax write-offs, ending corporate personhood, breaking up the biggest banks at the heart of the Wall Street inequality machine, and shifting toward a more community-based financial and business model. Ultimately, as is seen by all neo-Marxists, the solution is a massive change in power from corporations to ordinary people and a transformation in the culture from accumulation of money to social justice and public life.[59] The outburst of the Occupy movement, which brought extreme inequality to the center of the political conversation, confirms the neo-Marxist view that extreme inequality will ultimately create class-based protests helping to unify the 99 percent across race, gender, and ethnic lines against the 1 percent to create a more egalitarian system.

Nonetheless, Collins recognizes how tough the systemic change will be. He observes wryly that the 1 percent believe their own propaganda—that they hit a home run—and have persuaded many in the 99 percent. Instead, the 1 percent were born on third base, a mark of the shutting down of social mobility in America. Mass protests such as Occupy are possible, and local community-based changes, creating a more localist and fair economy, are going on in neighborhoods and towns around the nation. But these remain small-scale and Occupy, brutally suppressed by police on Wall Street and in cities around the country, did not sustain itself to create national and global change. New mass movements focusing on overcoming inequality, which are desperately needed, have yet to resurface.

The neo-Marxist analysis of inequality is, nonetheless, a profound challenge to both neoclassicists and Keynesians. It shows that the neoclassical idea of the perfect market is perfect only for the 1 percent, because they make the market rules and enforce them. This is a fatal challenge to the idea of the market as natural law, since neo-Marxists show that the market is socially and politically constructed. Since the market is based on laws and ideas about property created by government and courts, and there can be no property or market without the active intervention of the state in creating them, the very idea of a "natural" or "free" market is an illusion. It is rather a creation of powerful people who use both economic leverage and political influence to ensure that the market is designed and operates in their favor. Even Milton Friedman acknowledges the crucial rule of the state in creating and "umpiring" the market system, but then backs away from the obvious implications that neo-Marxists draw.[60] The capitalist market is programmed to create a 99 percent suffering from chronic social problems—poverty, low wages, hunger—that are an inevitable consequence of a rigged market and a state of, by, and for the capitalist class.[61]

As for Keynesians, who also embrace capitalism, the neo-Marxist onslaught is equally devastating. Keynesians see that capitalism is far from perfect and that power operates to influence the market and to decide who benefits. Paul Krugman, Joseph Stiglitz, and Robert Reich all argue that the 1 percent has dominant power in capitalist America today. But they do not see this as inherent or inevitable in capitalism, always leading within a capitalist framework to economic and political control by a tiny fraction of the population bent on making money by driving most of the population into servitude at the margins of poverty. Neo-Marxists make an argument about class exploitation as essential to profit-maximization—and therefore a permanent condition of capitalism—and thus argue that Keynesian regulation and other reforms will never scale up to the necessary structural changes, ones that only massive protest movements such as Occupy have any chance of creating. In contrast,

Keynesians believe that political elites, as in the New Deal, can reform capitalism and reduce inequality through social spending and regulation, a highly problematic argument as seen in the failures of the Obama era.

The problem for the Keynesians, highlighted by neo-Marxists, is this: What if the regulators are the 1 percent themselves, or driven by their paid lobbyists? Neo-Marxists argue that the political tools to soften capitalist exploitation and crisis are permanently in the hands of the capitalists themselves—and Keynesians have not been able to refute that effectively either. Moreover, the very need for regulation at the heart of Keynesian thinking suggests that Keynesians see exploitation—and all the social problems of joblessness and poverty that it creates—as built into capitalist machinery. They fall back on the idea that government can create seatbelts and engine modifications to protect the passengers and ensure their security, but the political arguments to the contrary by neo-Marxists are persuasive. Historical studies by Marxists such as Gabriel Kolko, who studied regulatory reforms during the early-twentieth-century Progressive era, showed that many progressive reforms did improve the lives of the 99 percent but were really designed to protect the wealth and power of the 1 percent and helped them more than they helped the rest of the population.[62]

Neo-Marxists make a powerful case that social problems of unemployment, joblessness, and inequality are the heart of darkness in the capitalist system. They are the social externalities of the capitalist markets and profit engine, costs to the mass of the population subjected to control by elites that the elites do not have to bear. These brutal externalities are inevitable because profit—the central aim of the system—depends on them.[63]

This suggests that capitalism, at least in its US form, is, as noted above, inherently sociopathic because it requires exploitation to function profitably. The externalized cost of treating workers as objects—or costs of production—will ultimately undermine the social fabric and the values required to sustain society. Its hurling of the masses into the worlds of the working poor and surplus people not only harm the great majority of the population but terminally weaken the society and the capitalist system itself. The social world becomes a subjugated and impoverished underworld, gated off from the estates of the 1 percent who use police and private security forces to protect their separate universe.[64]

Despite its power, neo-Marxism has its own limitations in explaining social problems. For one thing, for parts of the twentieth century, especially following World War II, many workers did not live in poverty and enjoyed relatively good wages and working conditions. Progressive politicians and liberal ideals dating from the New Deal permitted significant regulation and public investment. This helped to keep capitalist crises from reverting to catastrophes such as the Great Depression, at least until the 2008 meltdown.

Significant inequality has always been present as have poverty and homelessness, something validating neo-Marxist thinking. But unemployment was kept at 4 percent or below for much of the post–World War II era. Credit systems allowed workers to enjoy a middle-class standard of living in a thriving American capitalism for a much longer period than Marx thought possible, although more contemporary neo-Marxists, such as Paul Baran and Paul Sweezy, explained why capitalism would remain more resilient and raise living standards for a longer period than Marx expected.[65]

However, even as things got worse after the Reagan revolution, with expanding poverty, joblessness, and inequality, just as neo-Marxists predicted, the consciousness of the exploited workers did not correspond to Marx's predictions. Marx expected "false consciousness" propagated by capitalist media, schools, and intelligentsia, but he thought that as things got worse, the masses would see their interests and how the capitalist system would have to be transformed. But the reality of recent decades is how many workers and small-business people have acted against their own interests and supported economic agendas that locked them further into poverty, low wages, and job insecurity. This has become a major topic of neo-Marxist thinking for a long period, as we witness worker exploitation often leading to right-wing movements such as the Tea Party or leaders such as Reagan.[66]

What seems fair to conclude is that Marx was prophetic in predicting great social crises of inequality, joblessness, poverty, and social insecurity among a large and growing percentage of people in capitalist societies, especially in the United States. The Marxist systemic explanation for these social problems is more persuasive than the neoclassical view of personal laziness or dependency among a population of parasites. It is at least as persuasive as Keynesians, who have not been able to show that capitalist political realities will prevent their own reformist remedies from being enacted at the scale necessary. And when we consider the scale required to deal with new catastrophic threats such as climate change, as well as the existence of the truly massive and permanent social underworld of dispossessed and surplus people who don't seem to live in the same universe as the 1 percent billionaires, the Keynesian optimism becomes more problematic. None of this proves that neo-Marxism has all the answers, but it suggests that the failure of most Americans to give any thought to neo-Marxist ideas is irrational and potentially suicidal.

CHAPTER 7

Democracy

Do capitalism and democracy go together like love and marriage? Are they permanently divorced, incapable constitutionally of coexisting? Or are they in a troubled, rocky marriage and stay together in constant turmoil?

Most conservatives would probably agree with Sarah Palin, who ran for vice president in 2008 on John McCain's Republican ticket. Palin suggests that capitalism is married happily to a free, democratic way of life: "A free market system allows all parties to compete, which ensures the best and most competitive project emerges, and ensures a fair, democratic process."[1]

Conservative economic icon, Milton Friedman, agrees, arguing that the natural marriage between capitalism and democracy lies in the fact that "economic freedom is an essential requisite freedom of political freedom." The capitalist market provides the economic freedom underpinning the political freedom of democracy.[2]

But more liberal Americans have questions about this view. They worry about the huge role of giant corporations—the concentration of vast capitalist wealth and corporate lobbies in Washington—and see a very troubled marriage. In this view, big money and the huge inequalities of capitalism play havoc with democracy—and perhaps may destroy it in the long run. No less an American icon than President Abraham Lincoln expressed these serious reservations in 1864: "Corporations have been enthroned and an era of corruption in high places will follow, and the money power of the country will endeavor to prolong its reign by working upon the prejudices of the people until all wealth is aggregated in a few hands and the Republic is destroyed."[3]

Supreme Court Justice Louis Brandeis put forward a similar view to Lincoln's that appeared to suggest capitalism and democracy were incompatible: "We can have democracy in this country, or we can have great wealth concentrated in the hands of a few, but we can't have both."[4]

Noam Chomsky, like many fierce critics of capitalism, put the point even more sharply: "Capitalism is a system in which the central institutions of society are, in principle, under autocratic control.... I think that until the major institutions of society are under the popular control of participants and communities, it's pointless to talk about democracy."[5]

And humorist and writer, Fran Lebowitz, puts Chomsky's point in a lighter vein: "In the Soviet Union, capitalism triumphed over communism. In this country, capitalism triumphed over democracy."[6]

Deciphering the truth about the "marriage" is a central issue in political economy (PE). To a large degree, the reality has been distorted in most Western developed nations, including the United States. The purpose of political economy is to get at the truth, for it will help determine the future of both capitalism and democracy.

Neoclassicists

Neoclassicists such as Milton Friedman tend to see a happy marriage born of necessity and mutual compatibility. They argue that democracy—defined as a constitutional republic of representation based on elections, freedom to own private property, and rule of law—is not possible without capitalism as its economic foundation, a point at the very heart of neoclassicism.

Neoclassicists, we should note right away, are not proponents of participatory democracy, but of representative rule, characteristic of republics. They fear what Harvard political scientist Samuel Huntington calls "surplus democracy," which can express itself in popular protest or heightened worker participation, and is viewed by many neoclassicists as a prelude to mob rule. So, in speaking of democracy, neoclassicists are really talking about limited democratic models that do not encourage mass participation (beyond voting if citizens choose it). They support representative government but also strong limits on majoritarian participation and rule, an important qualification and something that sets the neoclassicists apart from many Keynesians and virtually all neo-Marxists.

The neoclassicists worry, though, that even their ideal model of representative democracy with limited popular participation—which they see as capitalism's natural partner or expression in the political world—is constantly under assault, because capitalism must constantly ward off seductive pressures toward "collectivism" or "big government." In the neoclassical worldview, best articulated by Milton Friedman, big government is inherently "coercive" and is the greatest challenge to democracy that capitalist societies must fight to the death.

These challenges tend to come from what conservative icon Ayn Rand called in her famous novel, *Atlas Shrugged*, the "moochers and looters" who feel entitled to the wealth created by others—and thus always push for more government and social redistribution.[7] In his 2012 race for president, Mitt Romney spoke famously of the dependent "47 percent" who represent the threat to both capitalism and democracy that Rand predicted.

These "moochers" are inevitably a huge mass of the working population in capitalism and threaten capitalist democracy by building up pressure—such as the high level of popular protests on the streets in the 1960s supporting the Great Society—for big government. That is a continuing, inevitable threat in all capitalism. Capitalists must fight the expansion of government and decisively win if democracy is to survive.

That fight goes to the root of the neoclassical view of the natural fit between capitalism and democracy. Capitalism enshrines free markets and the freedom at the heart of democracy. It requires limited government that "would refrain from a host of activities that are now undertaken by federal and state governments," including "minimum wages," "detailed regulation of industries," and "social security programs, especially the old-age and retirement programs" that Friedman views as forms of coercion.[8] Big government is inherently coercive—the heart of Milton Friedman's moral philosophy—and is always subverting free markets, expanding confiscatory taxes, and bringing the threat of tyranny.[9]

Capitalists' support for democracy is rooted in their basic self-interests and their core values. Capitalism depends on private property and free markets. If government seeks to own and run businesses, it substitutes bureaucratic control for private property and democratic freedom. If it replaces or highly regulates markets, it destroys the "free market" that guarantees broader democratic freedoms and defines capitalism itself. In Milton Friedman's vocabulary, government always substitutes the "command" principle for the "voluntary" principle of the market, since government is always hierarchical and limits individual choice, while the market is the perfect embodiment of voluntary exchange.[10] Capitalism depends on democratic checks on government encroachments, with publicly owned businesses or market interventions a red line. Crossing it even modestly chips away at capitalist bedrock and at democracy itself.[11]

The red-line encroachments include taxation, social welfare, public investment, and regulation, not just government ownership of property. Neoclassicists view most taxation as a confiscation of wealth and subversion of incentives to work and of personal responsibility on which capitalism and democracy both depend. They point to President Calvin Coolidge, the resurrected hero of the US conservative movement, who virtually eliminated income taxes as a model of neoclassical governance. Amity Shlaes, whose recent biography of Coolidge has excited contemporary conservatives, claims that Coolidge is the only president who said truthfully that "perhaps one of the most important accomplishments of my administration has been minding my own business."[12] That meant keeping government social spending, taxation, and regulation of big business to a bare minimum. Regulation—which Coolidge despised—distorts capitalist pricing mechanisms and the market's perfect ability to allocate resources efficiently, while also expanding government's bureaucratic control, thus endangering democracy.

If capitalism needs democracy, so too, for many of the same reasons, democracy needs capitalism. Democracy is based first and foremost on liberty, which, neoclassicists such as Milton Friedman argue, can only be ensured by the right to own property and exchange it freely in the markets. Freedom is indivisible: if it is not guaranteed in the economy it can never sustain itself in the polity.[13]

Friedman is very explicit that this means democracy is grounded in the free exchange offered only by markets: "The kind of economic organization that provides economic freedom directly, namely competitive capitalism, also promotes political freedom because it separates economic power from political power and in this way enables the one to offset the other."[14]

Friedman goes on:

> The fundamental threat to freedom is power to coerce, be it in the hands of a monarch, a dictator.... The preservation of freedom [and democracy] requires the elimination of such concentration of [political or government] power to the fullest possible extent.... By removing the organization of economic activity from the control of political authority, the market eliminates this source of coercive power.[15]

Friedman claims history is the ultimate proof of his bold assertion:

> Historical evidence speaks with a single voice on the relation between political freedom and a free market. I know of no example in time or place of a society that has been marked by a large measure of political freedom, and that has not also used something comparable to a free market to organize the bulk of economic activity.[16]

Friedman is defining freedom here as limits on the state's ability to intrude in the life of the private citizens and the right of those individual citizens to freely pursue their choices in the market. Private citizens cannot interfere in the rights and freedom of other citizens. All individuals freely contract with other citizens. The government standing outside the market, outside civil society, will interfere with free voluntary associations, including the market itself.

The US Constitution, in the view of neoclassicists and their political allies in the Republican and Tea parties, embodies this concept of government as the central threat to liberty and rights. Consider the actual text of the First Amendment, which defines rights as "negative"—the right to be left alone (mainly by government). Republicans and Tea Partiers brandish the slogan, "Don't tread on me!" And they point to the Constitution as the basis of this philosophy. The First Amendment is clear: "Congress shall make no law respecting an establishment of religion, or prohibiting the free exercise thereof; or abridging the freedom of speech, or of the press." This is a restriction upon Congress and says it must leave free citizens alone. Government is conceived mainly as a threat to freedom, the one institution that takes upon itself the right to interfere in the name of the public interest with private freedom.

Neoclassicists say democracy is based on making every man the king of his property and sole decision-maker over how to spend his income. It is for this reason that Milton Friedman argues that even government-mandated Social Security is antidemocratic, limiting personal freedom over how to spend one's money: "The citizen of the United States who is compelled by law to devote something like 10% of his income to the purchase of a particular kind of retirement contract, administered by the government, is being deprived of a corresponding part of his personal freedom."[17]

Personal responsibility and the rule of law also are rooted in the market and are a precondition of democracy. Democracy requires a responsible citizenry. Personal responsibility and the willingness to accept enforceable legal contracts are at the heart of capitalism. Capitalism breeds the culture of responsibility and independence that democracy requires—while socialism or other forms of government-based systems create "dependency," a culture creating moochers or dependents who lack the responsibility to sustain either a job or a democratic society.

Newt Gingrich captured the "dependency" argument of neoclassicists in his 2012 attack on President Obama as the "food stamp president." Gingrich proclaimed, "The average American understands exactly what I am saying. This president has a deep commitment to maximizing dependency in America. He wants Americans to be small and government to be big. And I think 'food stamp president' is an easy way to capture what I've said all along."[18] And what he is capturing is the idea that we will destroy our democracy if we turn our economy into a government welfare machine breeding parasites and takers.

Neoclassicists also argue that democracy means governance by citizens rather than by government bureaucrats who dominate socialist or welfare economies. Capitalism protects democracy by limiting the inexorable tendency, described by sociologist Max Weber, for government bureaucracies to expand and ultimately take the power of the people into their own hands. Weber was not a neoclassicist, but he provided ammunition for the neoclassical antipathy to the state by emphasizing its role as a bureaucratic "iron cage." Yet he realized that all big bureaucracies could be authoritarian iron cages, including corporations, something the neoclassicists ignore.[19]

Frederick Hayek, the prophetic neoclassical critic of big government, argued that the rise of the New Deal and the European welfare state represent authoritarian "collectivism." Collectivism moves "away from the basic idea"—individualism and democracy—on which Western civilization has been built. Indeed, Hayek proclaims government planning, as in the New Deal, shows, "We have progressively abandoned that freedom in economic affairs without which personal and political freedom has never existed in the past.... Socialism means slavery," and all government intervention is inevitably a spear thrown at the heart of democracy.[20]

One great limit of the neoclassical view is to fail to recognize that corporations are giant bureaucracies that, themselves, can take away the power of people central to democracy. Neoclassicists have too narrow a view of the kind of power that can threaten democracy. Yes, overreaching government can be dangerous. But it is obvious in today's world of huge global companies, many as large and wealthy as entire countries, that corporations can themselves become a primary danger to democracy.[21] David Korten, an economist and corporate critic who wrote *When Corporations Rule the World*, argued that corporations have already undermined popular democracy: "Capitalism is ... about concentrating capital, concentrating economic power in very few hands [and] using that power to trash everyone who gets in their way."[22] Concentrated economic power has long led to concentrated political power heading to "corpocracy"—or rule by corporation—rather than democracy.[23] Neoclassicists are blind to this threat, since they see no possibility of enduring antidemocratic power in capitalist free markets, one of the reasons that neoclassicism is embraced by the corporate elites.

The threat of corporate big money, especially after the 2010 *Citizens United* Supreme Court case banning limits on contributions by corporations and the wealthy to political advertising, has become obvious. Polls show 80 percent of the public views corporate money as weakening and corrupting democracy. The failure of neoclassicists to see this danger—when more than $6 billion, mostly from corporations and the wealthy, flood into presidential year campaigns—speaks to the inability of the neoclassical paradigm to even consider the most basic threats to democracy. In the United States, these threats are already leading to a government that serves the biggest banks and companies rather than the people. In the 2008 meltdown, this became obvious when the government shoveled billions to save the big banks and did little to help anybody else. Neoclassicists tend not to be concerned because, while some recognize the problems of what they call "crony capitalism," by definition, only the state, not a private institution such as a corporation, can intrude upon freedom.

The inability of neoclassicists to see this reflects a profound limit in their basic assumptions. They assume that power itself cannot be concentrated in free markets, made up of millions of competing consumers, investors, workers, and companies. The marketplace is inherently democratic, both because it involves voluntary exchange and because competition limits concentration of power.

There are other deep problems with the neoclassical view. Government plays a huge role in all capitalist societies, including the United States. Even Milton Friedman acknowledges that government must provide safety and defense, a judicial and legal system creating private property, and supervision of the money supply. It must act as an umpire to ensure market rules are both created and enforced fairly.[24] In reality, corporations depend on massive "corporate welfare": subsidies that include tax breaks, loopholes, and direct grants amounting to billions of dollars annually. They depend on bailouts in crises. They depend on high military spending and infrastructure investment to secure resources profitably and operate their businesses.[25] The notion of "small government" capitalism is a myth, unseen in any major capitalist society around the world. If, then, capitalism requires big government, it should serve the people rather than the corporations, a reasonable definition of what democracy is all about.

Keynesians

Keynesians are not subject to the same blindness as neoclassicists, although they have their own myopia. The Keynesian paradigm veers toward the view of a stable but troubled marriage between capitalism and democracy.

Keynesians tend to hold a more expansive and participatory model of democracy than the neoclassicists. Like neoclassicists, they favor the representative republic, as framed in the US Constitution, over more direct and participatory democracies. But because they recognize realities of capitalist concentration of wealth and power, which can subvert a government accountable to the people, they tend to be more supportive than neoclassicists of political participation by workers and ordinary citizens. This is limited though, both by Keynesian embrace of capitalism and the framing of Keynesianism as a school for policy wonks rather than an inspiration for popular movements.

Keynesians agree with neoclassicists that capitalism "fits" with democracy in a general sense, because both depend on freedom, built into the markets and private ownership, as well as personal responsibility and the rule of law. They also share the view that government should be limited and a last rather than first resort to building civil society. While Keynes opposed Hayek's view of collectivism as a "road to serfdom," he and Hayek were friends and Keynes sympathized with some of Hayek's observations about the dangers of central planning and its potential to undermine democratic freedoms and lead toward totalitarianism.

But Keynesians recognize that capitalism without planning can easily destabilize democracy—and that the marriage is always troubled. After all, Keynes himself lived in a period when a young, democratic Weimar Republic, in the midst of a horrific capitalist crisis of hyperinflation, lost its democracy and embraced Hitler and dictatorship.

At the heart of Keynesianism is the analysis of the vulnerability of capitalism to crisis and depression. Historically, these crises, when not resolved, have led to political instability, often extreme and antidemocratic, as in Germany and Italy. Keynes saw his main task as managing these crises, not only to save capitalism but to save democracy.

While Keynes vigorously supported capitalism, he never embraced Adam Smith's sanguine doctrine of the invisible hand. While he saw capitalism as a foundation of democracy, it can easily degrade into an antidemocratic nightmare, particularly when capitalists fail to manage the crises that they inflict on themselves. Laissez-faire capitalism, from a Keynesian framework, is doomed to political instability, since it will impose hardships on the population that often lead to the type of right-wing antidemocratic forces that emerged in Weimar Germany. Only Keynesian capitalism, then, is seen as a bulwark of a stable democracy.

Paul Krugman, one of the most influential Keynesians today, has argued that Western capitalist democracies are in similar political danger because of their folly about how to respond to the current crises facing the economies of Europe and the United States. Regarding Europe, Krugman wrote in 2011 that failed austerity policies are provoking frightening right-wing authoritarian movements:

> Right-wing populists are on the rise from Austria, where the Freedom Party (whose leader used to have neo-Nazi connections) runs neck-and-neck in the polls with established parties, to Finland, where the anti-immigrant True Finns party had a strong electoral showing last April. And these are rich countries whose economies have held up fairly well. Matters look even more ominous in the poorer nations of Central and Eastern Europe.[26]

Krugman explicitly evokes the German nightmare in referring to the rise of neo-Nazi movements in a Hungary undergoing severe economic and financial crises: "Democratic institutions are being undermined as we speak. One of Hungary's major parties, Jobbik, is a nightmare out of the 1930s: it's anti-Roma (Gypsy), it's anti-Semitic, and it even had a paramilitary arm."[27]

In the United States, Krugman sees the same dangers. Obama's failures to mount a robust stimulus and regulatory response to the 2008 Wall Street meltdown has led to what Krugman calls a Depression lasting well into Obama's second term. The political implications are ominous: Krugman devotes much of his writing since the US financial meltdown to the rise of the Tea Party and a Far Right Republican Party whose austerity measures threaten not only economic disaster but an authoritarian right-wing regime that is weakening American democracy. Only Keynesian policies, elaborated by Krugman in his bestseller, *End This Depression Now!*, can solve the economic crisis and the political one.[28]

The critical question for Keynesians, then, is whether the political will to enact their solutions to capitalist crises exists. Keynes himself played a role in helping end the Great Depression of the 1930s, and Keynesians have thus remained optimistic that the political will for their policies can be mobilized. But as Krugman sees—with even the Obama administration failing to implement the necessary Keynesian approaches—there is a difficult political struggle to keep both capitalism and democracy alive and mutually harmonious.

Keynesians understand what neoclassicists ignore: the threat to democracy by the huge concentrations of wealth in capitalist societies—that is, by the big banks and corporations and the wealthiest 1 percent. These threaten democracy in several ways, for example, in mobilizing political resistance to public investment and other Keynesian solutions. Keynesians, unlike neoclassicists, understand that private power, in the giant corporations, can threaten democracy as much as unfettered government. They are also not blind to the reality that globalization has increased the size and wealth of corporations and limited the power of governments, thus making the threat of corporate rule—one that can ultimately bring down democracy—a realistic twenty-first-century threat. This has been a focus of many of the most influential contemporary Keynesians, including Krugman, Robert Kuttner, Joseph Stiglitz, and Robert Reich.[29]

All contemporary Keynesians on this theme owe a major debt to John Kenneth Galbraith, the leading US Keynesian political economist in the mid-twentieth century, who wrote several books about the antidemocratic dangers of corporate political influence, including his work, *American Capitalism: The Concept of Countervailing Power*. In that book, he argued that democracy required limiting the potential of unchecked corporate power.[30] The United States needs checks and balances not just among the different branches of government but among the different sectors of society.

Galbraith was astute about the fragility and potentially illusory character of capitalist democracies that tended to narrow the idea of democracy to voting. He wrote,

When people put their ballots in the boxes, they are, by that act, inoculated against the feeling that the government is not theirs. They then accept, in some measure, that its errors are their errors, its aberrations their aberrations, that any revolt will be against them. It's a remarkably shrewd and rather conservative arrangement when one thinks of it.[31]

Galbraith argued that to sustain a true democracy in capitalism, one had to go beyond these manipulated perceptions of democracy-as-simply-voting. An authentic democracy requires thoroughgoing countervailing power in all sectors of capitalist society, with government as the most important check on corporate power. Both had to check each other to protect democracy. But government was not the only vital countervailing force. Labor and social movements could check corporate power. And even more important, capitalist competition led to corporations checking the power of each other.[32]

Galbraith's focus on countervailing power in the markets themselves helps explain the Keynesian commitment to capitalism. They see that the markets generate high concentrations of power but believe that competition within markets tends to check and balance the potentially dangerous takeover of the economy and society by one set of companies. They share with neoclassicists the view that the market has built-in tendencies toward democratic checks and balances.

Unlike the neoclassicists, though, they realize that the market is not a perfect check and balance on itself. Government is crucial to fine-tuning and preserving the kind of competition and corporations that are compatible with democracy. Keynesians' view that government is a guarantor of democracy rather than a threat to it marks a big difference between Keynesian and neoclassical thought.

Galbraith sees democracy as a system that runs up against the fundamental nature of capitalism—unless government intervenes in major ways. He embraced the view of early civil rights activist A. Philip Randolph who proclaimed, "A community is democratic only when the humblest and weakest person can enjoy the highest civil, economic and social rights that the biggest and most powerful possess."[33] Galbraith also noted that "as I would not be a slave, I would not be a master. This expresses my idea of democracy."[34] To meet these criteria, capitalism obviously needs, indeed, very big government.

In Keynesian thinking, it is true, big government can be too big and needs restraint to save both capitalism and democracy. But small or "not-big" government is also a threat since government must be large enough not only to check huge corporations but also to provide everyone with the freedom to enter the market and get the education, health care, and jobs that guarantee a large middle class, one of the social bulwarks of democracy. And, of course, it must be large and strong enough to counter capitalist crises with Keynesian policies of stimulus, regulation, and full employment. Jobless people are not free and their desperation is a threat to the economy and to democratic stability. Government, then, is a Keynesian elixir, providing many different guarantees of democracy that the market itself cannot deliver. Without government, market inequalities and lacks of checks and balances could spell the end of democracy, a theme made strongly by contemporary Keynesians such as Robert Kuttner and Robert Reich.[35] In a piece called "How Capitalism Is Killing Democracy," Reich urged,

> Let us be clear: The purpose of democracy is to accomplish ends we cannot achieve as individuals. But democracy cannot fulfill this role when companies use politics to advance or maintain their competitive standing, or when they appear to take on social responsibilities that they have no real capacity or authority to fulfill. That leaves societies unable to address the tradeoffs between economic growth and social problems such as job insecurity, widening inequality, and climate change. As a result, consumer and investor interests almost invariably trump common concerns.[36]

Corporate power is inextricably intertwined with one other central threat to both capitalism and democracy at the heart of Keynesian thinking: extreme inequality. Keynes himself understood the political implications, and Galbraith made it a central part of his analysis. Galbraith argued that inequalities in income and wealth have a powerful effect on political resources and influence. He called repeatedly for more progressive income taxes and stronger social welfare to limit the political power of the wealthy and the apathy of the middle classes, who often succumbed to the illusion that the guarantee of the vote ensured authentic democracy.[37]

Reich and Kuttner have brought the Keynesian focus on inequality up-to-date, concentrating on the growth of extreme inequality that the Occupy movement highlighted, with their discussion of the division between the 1 percent and the 99 percent. Keynesians did not give rise to Occupy, but they have made important contributions to the public conversation about inequality. In *Aftershock*, Reich argued that extreme inequality was the central cause of the Great Recession and there can be no recovery without closing the income gap, since most workers simply will not be able to consume enough to spur recovery, a point also repeatedly made by Paul Krugman.[38] In his sequel to *Aftershock*, *Beyond Outrage*, Reich argues that closing the gap in Obama's second term is also vital for democracy and the public good, a central argument also of Robert Kuttner, who, like Reich, focuses strongly on inequality as a rising killer of democracy.[39]

But what is the Keynesian strategy to build the kind of robust government that can save the public interest and democracy? Keynesians assume it is possible to save capitalism and democracy together, with a political strategy of vigorous regulation, social spending, and public investment, orchestrated by government. What Keynesians fail to acknowledge is that capitalism creates so much concentrated corporate wealth that the rich can always turn government to its own interests, and prevent it from carrying out the activist, public interest agenda that Keynesians seek.

Keynesians believe that capitalism does not have to be a corpocracy; it can be a true democracy if countervailing power and progressive control of government prevail, which is possible under capitalism, a Keynesian view that fundamentally differentiates it from the neo-Marxist perspective. The New Deal, which Keynes helped craft and legitimate, is the fallback proof for Keynesians that they can push through the progressive public interest led by government. FDR saved both capitalism and democracy. But only World War II and the expansion of the military—or military Keynesianism—ultimately pulled the country out of the Depression and allowed the vast government spending that Keynesians see as necessary.

The failures of the Obama administration reinforce the idea that even liberal presidents cannot mobilize the countervailing power necessary to save democracy and protect the public interest. When the economy melted down in 2008, Obama bailed out the big banks and mortgage companies while doing little to protect ordinary citizens. His regulation of Wall Street, made possible by Dodd-Frank, the congressional law seeking to right financial wrongs and limit Wall Street power, has proved weak and nearly impossible to implement. Obama has also been unable to push through climate legislation, limit corporate funding of elections, significantly increase corporate taxes, reduce corporate subsidies, or resist cuts in crucial social spending and entitlements such as Medicare and Medicaid.

Backed by Republicans and conservative Democrats, corporations have been able to block any major limits to their power and stymie new legislation that would support the masses of Americans who need precisely the kind of social spending and public investment that Keynesians advocate. Obama's signature first-term accomplishment—Obamacare—was supported by health care insurance corporations who reaped a bonanza of new clients forced to pay them premiums. What corporations really feared—single-payer health care as in Europe that would have stripped Aetna, Hancock, and other health insurance giants of billions in health care money—was not even on Obama's table, though the original plan included a public option, killed in congressional negotiations.

The Keynesians have no real answer. In 2008, in his book *Obama's Challenge*, Robert Kuttner voiced the historical optimism of Keynesians that the Democratic Party, under Obama, can become the democratic vehicle for fighting corporate power and implementing a major, new, progressive Keynesian agenda.[40] Kuttner laid out an ambitious Keynesian plan, similar to solutions proposed by Krugman, that could save both capitalism and democracy. But in his sequel on Obama, *A Presidency in Peril*, Kuttner had to backtrack, recognizing that Obama had failed, and there was the hope—but little evidence—that a second Obama term will succeed where the first one failed.[41]

The historical evidence—and the headlines today—converge on the idea that within capitalism, capitalist priorities will win over the public interest. This is nobody's idea of real democracy (although neoclassicists, of course, equate capitalist priorities with the public good). It is a body blow to the credibility of the entire Keynesian school.

Neo-Marxists

Enter the neo-Marxists. Obama's failures, they argue, are totally predictable. After all, capitalism depends on—and always ensures—that the capitalist class will control the state.

The core of capitalism—private ownership and class division—makes democracy impossible. The capitalist class has the wealth and power necessary to control the state. The working class, the majority of the people, can never take control under capitalism itself. This means that capitalism and democracy can never coexist in a marriage that is real.

Marx and Engels were definitive about this in the *Communist Manifesto*: "The executive of the modern State is but a committee for managing the common affairs of the whole bourgeoisie."[42] In other words, the elected government is a fig leaf masking capitalist control of the political system. Corporations run the show while maintaining a credible illusion of democratic procedures such as voting. Marx mocked the process: "The oppressed are allowed once every few years to decide which particular representatives of the oppressing class are to represent and repress them."[43] This has a remarkably contemporary ring, when many US progressives view recent elections as a choice between Bush and Bush-lite. Marx rejected decisively both neoclassical and many Keynesian views that elections and rule of law represent democracy. Since all leading parties and electoral procedures are controlled by the wealthy of the capitalist class, elections are ritual procedures—between Tweedle-dee and Tweedle-dum—that seek to legitimate capitalism but cannot erode the reality that the state in capitalism is always determined by the underlying structure of the economy and the power of the "possessing" class.

Rejecting prevailing notions of democracy, Marx defined it in a way alien to both neoclassicists and Keynesians: "Democracy is the road to socialism."

In other words, Marx saw democracy as something incompatible with capitalism, and taking form only in the political process emerging as capitalism disappears and socialism emerges.

Engels agreed, reinforcing the argument that capitalism was inherently a marriage of the capitalist class (and their corporations) and the state. He argued that such corpocracy was especially developed in the United States, where there is not only "direct corruption of officials" but a striking marriage of corporations, especially large banks, and the state: "In the form of an alliance between government and Stock Exchange, which becomes the easier to achieve the more the public debt increases and the more joint-stock companies concentrate in their hands not only transport but production itself, using Stock Exchange as their centre."[44] This evokes the contemporary view of the US government as hitched to Wall Street money, and makes clear that it is not just an aberration of the Great Recession but the permanent condition of capitalist politics.

Marxists argue that Keynesian political views, such as those expressed by Reich and Kuttner on creating authentic political democracy within capitalism, can never be realized in the United States. In 1892, Engels himself, again writing on US politics, argued that the mainstream US political parties could never become a vehicle for authentic and substantive democracy, for a government that would represent ordinary people rather than the corporations. Engels wrote,

> The divergence of interests even in the same class group is so great in that tremendous area that wholly different groups and interests are represented in each of the two big parties, depending on the locality, and almost each particular section of the possessing class has its representatives in each of the two parties to a very large degree.... The apparent haphazardness of this jumbling together is what provides the splendid soil for the corruption and the plundering of the government that flourish there so beautifully.[45]

Engels is prophetic here, writing in 1892 that neither major political party in the United States could free itself of the corrupting influence of corporations and the capitalist ("possessing") class. He would not be surprised by the progressive disenchantment with Obama and Obama's failure to create the democracy of, by, and for the people that Keynesians such as Kuttner and Reich envisage.

Why do capitalists need to control government? Because, say neo-Marxists today, the corporation can profit only if the state protects its property; subordinates workers; provides research, subsidies, and tax breaks that make profit possible; carries out wars that secure foreign resources, especially oil, and cheap labor abroad; and manages dissent at home. Corporations need the state to provide the official ideology that justifies private property, great concentrations of wealth, and the huge inequalities that capitalism breeds. It also needs police, prisons, and other coercive government to physically control anyone who seeks to overturn the system.[46]

Capitalism thus needs to control government for both economic and political aims. Economically, the government provides taxpayer money and favorable policy in every industry—energy, medicine, agriculture, finance—to keep companies maximally profitable. It keeps regulation low and corporate welfare high, freeing corporations to dominate their respective industries and transfer public funds to ensure private profits. It socializes corporate risk and privatizes profit, the essential precondition of capitalist success, as a kind of socialism for the wealthy.[47] Politically, as well, control of government legitimates the system itself and crushes those, abroad or at home, that would challenge its rule.

Despite these antidemocratic outrages, Marx recognized that capitalism upset traditional hierarchies and insisted on equal rights under the law. In *The Communist Manifesto*, he wrote that capitalism has "pitilessly torn asunder the motley feudal ties that bound man to his 'natural superiors.'"[48] In arguing that capitalism "put an end to all feudal, patriarchal, idyllic relations," he was recognizing that capitalism required everyone be treated equally under the law—with the same rights to private property and enforceable market contracts.[49] This meant that capitalists could produce a compelling illusion of democracy—and some very real advances from the permanent authoritarian regimes of feudalism.

Capitalism creates an illusory quasi-democracy because it provides "limited government," powerful enough to protect individual rights, especially private property, but not powerful enough to interfere with those rights. All are equal before the law and all are entitled to have their rights protected before the law. Everyone has the same right to use their property as they see fit. Billionaires have the same right to control their banks, factories, airlines, and oil wells as paupers to eat their crusts of bread. If all property is entitled to equal protection under law, then the government provides individual people (corporations are people) protection in proportion to what they own. Marxists give due credit to capitalism's advances and progress, while simultaneously showing the absolute limitations of the procedural and limited democracy that capitalism offers.[50]

Marx said that capitalism survives because it creates mirages or "false consciousness" that leads the masses to support a system that exploits it. Democracy is arguably the most potent form of false consciousness. It offers the impression that capitalism provides freedom and self-governance when, in reality, it operates to ensure that true democracy will never break out.

Almost a century after Marx's death, neo-Marxists in the United States—a high percentage of them sociologists—have updated the argument and the data showing that the capitalist class dominates the US government. Starting in the mid-twentieth century, as discussed in Chapter 2, C. Wright Mills published *The Power Elite*, arguing that a tightly intertwined group of wealthy corporate executives, state officials, and military commanders at the top of the Pentagon run America. Mills's work, drawing heavily on Weber as well as Marx, was a game-changer in political sociology and generated a new sociological PE challenging the common wisdom that America is a democracy.[51]

The most important figure following Mills was G. William Domhoff, who published a series of major works on the US power elite, the two most important being *Who Rules America?* and *The Higher Circles*.[52] Domhoff argued, "Who has predominant power in the United States? The short answer, from 1776 to the present, is: Those who have the money—or more specifically, who own income-producing land and businesses—have the power."[53]

Domhoff explained further that,

> The key reason why money can rule—i.e., why the business owners who hire workers can rule—is that the people who work in the factories and fields were divided from the outset into free and slave, white and black, and later into numerous immigrant ethnic groups as well, making it difficult for workers as a whole to unite politically to battle for higher wages and better social benefits.[54]

By focusing on money and the leaders of the corporate class as a ruling class, Domhoff clearly embraces a neo-Marxist sociological analysis, with works that analyze the cohesion of the capitalist class, how it mobilizes collectively to shape political decisions, and the fragmentation of the working class, a theme also taken up by the neo-Marxist sociologist Stanley Aronowitz in his seminal work, *False Promises*.[55] Aronowitz examines the religious, racial, and ethnic differences that historically have undermined the ability of US workers to unite in a more powerful labor movement that could transform capitalism. Capitalist elites divided and conquered, a key means of subverting democracy.

The power of Aronowitz's work is in the insightful historical analysis, always central to the best PE work, while Domhoff's great strength lies in the meticulous depth of his empirical analysis of capitalist elite networks and their political means of influence. Domhoff's work is also nuanced, recognizing that capitalist elites do not control everything:

> The simple answer that money rules has to be qualified somewhat. Domination by the few does not mean complete control, but rather the ability to set the terms under which other groups and classes must operate. Highly trained professionals ... win governmental restrictions on some corporate practices. Wage and salary workers ... sometimes have been able to gain concessions on wages, hours, and working conditions.

Most of all, there is free speech and the right to vote. While voting does not necessarily make government responsive to the will of the majority, under certain circumstances the electorate has been able to place restraints on the actions of the wealthy elites.[56]

Nonetheless, Domhoff is clear that the capitalist elites have so much power that the mainstream view of a pluralistic American democracy is wrong.

Rule by the wealthy few is possible despite free speech, regular elections, and organized opposition:

- "The rich" coalesce into a social upper class that has developed institutions by which the children of its members are socialized into an upper-class worldview, and newly wealthy people are assimilated.
- Members of this upper class control corporations, which have been the primary mechanisms for generating and holding wealth in the United States for upwards of 150 years now.
- There exists a network of nonprofit organizations through which members of the upper class and hired corporate leaders not yet in the upper class shape policy debates in the United States.
- Members of the upper class, with the help of their high-level employees in profit and nonprofit institutions, are able to dominate the federal government in Washington.
- The rich, and corporate leaders, nonetheless claim to be relatively powerless.
- Working people have less power than in many other democratic countries.[57]

A political economist and political scientist, Thomas Ferguson, in his influential book, *The Golden Rule*, helps confirm the Domhoff thesis.[58] Ferguson argued that democracy is impossible in US capitalism because the two political parties are competing blocs of investors rather than voters. They ensure that corporate and financial elites will control government, that politics is organized to ensure their business interests, and that policies will serve business whether Republicans or Democrats win.

Ferguson's work is an "investor" theory of politics, consistent with the neo-Marxist view that capitalist elites rule America through what might be called the "political market." Most voters lack the money or time to become significant "investors" in this market, and it is taken over by the financiers and other corporate elites, according to Ferguson: "The real market for political parties is defined by major investors, who generally have good and clear reasons for investing to control the state.... Blocs of major investors define the core of political parties and are responsible for most of the signals the party sends to the electorate."[59]

Ferguson argued that Democrats attract coastal capital-intensive and high-tech firms who don't depend as much on domestic workers as labor-intensive corporations, who tend to support Republicans. Democrats have historically had more support from the financial firms on Wall Street while Republicans attract the midwestern and southern manufacturing firms concentrated in the Chamber of Commerce. Despite party competition, both investor blocs controlling the two parties share the fundamental capitalist concern of wealthy investors maintaining control of government rather than ordinary citizens. Democracy is a facade.[60]

In a succession of recent books, including *Corporation Nation*, *People before Profit*, *Hidden Power*, and *Marx's Ghost*, sociologist Charles Derber reinforces Domhoff's and Ferguson's view. He offers several new perspectives on "corpocracy": corporate rule dressed up through elections and party competition as democracy. First, the expansion in the size of corporations in late-twentieth-century globalization shifted the balance of power between the capitalist and working classes, eroding the countervailing power of labor, community, and other citizens' groups throughout society. Corporate power is now exercised by a global corporate elite, which uses "exit power" to cement political and social control of America:

> As anyone in a marriage knows, one of the great sources of power is the freedom to exit. In any relationship, the person who can leave has enormous leverage over the person who has to stay because he or she lacks the emotional or financial resources to leave. Now extend that way of thinking to globalization. Corporations now enjoy huge new forms of exit power. By threatening to leave, they can extract enormous concessions from unions or governments.[61]

Globalization is essentially organized exit power, providing corporations with a consummate tool to cement control over national governments. Derber also shows that capitalist exit power *within* nations such as the United States—through corporations moving from New York to New Jersey to Delaware—has also consolidated capitalist control. The result: corporations largely run the country through the "hidden power" of what he calls "corporate regimes."[62] Regimes are institutionalized systems of power with dominant institutions and political discourses largely embraced by all mainstream parties; in a corporate regime, the dominant regime is the corporation and democracy becomes feeble, whichever party is in power. The Robber Barons ran America in the first corporate regime of the 1890s, followed by a "regime change" to a more democratic "New Deal regime" presided over by FDR in the Depression era, followed by another regime change in 1980 when President Reagan was elected to our current corporate regime, the most corporatized and least democratic.[63] Derber summarized,

> The idea of regime helps capture the changing balance of power and different zeitgeists of different US capitalist eras. The change from one regime to another is a political tidal wave—for better or worse—in the lives of ordinary Americans and in the fate of American democracy and morality. In corporate regimes, the balance of power swings toward money and away from democracy.[64]

Neo-Marxists make formidable arguments about the limits of democracy within corporate capitalism. The limits of the Marxist analysis, like those of the Keynesian one, have to do with its strategies for solving the problem. Clearly, it would require overturning capitalism and creating an alternative system to ensure democracy. That new system would have to eliminate major class differences and promote equality in both the economy and the polity. But Marxists fail on two accounts: (1) no clear vision of that alternative economy (Marx himself, a brilliant analyst of capitalism, offered very little of what socialism would look like) and (2) even less of a realistic strategy about how to get there.

Moreover, to the extent that Marxists offer a strategy, it has authoritarian overtones, which burst out in terrifying proportions in self-proclaimed communist regimes such as the Stalinist Soviet Union or Maoist China. This is less of an issue for many contemporary neo-Marxists, whose work emphasizes a commitment to economic democracy. But by writing about the "dictatorship of the proletariat" Marx himself appeared to justify authoritarian strategies and alternatives that violated his fundamental beliefs in freedom and self-determination—and this is worth considering once again because even highly democratic contemporary neo-Marxists have been stained by the historical legacy of Marxist authoritarianism. In famed disputes with the renowned anarchist of his era, Mikhail Bakunin, Bakunin attacked Marx for supporting governments that would inevitably become authoritarian: "Where there is a state there is inevitable domination," charged Bakunin, "if the proletariat is to be the ruling class, over whom will it rule? This means that another proletariat will remain which will be subject to this new domination, this new [Marxist] state."[65]

Marx responded that a "dictatorship of the proletariat" was a temporary but necessary evil, necessary to destroy capitalism and prevent restoration of capitalism by the wealthy. He acknowledged that this would require violence and despotic means to establish a highly centralized regime: "The proletariat will use its political supremacy to wrest, by degrees, from the bourgeoisie, to centralize all instruments of production in the state.... Of course, in the beginning, this cannot be effected except by despotic inroads on the rights of property."[66]

Marx was right about the need for progressives to engage in politics and claim a state strong enough to withstand counterrevolution. But in the process, he laid the ground for a perception of his entire philosophy as antidemocratic and dictatorial. That was far from his ultimate intention—which was to abolish the state itself and replace it with self-government communities and co-ops—but it left an indelible stain on Marxism among those prizing democracy.[67]

The tension between liberation as a democratic alternative brought about by violent or authoritarian strategies has limited the appeal of Marxism and pointed to the need for either a new Marxism that overcomes these deficiencies or a different political economy of liberation for the twenty-first century.[68]

A Leninist version of structural/scientific Marxism has been implemented as the ruling ideology in Russia, China, and other countries and produced regimes worse than capitalism. In European social democracies, Marxism has been melded with Keynesian thinking, with respect for civil liberties preserved, and perhaps has created a more substantive democracy than in the United States. Critical Marxism has never assumed state power and its commitment to individual autonomy may not build the discipline for managing a state or corporate bureaucracy. However, it does show how corporations and the state manipulate and control people. The only way real freedom and democracy can be achieved is through their total transformation.

CHAPTER 8

Individualism versus Community

The American narrative declares that we are "the land of the free," free to do pretty much what we want. Guns illustrate the idea. I have a right to buy and carry semiautomatic weapons even though Newtown and Columbine and Aurora show, sickeningly, that the social consequences can be deadly. Many Americans no longer feel safe in their homes, schools, or neighborhoods. But gun owners say that their individual freedom trumps everything else—and that is what makes America great. As the band Lynyrd Skynyrd sings in "God and Guns,"

> Well we might as well give up and run
> If we let 'em take our God and guns

The gun issue is a gut-level illustration of the dilemma faced by every society: how to balance individual and community rights. This is a key issue in sociology and also one of the great moral, political, and economic issues in every society. Each of our three paradigms of political economy takes a stance on the issue because the economic system itself depends to a large degree on the balance that is struck, a balance in American capitalism that is unlike any in the world.

Neoclassicists

Neoclassicists take a no-holds-barred theoretical approach. The individual reigns supreme. Milton Friedman was blunt and clear about this: "We take freedom of the individual ... as our ultimate goal in judging social arrangements."[1] His "freedom of the individual" is conceived tightly around ideas of the market. Neoclassicists define freedom as the right to amass private property and do with it as you choose. Anything that limits your freedom to acquire or use property, including government laws seeking to constrain property rights (such as gun ownership), is contrary to the idea of freedom. Moreover, social freedoms to be protected from poverty or homelessness or hunger, or to be guaranteed a job or home or education—key parts of the UN 1948 Universal Declaration of Human Rights—are not part of the concept of freedom that neoclassicists espouse—neoclassicists conceive these rights as coercive government limitations on freedom.[2]

Neoclassicists do believe in political freedom, but see it as rooted in the market or the "economic freedom" to acquire and dispose of property as you see fit. Milton Friedman said individual freedom has two components, economic and political, with the latter dependent on the former: "Economic freedom is an end in itself.... Economic freedom is also an indispensable means toward the achievement of political freedom."[3] Friedman stressed market freedom because it is "voluntary exchange" that is the foundation of other freedoms and because, he argued, "Intellectuals have a strong bias against regarding this kind of freedom as important. They tend to have contempt for material aspects of life," which they see as lower than their own lofty creative pursuits.[4]

Neoclassicists thus see themselves speaking for the common man and woman, whose lives revolve around their dignity as free property holders.[5]

Neoclassicists also claim that their idea of freedom (and private property) is rooted in natural law and must not be compromised or limited, except under very specific circumstances when one person's freedom restricts the freedom or property rights of others. Fortunately, neoclassicists argue, maximizing personal freedom and rights to property rarely limits and usually increases the freedom of others; as Adam Smith wrote, "The individual who intends only his own gain" is "led by an invisible hand" to promote both his own and social well-being.[6] For that reason, their focus rests on the individual and offers an impoverished theory of community interest or action.

This neoclassical view of freedom has always been uniquely potent in US politics, and Milton Friedman traces it back to Thomas Jefferson and the Declaration of Independence.[7] It is now at the heart of the conservative movement of the Tea Party, the larger Republican Party, and the libertarian movement. These forces, at this writing in the Obama era, are waging a scorched earth political agenda to entirely dismantle FDR's New Deal and demonize the socialist or collectivist ideas of the 1960s New Left. Since 1980, the Reagan revolution has been one of the most powerful historical campaigns—actually a political regime change[8]—to guarantee that individuals (and the individual corporation, another free market player) are unfettered by government limits of any kind, and that New Deal social welfare systems are obliterated in the name of individual freedom and personal responsibility. The Reagan revolution has turned into a relentless war on government (or, more precisely, the nonmilitary, nonprison, and social welfare sides of government), wrapped in the neoclassical view that government is inherently tyrannical and that its simple presence threatens individual liberty at the heart of the American experiment. Thus in the 2012 election, Republican candidate Mitt Romney ran against Obama, whom he deemed a "European socialist" who would bury individuals in European-style big government, and Romney's vice-presidential running mate, Paul Ryan, launched an assault to end Social Security, Medicare, and Medicaid as we know it, since as government programs they threaten to bankrupt both the economy and our individual freedom.[9]

Meanwhile, Democrats have joined the parade in their own way. President Clinton vowed to end the era of big government and President Obama repeatedly proclaimed his ardent faith in the free market. This is the meaning of corporate regimes in the United States, where both mainstream parties embrace, in this case, a shared discourse of capitalist individualism and freedom.[10]

This rhetorical focus on the individual is not just a neoclassical preference; it is built into the paradigm's basic vocabulary and is also its cardinal article of faith. Neoclassicists have no theory of the community—nor any developed language for discussing societal rights or welfare, or indeed society itself. You are free to sink or swim on your own. Their economic analysis rests on the assumption that the individual is the relevant actor or "unit of analysis." Drawing on their interpretation of Adam Smith (which is problematic because it ignores Smith's view about the crucial importance of community in his classic work on moral sentiments[11]), their entire philosophy rests on an economy they view as maximizing liberty and "utility" for individuals—and an economic system that cannot exist or be justified except in terms of its protection of individual freedom and choice.[12]

Milton Friedman's language reveals how the concept of society is nearly obliterated by the neoclassical focus on the individual. He suggests that a simple society "consists of a number of independent households—a collection of Robinson Crusoes.... [Each] household has the alternative of producing directly for itself, it need not enter into any exchange."[13]

The Robinson Crusoe image is telling. Friedman said elsewhere that the freedom of a totally isolated Robinson Crusoe is not identical to the freedom of the individual in social life. Nonetheless, just using the image of Robinson Crusoe communicates the idea of society as a collection of separate and independent individuals—each essentially on an island by themselves. They may choose to exchange through the market but society is, if not an afterthought, simply an option for people essentially in command of their own island.

Friedman argued that capitalism is the only system compatible with individual liberty. "History," he wrote, proves "that capitalism is a necessary condition for political freedom."[14] Friedman defined the market as "voluntary"—and the only possible economic foundation of individual freedom. Since he defined the government as inherently coercive, any economic model organized around government ownership, regulation, or intervention strips the individual of liberty and is unacceptable tyranny.

Neoclassical theory in the Anglo-American tradition is associated with the great British philosopher John Locke. Locke argued that the individual was paramount, that individual rights were rooted in natural law, and that private property is the only way to protect the individual. The economy had to be based on natural law, which required individual property rights to be sacred. This was the basis of the social contract and of society itself, a minimalist view of society and a maximalist view of the individual. Locke wrote,

> To understand political power right, and derive it from its original, we must consider what state all men are naturally in, and that is, a state of perfect freedom to order their actions, and dispose of their possessions, and persons as they think fit, within the bounds of the law of nature, without asking leave, or depending on the will of any other man.[15]

The United States took Locke's philosophy as its touchstone. The United States has rhetorically sanctified the individual, putting a Lockean vision of the individual and individual liberty at the heart of the Constitution. Locke basically believed the state was formed as a contract signed by property owners to protect their rights against the property-less. The implication is that those without property are without state-sanctioned rights. The more property you have, the more rights.

The US idea of individual freedom or rights is a "negative" idea—that is, the right of the individual is to be left alone and not be hemmed in by government or other people. Positive rights—the right for social welfare in the form of education, health care, a living wage, and a caring community—have no place in the Constitution. The first and longest-serving justice of the US Supreme Court, John Marshall, almost single-handedly shaped US law to ensure that private property and market contracts—the foundations of US capitalism—were the only constitutional options in America, and that negative rights were the only ones protected. The great essayist, Max Lerner, regarded Marshall's legacy as the biggest gift that a chief justice ever bestowed on capitalists in America.[16]

This legal and moral vision connects perfectly with the neoclassical theory of the economy. It is based entirely on a view of individual market actors seeking to maximize their personal interests and freedom, and it attempts to demonstrate mathematically that this is the only system that can ensure both economic efficiency and liberty. Neoclassicists view the market as nothing but individuals seeking to freely maximize their self-interest or utility, a principle drawn from the master, Adam Smith. He saw the market as ensuring "the uniform, constant and uninterrupted effort of every man to better his condition, the principle from which public and national, as well as private opulence is originally derived."[17] Smith meant that self-interested action in the market creates such efficiency that it ensures collective benefit and the common good far more than any government can provide. Milton Friedman argued that Smith had touched on the secret of all prosperity. He argued that the market is so efficient, "It has been powerful enough to maintain the natural progress of things toward general improvement in spite of the extravagance of government and the greatest errors of administration."[18]

This voluntary and natural "efficient market" leads to the best pricing and a dynamic equilibrium in which the economy will constantly readjust to ensure that all individuals' preferences are safeguarded. The efficient market, driven by rational individual choices and no higher political power or community intervention, links supply to demand, maximizes growth and wealth, and prevents any long-term downturns or instability.

But how can a political economy based exclusively on the idea of the individual and personal negative rights be viable since society obviously exists and must survive if individuals themselves are to live together and sustain themselves? Society is a voluntary association of autonomous individuals conducted through the market, but without society there can be no market.

Neoclassicists resolve this apparent tension in three ways. One is based on the invisible hand theory of Smith, as interpreted—wrongly, it turns out, in the light of Smith's theory of moral sentiments—by neoclassicists today. The invisible hand always links the pursuit of self-interest in the market to social well-being. In fact, it is the only way to ensure the health of society. If one believes in the invisible hand, then the focus on the individual and neglect of community and government is logical and benign, because focusing on the individual is the only and best way to protect the community. Even Smith, though, saw these benefits only in a society, like his own, where feelings of moral solidarity in the community were strong and the community itself a powerful force.[19]

Second, and this is a major weakness of the paradigm, the neoclassical theory of the individual has little relation to the actual policies that neoclassicists and their political allies support. The conservative movement, Republican Party, and corporate elites pay lip service to Milton Friedman's neoclassical nostrums of small government to protect free individuals but depart radically in practice from their own rhetoric. It is no secret that the Reagan administration built up huge government, especially in military spending and in corporate welfare or subsidies, massively increasing the deficit and subverting free market ideas, a feat also achieved by another self-proclaimed antigovernment conservative, George W. Bush, whose bailouts of Wall Street dramatized the huge chasm between neoclassical theory and practice. The 2007 bailouts of the biggest Wall Street banks, in particular, supported by most leading neoclassical economists, such as Alan Greenspan, put on lurid display the neoclassical tacit recognition that free markets were not free and that society and government were an unspoken necessity to protect capitalism itself. Neoclassicists want social protection and corporate welfare for the rich and their cherished free market laissez-faire is meant only for the hard-pressed working class.[20]

A third and closely related contradiction—going to the heart of neoclassical thinking—is the use of government to control individuals, something that became apparent in the Reagan war on communism and in the George W. Bush war on terrorism. Reagan and Bush put in place repressive policies on individual dissent, free expression, and civil liberties in the name of national security, policies continued on a bipartisan basis by President Obama in keeping the prison at Guantanamo open, pursuing drone warfare by executive order, enshrining a regime of warrantless and massive surveillance (revealed by the whistle-blower Edward Snowden), and detaining alleged terrorists without elementary rights of habeas corpus or judicial review, the legal bulwarks of individual liberty, putting into question the political commitment of neoclassical conservatives to their cherished rhetoric of personal freedom.

This shows that the neoclassical idea of individual freedom has to be "deconstructed." Freedom for neoclassicists in practice means compliance with the norms of corporate capitalism and its national security state. Dissent and personal freedom mean little to those fired for supporting a union or put in jail for sleeping overnight in an Occupy tent on Wall Street. Neoclassical personal freedom is actually the "freedom to comply" with corporate and state edicts, an idea that has persisted throughout US history and is on display in the long, ruthless use of police and military power to control or suppress personal freedom that does not toe official lines. Neoclassical practice is actually a politics of social conformity.

This means we need to distinguish the neoclassical idea of freedom and the individual from authentic free-thinking and creative individuality. Neoclassicists want the freedom of the market—the freedom to consume, profit, and play by the rules of national security and the corporate state. That is, it offers essentially the freedom to obey the ruling or official norms of the corporate capitalist system, the kind of freedom enshrined in the conventional American Dream of getting rich and enjoying the high life. It seeks social conformity rather than true personal freedom, the latter a kind of nonmarket individuality that is to be much prized and was celebrated by 1960s activists in the New Left.

The irony is that, by this interpretation, neoclassical thinking points toward a slavish adherence to social norms, in this case those of capitalist society.

In the name of the individual, and without serious analysis of society as an entity different than an aggregate of individuals, neoclassicists contradict their own basic metaphysics and offer a definition of individual freedom that does the very opposite of what it claims: subordinates the individual to the dictates of society, specifically capitalist or market society.

Keynesians

In the Great Depression, President Roosevelt helped pass laws and judicial policies that broke market contracts—such as mortgages that people couldn't pay—to help them stay in their homes. He also spent billions of public funds to directly employ the unemployed. He introduced a new social welfare system involving unions, Social Security, and welfare for the poor. Neoclassicists call this socialism, tyranny, and "the road to serfdom";[21] Keynesians view it as the only recipe to save capitalism and the very possibility of a civil society.[22]

All these programs broke sharply from the neoclassical focus on individual negative rights and pure market mechanisms. They involved ideas of positive rights—rights to a decent living for all in society. The Great Depression and the election of FDR created a regime change at home, leading to the ascendancy of Keynesianism as the new reigning paradigm of political and economic thought and a new view of the balance between individual and community.[23]

Unlike the neoclassicists, Keynesians recognize the great importance of the community and the public interest. Keynes himself rejected the idea of the invisible hand, with a memorable phrase: "Capitalism is the astounding belief that the most wickedest of men will do the most wickedest of things for the greatest good of everyone."[24]

The rejection of the "invisible hand" requires Keynes and his followers to focus on society and the common good, since the market does not automatically protect it. Keynesians argue that government and other countervailing power must intervene to protect the general social interest against the purely private interests of individuals and corporations. New Deal policy, rooted partly in the desperation of people who saw their own lives and the entire economy collapsing around them, became a credible alternative to neoclassicism. The Depression led to a Keynesian paradigm shift that focused on society and how to promote what Keynes called "the general welfare." The shift was enormous, as economist Robert Heilbroner wrote in his assessment of Keynes's most famous work, *The General Theory of Employment, Interest and Money*:[25] "The book was revolutionary: no other word will quite do. It stood economics on its head, very much as the *Wealth of Nations* and *Capital* had done."[26]

This is not to say that Keynesians rejected markets or a central concern with individual rights, both negative and positive. Keynesians saw their job as saving capitalism, which they view as imperfect but better than any alternative. They share the neoclassical focus on the market and private ownership as desirable because they are essential to individual freedom and the efficiency that promotes social well-being.

Unlike neoclassicists, though, Keynesians see the market and private ownership as necessary but not sufficient to protect either the truly free individual or the community. Once Smith's invisible hand loses credibility, the need for a "visible hand" becomes crucial to protecting the economy and society itself. The visible hand is government. It must regulate the markets, invest billions to guarantee full employment, and intervene actively to ensure that the public interest is protected. Since the individual and the market are neither perfect nor self-correcting, guaranteeing individual market freedoms will not automatically translate into a public good. The community voice must be heard—and that can only be done through government and the community itself.

Keynes's core new insight that individual self-interest does not guarantee social well-being was tightly linked to another transformational idea: capitalist crises would not self-correct. Both insights pushed the needle from a focus on individuals and the market to a focus on society and government as its voice. During the inevitable deep downturns of capitalism, only government spending to create jobs and ensure greater demand could save capitalism and society itself, leading Keynesians to support the right to protection of the individual from want and misery. Both Keynesianism and neoclassicism are concerned with individual rights, but they have a different understanding of what those rights are and how to prioritize them. Keynes's relentless focus on full employment was not only an economic goal but a recognition that society itself depended on everyone having access to a job. This aim, when understood and followed properly, led, even in individualistic America, to a Keynesian social revolution embodied in the Employment Act of 1946, which enunciated a transformational "Declaration of Policy" proclaiming that "all Americans able to work and seeking work have the right to useful, remunerative, regular and full-time employment, and it is the policy of the United States to ensure the existence at all times of sufficient employment opportunities to enable all Americans ... freely to exercise this right."[27]

Here, we see Keynesian social as well as economic philosophy, promoting a new US idea of "positive" rights—such as rights to a job—rather than the negative rights embraced by neoclassicists, which are rights simply to be left alone. Keynesian positive rights include the right to a job, to a good retirement, to housing, and to be free of hunger. As we show shortly, American presidents, such as FDR and LBJ, endorsed such rights in their roles as

Keynesian political leaders, as have many Keynesian European leaders and labor parties. In contrast, the neoclassical "negative" rights are the rights of the individual simply to say "Don't tread on me!" Negative rights are assured by constitutionally limiting government from constraining personal freedom, whether to own a gun or drill for oil on one's own land. These are rights associated with property, and they protect, in large measure, the propertied class.

Keynesian positive rights are rights of the individual to social benefits or well-being that only society can provide. Keynesians support far less extensive positive rights than those supported by neo-Marxists, and Keynesians remain mainly concerned with protecting property rights rather than expanding either individual social benefits or protecting the larger well-being of workers and communities. Nonetheless, the very idea of positive rights reflects the Keynesian appreciation of community and social entities larger than the individual—and of the individual's need for social protection and the benefits of community that are antithetical to neoclassical thinking. Keynesians believe that government has the affirmative obligation to ensure positive rights, both to prevent economic collapse and to sustain a civil society. When FDR implemented New Deal positive rights—to a job and Social Security—during the Great Depression, he helped individuals, built community, saved capitalism, and also created a paradigm shift from a neoclassical view of a Robinson Crusoe America to an America based on a balance of the individual and community, though still focused most on protection of the propertied class.

Keynes and his followers saw other problems with the neoclassical way of thinking about individuals and society. Individuals were not the rational beings that neoclassicists imagined. As was clear in the speculative mania of the 1920s, "animal spirits," the lust for fast money, and other irrationalities in people, especially in the world of high finance, crashed the economy in 1929 and almost destroyed US society. Neoclassical policy of laissez-faire only made things worse. This reinforced Keynes's view that active government intervention was essential both economically and morally to save the individual, the community, and capitalism itself. Keynes essentially anticipated Gordon Gekko in Wall Street, who famously proclaimed, "Greed is good." And Keynesians argue that this sociopathic impulse threatens both capitalism and society.[28] John Kenneth Galbraith, the great mid-twentieth-century US Keynesian, wrote that the bankers' feeling of responsibility for the larger society beyond Wall Street is virtually nonexistent.[29]

Unlike neoclassical thinking, Keynesian theory requires an explicit idea of the public interest and of the community itself, ultimately because Keynesians reject the neoclassical doctrine of the invisible hand. Keynesians see that individuals driven by irrational greed and government policies purely protecting negative rights cannot sustain a capitalist economy or the society that hosts it. Galbraith thus devoted much of his work to fleshing out his concept of an enlightened vision of the public interest in capitalist society, which meant satisfying in some measure—not to a point that neo-Marxists would find acceptable—the interests and well-being of the great majority of ordinary people rather than just the interests of the capitalist elite. His work commanded great interest, because it directly challenged the classical American idea that individual self-interest and the market freedom of individuals superseded or guaranteed a good society.

In his most famous work, *The Affluent Society*, Galbraith argued that the market was channeling resources into private, trivial consumer goods rather than the education, health care, living-wage jobs, arts, and other public goods that made for a good society. As the market economy grows, society declines:

> The family which takes its mauve and cerise, air-conditioned, power-steered and power-braked automobile out for a tour passes through cities that are badly paved, made hideous by litter, blighted buildings, billboards and posts for wires that should long since have been put underground. They pass on into countryside that has been rendered largely invisible by commercial art. (The goods which the latter advertise have an absolute priority in our value system. Such aesthetic considerations as a view of the countryside accordingly come second. On such matters we are consistent.) They picnic on exquisitely packaged food from a portable icebox by a polluted stream and go on to spend the night at a park which is a menace to public health and morals. Just before dozing off on an air mattress, beneath a nylon tent, amid the stench of decaying refuse, they may reflect vaguely on the curious unevenness of their blessings. Is this, indeed, the American genius?[30]

Galbraith's most useful argument was that power was a corrosive factor in the market, and that the neoclassical focus on millions of competing and equal individuals disguised dangerous inequalities of wealth and power. Once great differences in power among individuals and institutions are acknowledged, it is obvious that just letting private interests run free does not guarantee the public good. Rather, it is likely to protect only the interests of the most wealthy and powerful, condemning the larger community to misery. Galbraith wrote, as part of a large body of his works focusing on the antisocial impact of growing corporate power,

> Were it part of our everyday education and comment that the corporation is an instrument for the exercise of power, that it belongs to the process by which we are governed, there would then be debate on how that power is used and how it might be made subordinate to the public will and need.

This debate is avoided by propagating the myth that the power does not exist.[31]

This marks the critical difference between neoclassicists and Keynesians. The latter recognize what the former deny: that markets are organized and managed by powerful interests and that this leads—without Keynesian social and economic reform—toward destruction of society by corporations interested only in money—their own money. The result is a society gaining a massive impoverished underclass and losing its communal soul, deceiving itself that private enterprise always creates a common good:

> Capitalism has never anywhere provided good houses at moderate cost. Housing, it seems unnecessary to stress, is an important adjunct of a successful urban life. Nor does capitalism provide good health services, and when people live close together with attendant health risks, these too are important. Nor does capitalism provide efficient transportation for people—another essential of the life of the Metropolis. In Western Europe and Japan the failure of capitalism in the fields of housing, health and transportation is largely, though not completely, accepted. There industries have been intensively socialized. In the United States there remains the conviction that, however contrary the experience, private enterprise will eventually serve.[32]

In a succession of books such as *Countervailing Power, The New Industrial State*, and *The Affluent Society*, Galbraith showed that US capitalism was creating poverty for millions in the midst of great affluence for the few, undermining the very foundations of a good society. As Keynes's own work had helped frame the New Deal, Galbraith's work helped sustain President Kennedy's New Frontier and President Johnson's progressive domestic agenda, showing that a "Great Society" was as necessary to protect individual rights as individual rights were to protecting society.[33]

This did not lead Galbraith, or other Keynesians, to reject capitalism. Having seen the success of the New Deal and the Keynesian consensus that extended from Roosevelt to Lyndon Johnson, they remained optimistic that countervailing power to the corporations could be mobilized within capitalism to protect the public good. There would always remain the dark side of capitalism but there was no better alternative. And capitalism, once the political will was mobilized, could be fixed, much like a basically sound car could be taken to the garage for a tune-up by a good mechanic, the metaphor used by contemporary Keynesian luminary, Paul Krugman. Yes, the vices of laissez-faire capitalism are awful. But, no, they are not fatal. The Keynesian policies are not much different than a good tune-up, perfectly capable of making the capitalist engine run soundly and protect both the economy and the larger society.[34] One simply had to maintain the countervailing power and progressive political will that had sustained Keynesian policies from Roosevelt until Reagan.

By the 1970s, though, globalization, the Vietnam War, and stagflation began to undermine the credibility of Keynesian ideas and the political consensus that had sustained them. A New Right rose up to resurrect neoclassical thought, arguing that the Left collectivism of the 1960s and the social welfare government of the Great Society had eroded the work ethic and individual responsibility, creating mass dependency or parasitism among the masses (which in 2012 Mitt Romney memorialized in his famous comment about the 47 percent dependents—Ayn Rand referred to them as "moochers and looters").

There are 47 percent of the people who will vote for the president no matter what. All right, there are 47 percent who are with him, who are dependent upon government, who believe that they are victims, who believe the government has a responsibility to care for them, who believe that they are entitled to health care, to food, to housing, to you-name-it.... My job is not to worry about those people. I'll never convince them they should take personal responsibility and care for their lives.[35]

The New Right made the individual entrepreneur the new hero who could save the economy from its new troubles. By electing Ronald Reagan, they created the regime change that would shift the nation back to belief in the invisible hand and the ideology that a renewed focus on the individual and his or her negative rights was the only way to save the American individual and American society itself.

This shows the limits of Keynesianism. On the one hand, it cannot produce a robust enough view of the public interest and of community because of its commitment to capitalism. Keynesianism is intellectually locked in by its belief in the viability of US corporate capitalism. It refuses to acknowledge that the market and private property regime it wants to save might not permit the kind of vision or practice of community strong enough to ensure the public interest and either social or economic health. And it fails to develop a robust concept of community or the public interest that is compatible with the privileges of private property and profit-maximization that capitalism prioritizes.

Just as important, Keynesians underestimate the political constraints within capitalism that prevent their achieving the reforms they seek. FDR's successes nurtured Keynesian faith today that we can achieve a new New Deal within the US capitalist order. But times have changed, and the New Deal itself ultimately was far too intellectually timid, resurrecting the economy and society not because of its visionary idea of community but because of World War II, which allowed the visible hand of government to overcome all the inherent political obstacles to the reforms necessary to even temporarily put the country back to work. Even many Keynesians today acknowledge that the rich tend to dictate economic policy, as Paul Krugman argued in his view of how the doctrine of austerity took root in Europe and the United States after the 2008 meltdown, when it was so patently destructive: "The austerity agenda looks a lot like a simple expression of upper class preferences, wrapped in a façade of academic rigor. What the top 1 percent wants becomes what economic science says we must do.... We have policy of the 1 percent, by the 1 percent, for the 1 percent."[36]

At this writing, the same political obstacles are limiting not just President Obama's reforms but the ability of great Keynesians, such as Krugman, Joseph Stiglitz, Robert Reich, and Robert Kuttner, from seeing their ideas implemented. Obama has politically marginalized figures such as Krugman and Stiglitz, who are the best political economists in the mainstream arena (and are indeed brilliant and enormously important public intellectuals who have played starring roles in debunking the New Right's resurrected neoclassical ideas, particularly the idea of austerity as a way to solve the great economic crises in the United States and Europe after the 2008 Great Recession). Nonetheless, even Keynesians such as Krugman tend not to embrace the more radical visions of change and a more expansive vision of community and the "commons" that can protect the public interest against the overwhelmingly dominant private interests of wealthy individuals and corporations. For that task, neo-Marxists step in and offer their own more transformative ideas of a political economy beyond capitalism.

Neo-Marxists

Americans hear Marx and see red. They associate him with authoritarian government crushing individuals in the name of community. Marxists, typified by Stalin or Mao, appear to represent a tyrannical idea of collectivism incompatible with individual freedom. This makes sense regarding Stalin and Mao, but it has nothing to do with current neo-Marxist thinking. Neo-Marxists today view Stalin and Mao as Marxists in name only. Soviet and Chinese dictators used Marxist vocabulary and elements of Marx's theory to justify a system totally at odds with the core ideas of Marxism, and particularly with the central values of the critical Marxist school.[37]

As discussed in an earlier chapter, Marx used language—specifically in *The Communist Manifesto* of the "dictatorship of the proletariat"—that could be exploited by dictators seeking total control in the name of Marxist concepts of revolution. Marx wrote, "The proletariat will use its political supremacy to wrest, by degrees, all capital from the bourgeoisie, to centralize all instruments of production in the hands of the state of the proletariat organized as the ruling class.... Of course, in the beginning this cannot be effected except by means of despotic inroads on the rights of property."[38]

Lenin, Stalin, and Mao all developed a Marxist rhetoric and political practice derived from this idea that communism required a working-class dictatorship, a total "despotic" control of the collectivity over the individual. The interests of the people, collectivity, the working class, the party, and the state override the individual. Within the Leninist model, anyone who does not acknowledge this is an "enemy of the people" and forfeits all rights. If the state represents the people, then it represents your true ultimate interests. If you deny this, that only proves you do not know what is best for you and you must submit to its authority for your own benefit. Once we have the right rulers, we no longer have need of formal devices to protect the individual from the state. Rather, the state can assume almost parental authority over citizens, acting in their best interests, often contrary to individuals' conscious desires. You must have "faith in the people" or "faith in the 'Dear Leader.'" The leaders are often presented as the embodiment of the people.

This had many frightening implications—appearing to destroy both individuality and society—by setting an authoritarian state over both of them. One cannot dismiss Marx's (or Lenin's) words as meaningless or benign. Yet, they can be misleading, since Marx's larger philosophy was a passionate affirmation of both individuality and society, and he opposed capitalism because he thought it inevitably destroyed both the individual and the very existence of civil society.

Marx did not seek a permanent state of any form, but a healthy civil society that unleashed the full self-governing powers of the free individual. A close reading of Marx, especially his early writings, makes clear that he saw government as a necessary evil in a class-based society, and that he wanted to move as quickly as possible (i.e., when capitalists could no longer mobilize a counterrevolution) toward the end of central state command and toward a self-governing society of free individuals and communities. Marx wrote that as socialism emerges, "The system starts with the self-government of the communities.... The entire people will rule, and no one will be ruled.... When class rule has disappeared there will be no state in the present political sense."[39]

Marx, in other words, was committed to the self-governing individual and the self-governing society that could produce true individuality. Marx recognized that individuality was inherently social. The human individual was a product of the language, reasoning, interactions, and knowledge that only a society and community can create, though Marx did not believe that society, especially capitalist society, should be considered "natural" or be preserved in its current form. Marx's view of "society" is that it is a set of arrangements and norms typically constructed by elites to serve their own interests rather than those of the general population. Nonetheless, in every social order, individuals are shaped by the ruling social system and are a product of society, even if they need to become revolutionaries and transform it. Here is Marx on the individual and society:

> But also when I am active scientifically, etc.—an activity which I can seldom perform in direct community with others—then my activity is social, because I perform it as a man. Not only is the material of my activity given to me as a social product (as is even the language in which the thinker is active): my own existence is social activity, and therefore that which I make of myself, I make of myself for society and with the consciousness of myself as a social being.[40]

Marx thus broke with the atomized view of neoclassicist men as "Robinson Crusoes." Instead, he advanced the sociological idea of individuality as a reflection of healthy social ties and interrelations: "Society does not consist of individuals but expresses the sum of interrelations, the relations within which these individuals stand."[41]

The sociological Marx saw society as far more than the aggregate of atomized individuals, rejecting the individualistic market notions of David Ricardo, Jean-Baptiste Say, and Jeremy Bentham—the neoclassicists of his era. He sought ultimately not a centralized hierarchical state but a highly developed and networked social order that he viewed as essential to the creation of individuality or the free individual. Common wisdom is that Marx valued neither the individual nor society, a distortion created by capitalist ideology and later Leninist doctrine, both of which obscured Marx's Enlightenment commitment to the free individual and the self-governing community.

Marx, in a sense, it is true, dug his own grave with his language about proletarian dictatorship. But an in-depth study of his work suggests his entire philosophy was driven by a belief in self-government and on the critical importance of individuality as well as community. Marx always argued that the dictatorship of the proletariat is temporary and will "wither away" as the class structure is abolished: "this dictatorship itself only constitutes the transition to the abolition of all classes and to a classless society."[42]

While Leninism deeply influenced Marxist practice—and shaped public perceptions of it—it departs in extreme ways from the essence of Marx's own critical Marxism and from most contemporary neo-Marxist thinkers, about personal freedom and self-governing communities. Marx spent his life attacking capitalism because he felt it destroyed individual freedom, particularly in the workplace because of the capitalist monopoly of productive private property. Marx's most important work, *Capital*, showed how capitalists inevitably took dictatorial control over the worker, prescribing what job to do and precisely how to carry out the physical motions required. Frederick Taylor's system of scientific management and time-and-motion studies are the perfect core of the broader capitalist model, dictating not just what would be produced but precisely how the product would be made as well as marketed and sold.[43] Marx himself wrote that capitalist manufacturers "prosper most when the mind is least consulted and where the workshop may be considered as an engine, the parts of which are men."[44] This capitalist dictatorship of the workplace enraged Marx because he thought humans realized their creative individuality through labor and that capitalism inherently crushed the very possibility of becoming a free individual. Marx wrote, "In bourgeois society capital is independent and has individuality, while the living person is dependent and has no individuality."[45]

Marx is explicit above about the crushing of individuality by capitalism. Below, he makes clear this is because capitalists control every aspect of the work-life of the individual, who has no choice but to work for the owners of wealth and property: "Under the presupposition of private property [work] is an externalization of life because I work in order to live.... Working is not living. My individuality is externalized to the point where I hate this activity."[46]

Marx made clear that the purpose of anticapitalist revolution was to restore individual freedom and individuality to the work process and larger social life, for in a postcapitalist world, "My labor would be a free manifestation of life and an enjoyment of life. In my work, the particularity of my individuality would be affirmed because my individual life would be affirmed." Marx also hated capitalism's destruction of the individual's voice and freedom in politics. The capitalist class used its wealth to buy politicians and control state policy. Yes, individuals could vote, but Marx saw elections as a fig leaf disguising the reality of corporate control over all mainstream political parties. Marx thus saw the crushing of the individual both at work and in the "democratic" politics of capitalism. Democracy in capitalism was not the self-governance of free individuals but the rule of corporate bankers and their political handmaidens.

Marx himself, we repeat, called for the end of capitalism because it destroyed both individuality and the collectivity. It not only created a corporate dictatorship imprisoning the individual worker and creating a fictitious democracy, but it subverted the very possibility of authentic social bonds and collectivity that went beyond the "icy calculations" of the market. Marx wrote in *The Communist Manifesto* that capitalism "has left remaining no other nexus between man and man than naked self-interest, than callous 'cash payment.' It has drowned the most heavenly ecstasies of religious fervour, of chivalrous enthusiasm, of philistine sentimentalism, in the icy water of egotistical calculation."[47]

Capitalism could only produce a society based on the "cash nexus," undermining the very possibility of trust and civil society. The capitalist class, through private ownership and its own great wealth, would take control of all social institutions—the school, the workplace, the government, the media—and reconstruct society itself as an instrument for its own interests and pleasure, a sociopathic tool that destroyed the prospects of community and a civil society that would promote the general welfare of the entire population.

This view of capitalism as sociopathic, ending the possibility of humane civil society and social relations, as well as personal freedom, is at the heart of the neo-Marxist paradigm.[48] Society itself is a fiction, masking the reality of a class-divided and disintegrating social order designed to reward the capitalist class at the expense of all other classes. From the Marxist perspective, capitalism is incapable of producing a society or state representing the general interest and the welfare of all, since it is scripted to subordinate all of society, including the great majority of the populace in the working and poor classes, to the will and interests of the tiny capitalist class, which is increasingly globalized. National "societies" are increasingly mirages, disguising the reality of global capitalist systems including global companies, that are the only form of "society" remaining. This is the basis for Marx's famous lines: "The Communists are further reproached with desiring to abolish countries and nationality. The working men have no country. We cannot take from them what they have not got."[49]

Contemporary neo-Marxists have taken up Marx's themes that capitalism cannot create strong communities or a sustainable civil society. The most common theme concerns the unraveling of community and the breakdown of society in the late twentieth and early twenty-first century, an issue also highlighted by conservative neoclassical and liberal Keynesian political economists and sociologists. Conservatives such as William Bennett, Lynne Cheney, and David Brooks, as discussed elsewhere, see societal breakdown as a cultural collapse, triggered by the hedonistic countercultural revolution of the 1960s, the weakening of religion, and the rise of feminist, gay, and other progressive identity movements that challenge "family values" and other traditional foundations of society. Capitalism, they argue, can help restore the individual responsibility, family and neighborhood traditions, and moral restraints essential to rebuilding civil society.

Neo-Marxists, however, view the problem as in the DNA of capitalism itself, an inherently atomizing system that promotes greed, competition, and self-centeredness while undermining the economic foundations of community and social solidarity. Neo-Marxists argue that these atomizing forces are intensifying as global capitalism leads to deeper class warfare, heightened in the United States by the anti–social welfare and anti-labor policies of the Reagan revolution.

The breakdown of community is where PE joins most naturally with sociology. Sociologists have always been centrally concerned with the idea of community and the forces that can sustain it. Many sociologists who are not neo-Marxists, including many following the Durkheimian tradition, join Keynesians in viewing the problem as serious but solvable within a capitalist framework. PE sociology, as advanced by neo-Marxists, breaks from both Keynesians and many traditional sociologists by arguing the problem is endemic to capitalism and can be solved only by changing capitalism itself.

In several books, Charles Derber has argued that capitalism, especially in the United States, breeds a sociopathic individualism, codified in the American Dream, that is incompatible with community or any form of social solidarity. In his book, *The Wilding of America*, Derber described *wilding* as self-interested behavior that harms others and weakens the social fabric, whether carried out by individuals, corporations, or government. He argued that wilding is a form of egoistic individualism—focusing on "me, me, me"— now emerging at the heart of a perverted American Dream.[50]

While his focus on the American Dream obviously involves culture, Derber's argument is an indictment of capitalism.

> American Dream is capitalism's master script. It dictates that each of us look out for "number one." If we fail to play our egoistic, competitive role in this capitalist script, profits are threatened and capitalism itself would unravel.... The capitalist elites script the individualistic American Dream because their wealth and power depend on the population believing fervently in the script's economic rationality and moral legitimacy.[51]

Derber takes a neo-Marxist view about how economics shapes culture: "For Marx, values themselves are the most carefully crafted 'products' of the economic system.... While this script [the American Dream] might seem pure greed or selfishness, it comes wrapped in high morality."[52]

Derber argues that the capitalist-driven "high morality" of greed and selfish behavior not only harms most citizens and undermines community but inverts traditional ideas of sociopathic behavior. Wilders are not undersocialized, or rebelling against society, but scrupulously following its norms. They are "oversocialized," lacking the inner capacity to resist the norms promoted by capitalist society. And, although millions of individuals pursue this script, they are minor sociopathic players compared to the large corporations, such as the Wall Street banks in the 2008 meltdown, that played by the same script and almost destroyed the entire economy.

The larger argument, that Derber advanced in his book, *Sociopathic Society*, is that capitalism is inherently sociopathic.[53] It socializes both individuals and core economic and political institutions toward antisocial rules and behavior that—in the service of money and profit—will attack and consume the society itself. The main perpetrators are large corporations:

> The range and types of corporate sociopathy are large and varied but not surprising since they reflect the sociopathic programming of capitalist culture and the corporate charter and law, which mandates profit-seeking without regard to "externalities" involving worker, human, or environmental harm (corporations that do not seek to maximize shareholder value or profit in this manner can be sued by their shareholders for violation of their fiduciary obligation). Lockheed-Martin, Boeing, General Dynamics, and other giant defense contractors produce bombs, tanks, planes, drones and missiles for enormous profit, lobbying to keep US military expenditures—which are greater than the next 17 biggest military countries combined—far higher than necessary, bleeding funds from essential job and social welfare spending. Giant retailers such as Walmart pay miserably low salaries and benefits to part-time workers—particularly females and minorities—from whom they extract huge profits. The biggest food and beverage companies such as McDonald's and Coca Cola, sell unhealthy products dished out by low-paid workers or school vending machines, targeting low income and young consumers. The biggest agricultural companies, such as ADL, take huge government subsidies as they produce monoculture industrialized crops that destroy the soil and spread fossil fuel toxins into the water and air. The giant oil companies such as Exxon and Shell and huge coal companies such as Duke Energy engage in extreme sociopathic climate denial and greenwashing, while engaging in environmentally toxic drilling such as fracking and fighting climate control treaties and law to protect their profits. Most of this sociopathic behavior conforms to the expectations of investors who seek and are legally entitled to profit maximization despite the high social costs just enumerated.[54]

These are perfectly legal forms of corporate conduct—in fact, to a large degree fiduciary requirements—that undermine the well-being of workers, the environment, and, of course, communities and society itself. The only way to rebuild community and social solidarity is to transform the corporate capitalist order and the values of the economic system. Derber enumerates a host of alternative economic possibilities, from a cooperativist worker-ownership economy to one organized around local and community production to the breakup or socialization of the largest banks and energy companies, to the more socialized system of European systems with strong labor parties and unions, to name just a few.[55]

Derber is hardly alone in the contemporary neo-Marxist search for economic alternatives aiming toward justice for workers, preserving the environment, and rebuilding the fabric of communities and the larger society. A school of "new economics" or "living economies" is emerging, driven by PE sociologists with a central concern for ecological sustainability and community renewal. These include PE sociologists such as Juliet Schor, Gar Alperovitz, and David Korten, all of whom have developed ecological critiques of capitalism and proposed alternatives focusing to a large degree on community-based systems of local ownership and control of banks, food, construction, transportation, and much of the service economy. They are also concerned with national and global structural changes that can promote both local and global communities. In the last chapter, we shall look in more detail at these ideas, because they are the beginning of a new ecological political economy that constitutes a promising theory and practice of a new twenty-first-century political economy and society.

Neo-Marxists of all stripes depart radically, as noted above, from both neoclassicists and Keynesians, because they see no possibility of true individuality or sustainable community within capitalism. Neoclassicists see the market as the only sustainable foundation of society, since its invisible hand coordinates otherwise anarchistic individuals into a social order respecting and protecting autonomous individuals. Without the market, there is either dictatorship or the Hobbesian jungle.

The contrast between neo-Marxists and neoclassicists is obvious but different than traditionally conceived. The neoclassicists present individualism as their holy grail, while neo-Marxists see neoclassical individualism as pure social conformity to the market, a travesty of true individualism—or more accurately put, individuality—that Marx himself embraced. In other words, Marxists, especially those of the critical rather than structural school, view themselves in pursuit of the authentic individual and the freedom that neoclassicists claim to celebrate but actually refuse to countenance. Likewise, the invisible hand concept of the market embraced by the neoclassicists to guarantee a good society and social welfare is totally at odds with neo-Marxists' views of a class economy, in which market pursuits are simply vehicles for giant corporations and the capitalist class to increase their own profits and power. The capitalist class has no true interest or capacity to advance the general public interest, which is an untenable concept in a social order divided by private ownership and class warfare endemic to capitalism.

The difference between neo-Marxists and Keynesians is also profound regarding both individuality and community. Keynesians also do not question the idea that a free individual or sustainable community and society can be created within the bounds of a capitalist order. Keynesians see the market as protecting the individual and the progressive capitalist state as helping protect a civil society that is real within capitalism and can be sustained through the wise guidance of an interventionist state dedicated to the public interest.[56]

Because they dismiss Marx's view that capitalist society is a fiction disguising class divisions and the inherent rule of the capitalist class, Keynesians, unlike Marxists, see no irreconcilable conflict between capitalism and community, a very profound disagreement between the two paradigms. Likewise, Keynesians see the market as imperfect but correctible through state regulation that can ensure individual freedom, while neo-Marxists show that there is no prospect for a sustainable individuality within the framework of capitalist ownership and dictatorial control of the workplace and the state itself.

Neo-Marxists are flawed, though, by some of the same problems plaguing Keynesians. First, while they put great emphasis on it, they have never fully fleshed out or constructed a liberated postcapitalist society and way of life. Marx himself never developed a robust vision of socialism or communism. Neo-Marxists, such as Gar Alperovitz, Erik Olin Wright, Robert McChesney, Juliet Schor, John Bellamy Foster, Michael Albert, Robin Hahnel, Howard Zinn, and many other important thinkers, have spent time trying to develop models of postcapitalist societies, and they have studied experiments from co-op, worker-owned, or participatory economies to localist, green, and indigenous socialist models. But none have proved successful in practice for large societies nor has the design—while often ingenious and a foundation for further study—moved beyond the drawing table.

The second problem—also shared with Keynesians—may be yet more challenging. Marx is a four-letter word in the United States. Marxism, while it has had a surprising influence in American history, has today been demonized and virtually eliminated from mainstream and even academic discourse. The tragedy of self-described communist regimes such as Stalinism and Maoism has contributed to the power of the propaganda directed against any anticapitalist politics, and the New Right, the Reagan revolution, and the evolution of mainstream liberalism and Keynesianism have also made neo-Marxism appear a relic of the nineteenth century. Occupy movements showed that the spirit of anticapitalist and neo-Marxist ideas and politics has far from disappeared in the general public. But their crystallization into a political movement that can gain great influence in the United States and change the direction of the nation and the world requires a giant leap of faith.

CHAPTER 9

Globalization

As we started this chapter, in early 2013, we Googled the word "globalization." We found just under 50 million Google entries on this topic. Now, admittedly, that's not as many as "Lady Gaga," who had over 313 million Google entries. But 50 million is a very large number. And Lady Gaga is a global icon, with all her Google hits an awesome symbol of the globalization of popular culture.

Globalization is one of the great transformations of our time. Globalization is not new—it began at least as early as European colonialism, perhaps going back to the trade practices of the Italian city-states in the Renaissance—and it's a work in progress.[1] But there is no question that it has revolutionized our economies, political systems, personal lives, and, yes, the pop singers we hear and adore.

Globalization is also a hot topic of controversy. In 1999, thousands of protesters against corporate globalization marched in the streets of Seattle, ultimately met by police in tanks in what became called "the Battle of Seattle." In nearly every annual meeting of global governing bodies such as the World Trade Organization (WTO), the International Monetary Fund (the IMF), and the World Bank, thousands of protesters gather to protest trade agreements, genetically modified food, giant transnational corporate power, global sweatshops, and the global policy threatening the environment. Few issues generate so much heat and passion over such a long period.

Many see globalization as an inevitable and virtuous "race to the top," with bumps in the road and some short-term losers but ultimately raising up all nations.[2] Journalist Tom Friedman has shaped Americans' view of globalization perhaps more than any other pundit:

I feel about globalization like I feel about the dawn. Generally speaking, I think it's a good thing that the sun comes up every morning, especially if you wear sunscreen and sunglasses. But even if I didn't much care for the dawn there isn't much I could do about it. I didn't start globalization. I can't stop it—except at a huge cost to human development—and I'm not going to waste time trying.[3]

Others, including most of the protesters, see it quite the opposite, dragging down both rich and poor countries, something that must be transformed if not totally stopped.[4] Jeremy Brecher and Tim Costello argued that "globalization promotes a destructive competition in which workers, communities and entire countries are forced to cut labor, social and environmental costs to attract mobile capital. When many countries each do so, the result is a disastrous 'race to the bottom.'"[5]

Many critics of the race to the bottom focus on the wretched life of globalized sweatshop workers like Samima in Bangladesh, who produces Disney's "Pooh" label and says she has "to work from 8AM to 10PM each day.... I get a regular wage ... of 14 cents an hour. Because we have to work very long hours, seven days a week, we have no family life, no personal life, no social life."[6]

Our three political economy paradigms provide three dramatically different views on the subject. Globalization is a crucial topic that helps us understand what the neoclassicists, the Keynesians, and the neo-Marxists are really all about.

Neoclassicists

Since neoclassicists see the market as perfect, its global spread is the best way to bring blessings to the whole world. Globalization creates single worldwide markets—in wine, widgets, and workers. Most important, it creates a unified global financial or money market, allowing capital to be invested in the most efficient and profitable sectors or companies anywhere on the planet. If national barriers are torn down, everybody will benefit from the inevitable explosion in prosperity and democracy.

Ronald Reagan challenged Mikhail Gorbachev about the Berlin Wall: "Tear this wall down!" Neoclassicists say the same to defenders of national barriers to trade: "Tear *all* these walls down!" They mean just what Reagan did. Trade walls, as neoclassicists see it, are barriers to freedom far more terrible than the Berlin Wall. They allow tyrannical governments and inefficient economies everywhere on the planet to survive and hurt the people imprisoned within them. It is only when these walls are torn down that people all over the world can be free and become prosperous.

The neoclassical economic case for "free market" globalization—often called "neoliberal," which is confusing because it represents what most

Americans would call "conservative"—has to do with cost, choice, and efficiency. National barriers to trade are just like any other government intervention in the market. They artificially prevent flows of capital and other resources across national boundaries, an assault on market efficiency. Government is preventing investors or workers from making the free choices that create market magic. Once you remove this harmful government blockage, you massively increase efficiency, allowing the magic of the liberated invisible hand to benefit the entire world community.

The founder of neoclassicism, Adam Smith, made no bones about the virtues of international trade, based on the idea that it allows consumers everywhere access to the most efficiently produced and cheapest goods. Smith wrote that if "a foreign nation can supply us with a commodity cheaper than we ourselves can make it, better buy it of them.... In every country it always is and must be the interest of the great body of the people to buy whatever they want of those who sell it cheapest. The proposition is so very manifest, that it seems ridiculous to take any pains to prove it."[7]

The neoclassical "efficient market" is limited by any political constraint on the free flow of capital, none more so than protectionist trade barriers. Such barriers impinge on the core neoclassical theory of "comparative advantage." Developed by nineteenth-century economist David Ricardo, this theory, almost as sacred as the principle of the invisible hand itself, says that every region, nation, or community in the world has relative comparative advantages in specific products or services, because of weather, richness of soil or resources, human skills, low wages, low taxes, or any other factors. The theory—expressed in mathematical equations—says that all nations benefit if they specialize in the production of the area where they are *relatively* most efficient—and let others produce goods in which they are most efficient, even if they are less efficient in absolute terms. If trade barriers prevent exploitation of this comparative advantage, then market efficiency—and prosperity—is deeply compromised.[8]

When capital is free to flow anywhere, it creates irresistible incentives for every nation to "get its act together," meaning to restructure itself rationally so as to attract the alluring multitrillion-dollar pools of global capital swooshing across the planet in search of profit. In practice, this means creating a "free market" capitalism built on the US example. Socialist or "big government" societies have to privatize their economies and "tear down the walls," eliminate protection of their banks, farmers, or local factories, so that foreign investors or companies—what Tom Friedman calls the "Electronic Herd"[9]—can come and buy whatever they want or compete on the open market and a level playing field. There is no tolerance for favoritism to your own country. This brings massive capital from the Electronic Herd to the newly open country and ensures that former big and corrupt bureaucracies run by the government in scores of countries will be taken over by private business managers who know how to reengineer business to be lean and mean. There will be short-term costs to workers laid off or bureaucrats weaned from their plush patronage jobs but the long-term benefits to the nation will be magic for nearly all, fueled by the huge pools of money invested by the Electronic Herd and the ruthless efficiency of the new private markets.[10]

Tom Friedman argues that globalization works because the Electronic Herd enforces a neoclassical model of free market capitalism on every nation that wants its money. And Friedman, with neoclassical exuberance, argues that nobody can argue with globalization because nobody can dispute the efficiency of the underlying capitalism it imposes: there is no alternative. No other system "can generate income to distribute as efficiently as free-market capitalism."[11]

Yes, neoclassicists acknowledge, attracting the trillion-dollar pools of big global money can have short-term painful drawbacks for the poor, since it means putting the entire national budget on an austerity diet. Too many countries are subsidizing their own people with free food, health care, or other welfare benefits, as well as sometimes propping up wages or enforcing taxes and regulations on foreign companies, usually to legitimate corrupt government regimes and pacify the population. But these benefits by leftist governments in poor (or rich) countries, while appearing to be humanitarian, create, say neoclassicists, dependency and severe economic costs. They divert capital from private investments and prevent development of a rational capitalist market infrastructure to attract foreign investment. Shrinking these governments is, for sure, a form of austerity and can hurt the poor in the short term. But as austerity sends out bright flares to global investors that they have a fertile field to plow, uninhibited by government protections, regulations, and wage or environmental constraints, the global money train will stop at their station. The result is pure gold.[12]

The political benefits come hand in hand with the economic ones. As corrupt bureaucratic dynasties crumble, a leaner democratic political system will emerge. Global investors require a nation of laws, not despots, and global companies seek a transparent, enforceable system of contracts and political leadership that is trustworthy and legitimate, thereby ensuring the stability global business craves. Globalization, then, spreads markets and democracy together, because they are mutually interdependent and neither can survive without the other. Milton Friedman wrote, "Few measures that we could take would do more to promote the cause of freedom at home and abroad than complete free trade."[13]

Friedman thought that to spread freedom, we should say to the world, "We cannot force you to be free. But we can offer full cooperation on equal terms to all. Our market is open to you without tariffs or other restrictions.

Sell here what you can and wish to. Buy whatever you can and wish to. In that way cooperation among individuals can be world-wide and free."[14] If globalization is spreading markets and a market system like the United States, it is spreading freedom itself. Globalization is the foundation of a new liberty everywhere, essentially the globalization of democracy. What higher moral end could one ask of any economic system?

Neoclassicists believe that globalization, newly fueled by technologies such as the Internet, is irreversible. The countries that opt out of its "free market" and "free trade" rules become outlaws and lose access to international capital. They will either comply or die. While this seems harsh, neoclassicists point out that countries opting in—whether it is Brazil or Vietnam or Mexico or South Korea—are exploding with growth and lifting hundreds of millions out of poverty. The jury is in—and nobody can contest the evidence. Milton Friedman dismissed any possible disagreement: "Economists often do disagree, but that has not been true with respect to international trade. Ever since Adam Smith, there has been virtual unanimity among economists, whatever their ideological position on other issues, that international free trade is in the best interest of the trading companies and the world."[15] End of story!

Of course, there is another reason globalization and its new "free trade" and "free market" rules are spreading. The global governance bodies—the WTO, IMF, and World Bank—create huge penalties for countries that don't play along. Corporations or their political allies can take nations to "court" at the WTO and enforce sanctions against an offending regime. And the IMF will refuse to extend essential loans to countries that maintain a desire to protect infant industries or refuse to sell to foreign companies their own banking or telecommunication systems. The World Bank acts the same way, refusing development loans to countries that resist austerity. Beyond just the capital markets, then, hugely powerful international agencies—dominated by neoclassical economists and large corporations—ensure that neoliberalism is the only game in town.

Neoclassicists tend to ignore obvious problems. As globalization has spread, disparities in wealth have grown in almost every country. Yes, globalization creates billionaires and a growing middle class but it also creates extreme inequality and a new desperate class of very poor people without the previous safety nets. Many are young, mainly female, sweatshop workers, such as Nisran, a Bangladeshi worker in a textile plant that sends the clothes it produces to the United States:

> I had to leave school after the fourth grade. For the last yen years, even as a child worker, I have had to work twelve to fourteen hours a day and sometimes up to twenty hours.... Now I work for Actor garments, where I produce caps for many universities in the United States.... We have

to work nineteen or twenty hours until 3 or 4AM. There is no space to sleep, so I have to curl up next to the machine to sleep for three or four hours.[16]

The majority of people hurt by globalization live in rural areas of developing nations, such as Mexico and China, dispossessed by foreign investors buying up resources or setting up power companies, in nearly all the countries that the neoclassicists call success stories. Millions of workers lose their jobs in rich nations and lose their land in poor countries. But neoclassicists call these short-term disruptions. Most short-term losers—such as the Mexican rice farmer who cannot compete with giant American agri-business—will be winners in the long run, finding better paid jobs in factories in Mexican export zones. Some groups may disappear or move into entirely different sectors of the economy, but they will be more prosperous.

Neoclassicists also ignore the issue of power. Globalization, they say, is not run by any powerful elite, since it is simply a free worldwide market, too big and competitive and free to be dominated by any country or company. Recall that neoclassicists argue that markets are a guarantee of liberty because nobody can control them. Thomas Friedman wrote "that the most basic truth about globalization is this: 'No one is in charge.'"[17]

Since globalization is the spontaneous action of millions of investors, workers, and consumers, there is nobody to call. This is economic democracy in action!

Keynesians

While forms of globalization began with trade and empire many centuries ago, many historians argue that the contemporary form of globalization began in the tiny New Hampshire ski town of Bretton Woods in 1944. Western leaders, especially from the United States and Great Britain, gathered to plan the world order—and especially the world economy—that would emerge from the destruction of World War II. The United States was by far the most powerful participant, but Britisher John Maynard Keynes was the most brilliant and influential economist and architect of the emerging global order. He was eager to craft a new global capitalism integrating all the world's major—and many minor—economies that would spread the magic of the market around the world and retain as much power as possible for Britain in the face of rising and aggressive US ascendancy.[18] But it would also permit nations enough sovereignty to ensure that they could maintain control over their fiscal policies and retain enough regulatory power to preserve full employment and public investment to reverse national downturns. Keynes had fought his whole life for this—the elimination of an economic regime that would deny the rights of all states to ensure full employment—and he said he would never abandon it in his postwar planning.[19]

As long as Roosevelt was alive, US trade representatives entertained Keynes's vision to promote an extension of New Deal policies around the world. But when FDR died, and President Truman replaced him, a new and more neoclassical team of economists took over. They created an IMF and World Bank that would enforce the neoliberal rather than Keynesian model. The Keynesian vision that had originally gained consideration at Bretton Woods died a premature death, along with Keynes himself, who died on a train after the shock of a meeting with the new US representatives, who repudiated the principles for globalization that Keynes had fought so hard to implement.

If Keynes's model of globalization had triumphed, the world economy would look very different today. It would still be capitalist, and it likely would still be shaped and enforced by a hegemonic US foreign and military imperial policy (with a much stronger British counterpart), promoting the interests of global companies and undermining socialist nations or movements. But Keynes's global economy, as he designed it in his blueprints of trade rules and the early IMF and World Bank, would be highly regulated to prevent some of the prevailing corporate abuse and protect the world's poor. It would endorse essential protectionism for infant industries, fair trade agreements, limits on short-term capital flows, and rights for national public investment and social welfare programs. We would still have a capitalist world dominated by the United States but one based on New Deal principles rather than neoclassical ones, a kind of globalization that many prominent Keynesians critical of today's globalization, such as Joseph Stiglitz, argue forcefully for today.[20]

In the first decades after World War II, globalization policies combined elements of neoclassical and Keynesian thinking. It was capitalist but not neoliberal; it encouraged free trade but also essential protections to permit countries, especially poor nations, to safeguard their poor and develop their own economies.[21]

In the 1970s, though, as Keynesian economics began to crack in the face of war, stagflation, and the rise of right-wing politics leading to Reaganism in the United States and Thatcherism in Great Britain, a dramatic shift took place. The IMF and World Bank, dealing with crises in scores of poor nations that had gone into excessive debt based on first world lending of their excess profits from oil industries, turned to hard-line neoclassical or neoliberal policies. The neoclassical economists in the Bretton Woods agencies argued that the only solution for third world debt and poverty was to force an austerity regime, in the form of "structural adjustment programs." As sociologist Kevin Danaher has written, structural adjustment was a devastating recipe to "radically reduce government spending on health, education and welfare, privatize and deregulate state enterprises, devalue the currency, liberalize imports and remove restrictions on foreign investment, cut or constrain wages and eliminate or weaken mechanisms protecting labor" and all these policies "triggered a sharp rise in inequality" and general misery for the masses.[22]

If poor countries wanted IMF loans to avoid bankruptcy, or World Bank loans for development, they would have to shrink drastically their public spending, especially for the poor, and tear down all their trade barriers while privatizing their public enterprises. It was a preview of what the German banks would demand of the Greek and Portuguese governments in the desperate Eurozone crises following the 2008 Great Recession.

Keynesians opposed many of the new neoclassical austerity programs beginning in the 1970s. IMF and World Bank austerity validated Keynes's own worst fears that globalization could become a vehicle for undermining Keynesian national policies of full employment and public investment. Keynesian, as well as neo-Marxist, objections to neoliberal globalization in this era were centered in the development agencies of the UN, staffed by progressive economists, many from the third world, who protested what the neoclassical elites in the Reagan and Thatcher administrations and in the IMF and World Bank were doing. But Reagan and the IMF held the upper hand, backed by the world's most powerful corporations and investors.

After Reagan came into power, US corporate elites began to see globalization as a vehicle for dismantling the New Deal in the United States, by threatening to leave the country unless unions gave up demands for better wages and benefits and accepted a major cut in their standard of living. Neoclassical policies allowed US corporations to make good on that threat, shutting down car companies in Detroit and rebuilding them in Mexico, while shutting down most other manufacturing and outsourcing production to China and other developing nations, triggering what Barry Bluestone and Ben Harrison called "the deindustrialization of America."[23] The pace of globalization and outsourcing has accelerated over recent decades, and it can be viewed as a decision to disinvest so massively in the US infrastructure that it will be difficult to reverse.[24]

Leading contemporary Keynesians, including Stiglitz, Robert Reich, and Robert Kuttner, have been speaking out since 2001, particularly against the proliferation of "free trade" treaties, structural adjustment programs, and other neoclassical globalization policies. Western elites have now forced privatization and austerity on much of the world, with poor nations and now many richer ones unable to defend themselves with Keynesian fiscal stimulus or regulations, deemed protectionist or out of compliance with WTO rules. The harsh global regime is also creating environmental hazards and making it difficult to create any global response to climate change.[25]

Joseph Stiglitz, the Keynesian Nobel laureate who was once chief econo-mist at the World Bank, has been particularly outspoken and incisive in his critique of the neoliberal globalization agenda, which he labels "the Washington consensus." He has advocated in several influential books a powerful Keynesian critique of the structural adjustment programs created by the International Monetary Fund that impose neoclassical austerity and privatization on poor indebted countries and of free trade agreements that ignore labor and environmental rights. He also argues that the IMF, the World Bank, and World Trade Organization are mistakenly and unjustly preventing implementation of "capital controls" that would allow national governments to restrict or penalize short-term money flows—or speculative "hot money"—that flood into a country and then just as rapidly drain away, leaving a host of half-built office buildings, ports, or bankrupted banks and businesses. His critique of the IMF in particular has been severe:

> The IMF is pursuing not just the objectives set out in its original man-date, of enhancing global stability and ensuring that there are funds for countries facing a threat of recession to pursue expansionary policies. It is also pursuing the interests of the financial community.... The change in mandate and objectives, while it may have been quiet, was hardly subtle: from serving global economic interests to serving the interests of global finance. Capital market liberalization may not have contributed to global economic stability but it did open up vast new markets for Wall Street.[26]

This is moving closer to a systemic indictment of globalization as an agenda serving capitalists. Stiglitz has, in this spirit, argued for regulations and social programs to protect the global poor and reverse the growing global inequality within and across nations. And he argues powerfully for a global carbon tax to stop climate change.[27]

Keynesians such as Stiglitz have been important voices seeking to reform globalization and soften its harsh neoliberal policies. The Keynesians have helped bolster global labor movements against free trade treaties and helped global social justice groups mount campaigns against dangerous tsunamis of short-term capital flows, as well as promote a movement for more global regulation of sweatshops and the environment. They are putting pressure on the Bretton Woods institutions to shift away from structural adjustment and austerity regimes, and to move toward global investment in health and education and infrastructure that can support development and protect the environment.[28]

Nonetheless, Keynesians remain committed to capitalist globalization and bear responsibility for some of the harms that have been perpetrated in the name of free and efficient markets. Stiglitz, one of the Keynesians' most vocal critics of globalization as currently practiced, still supports capitalist globalization, but with different rules:

> The problem is not with globalization, but with how it has been managed. Part of the problem lies with the international economic institutions, with the IMF, World Bank and WTO, which help set the rules of the game. They have done so in ways that, all too often, have served the interests of the more advanced industrialized countries—and particular interests within those countries—rather than those of the developing world.[29]

Stiglitz, though, goes on to say, "I believe that globalization can be reshaped to realize its potential for good and I believe that the international economic institutions can be reshaped in ways that will help ensure that this is accomplished."[30]

Here, however, is where Keynesians, even the most enlightened and critical like Stiglitz, display a reformist and ultimately inadequate vision. It reflects their embrace of capitalism, their support for its expression on a worldwide scale in globalization, and their view of the political possibilities of major reform supporting the poor in the global capitalist framework, which we view as problematic. It leads them to overlook the ways in which the very problems that Stiglitz highlights are programmed to be part of any system of globalization that remains linked to global capital and a worldwide capitalist framework.

Keynesians are locked into a limited understanding of globalization and its injustices by their commitment to saving capitalism, both nationally and globally. They generally embrace the doctrine of comparative advantage and historically have supported free trade agreements and privatization or structural adjustment, as well as the great global power of the United States and the developed nations over developing nations. Keynes himself played a key role in seeking to perpetuate British global power, fearful that the United States would take over global hegemony at British expense.[31]

All of this reflects serious weaknesses in Keynesian perspectives on US foreign policy, militarism, and global security arrangements during and since the British Empire. Keynesians have not been outspoken opponents of US hegemony and its militaristic foreign policy, even though writers such as Stiglitz have been critical on economic grounds of wars such as the 2003 US invasion of Iraq. Few Keynesians write about the outrages of US intervention and regime change from Chile to Iran to cement control of critical resources and prevent socialist regimes from succeeding. Their faith in capitalism and the ability to mobilize the political will to regulate it reflects the same position they take toward globalization and global capitalism. Capitalist globalization is imperfect, but it is the best system we can achieve when properly regulated;

underneath this lies a belief in the fundamentally benign quality of both US capitalism and its global policies and power.

Keynesians have failed to take seriously one of the greatest challenges of political economy: to integrate an analysis of globalization within a broader analysis of economic, political, and military aims of global capitalist nations and corporations. Globalization is part of a US hegemonic foreign policy that has subordinated the world to its own economic and military power. Any assessment of contemporary globalization has to involve an integration of economic analysis with the larger political and military aims of the major players, particularly the United States and the world's largest corporations, an analysis that most Keynesians have ignored or downplayed in their writing.

This helps explain why Keynesians have not questioned the underlying inevitability or desirability of globalization itself. They tend to assume the ultimate altruistic intentions of US economic and foreign policy, even if they are unwisely implemented. They recognize that capitalism will not survive except as a global system, and they are committed to supporting that system through Keynesian principles.

Neo-Marxists and others regard globalization as a form of soft power that helps Western corporate elites sustain global control under the benign guise of economic policies rather than guns and conquest. These policies include "free trade" agreements that do not provide labor or environmental protections, forced selling of national public utilities or banks to the highest private bidder, unfettered capital mobility that can unhinge whole economies, intellectual property rights that restrict use of generic drugs that could cure massive epidemics, structural adjustment programs that force governments to stop subsidizing food and medical care for their poor, and forced opening of entire national economies to foreign investments that turn national sovereignty over to the largest global multinationals and banks. Stiglitz seems to recognize that globalization feels like an assault on national sovereignty to many poor countries: "Much of the rest of the world feels as if it is being deprived of making its own choices, and even forced to make choices that countries like the United States have rejected."[32]

Keynesians may critique some of these policies, but they have not developed a systemic critique of globalization as soft power perpetuating the hegemonic corporate and Western state power that for centuries was maintained by the hard power of colonial militaries. Keynesians need to state what is obvious to many people around the world: that globalization is the velvet glove replacing or supplementing the iron fist.

While environmentalists have made powerful arguments for localizing many economic sectors, such as food, and neo-Marxists have long made forceful arguments against the entire globalization system as a vehicle for giant corporations and the capitalist class to expand their power and profit around the world—essentially seeing globalization as both the economic and the military face of hegemonic global capitalism—Keynesians remain steadfastly committed to globalization. Keynesians believe that the Bretton Woods institutions can move toward a Keynesian model of regulation that will promote global growth and social welfare—the ideal that Keynes himself espoused. However, they have not questioned the ideal of growth itself, nor have they taken seriously enough the concerns that neo-Marxists voice: that globalization as soft power is the most dangerous force undermining collective security and global democracy in the name of national security and the moral virtues of the US-led "free world." And Keynesians have not taken seriously enough the concerns about globalization that Keynes himself voiced: globalization's potential to undermine the ability of national governments to carry out Keynesian policies of public investment, full employment, and public welfare.

Neo-Marxists

Though he was writing 150 years ago, Marx saw globalization, along with capitalism itself, as the most revolutionary force of the modern era. He believed correctly that capitalism could not survive without expanding, and that capitalists would use whatever means possible to gain access to land, resources, labor, and markets everywhere in the world. Marx wrote that "the need of a constantly expanding market for its products chases the bourgeoisie over the whole surface of the globe. It must nestle everywhere, settle everywhere, establish connections everywhere."[33]

He realized this would transform the planet but not in the way that founding neoclassical thinkers such as Adam Smith and David Ricardo, the early champions of globalization, thought. Rather, Marx saw globalization as the conquest of the world by a globalizing capitalist class, who would not be satisfied until every worker and government was under their control and harnessed to their lust for endless profits. Unlike Keynesians, Marxists do not hold any illusion that the intentions of the United States or other Western imperial powers are benign.

Marx saw globalization as a race to the bottom, designed to cheapen costs of production and maximize profits for capitalist corporations, whatever the social and environmental costs. It was the logical extension of capitalism, and it would create a planet designed to serve the capitalist masters of the universe.

Marx saw globalization as a violent process, involving overcoming hatred and resistance of foreigners. But their walls would succumb to cheap prices, ironically one of the arguments made by neoclassicists. Marx wrote of capitalism that "the cheapness of its commodities are the heavy artillery with which it batters down all Chinese walls, with which it forces the barbarians' obstinate hatred of foreigners to capitulate. It compels all nations, on pain of extinction, to adopt the bourgeois mode of production."[34]

Marx saw freedom as the ideology of capitalist globalization. But while neoclassicists view such freedom as globalization's great virtue, Marx wrote of it as a rhetorical grand manipulation, worthy of George Orwell's doublethink in *1984*. Marx wrote that globalizing capitalism stripped away "numberless indefensible chartered freedoms ... and has set up that single, unconscionable freedom—Free Trade.... [Free Trade] is veiled by religious and political illusions, it has substituted naked, shameless, direct, brutal exploitation."[35]

Marx always saw nation-states as artificial entities, masking the reality of global class divisions and exploitation. He argued that workers' identification with their nation was a form of false consciousness.[36] The enemies of workers are the rulers of their own countries, not the people of other countries. National identity was a capitalist tool to create conflicts within the global working class and pit them against each other on patriotic grounds rather than allowing them to unify and confront the global capitalist elite. Patriotism was a spectacularly successful means of creating "false consciousness" and preventing workers from seeing that their identity and interests lay with workers of all nations rather than the leaders of their own country. They proudly marched to their deaths.[37]

Marx's most important political action was to create the First International Workingmen's Association, and he spent ten years leading an effort to bring together workers across Europe and the world to confront the rising global capitalist system. Marx believed it was important to organize at local and national levels, but the ultimate revolution would have to be global, because that was where capitalist power was centered. The capitalist class is so intertwined worldwide that the success of revolution anywhere depends on revolution everywhere. Leon Trotsky, in particular, saw the Russian Revolution as a way to provoke revolutions in more advanced countries, especially Germany. Marx felt that nationalism would have to be curbed and national wars ended in order to unify global workers against global capitalists.[38]

Marx had these words inscribed on his tombstone: "Workers of the world unite."

Marx knew that globalization began long before the 1944 Bretton Woods meeting or the rise of the Internet. It began with capitalism itself, which early on used trade and war to expand production and profits. He wrote, "The discovery of America, the rounding of the Cape, opened up fresh ground for the rising bourgeoisie. The East-Indian and Chinese markets, the colonization of America, trade with the colonies, the increase in the means of exchange and in commodities" were the engine of capitalism from the beginning.[39]

Marx lived during an era in which capitalism was spreading across Europe and expanding overseas in European colonial empires. He saw that capitalists would fight each other to gain competitive edges but that the true goal was to create the architecture of a capitalist planet in which the capitalist class could manage the world to serve their own ends.

This historical idea of Marx—that capitalism has for centuries been a global project—became the core argument of contemporary neo-Marxist thinkers such as Immanuel Wallerstein, often seen as the founder of "world systems theory."[40] Wallerstein and his colleagues argue that capitalism is a world system divided into a "core" of advanced nations and a "periphery" of poor countries, as well as a "semiperiphery" of more rapidly developing nations. The division between core and periphery is a global class divide, with global capitalists operating mainly in the "core" of the United States, Europe, and Japan to control the global labor of the "periphery" in Africa, Latin America, and Asia.[41] While this developed over centuries during Western colonialism, the core and periphery in the postcolonial era are becoming "deterritorialized." The periphery is increasingly found in the slums of Detroit and Los Angeles as well as those of Beijing and Capetown or Rio, and billionaires and global banks in New York join with those in Mexico City or Shanghai to extract profit and resources from the global working class.[42]

We have argued in Chapter 7 and in earlier works that globalization creates "exit power" for corporations, increasing their leverage over ordinary workers.[43] Exit power is the power arising from a credible threat to leave. Globalization makes credible the corporate threat to shut down plants and move abroad, if workers in advanced countries do not agree to drastic reductions in wages, pensions, and working conditions. Those without exit power in any institution are vulnerable to abuse and may have little recourse. Capital can move much more easily than labor, which faces rigid immigration restrictions. Exit power by capital is decimating unions and workers' standard of living in the United States and other developed nations, creating severe austerity at home resembling the structural adjustment programs inflicted on poor nations.[44]

In the twenty-first century, US global elites have made a momentous decision to relocate overseas and disinvest in much of the US labor force and infrastructure. Why should they pay higher wages and submit to regulations here if they can find low-paid, unskilled, and skilled workers in China or Vietnam, without having to abide by environmental regulations or submit to taxes in "free trade" zones? When Steve Jobs told President Obama that US workers would not be the ones making computers anymore, he was hinting at the larger truth of US companies abandoning the United States itself.[45]

The consequence is the creation of a huge US and European "surplus people" crisis.[46] As jobs go overseas, or workers are replaced by robots, new generations of workers in the advanced world have dimming job prospects. Even the college-educated find it harder to secure jobs, especially well-paying ones. The surplus population experiences a sense of decline and despair. The young people in the surplus pool are not only the first generation likely to live less well than their parents but also arguably the first to face a jobless future.[47]

Neo-Marxists see the WTO, IMF, and World Bank that create and enforce free trade agreements and global neoliberal rules as key parts of a rising world capitalist government. Their aim is to open all countries to access, control, and exploitation by global companies and investors, in the name of free markets, efficiency, and liberty. The reality is that neoliberal rules—crafted and enforced by the Bretton Woods institutions and their corporate sponsors—are the global economic "constitution" that reshapes the world economy into a profit machine for a small and extremely wealthy and powerful global governing class. Lori Wallach, a brilliant globalization critic and activist, wrote that "the WTO is carrying out a slow motion coup d'état over democratic governance worldwide."[48]

Neo-Marxists differ from neoclassicists in their view that globalization is not a part of natural law or a "natural" extension of efficient markets. It is a project created and designed by the capitalist class, seeking to expand their wealth and control. Neoclassicists argue that globalization creates a free world in which nobody has centralized power. Thomas Friedman wrote that nobody is in charge of globalization, quipping that if you want to complain to somebody about globalization, "guess what, there's no one on the other end of the phone. It's like telling people there's no God."[49] But neo-Marxists argue that globalization is entirely a project built of, by, and for the powerful.

Neo-Marxists note that neoliberal rules are hypocritical, since the United States and Europe do not live up to them. They protect and subsidize key industries such as agriculture, oil, mining, and pharmaceuticals.[50] This is hardly new. Many believe that the Civil War was fought by the US North to allow its new industrial steel and oil companies to continue high protectionist measures against British manufacturing companies, while the South wanted a free trade regime to sell its cotton and other products to Britain cheaply.

Ironically, Southern agrarians were acting like neoclassicists. This exposes the hypocritical nature of neoclassical laissez-faire. Northern industrialists who professed neoclassicism wanted prototypical Keynesian protectionism. The South may have professed "states rights" but they expected the federal government to prevent Northern abolitionists from protecting escaped slaves. The history of the United States is one of perpetual protection and corporate welfare that permits the United States to compete on a nonlevel playing field, as it seeks to end all protection and subsidies offered by other countries to their own companies.

In other words, neoliberal or neoclassical globalization is utter hypocrisy, with dominant nations espousing rules that they don't follow themselves. It is a rigged system, in which giant global corporations get huge benefits from their protectionist governments and trade arrangements, in the name of a free market, antiprotectionist global regime.[51] The system is a farce, setting up a stacked system in which the giant corporations cannot lose and rising competitors in poorer nations—not to mention the world's poor and workers—cannot win.[52]

Neo-Marxists believe that by changing capitalism, the world's people can create new forms of democratic globalization. Since globalization was created historically by ruling classes, it can be restricted or dismantled by subjugated classes. If it is not the product of natural law or new technology like the Internet, then we can return to more localized economies even in the electronic digital age. The victor in the class struggles between global elites and global workers will decide globalization's future.

Neo-Marxists, though, are divided on the future they want.[53] Some believe in a globalized economy but one organized democratically and built around ecological rules and social justice, and governed democratically from the ground up. They argue that global businesses can be rechartered in line with the UN Universal Declaration of Human Rights, and that global trade treaties can be transformed to ensure protection of labor and the environment. A global economy can be socialist rather than capitalist, if labor and social movements around the world rise up to create a new global economic order.[54]

Other neo-Marxists, including many green Marxists, want to eliminate much of the global economy and replace it with a localized community-based economy. Their argument is that any form of global economy is ecologically unsustainable because of the costs associated with global transport, marketing, wars for resources, and the construction of global mass consumerism. They also argue that the size of global companies will inevitably concentrate power and wealth in these businesses and make a democratic or socially just global economy a pipe dream. Only smaller, community-based companies and banks, owned by workers or the community itself, will support the new type of socialist and green economy that is fair and sustainable.[55]

CHAPTER 10

Environment and Climate Change

Are Americans who are doubting or denying climate change sleeping well now? Those who lived in the path of Superstorm Sandy in October 2012—the most ferocious storm, also dubbed "Frankenstorm," ever to hit the entire East Coast—may be having nightmares about climate change. That is, if they have any place to sleep. Sandy's massive winds and waves demolished homes, cars, office buildings, roads, bridges, and everything else in its path and created at least $50 billion in damages. A year later, thousands were still trying to put their lives back together.

According to a team of eminent climate scientists, the victims of Sandy—and all the rest of us—certainly ought to be having climate change nightmares. Scientists offer strong evidence that unexpectedly fast Arctic ice melting played "a significant role in Sandy's evolution as an extra-tropical superstorm." They suggest Sandy's monstrous impact was likely a man-made disaster rather than "a freak of nature."[1]

The climate change deniers among those hit only weeks after Frankenstorm Sandy by the great Nor'easter blizzard that buried Boston and other New England cities with up to three feet of snow, also may have begun to reconsider. In the year or two prior to Sandy, huge fires in California, drought in large areas of the Great Plains, and the movement of tropical insects and disease into parts of the Gulf Coast and farther north, along with the rapid melting of Arctic and Antarctic ice and rising sea levels didn't make things any easier for climate deniers. Nor did the fact that 2012 was the hottest year in recorded history, and that ten of the fifteen hottest years ever recorded occurred between 1997 and 2012. Eight of the hottest years ever recorded have happened in the ten years between 2002 and 2012. In 2012, "34,008 daily high records were set at weather stations across the country, compared with only 6,664 record lows."[2]

Worse, the concentration of CO_2 in the atmosphere rose over the dreaded number of 400 parts per million, on May 9, 2013, for the first time in millions of years. Scientists reacted with alarm. Maureen E. Raymo, a scientist at the Lamont-Doherty Earth Observatory, a unit of Columbia University, said, "It feels like the inevitable march toward disaster."[3]

The scientists report that the last time carbon dioxide occurred at such a high rate was during the Pliocene era, three million years ago. In that era, long before humans existed, the earth was much warmer, glaciers were smaller and *sea levels were sixty to eighty feet higher than now.* During the roughly 8,000 years of human civilization, the concentration of carbon dioxide ranged between 180 and 280 parts per million.[4] A measurement of 400 suggests we are likely to displace or drown roughly half the people living near the coasts of the planet.

Virtually all climate scientists across the globe agree that we humans are creating global warming and leading the planet toward irreversible and catastrophic changes. Millions of people on every continent are now experiencing climate change creating devastating crop loss, lack of clean water, and flooding.[5] But the denial continues. Since 2003, tens of millions of dollars—put up by conservative billionaires such as the Koch Brothers, who are Texas oil and gas tycoons, and by big oil and coal companies such as Exxon—have funded secret networks of foundations and think tanks spouting continued denial. These are foundations and think tanks supported by the same corporate elites and staffed by the same scientists and lobbyists paid by Phillip Morris and other cigarette companies to deny that cigarettes kill.[6]

Sandy may have helped catalyze a turning point, as Americans became more concerned about climate change, emboldening President Obama to proclaim in his 2013 Inaugural Address that global warming was one of the greatest threats facing the world and had to be a top priority of the US government:

> Some may still deny the overwhelming judgment of science, but none can avoid the devastating impact of raging fires and crippling drought and more powerful storms.... We will respond to the threat of climate change, knowing that the failure to do so would betray our children and future generations.... That is how we will preserve our planet, commanded to our care by God. That's what will lend meaning to the creed our fathers once declared.[7]

If climate change is man-made, as science shows us, then we need a sustainable political economy that can slow or stop climate change. Each of our three political economy schools has an approach but whether any is up to the job is another question, perhaps the most important they face.

Neoclassicists

Neoclassicists have their own approach. Neoclassical thinkers argue that the invisible hand of the free market can solve environmental problems with the same power that they solve all other great issues. Since the invisible hand ensures maximum personal utility of individuals while guaranteeing social well-being, we can rely on the market itself—with little outside interference from government or popular movements—to cure the problem.

Moreover, neoclassicists make clear that just because people are self-interested doesn't mean they don't care about larger issues concerning society. Milton Friedman contended that "self-interest is not myopic selfishness. It is whatever it is that interests the participants, that they value."[8] In a world of climate change, that might easily come to mean environmental values, and lead individuals to factor environmental costs and benefits into their personal market calculations.

The core argument is that the market always responds to the preference of rational investors and consumers. Investors will be sensitive to profit and price—and if the costs of fossil fuel business increase while the profits decrease—they will shift capital into renewable energy. If consumers want energy, they will be willing to pay for it, creating a new mass and profitable market for green energy business. Since the assumption is that both investors and consumers are rational, the hard reality of climate change—if in fact it is a scientific truth—will lead all market participants to make these rational "green" choices, for it is in their own interests of survival.

Why then are pollution and climate change becoming worse—with frightening speed? Neoclassicists argue that one of the reasons is precisely that we don't actually have "environmental markets." Most air and water are part of a precapitalist "commons" and are not privately owned and exchanged on free markets. This is how neoclassicists explain the crisis of the environment—exactly the opposite of what neo-Marxists and many Keynesians believe.

For neoclassicists—using an analysis codified into the Coase theorem, named after economist Ronald Coase—the problem is not market failure but the very absence of markets. The Coase theorem proposes that we privatize the environment—land, air, and water—and subject it to routine free market private property principles and prices, thereby immediately allowing the market to operate and solve environmental problems. The tragedy of the commons lamented by environmentalists is the very perpetuation of the commons.[9]

The answer is thus subjecting more of the environment to the free market.

Yet neoclassicists recognize that this will not solve all the problems of "externalities," the social or environmental costs and benefits of market transactions that extend to other people not directly involved. Such externalities are a huge problem but neoclassicists have answers. They propose that all people subject to environmental pollution or "externalities" from a particular market transaction join private negotiations to work out a system of costs and prices that is optimal or efficient. Another involves "contingent evaluation" in which market actors are asked to include in their preferences the costs and benefits to the environment. The aim is to incorporate more accurately pollution costs into market mechanisms without having to bring in the distorting effect of government.[10]

Once markets are fully introduced—and water, air, or wild animals become private property—most environmental disasters, including climate change, will be solved. Private incorporation of externalized costs will lead companies to spur innovative technology for cleaner and more efficient, less costly products and energy sources. Changing costs of increasingly scarce oil and coal and increasingly cheaper solar, wind, and natural gas will also lead to market self-correction. Fossil fuels are reaching peak and beyond, meaning their supply is becoming scarcer. Investors and corporations, being rational, will see the writing on the wall and make new decisions that ensure future return on investment.

These new decisions will drive technological innovation in clean energy, the great strength of markets. Neoclassicists see climate change as above all a problem of technology, something that the free market is superb—cannot be surpassed—at creating. Climate change requires dramatic, revolutionary, new, clean energy technologies and efficiencies. For neoclassicists, only the competitiveness and entrepreneurship of the market—symbolized by all those inventors in Silicon Valley and in garages or labs everywhere—can create the clean energy revolution we need. While Thomas L. Friedman moved partly toward Keynesian thinking in his bestseller on climate change, *Hot, Flat, and Crowded*, he put the neoclassical view of climate change as a technological problem—only solvable by market-driven innovation—very, very clearly:

> If you take only one thing away from this book, please take this. We are not going to regulate our way out of the problems of the Energy-Climate era. We can only innovate our way out, and the only way to do that is to mobilize the most effective and prolific system for transformational innovation and commercialization of new products ever created on the face of the earth—the US market place. There is only one thing bigger than Mother Nature and that is Father Profit, and we have not even begun to enlist him in this struggle.[11]

Friedman is thus proposing a climate change version of the Coase theorem: the only way to solve the crisis is to create more capitalism.

Friedman goes on to argue that "We don't need a Manhattan Project for clean energy. We need a market for clean energy."[12] And he is crystal clear that only the US capitalist market can achieve the breakthroughs in technology that are essential:

> But the only thing that can stimulate this much innovation in new technologies and the radical improvement of existing ones is the free market. Only the market can generate and allocate enough capital fast enough and efficient enough to get 10,000 inventors working in 10,000 companies and 10,000 garages and 10,000 laboratories to drive transformational breakthroughs: only the market can then commercialize the best of them and improve on the existing ones at the scope, speed and scale we need.[13]

Of course, big questions face this neoclassical approach. One is something that Friedman acknowledges. The market needs incentives to drive this innovation, because existing externalities and the power of Big Oil and Big Coal mean that the market won't create this magic on its own. Friedman melded into his neoclassical market infatuation a view that we need government to incentivize this change, with tax policies, subsidies, and regulations providing a huge kick in the pants to entrenched market interests. Now sounding more like a Keynesian, as we see below, he said, "Markets are like gardens. You have to intelligently design and fertilize them—with the right taxes, regulations, incentives and disincentives—so they yield the good, healthy crops necessary for you to thrive."[14] Friedman also recognized that big companies wield huge influence to preserve existing fossil fuel capitalism. They are subsidized and return huge profits now. Only populist and government countervailing power can get them into the energy revolution we need. But this goes against the neoclassical mandate, which argues that such powerful government intervention will destroy the very market magic that Friedman is trying to exploit.

Despite his core belief in the market as the solution, armed with some Keynesian corrections, Friedman succumbed to two key further neoclassical fatal flaws. One is the failure to recognize the inability of capitalist markets to overcome and correct their built-in externalities. One reason is there are simply too many of them to correct rapidly enough when it comes to climate change—and a second is that the political influence of Big Oil and Big Coal is too large to correct them in time. The nature of climate change as a product of thousands of large and small externalities is simply too big for neoclassical markets to overcome, leading no less than Oystein Dahle, a former executive of Exxon, to say, "Socialism collapsed because it did not allow the market to tell the economic truth. Capitalism may collapse because it does not allow the market to tell the ecological truth."[15]

Because of massive environmental externalities, the market fails to register accurate costs and prices, leading to short-term strategies with irreversible harm, since once carbon is up in the atmosphere, it stays there for hundreds of years. It is already at a dangerously high level and cannot be sucked out. Markets can take time to adjust even under the most optimistic assumptions, and science suggests we don't have time left.

And there is one other crucial failure of the neoclassical approach. Climate change is a social and political, not just technological, challenge, so that even if one assumes capitalism to be the most innovative technological system, it cannot tackle the climate change crisis because it is actually the *cause* of it. As we show later, climate change is driven by a profit engine requiring endless growth and consumption, a way of life based on big homes, autos, and highways, and endless buying of "stuff" to make people happy. As long as we have capitalism, at least any capitalism looking like the system in the United States, we will have the political, social, and cultural roots of climate change baked into society. Even with clean energy systems, such as wind and solar, endless consumption drains scarce resources, changes delicate environmental balances and feedback systems, and endangers thousands on thousands of species. No matter what is done through technological change, it will take dramatic adjustments in our way of life—a shift from private consumerism to public life and pleasures—to solve our environmental crises.[16] And consumerism cannot be ended until we have transformed capitalism and its master script of unfettered consumerism.

The environment is *the* "commons"—the necessary foundation of all life that we share and depend on together. If the market—guided by individuals pursuing their own private objectives—fails to protect the commons by failing to limit its raiding of resources for endless consumption, the market, along with the rest of society, cannot long endure. This concept of protecting the environment simply cannot be integrated into neoclassicism, because it offers no vision of life beyond the consumption that the market views as the source of all pleasure and purpose.

Trusting in the perfection of the market, neoclassicists are not alarmed. They have failed to adequately answer any of these objections. Their influence has reinforced US inaction on this greatest of all twenty-first-century crises. The consequences are frightening.

Keynesians

After Superstorm Sandy, the prominent Keynesian writer, Robert Kuttner, wrote that America "has just become a much larger version of Holland." Holland, of course, is below sea level and could have already sunk into oblivion.

But, instead, Holland "spends billions of dollars on flood prevention" and "is a thriving, prospering society."[17] Public investment in a complex system of dikes, sea walls, and pumping stations is not only keeping Holland's economy afloat but literally keeping Holland itself above water.

Kuttner continued, "Sandy changes everything—maybe." What he means is that Sandy makes a Holland-style response more politically possible in the United States. "It just happens that the money that we need to invest in protecting our coasts and reducing carbon emissions can also power the recovery that the economy needs."[18] Kuttner noted that the "money needed easily reaches into the trillions of dollars" to reconstruct the energy infrastructure and protect the coasts.[19] This approach to saving the economy and environment—massive public spending—might be called "Green Keynesianism."

Keynesianism is far better suited than neoclassicism to address climate change and other environmental problems. First, it recognizes that market failures are commonplace—and environmental problems are perhaps the most important form. Second, Keynesianism sees government intervention as essential and benign, rather than coercive, and thus, Keynesianism is geared to support the kind of public investment and regulation that Kuttner discusses. Third, Keynesians understand that the market economy is driven by social and political power—typically of wealthy elites—and, to preserve the social good, must be managed aggressively by the public sector to ward off social crises and to ensure jobs, social welfare, and environmental protection.

Not surprisingly then, the most important Keynesian thinkers today, particularly Joseph Stiglitz and Robert Kuttner, have made efforts to address climate change and environmental problems. Keynes himself, it is true, was so preoccupied with the crises of the Great Depression and the building of the architecture of a viable global international economy after World War II, he did not himself devote much time to environmental issues. But the paradigm he created, as just noted, lends itself to thinking about solving environmental externalities and crises through public investment, regulation, and subsidies.

Keynesians offer a number of core solutions. The most straightforward is taxation. Since the market is not accurately reflecting externalized environmental costs, the government can do so, most simply by a global carbon tax, as advocated forcefully by the Nobel Prize–winning Keynesian, Joseph Stiglitz.

> There is a way out, and that is through a common (global) environmental tax on [carbon] emissions. There is a social cost to emissions, and the common environmental tax would simply make everyone pay the social cost. This is in accord with the most basic of economic principles, that individuals and firms should pay their full (marginal) costs. The world would, of course, have to agree on assessing the magnitude of the social cost

of emissions; the tax could, for instance, be set so that the level of (global) reductions is the same as that set by the Kyoto targets. As technologies evolve, and the nature of the threat of global warming becomes clearer, the tax rate could adjust, perhaps up, perhaps down.[20]

Taxing oil, coal, or other greenhouse gas emissions is the obvious path to "internalizing the externalities." The tax adds to the price at the pump the longer-term social and environmental hidden costs that the oil companies and current consumers do not have to pay today. The idea of a carbon tax reflects Keynesian concerns that externalities lead to market distortions and failures, a major theme in Stiglitz's work, which won a Nobel Prize for pointing out how incomplete information in both the short and long term is a serious problem for market theorists and actors. Neoclassicists recognize the existence of environmental externalities, incomplete future information about environmental costs, and the need to accurately price the full costs of market products or services. After all, the failure to internalize the true cost represents a subsidy; Stiglitz notes that "a subsidy means that a firm does not pay the full costs of production. Not paying the cost of damage to the environment is a subsidy, just as not paying the full costs of workers would be."[21] Neoclassicists would mainly agree in principle, since they reject subsidies and assume that prices accurately reflect costs. But they are reluctant to endorse major taxation such as global carbon taxes, since they believe that government mismanagement or overextension will get the world into even deeper problems.

A second Keynesian approach is regulation. Market failure, say Keynesians, almost always requires governments to step in and restrain the investor and corporate greed or "animal spirits" that can create bubbles and short-term blindness to long-term crises such as climate crisis.[22] In this case, government must regulate greenhouse gas emissions—at power plants, in car production, and in building standards—to cap annual totals, reducing the level over time, the approach advanced by international climate agreements such as the Kyoto Protocol. Europeans have drastically reduced their carbon footprints because they have not only taxed carbon but also put strict regulations on buildings, cars, and homes to ensure minimal greenhouse gas emissions.[23]

A third Keynesian approach—the one highlighted by Kuttner in his discussion of Holland—is public investment. Only government can mobilize the huge resources involved to rebuild the entire energy infrastructure. So Keynesians see European governments—and the Chinese government too—as a model for investing in and subsidizing wind and solar, while more broadly investing in electric charging stations for cars, new public transit for urban populations, and a total transformation away from roads, suburbs, and fossil fuel power.[24] Ultimately, this requires not only public investment in clean energy and energy efficiency, but in expanding public and community space—the social commons—so that people have an alternative to privatized consumerism.[25]

In 2008, running for his first term, Obama gave a strong speech proposing Keynesian-style investment in an Infrastructure Reinvestment Bank with initial funding of $60 billion, creating millions of new jobs. He went on to emphasize the need for public investment in clean energy: "We need to invest in green technology.... We should be investing in American companies that invest in American-manufactured solar panels and wind mills.... That's why I've proposed investing $150 billion over the next ten years in the green energy sector."[26]

This was far too modest a sum, but even that was derailed by Big Oil and Republicans in Congress. This reflects one of the most serious problems of the Keynesian approach: political resistance. Huge oil and coal companies, along with most other corporations, military and civilian, are locked into the fossil fuel infrastructure. It will cost them heavily to change, requiring a revolution in their business strategies. They have the political power to resist the major government taxation, regulation, and public investment Keynesians want. And corporations have proven their avid willingness to do this, whatever it costs.[27]

Two other intertwined problems indicate the severe limits of Keynesianism in its ability to solve the emergency of climate change. One is that most Keynesians, like the neoclassicists and even many neo-Marxists, are committed to growth as a central aim. And we know that endless growth, combined with population growth, is a guaranteed recipe for climate catastrophe. You cannot have infinite growth on a finite planet without destroying the planet.[28]

Similarly, Keynesians do not tend to discuss limiting consumer demand to save the environment, since that could create recessions or depressions that Keynesians seek to prevent. Yet mass consumerism, as noted above, is at the heart of the problem of climate change. As economist and sociologist Juliet Schor has argued persuasively, there can be no solution to climate change without shifting away from a consumer society.[29] It would take seven planets to support everyone on earth at the level of consumption and per capita carbon emissions that the United States embraces.

Stiglitz, among other Keynesians concerned with climate change and the environment, takes up the question of growth, indicating openness to restraints on growth. Yet the core problem for all Keynesians is that they remain committed to capitalism, and nobody has conceived a persuasive model of how to create a capitalism that limits both consumerism and growth. Both are central to the profit engine driving capitalism. Since Keynes invented Keynesianism to save capitalism, it cannot effectively embrace a robustly ecologically sane way of thinking, because solutions to climate change, as neo-Marxists and many other environmental thinkers point out, cannot occur within a capitalist system.

Neo-Marxists

For neo-Marxists, the climate crisis is a symptom of the irrationality of the capitalist system itself. Capitalism, particularly the US variety, causes climate change because the DNA of the system demands exploitation of both workers and the environment. The implication is clear: if you want civilization to survive, you have to get behind an alternative to capitalism.

This is something that both Karl Marx and his main collaborator, Friedrich Engels, understood well. Engels wrote prophetically, "Let us not however flatter ourselves over much on account of our human conquest over nature. For each such conquest takes its revenge on us."[30] Capitalism is based on private property ownership tied to class divisions and warfare. Owners and employers can survive only by cheapening the cost of production, including the cost of labor and environmental resources. Marx and Engels were very explicit about capitalist agriculture's inevitable destruction of the environment: "All progress in capitalist agriculture is not only a process in robbing the labourer but robbing the soil. All progress in increasing the fertility of the soil for a given time is a progress towards ruining the last sources of that fertility."[31]

Marx generalized environmental degradation as an inexorable consequence of the development of capitalism: "The more a country develops its foundations of modern industry, the more rapid is this process of destruction ... only by sapping the original sources of all wealth, the soil and the labourer."[32] Of course, when you degrade the workforce and the environment there are both short- and long-term grave consequences, but these are "externalities" and they will not deter capitalists who are short-term in their calculus, legally bound to maximize return on investment, and hostage to financial markets that withdraw capital if they don't get big and fast returns, whatever the cost to society.[33]

Capitalists do what is individually profitable for them. What is rational for the individual may not be rational for society or even the capitalist system as a whole. If the environment is destroyed, if all resources are depleted, it will destroy capitalism. There is a profound contradiction between the short-term and long-term interests of capitalism. Marx argued that as capitalists compete and pursue their short-term individual interests, they will bring down the very system that sustains them. The focus on short-term profit, on market blindness to long-term environmental externalities, on unlimited consumerism, and the privatization of the commons all make capitalism inherently destructive to the planet and the common good. This is the exact opposite of the invisible hand—and it means that capitalism is a central cause of climate change and a new tragedy of the commons or common good, an argument made by contemporary neo-Marxists, such as John Bellamy Foster and David Harvey. Foster, in particular, has written a series of important scholarly works documenting the centrality of Marx's critique of the environment in his overall analysis of capitalism.[34]

Friedrich Engels summed up the idea concisely: "And the original appropriation—the monopolization of the earth by a few, the exclusion of the rest from that which is the condition of their life—yields nothing in immorality to the subsequent huckstering of the earth."[35]

Wait a minute, you say, we have good and responsible green companies who practice "conscious capitalism," as CEO John Mackey of Whole Foods says in his book of this title.[36] Yes, some companies practice "triple bottom line" accounting, claiming to live up to environmental and labor as well as profit measures. But these are exceptions to the rule—usually small companies such as Ben and Jerry's that will get bought by bigger ones if they succeed, as happened with Ben and Jerry's—and cannot change the climate change crisis even if some do survive and thrive.

Sociologist John Bellamy Foster's response is that this is just another more sophisticated form of denial:

> [This] stage of denial has the look and feel of greater realism, but actu-
> ally constitutes a more desperate and dangerous response. It admits that
> capitalism is the problem, but also contends that capitalism is the solu-
> tion. This general approach emphasizes what is variously referred to as
> "sustainable capitalism," "natural capitalism," "climate capitalism," "green
> capitalism," etc. In this view we can continue down the same road of capital
> accumulation, mounting profits, and exponential economic growth—while
> at the same time miraculously reducing our burdens on the planetary
> environment. It is business as usual, but with greater efficiency and greater
> accounting of environmental costs. No fundamental changes in social or
> property relations—in the structure of production and consumption—are
> required. This is the magical world view advanced by such diverse figures
> as Al Gore, Amory Lovins, L. Hunter Lovins, Paul Hawken, and Jonathon
> Porritt—if not Thomas Friedman, Newt Gingrich, and the Breakthrough
> Institute, as well.[37]

This brings us back to bigger forces in capitalism to which we now return: endless growth and mass consumerism. One is the need for expansion built into the system, requiring ever-more production and ever-more growth to avoid declining profit levels. As Foster noted,

The main problem, which all of this denies, is the nature and logic of capitalism itself. Capitalism, as its name suggests, is quite simply, the system of capital. Its sole purpose is the accumulation of capital through the exploitation of human labor. It is a grow-or-die system dominated by the 1% (the capitalist class) and giant corporations. It is prone to periodic economic crises, and constant—and today deepening—unemployment. Capital accumulation and economic expansion occur by means of gross inequality and monopolistic competition, generating a war of all against all and a world of waste. The wider public/social/natural sphere is an object of theft—a realm in which to dump "externalities" or impose unpaid social costs, which then fall on nature and humanity in general.[38]

Foster highlighted the peril of a system devoted to endless growth:

Endless capitalism requires unlimited economic growth. Economists generally consider a 3 percent average rate of economic growth over the long run as absolutely essential for the stability of the capitalist system. Yet, if we were to have a continual 3 percent rate of economic growth, world output would expand exponentially by around sixteen times in a century, 250 times in two centuries, and 4,000 times in three centuries. Already we are overshooting planetary limits—consuming resources as if we had multiple planets at our disposal, undermining the very basis of our existence.[39]

Foster concluded,

Nevertheless, where capitalism is concerned, expansion is a requirement for the existence of the system itself. "Capitalism," as Murray Bookchin observed, "can no more be 'persuaded' to limit growth than a human being can be 'persuaded' to stop breathing. Attempts to 'green' capitalism, to make it 'ecological,' are doomed by the very nature of the system as a system of endless growth."[40]

True, different energy systems could conceivably provide an even more comfortable standard of living—and modest growth levels—with less environmental cost than in the United States. We are seeing a small example of this in Europe, where each nation's carbon footprint is half or less per capita than here. But European capitalist reforms don't solve the long-term fundamental problems:

Problem 1: The cost of the transition and replacing technologies that are still functional, but not the most efficient or the least environmentally destructive. Capitalist corporations—particularly Big Oil and Big Coal—will block the transition because the current system is so profitable for them and they are among the most influential global corporations.

Problem 2: Even, as in Europe, where some corporate political resistance is overcome, the irreducible elements of growth and mass consumerism in any form of capitalism make capitalist reform too timid, and capitalism inevitably creates growth that is unsustainable.

Problem 3: European capitalist and climate reforms are a short-term palliative and not a long-term solution. We need a systemic change toward a steady state system that has rejected the consumer society.

Mass consumerism deserves our attention again—for it is a guaranteed recipe for climate change, the leading capitalist means of expansion and growth, and thus arguably the most important reason why capitalism and climate sanity are incompatible. As the population grows globally toward 9 or 10 billion people in the next decade, the recipe becomes fixed, even with efficiencies and technological innovation. Capitalism sees nothing here but new markets for more profit. It will put all money necessary into seeing that all the new people are programmed from birth with bigger appetites to buy.[41]

Consumerism is the engine driving US capitalism. Domestic demand drives production and keeps the economy humming; 70 percent comes from private consumers. American capitalism is thus totally dependent on an American Dream requiring that people equate personal happiness with buying stuff at the mall. Advertising operates 24/7 to ensure that this culture of consumerism is the religion of the nation—it produced a "coerced consumerism" even though most Americans now may believe that the freedom to buy what they choose is the only freedom they have left in America.[42]

But mass consumption is the central engine—along with profit—of both climate change and capitalism. This is something that Marx recognized and wrote about in the very first chapter of his most important work, *Capital*. Marx would not be surprised by the popularity of the sitcom *Mad Men*. The advertiser's role is as the alchemist of capitalism, helping to create what Marx called "the mystical character of the commodity" that alienates the worker from his product but also enchants and magically seduces him into endless consumerism. Herein lies the "fetishism of commodities," the theme of Chapter 1 of *Capital*.[43]

Economist and sociologist Juliet Schor has become the leading new neo-Marxist and ecological critic of mass consumerism. Our mode of consumption, she argues, inexorably burdens the environment: "Let's start with stuff. There's no avoiding the fact that just as every purchase has a price in money terms, it also has an ecological impact. Some items tax the earth more, some less, but everything we buy puts carbon in the atmosphere, uses up resources and affects the functioning of ecosystems."[44]

And Schor documented the extraordinary increase in the sheer amount of consumption in the United States:

> From the perspective of fifty years earlier, when the nation was already very prosperous, the expansion of consumption is also striking. In 1960 the average person consumed just a third of what she or he did in late 2008. Since 1990, inflation-adjusted per-person expenditures have risen 300% for furniture and household goods. 80 percent for apparel.... Overall, average real per-person spending increased 42 percent.[45]

This has all happened as capitalism turns to the consumer to float the economy and generate profit. But mass consumerism, Schor argued, can sustain neither capitalism, as it ricochets into deeper crises, nor the environment, as ecocide becomes more imminent. Yet the largely neoclassical economists who embrace the current model of US capitalism are engaged in denial, since they assume that consumption will grow to refloat the economy and that the ecological costs are tolerable and can be borne by future generations.[46]

To mitigate climate change, we need to move beyond mass consumer society. Schor does not reject consumption per se, but suggests movement toward "slow spending," based on quality rather than quantity.[47] Schor also advocates a "share economy" and describes alternatives where people depend on public pleasures—concerts, community events, public debates, street theater, and the like—for happiness. Unlimited personal consumption with ever-more stuff—bigger houses, cars, and boats—will not only sink the planet but does not provide happiness. But since this religion of mass consumption is the heart of capitalism, neo-Marxists such as Foster and Schor argue that we need transformation in the economic system.

Neo-Marxists believe that the only survival strategy is to rebuild the economy as a green and more just system, based on a clean energy infrastructure, limits to growth and consumerism, localization of production, and robust economic democracy. This requires change in government, with public ownership of energy companies, of much of Wall Street (to finance this change), and expansion of the commons. The profit charters and corporate law must drastically change if we are to sustain ourselves.[48] Defining the public interest in terms of private property guarantees the tragedy of the commons. The environment must be entrusted to an institution responsible not for individual interests but for society as a whole.

And, of course, all this requires simultaneously a change in the American Dream and our dysfunctional ideas of "fast spending" and mass consumption.

Neo-Marxists, especially those focused on the environment, are developing new, creative, and important visions of change, attractive to many ordinary Americans. They deserve our sustained attention. Neo-Marxists, however, run into the political problems connected with massive change in the system itself. In America, Marxism is widely discredited. It seems a pipe dream to imagine the realization of a whole-system alternative when the US government has been captured by giant corporations and the capitalist class. Nor, despite the existence of many clear micro- and institutional alternatives, is there any clear model of a new postcapitalist economy on the macro level, or clarity of whether or how it might work, even if the political path were open.

This should not lead to despair. But it does suggest limits on all three paradigms and the need for visionary new thinking with realistic political possibilities. In Chapter 14, we shall look at the beginnings of new thinking of political economy that bring the problem of solving the catastrophe of climate change into central focus.

Chapter 11

Education

We don't need no education
We don't need no thought control

—Pink Floyd

One year, the state board of education required every fourth grader in Massachusetts to write an essay on this topic: *A Dream Come True! It is snowing and there is no school. What would you do on that happy day?* The people who run the education system cannot imagine that any child would choose to be in school if they could be someplace else.

Should schools be a place where children want to be? What is the purpose of school? Whom should they serve? How should they be structured and controlled? What should they teach? Should public schools even exist? All of these are hotly debated issues across our three paradigms.

Both neoclassicists and Keynesians accept capitalism as beyond question and turn to schools to train the required labor force. Although they have different tactics, they both acknowledge that capitalism has not lived up to all its promises, especially the promise of equal opportunity, and expect education to correct the defects. Neo-Marxists, however, consider capitalism to be fundamentally flawed. Inequality is not a correctable defect; it is at capitalism's core. No one institution, even education, can solve capitalism's problems. Neo-Marxists believe that as far as capitalism is concerned, schools are doing their job: to reinforce and justify inequality, not to overcome it. Let's now see how our paradigms deal with education.

Neoclassicists

Neoclassicists tend to laud schools as the "great equalizers," the proof that capitalism works and provides opportunity for advancement among those who are talented and willing to work hard. It is the place where poor children can compete with children from privileged backgrounds and prove they have the "stuff," that they have the ambition, drive, and ability to succeed and rise in wealth, status, and authority. Milton Friedman credited schools with creating a common American culture and spreading the harmonizing values of freedom, democracy, and capitalism throughout the entire society.

> The major problem in the United States in the nineteenth and early twentieth century was not to promote diversity but to create the core of common values essential to a stable society. Great streams of immigrants were flooding the United States from all over the world, speaking different languages, and observing different customs. The "melting pot" had to introduce some measure of conformity and loyalty to common values. The public school had an important function in this task.[1]

Neoclassicists assume that schooling is not something children choose for fun, but that is not a problem. It should be hard work and require struggle. It should be a test to see who has the gumption and discipline to sacrifice and thus deserves to advance. It is only fair that jobs requiring more years in school pay more because of the commitment that requires. The expectation of greater wealth is one of the main incentives for staying in school. The highly educated have given up the time they could spend doing other things and need to be appropriately compensated. Ironically, especially from the viewpoint of working-class students who can't afford higher education, this suggests that time they must spend spent flipping hamburgers in McDonald's, working on the assembly line, cleaning other people's houses, or checking out groceries in Wal-Mart is more enjoyable than time in school.

Neoclassical economists embrace a functionalist sociology of education, arguing that schools should select and train "smart" rather than "dumb" students, ensuring that the smart ones get the higher skills required at the top jobs. Schools sift and the market rewards handsomely the gifted who are sifted—the ones who get higher education. Thinking like neoclassicists, functionalist sociologists Kingsley Davis and Wilbert Moore doubted if anyone would endure the burden of medical school without the promise of high pay. "In many cases … the training process is so long, costly and elaborate that relatively few can qualify. Modern medicine, for example, is within the mental capacity of most individuals, but a medical education is so burdensome and expensive that virtually none would undertake it if the position of the M.D. did not carry a reward commensurate with the *sacrifice.*"[2]

So, yes, neoclassicists think education is necessary and time in school (for the gifted) is well spent, but compulsory education conflicts with the neoclassical ideal of maximum freedom and personal choice. If education must be compulsory, then parents should have the right to homeschool their children in order to guarantee the education their children receive reflects their values. Despite Friedman's and other neoclassicists' desire for a common national culture, communities should organize schools to meet local needs and tastes. If most residents find evolution offensive, then a neighborhood school should teach the idea that God created the world in six days as science. Largely in response to a proposal that science education encourage critical thinking skills, the heavily neoclassical Texas Republican Party Platform makes clear their contempt for critical thinking, condemning "The teaching of . . . critical thinking skills and similar programs that . . . have the purpose of challenging the student's fixed beliefs and undermining parental authority."[3]

Neoclassicist logic suggests that something as important as education should not be entrusted to government, especially the federal government. Parents know what they want for their children and state bureaucrats should not impose. Government has no motive to be efficient and can waste money without proving results. Public schools have largely succumbed to the teachers' unions and have let seniority and patronage override merit in determining teacher hiring, promotion, and salaries.

The neoclassical attack on public schools is an effort to turn education over to the private market, which is presumed to be more efficient and will enforce more discipline and offer more job skills than public schools. Teachers, in the eyes of neoclassical thinkers, are veterans of the 1960s and 1970s Left and permissive counterculture, are contemptuous of discipline and of authority, and embrace what they call "child-centered" learning, where students are encouraged to explore on their own and do not necessarily conform to a preset structured curriculum and pedagogy. These permissive teachers do not even arrange students in rows, all focused on the teacher. The Reagan restoration of neoclassicism brought a "back to basics" movement. Schools were to build respect for authority and patriotism, place more emphasis on memorizing facts than independent thinking, and teach basic skills like reading, writing, and arithmetic.

One of the strongest advocates of "back to basics" was Lynne Cheney, wife of former secretary of defense and vice president Richard Cheney, and herself chair of the National Endowment for the Humanities during the Reagan and George H. W. Bush presidencies. Alarmed that multicultural education was undermining patriotism and support for military adventurism, she wrote sarcastically,

As American students learn more about the faults of this country and about the virtues of other nations, . . . they will be less and less likely to think this country deserves their special support. They will not respond to calls to use American force, and thus we will be delivered from the dark days of the early 1990s, when President George Bush was able to unify the nation in support of war against Iraq, and be able to return to the golden days of the late 1960s and early 1970s, when no president was able to build support for Vietnam.[4]

Neoclassicists believe schools, like almost everything else, should be controlled by the market. Customers including parents and local communities should know what they are paying for. Teachers and school administrators are employees and need to be treated as such. They should be carefully scrutinized and tested. If schools are failing, it is not because they are inadequately supported or funded, but because they are not held accountable. "You can't throw money at problems."[5] Although the neoclassical paradigm suggests the federal government should stay out of education, President George W. Bush signed the No Child Left Behind Act[6] (NCLB). Despite NCLB's neoclassical assumptions, it was actually sponsored by a Keynesian liberal, Senator Edward Kennedy, and increases federal supervision of education. Its real purpose is to make sure schools conform to neoclassical values.

NCLB requires that a school's funding be dependent upon pupils' performances on standardized tests. It is almost all stick and no carrot. It does not offer schools additional funding to achieve the goals, but threatens to take funding from those that fail. Teachers are to make sure their students succeed. The child's family, cultural background, and type of neighborhood are not considered factors. Neither is class size. A gifted teacher should be able to succeed with poor children, in schools lacking support staff, textbooks, or other facilities. If they fail, the fault rests with the teacher or school administrator, not the education system. Former superintendent of the Washington, DC, schools, Michelle Rhee, a neoclassicist, insists,

> Poverty presents huge challenges in our schools. But expectations of academic success for a child should never hinge on the circumstances of his or her birth.... Our schools can and should be held accountable for ensuring all students are learning.... Schools can and must be an important part of that by providing educational opportunities to low-income kids that can help break cycles of generational poverty.... We have to give the parents of children stuck in these schools the tools and authority to demand change.... Principals also must be freed from bureaucratic rules that prevent them from hiring and rewarding their own team. Too often, principals in low-income schools are forced to fill their vacancies with teachers excessed from other schools regardless of whether they are a good fit. These teachers may not be performing particularly well but have to be retained by the system because of seniority-based job protections.[7]

Schools should be governed by the market; parents are customers. Ideally, parents who are dissatisfied with their local public school should be able to send their children to a private school or homeschool them, but even the neoclassicists who support this law recognize not all families can afford to do that. Under NCLB, where local public schools are deemed failing, parents will be given vouchers to buy their children education elsewhere. The funding for the local school will be reduced for each student who leaves. This will make it all the more difficult for the school to educate the children of the community and the vouchers will hardly be enough for parents to afford elite private schools.

The idea that schools should be run like for-profit corporations extends from pre-K all the way up to the university. Corporations have clear criteria to determine performance-profit. So schools' performance on standardized tests, job placement of their graduates, and possibly profit need to be tracked. A corporate model inflicts on education the neoclassical econometric assumption that everything relevant can be measured, while goals like creativity, love of learning, and independent thinking may not be quantifiable. For-profit corporations like The Edison Project run 157 "charter schools," without accountability to unions and without protections of teachers' rights. They drain the budgets of community schools by taking the money the town would have paid for each student they enroll. Using Edison's own criteria, their schools actually performed worse than troubled public systems like Cleveland.[8]

As neoclassical assumptions gain popularity, there has been an expansion of for-profit colleges and universities parallel to the growth of charter schools. From 1998 to 2008, enrollment in these schools tripled to 2.4 million students. According to a 2012 report issued by Iowa Democratic Senator Thomas Harkin, "Taxpayers spent $32 billion in the most recent year on companies that operate for-profit colleges, but the majority of students they enroll leave without a degree, half of those within four months."[9]

Harkin charged,

> In this report, you will find overwhelming documentation of exorbitant tuition, aggressive recruiting practices, abysmal student outcomes, taxpayer dollars spent on marketing and pocketed as profit, and regulatory evasion and manipulation.... These practices are not the exception—they are the norm. They are systemic throughout the industry, with very few individual exceptions.[10]

The neoclassical aim is the "corporatization of the university," a matter which has become a major concern among both professors and students. It restructures the university as a for-profit corporation, centering power at the top and stripping faculty and students of a voice. The primary aim is profit rather than learning. Much of the research and classroom funding comes from large corporations, who in turn gain direct or indirect control over content of students and classes. Professors increasingly are hired off tenure track and treated as temporary workers, much like workers in other sectors. Students accumulate overwhelming debt, as discussed later, crippling their lives for years to come. The line between education and the corporate world vanishes.

It appears the neoclassical approach to education has been profitable for corporations and their allies, but not for students, their families, or anyone committed to creating an educated, as opposed to trained, citizenry.

Keynesians

Keynesians agree with neoclassicists that schools are the "great equalizers," which provide the opportunity for success even for children from deprived backgrounds. Although most neo-Marxists would consider Keynesian policies preferable to neoclassical, they question the likelihood that schools can provide equality under capitalism. Therefore as we discuss the Keynesian education policy, we must also expose their weaknesses as seen through neo-Marxist eyes.

The main difference between Keynesian and neoclassical education policy is that Keynesians believe public schools are the best place to build equal opportunity, if for no other reason than that is where most children, especially poor children, can afford to go. When Keynesianism was the dominant paradigm in the 1960s and 1970s, the government created a number of programs to help poorer children, often black, compensate for their disadvantaged background. These included Head Start for preschool, Upward Bound to give a college experience, and Metco, which supposedly bused inner-city students to wealthy suburbs. Frequently, instead of sending inner-city black pupils to prosperous white neighborhoods, they were bused to poor white ghettoes where the schools were not much better than in the black communities. This hardly improved anyone's education, but bred resentment, undermined neighborhood cohesiveness, turned poor whites against poor blacks, and left wealthy whites unaffected. In the Boston area, the practice gave rise to the definition of liberal as someone from Brookline (a wealthy white suburb) who supported busing from Roxbury (a poor black neighborhood) to South Boston (a poor white neighborhood). To resist busing, whites from South Boston in the 1970s formed ROAR (Restore Our Alienated Rights). ROAR's spokesperson, a white, working-class, former congresswoman, Louise Day Hicks charged, "If the suburbs are so interested in solving the problems of the Negro, why don't they build subsidized housing for them?... I have guarded your children well. I will continue to defend the neighborhood school as long as I have a breath left in my body ... a racially imbalanced school is not educationally harmful."[11]

In this period, affirmative action laws were also enacted, but we will talk more about them in Chapter 12 on race.

Affirmative action and other Keynesian education programs were justified under the language of equal opportunity, an effort to create a "level playing field" so that everyone could compete within the capitalist marketplace. Keynesians share the neoclassicist faith in capitalism, but believe public education should compensate if some people are born with disadvantages. Education is necessary to qualify everyone for better jobs, but capitalist competition, even under the best educational circumstances, produces losers as well as winners, something Keynesians view as part of the efficient outcome of the market system.

Neo-Marxists point out that even if everyone is highly educated, gifted, talented, ambitious, and hardworking, the capitalist marketplace creates only a limited number of high-paying, fulfilling positions. More educated people simply means some will be left frustrated, angry, and feeling entitled to something they were denied. Education is not going to help people who qualify for careers that do not exist. The root of the problem, neo-Marxists point out, is something much deeper, the capitalist economy itself. Declaring education the elixir makes it responsible for something it cannot solve, which only breeds hostility toward the education system and deflects anger away from the real cause. Capitalism will be unchallenged and education will be scapegoated.

In America, public education is controlled and paid for by the local community. This is something neoclassicists applaud and Keynesians seldom challenge. However, rich communities obviously can spend more on schools than poorer ones. The neoclassical claim that you can't spend your way into success is completely unfounded. Neoclassical market logic says rich parents will only send their children to expensive private schools if they expect a better return. For those who attend public schools, the wealthier your neighborhood, the better your schools. This completely undermines the Keynesian claim that public schools will be equalizers. The opposite is true. Locally funded public schools reinforce existing inequality.

In the mid-twentieth century, when Keynesianism was the dominant economic ideology, America was also the unqualified world economic power. It could afford experiments, like "progressive" and "child-centered" education that might lead to joy in learning and self-fulfillment rather than vocational "success." Education did not have to be defined as equal job training—creating a labor force that meets the needs of corporate employers. In fact, Keynesian logic sees consumption for consumption's sake as inherent economic benefit. Education is a good luxury to consume, just like anything else. Although

President Lyndon Johnson saw education as part of the cure for poverty, when he proposed his Great Society, he spoke of education as more than job training but a way to unlock creativity and imagination. In contrast to neo-classicists, he pleaded that teachers and schools must be given the resources needed to cultivate their students.

> A place to build the Great Society is in the classrooms of America. There your children's lives will be shaped. Our society will not be great until every young mind is set free to scan the farthest reaches of thought and imagination. We are still far from that goal.... Nearly 54 million—more than one-quarter of all America—have not even finished high school.... In many places, classrooms are overcrowded and curricula are outdated. Most of our qualified teachers are underpaid.... So we must give every child a place to sit and a teacher to learn from. Poverty must not be a bar to learning, and learning must offer an escape from poverty.... It means preparing youth to enjoy their hours of leisure as well as their hours of labor. It means exploring new techniques of teaching, to find new ways to stimulate the love of learning and the capacity for creation.[12]

Some Keynesians, like Robert Reich, former Clinton labor secretary, praise critical thinking, what he called "the symbolic-analytic mind," for training the American workforce for an emerging labor market.

> The student is taught to get behind the data—to ask why certain facts have been selected, why they have been assumed to be important, how they were deduced, and how they might be contradicted. The student learns to examine reality from many angles, in different lights, and thus to visualize new possibilities and choices. The symbolic-analytic mind is trained to be skeptical, curious and creative.[13]

Reich acknowledged that only 20 percent of jobs really required symbolic-analytic skills. Although he recognizes that corporations have few qualms about exporting jobs, he hardly seriously considers the possibility, raised by neo-Marxists, that capitalist employers do not want most workers to be independent thinkers. His underlying assumption appears to be that if people are prepared for more fulfilling careers, the jobs will emerge. However, as other countries develop people with symbolic-analytic skills, corporations will gravitate to where wages are low and regulations are minimal. When Reich became secretary of labor, under Clinton, little was done to reverse the neoclassicism of the previous presidencies.

The Reagan restoration of neoclassicism took place as America entered its relative economic decline, essentially undermining the Keynesian approach to education despite its intent to strengthen the capitalist system. The Reagan neoclassicists created new demands for austerity—which the Keynesians could not prevent—to make sure the government or the ordinary citizen did not compete with the corporate elite. Progressive and child-centered education came under attack for wasting money on "luxuries" like art and music. Governments reduced support for higher education. In some states, the government went from paying 80 percent of the cost of public colleges and universities to 20 percent.[14] From 1980 to 2011, student tuition and fees have risen by 247 percent at flagship state universities.[15] Students have to borrow more and more money to pay for their education. Eventually, total student debt exceeded credit card debt.[16] The burden this imposes could impede students and their families from accruing the financial benefits of higher education and slow the overall economy.

> Total student debt outstanding appears to have surpassed $1 trillion late last year.... But as more people go to college and assume bigger loans for education, they may take longer than previous generations to hit key milestones such as buying a house or getting married.... Student debt could ultimately slow the recovery.... Student debt is a burden not just for recent college graduates in their 20s but also parents, who often co-sign their children's student loans.[17]

Student debt has become a deadly noose around the neck of the younger generation. The average student graduates college with about $25,000 in debt in 2013, facing a difficult, low-wage job market that makes debt repayment extremely difficult. Keynesians want to help through government aid, but (1) their proposals for debt relief are too modest to help middle- and low-income students, and (2) they lack the political power to get their proposals enacted by Congress.

Under these circumstances, fewer students can afford to major in the liberal arts and are forced to instead choose majors with direct career objectives. More students might aspire toward such careers, but as the job market declines, fewer graduates will achieve them. This will be all the more true as corporations increasingly outsource or export jobs to countries with lower wages like India. It is not only factory jobs that are outsourced, but also specialized professional careers, which require advanced education, like computer programming. Reich seems to think that improved education may reverse the trend.

> America isn't educating enough of our people well enough to get American-based companies to do more of their high-value added work here.... Our K–12 school system isn't nearly up to what it should be. American students

continue to do poorly in math and science relative to students in other advanced countries. Japan, Germany, South Korea, Canada, Australia, Ireland, Sweden, and France all top us. American universities continue to rank high but many are being starved of government funds and are having trouble keeping up. More and more young Americans and their families can't afford a college education. China, by contrast, is investing like mad in world-class universities and research centers.... The way we get good jobs back is with a national strategy to make Americans more competitive— retooling our schools, getting more of our young people through college or giving them a first-class technical education.[18]

However, Reich also quotes an Apple executive: "We don't have an obligation to solve America's problems. Our only obligation is making the best product possible." He might have added "and showing profits big enough to continually increase our share price."[19]

If that is the attitude of the corporate elite, as Reich admits, where is the evidence that a more educated labor force, which will have to be more highly paid, will attract jobs, industry, and investment back into the United States?

Rather than resisting the assault on public education, many Keynesian politicians accepted neoclassical logic and went along with it. As we saw, Edward Kennedy cosponsored No Child Left Behind. Public schools had to be held accountable and judged by the criteria of producing a labor force for the corporations. There has been an international "race to the bottom" competition among countries to see who could have the lowest wages; the worst environmental, occupational, health, and safety standards; and the least regulations, in order to attract corporate investment. In the midst of it, President Obama adopted the language of a "race to the top." He praised his own administration for starting what he described as "a competition that convinced almost every state to develop smarter curricula and higher standards, for about 1 percent of what we spend on education each year."[20]

Obama may have been moving away from neoclassicism and embracing Keynesian educational programs like publicly funded preschools. However, he was not calling for using resources to build love of learning, creativity, or independent critical thinking. Rather, he wanted schools that would "better equip graduates for the demands of a high-tech economy" and provide "the skills today's employers are looking for to fill jobs right now and in the future."[21]

But Obama's Keynesianism runs up against the same internal limitations within capitalism as does Reich's. Even if Americans have the skills employers want, corporations may still choose to move where they can find professionals with the same skills who are willing to work for lower pay under less regulation. Furthermore, the future is not predictable and people educated for independent thinking can more easily adapt to changing conditions than those technically trained for specific jobs.

Obama's new Keynesianism was infested with neoclassicism. He still expected families to bear much of the cost of education and his promised offer was to use federal resources to help them make more informed choices within the capitalist marketplace: "My Administration will release a new College Scorecard that parents and students can use to compare schools based on a simple criteria: where you can get the most bang for your educational buck."[22]

He certainly expected most families to interpret "the most bang" as direct training for a specific career. Keynesian educational policies may be preferable to neoclassical, but they still fail to address the fundamental issue: schools are constrained by having to operate within the limits of the capitalist system. They are seen as offering training for corporate jobs rather than critical thinking for an empowered citizenry. Inevitably, as students fail, the result will be what we summarized earlier: capitalism will go unchallenged and public schools will be scapegoated.

Neo-Marxists

Neo-Marxists do not believe schools are the "great equalizers"; rather they are the "great dividers." Ironically, many neo-Marxists share some of the neoclassical analysis of the public school system, although they reach different conclusions and have profoundly different values. Marxist economists Samuel Bowles and Herbert Gintis agree with Milton Friedman's history that the public schools were established during the industrial revolution to build a common American culture among peoples with very different backgrounds, values, and traditions.[23] Former black slaves and immigrants from Southern and Eastern Europe and later, Latin America, Asia, and Africa had to be taught patriotism and capitalist values. Bowles and Gintis quoted John Dewey, one of the founders of the modern universal school system: "The intermingling in the school of youth of different races, different religions, and unlike customs creates for all a new and broader environment. Common subject matter accustoms all to a new unity of outlook upon a broader horizon than is visible to members of any group while it is isolated."[24]

Robber Barons in the late-nineteenth-century Gilded Age, like Andrew Carnegie, were heavily involved in creating the public school system. Neo-Marxists part company with neoclassicists because neo-Marxists do not believe schools are really designed to benefit children and communities. They believe their real purpose is to build a labor force for the corporations and cannon fodder for the military.

Despite the "child-centered" and "progressive" education movements, most children, especially children from poorer urban and rural communities, perceive schools as an alienating experience. Under the Reagan neoclassical "back to basics" movement, schools seldom bred love of learning, but instead made learning something students wanted to avoid. As we saw, neoclassicism justifies class stratification on the grounds that staying in school is a sacrifice. Knowing the attitude children typically develop, Bill Cosby, who holds a PhD in education, began his Saturday morning kiddie cartoon show, *Fat Albert*, with the ironic warning, "If you're not careful, you might just learn something."

Schools in capitalist society, as neo-Marxists see them, usually teach that learning is work, not play. It is not a mode of exploration or creative self-expression. Students are not rewarded for being curious or involved; they should be passive and disciplined, often even silent, while sitting in regimented classrooms. They are expected to memorize established isolated facts by rote, without necessarily thinking about what they mean and almost never questioning their validity. They will copy the facts into workbooks or spit them back as short answers on tests for grades. Grades teach that students must compete with one another to win the approval of the teacher, representing authority and that the purpose of learning is to earn an external reward. It is not something valuable in its own right. This is effective training for jobs where you work for a paycheck, with almost no expectation of personal satisfaction or fulfillment. As Bowles and Gintis observed,

> The structure of social relations in education not only inures the student to the discipline of the workplace, but develops the types of personal demeanor, modes of self-presentation, self-image, and social class identifications which are the crucial ingredients of job adequacy. Specifically, the social relationships of education—the relationships between administrators and teachers, teachers and students, students and students, and students and their work—replicate the hierarchical divisions of labor. Hierarchical relations are reflected in the vertical authority lines from administrators to teachers to students. Alienated labor is reflected in the student's lack of control over his or her education, the alienation of the student from the curriculum content, and the motivation of school work through a system of grades and other external rewards rather than the student's integration with either the process (learning) or the outcome (knowledge) of the educational "production process." Fragmentation in work is reflected in the institutionalized and often destructive competition among students through continual and ostensibly meritocratic ranking and evaluation.[25]

From a capitalist point of view, schools like these are not failures but successes. Their purpose is not to develop students as people, but to transform them into potential employees and tools for profit, as assembly line workers, McDonald's fry girls, and Wal-Mart cashiers. These schools produce a complacent, obedient, controllable labor force, who will accept their fate and not interfere with decisions made by authorities.

The military, a major recruiter from public high schools, is, from a neo-Marxist perspective, a powerful force, along with corporations, in shaping education. The military needs blind obedience even more than the civilian workforce, and indeed, the No Child Left Behind Act considers high schools that send their graduates to the army to be as successful as those that send them to college. It requires schools that receive federal funds to actively assist the military in recruiting students.

> The new NCLBA military recruitment provisions require high schools that receive federal funds to meet two requirements. First, such schools must "provide, on a request made by military recruiters . . . , access to secondary school students' names, addresses, and telephone listings," and second, schools must "provide military recruiters the same access to secondary school students as is provided generally to post secondary educational institutions or to prospective employers of those students." Schools that fail to comply with either of these two requirements—access to student information or equal access to students themselves—risk losing federal funds.[26]

One of the best Marxist sociologists of education is British scholar Paul Willis, who sees that corporations and the military converge to subvert education as an engaging, creative, and empowering experience, especially for working-class kids. Willis has proposed that working-class youth rebel against the alienation, boredom, and tedium of school, but ironically, it is a rebellion that serves the very authorities against whom it is fought. With their intellectual interests destroyed, working-class youth compete against each other to show their indifference to school and to be "cool," often by becoming sports heroes, sometimes aggressive or even violent. They will strive for sex partners, alcohol, drugs, clothes, and cars that they cannot afford. To pay for these desires, they will take jobs at gas stations, McDonald's, and Dunkin' Donuts. The time and energy this absorbs makes their failure at school all the more severe. Many drop out of school altogether, but even if they graduate, they are trapped in low-level jobs, like the ones they held in high school, if they are able to find work at all. Those working at the worst jobs are told they are lucky and they better not do anything to risk them. Romancing violence and aggression, many working-class youth consider joining the army to be the coolest thing they can do. Maybe they can come back as war heroes. Their rebellion does not become an organized movement that threatens the authorities, but rather becomes a culture that the rich and powerful can manipulate to their benefit. It results in compliant workers and soldiers. Here are aspects Willis attributed to male working-class high school culture, drawing on his fieldwork in British schools.

> Many of their own mental activities and feelings are expressed and acted through the cultural, the stylish and the concrete ... what they take as mental work becomes for "the lads" mere "pen-pushing," "not really doing things" and most importantly, "cissy": it is not basically man's work or within the manly scope of action. We see at least why the "ear'oles" are likely to be regarded as effeminate and passive cissies.... Despite their greater achievement and conventional hopes for the future, "ear'oles" and their strategies can be ignored because the *mode* of their success can be discredited as passive, mental and lacking a robust masculinity.[27]

Neo-Marxists argue that, as adults, those who failed in school can suffer from a "hidden injury of class."[28] They see the college graduates, whom they had looked down upon as brownnosers or nerds, as successes, some of whom could now be their bosses, and come to believe they deserve their fate. The myth of equal opportunity, of schools as "great equalizers," says they had their chance but they blew it. Capitalist ideology teaches that if you fail, you ain't got nobody to blame but yourself. The successful had the stamina to endure boring, tedious, alienating schools, and they deserve to be where they are. Sociologists Richard Sennett and Jonathan Cobb described the deference that men who did not "make it" in school have toward the educated after they grow up:

> "Well, they're educated people, they must know what they are doing ... maybe there are things about this I don't know." ... The people in Washington must know something we don't know, and therefore they have some right to do what they are doing, even though from what we see it makes no sense.... The "higher knowledge" of those in power creates at once mystification of power and its legitimacy. The apportionment of mind and knowledge represents the divide between those who judge and those who are on the receiving end of judgment.[29]

What the failed students may not realize is that the "successful" students went to entirely different types of schools. Their schools may have been more progressive or child-centered. Bowles and Gintis imply that schools, as most neo-Marxists believe, are not equalizers, but dividers. Neo-Marxists are showing that there may really be two school systems. This is something that even Keynesians like Reich acknowledge, although he does not see it as intentional.

Capitalism may need docile obedient workers, but it also needs innovators and managers, those whom Reich calls symbolic-analytic workers. For corporations to compete and profit, they need scientists and engineers to discover and create. Corporations and governments are huge bureaucracies. They need middle managers, people schooled in psychology who can elicit worker cooperation, as well as social planners who can assuage discontent and control the general population. Unlike inner-city and rural public schools, private schools and public schools in wealthy suburbs are more likely to encourage creativity and critical thinking. Rather than punish students who challenge teachers, they may reward them. Students may feel their opinions are valued. These schools were given budgets high enough to educate their graduates as leaders rather than followers. Bowles and Gintis suggested the two school systems serve very different purposes.

> Schools do different things for different children. Boys and girls, blacks and whites, rich and poor are treated differently. Affluent suburban schools, working-class schools, and ghetto schools all exhibit a distinctive pattern of sanctions and rewards.... Colleges are different; and community colleges exhibit social relations of education which differ sharply from those of elite four-year institutions. In short, US education is not a monolithic.... [Some schools] provide the child with the freedom to develop "naturally" with a teacher as guide, not taskmaster. Intrinsic interest ... was to motivate all work ... and the aim was to sublimate natural creative drives in fruitful directions rather than to repress them.[30]

The back to basics movement was largely a reaction against the second type of school, the ones that fostered love of learning and creativity, being too successful. Students allowed to think independently came to believe that much of what they were taught was a myth and turned against the capitalist class, the state, and the military. In the 1960s and 1970s, many concluded that their country was not the world's beacon of freedom and democracy but a capitalist empire intent on global domination. From a capitalist point of view, so many students were being educated for critical thinking that they posed a threat. As a result, students growing up under the Reagan neoclassical restoration had reduced educational resources and were trained to think of school as something with little purpose other than a path to a job. This made, ironically, the probability that the American capitalist economy would stagnate all the greater.

Unlike Keynesians or neoclassicists, neo-Marxists do not believe the problems within schools are the result of misdirected good intentions. The problem is grounded in the fundamental purpose of schools: the maintenance and reproduction of the capitalist labor force. As long as capitalism exists, this problem cannot be solved. Marxist sociologist Stanley Aronowitz has little faith in schools.

> Contrary to the belief that schools were either actually or potentially forces for democratic ends, these institutions were established from the very beginning to achieve the opposite. Schools ... were assigned by capital the task of reproducing labor power for an industrial order whose jobs were organized hierarchically. There was no chance that schools could become democratic vistas, because they were structurally incapable of such outcomes.... Certain schools produced managers; others technicians or professionals.... [In others] the curriculum, the authority relations, and the life in the classroom all conspired to persuade the working class and the poor that, with few exceptions, their destiny was to remain at the bottom.[31]

Many neo-Marxists would like to see teachers go into the schools, build love of learning, encourage creative critical thinking, and expose "patriotic" capitalist myths. However, they recognize teachers like that can expect short careers. To survive and transform schools and the larger society, they must strive to build support in the community, with no guarantee of success. But many teachers are now dropping out because they cannot stand the testing, the assault on their independence, and what they must do to serve the corporation and the state. Such teachers have little to lose.

CHAPTER 12

Race

Almost everyone knows these words by Martin Luther King:

> Now is the time to open the doors of opportunity to all of God's children.... I have a dream that one day on the red hills of Georgia the sons of former slaves and the sons of former slave owners will be able to sit down together at a table of brotherhood.... I have a dream that my four children will one day live in a nation where they will not be judged by the color of their skin but by the content of their character.[1]

This sounds like an appeal for everyone, black and white, to have an equal opportunity to aspire to the American Dream. Everyone will be judged, hopefully fairly, but there is no expectation that equal opportunity will result in equal outcome. This is language you might expect from an American hero, honored with a holiday in his name.

But how familiar are these words?

> I knew that America would never invest the necessary funds or energies in rehabilitation of its poor so long as adventures like Vietnam continued to draw men and skills and money like some demonic destructive suction tube.... I knew that I could never again raise my voice against the violence of the oppressed in the ghettos without having first spoken clearly to the greatest purveyor of violence in the world today—my own government.... The war in Vietnam is but a symptom of a far deeper malady within the American spirit.... When machines and computers, profit motives and property rights, are considered more important than people, the giant triplets of racism, extreme materialism, and militarism are incapable of being conquered.... This has driven many to feel that only Marxism has a revolutionary spirit. Therefore, communism is a judgment against our failure to make democracy real.[2]

Rather than embracing American capitalism here, King was suggesting it is so intertwined with racial oppression that its total transformation is a prerequisite for ending racism. As long as America remains a capitalist militaristic empire, intent on world domination, it cannot solve the problems of its own people. Although King does not identify himself as a Marxist, he acknowledges its appeal. These hardly sound like the words of an American hero. Around the time King made this speech, he was linking resistance to racial discrimination to the need to transform American foreign policy, and the struggle to end poverty and class differences. He was assassinated as he expanded the fight for racial justice to a critique of American society at its core.

Before we discuss our three paradigms' treatments of racial differences, we must compare two concepts: class and caste. Marx technically defined class as a group with a shared relationship to the means of production, but we can think of it as a group with a shared level of wealth and power. Throughout life, it is possible to rise or fall in class. You can become richer or poorer, more or less powerful. In capitalism, there are at least two classes: a ruling class that controls most wealth and power, and everyone else. The Occupy movement referred to them as the 1 percent and the 99 percent.

Caste is a status, such as gender or race, you are born with and will virtually never change. And capitalism prides itself with reducing caste inequality. Even Marx gave it credit for doing that. However, class differences have, if anything, grown more intense. It is possible to be at the top of the class hierarchy but have low caste status. President Obama may be president, but he is still black. His friend, Henry Louis Gates, may be a millionaire Harvard professor, but he can still be arrested for his skin color in liberal Cambridge, Massachusetts.[3]

All three of our paradigms consider racial inequality to be something to overcome. Except for some neoclassicists, most recognize that in America, slavery and Southern segregation carry strong residues that affect life today. However, they dispute whether capitalism is a cause or a solution, and what, if anything, the state should do about it.

Neoclassicists

In the late-nineteenth-century age of the Robber Barons, some neoclassicist sociologists, like William Graham Sumner,[4] believed that racial inequality stemmed from innate biological differences. Later neoclassicists, like Jensen,[5] Herrnstein, and Murray[6] share this assumption. However, while most recent neoclassicists highlight that biology makes some people smarter, more ambitious, and talented, they accept that smart industrious people, as well as stupid lazy people, can be found in all races. If racial discrimination were eliminated, as most neoclassicists believe capitalism has done, people can rise or fall as their drive and ability permit.

While neoclassicists applaud capitalism for reducing caste inequality, they do not see class inequality as a problem. Class inequality is as natural as the law of gravity. It is something to embrace, not overcome. Trying to overcome it defies nature and is self-defeating, if not disastrous. The hope that individuals can rise in class is the primary motivator for almost all progress and growth. Society must reward the creative and ambitious with upper-class status and punish the lazy and parasitical. Among capitalism's great achievements was breaking caste barriers so people could rise or fall to their natural potential. The more purely capitalist a society is, the fewer caste obstacles it will have, but class differences will persist and they will be based on merit.

When the Civil War ended slavery, it eliminated a noncapitalist race distinction and allowed blacks to freely enter the labor market. Southern leaders instituted segregation in the hope of restoring a precapitalist barrier. The civil rights drive for integration was largely an attempt to guarantee blacks the opportunity to compete with whites under capitalism, a right supposedly won in the Civil War, but not really granted. Milton Friedman offered this history lesson:

> The Southern States after the Civil War took many measures to impose legal restrictions on Negroes. One measure which was never taken on any scale was the establishment of barriers to the ownership of either real or personal property. The failure to impose such barriers clearly did not reflect any special concern to avoid restrictions on Negroes. It reflected rather, a basic belief in private property which was so strong that it overrode the desire to discriminate against Negroes. The maintenance of the general rules of private property and of capitalism have been a major source of opportunity for Negros and have permitted them to make greater progress than they otherwise could have made.[7]

In a pure capitalism, all positions are rewarded on merit. Neoclassicists believe that a free market will eliminate racial discrimination, although it will not end class distinctions, nor should it. Interfering with the market by government, or anyone else, reduces efficiency, growth, and the opportunity for advancement.

Neoclassicists see liberal, Keynesian affirmative action by government to be as harmful to blacks as Southern laws designed to keep them in their place. Beginning with President Johnson, Great Society antipoverty programs provided welfare, dole for single mothers, food stamps, housing subsidies, free or subsidized medical care, and special education. In some cases, it was possible for "welfare queens" (a term President Reagan[8] used) to live better than people working at low-paying jobs. This provides just enough comfort to wallow, to not work and not strive to uplift yourself by your bootstraps. Keynesian attempts to eliminate black poverty end up reinforcing it, maybe even intensifying it. They breed a false sense of entitlement, that the world owes you as a compensation for your color, for the suffering your ancestors endured, whether or not you experienced anything vaguely comparable.

Neoclassical former Speaker of the House and presidential candidate Newt Gingrich virtually attributes welfare with undermining civilization. It destroys initiative and encourages the poor, largely black, to forfeit their independence and submit to arbitrary federal bureaucratic regulations. It undermines families and communities and breeds crime, violence, and child abuse.

> It is impossible to maintain civilization with 12-year-olds having babies, 15-year-olds killing each other, 17-year-olds dying of AIDS, and 18-year-olds getting diplomas they can't even read. Yet that is precisely where three generations of Washington-dominated, centralized-government, welfare-state policies have carried us....[9] Look at what the welfare state does. The welfare state reduces citizens to clients, subordinates them to bureaucrats, and subjects them to rules that are anti-work, anti-family, anti-opportunity, and anti-property.[10]

Welfare bureaucrats tell blacks they do not have to work as hard to compete with whites; benefits will come to you by virtue of your skin color. Black neoclassical economist Thomas Sowell claimed to find this attitude among black college students: "A study of black colleges in the United States similarly noted that even students planning post-graduate study often showed no sense of urgency about needing to be prepared 'because they believed that certain rules would simply be set aside for them.'"[11]

Sowell and other neoclassicists find affirmative action particularly troubling. It assumes certain groups like blacks are entitled to special consideration when applying for jobs or admissions to schools and other programs as a way of minimizing the impact of historical oppression. Affirmative action programs include a variety of policies. Among them are (1) requiring that if two applicants are equally qualified, the one from the preferred caste will be chosen, (2) quotas setting aside a number of positions for members of the preferred caste, (3) designating membership in a preferred caste as a special qualification, and (4) active recruitment of members of a preferred caste. To Sowell, affirmative action violates the laws of the free market. It substitutes caste membership for merit and does not permit equal open competition without considering caste. It can prevent the most qualified from winning and degrades the quality of society's leaders. It creates reverse racism or reverse discrimination and holds some people responsible for events that occurred long before they were born or rewards others for oppression they never personally experienced. No living white can do anything about slavery, but through affirmative action they are forced to pay for it and are denied opportunities they may deserve. Sowell questioned the moral justification for this: "Given the mortality of human beings, often the only compensation for historic wrongs is ... taking from individuals who inflicted no harm and giving to individuals who suffered none."[12]

Sowell is convinced that affirmative action benefits already relatively privileged blacks and hurts those who are most needy. Ironically, many neo-Marxists agree with him, as we shall see. Sowell continued,

> The less fortunate members of a preferred group may actually retrogress while the more fortunate advance under preferential policies. After "affirmative-action" policies took hold in the early 1970s, blacks with little education and little job experience fell further behind the general population—and indeed further behind whites with little education and little job experience.... The factual reality [is] that actual benefits from compensatory preferences tend to be concentrated in the already more fortunate elites among the preferred groups.[13]

Sowell has one concern that neo-Marxists do not share. Most desirable jobs blacks received were in government, not the private sector.[14] As a neoclassicist, Sowell does not believe that government can do anything as well as private industry. If affirmative action's success occurs within the state, it does not count. The private sector is the creator of all wealth and value. Sowell shares the neoclassical dogma that private industry will solve problems government cannot, but there is little evidence for that. The closing of auto and steel factories, which paid $40 or $50 an hour in 2013 dollars—once for many blacks, the entry to the middle class—suggests otherwise.

Sowell may profess more sympathy for the poor than many other neoclassicists, but resolving the plight of blacks and other racial minorities requires attention to class as well as caste. Since neoclassicists refuse to acknowledge the possibility of class inequality that is not based on merit, class differences can never be a problem. Because neoclassicists want to keep major class differences, many of which can be traced as far back as slavery, they can never end racial oppression.

Keynesians

In discussing the neoclassical treatment of race, we were forced to summarize much of the Keynesian position. Keynesians are much more accepting of state intervention than neoclassicists and are more willing to recognize poverty and class inequality as problems. They acknowledge race is a continuing major barrier to equal opportunity and a barrier that reinforces class inequality. The Keynesian commitment to capitalism rests in large part on the view that it is a system for ensuring equal opportunity—for everyone of all races.

Keynesians believe that the private market does not have the power to overcome racism alone. It needs the support, and possibly the pressure, of the state. Antidiscrimination laws, affirmative action, social services, antipoverty programs, and welfare are all necessary to achieve racial equality—and they are all important Keynesian tools for dealing with racial discrimination (and also overcoming economic downturns and ensuring human capital for long-term growth). This has been enshrined in Keynesian values since Eleanor Roosevelt, the widow of the first Keynesian president Franklin Roosevelt, wrote the UN Declaration of Universal Human Rights. In the second article, it proclaims racism a violation, one implicitly linked to class differences:

Article 2

Everyone is entitled to all the rights and freedoms set forth in this Declaration, without distinction of any kind, such as race, color....

Subsequent articles treat certain protections as fundamental rights, while neoclassicists regard these, at best, as privileges, which must be earned:

Article 23

(1) Everyone has the right to work, to free choice of employment, to just and favorable conditions of work and to protection against unemployment.

(2) Everyone, without any discrimination, has the right to equal pay for equal work....

Article 25.2

(1) Everyone has the right to a standard of living adequate for the health and well-being of himself and of his family, including food, clothing, housing and medical care and necessary social services.

Keynesians would insist that if the private sector fails to ensure these rights, the government must. When campaigning for president, Barack Obama rejected the neoclassical attitudes that each individual is responsible primarily for himself, that there are few collective social responsibilities, and that poverty is a result of individual failure. You cannot expect anyone to lift themselves out of poverty without resources.

> That's the promise of America, the idea that we are responsible for ourselves, but that we also rise or fall as one nation, the fundamental belief that I am my brother's keeper, I am my sister's keeper.... Out of work? Tough luck, you're on your own. No health care? The market will fix it. You're on your own. Born into poverty? Pull yourself up by your own bootstraps, even if you don't have boots. You are on your own.[15]

As a candidate, Obama decried a history of caste and racial barriers that had prevented blacks from receiving the opportunity that capitalism promised. He implied blacks are victims of forces beyond their control and might need Keynesian government policies to help them compensate for historical oppression.

> So many of the disparities that exist in the African American community today can be directly traced to inequalities passed on from an earlier generation that suffered under the brutal legacy of slavery and Jim Crow.... Segregated schools were, and are, inferior schools; we still haven't fixed them.... The inferior education they provided, then and now, helps explain the pervasive achievement gap between today's black and white students.... Legalized discrimination—where blacks were prevented, often through violence, from owning property, or loans were not granted to African American business owners ... meant that black families could not amass any meaningful wealth to bequeath to future generations. That history helps explain the wealth and income gap between black and white, and the concentrated pockets of poverty that persists in so many of today's urban and rural communities.... A lack of economic opportunity among black men, and the shame and frustration that came from not being able to provide for one's family, contributed to the erosion of black families—a problem that welfare policies for many years may have worsened.[16]

Obama was talking like a Keynesian. As a Keynesian, he shares with neoclassicists the faith that capitalism provides the tools for individual advancement and achievement. American capitalism is the path out of poverty and depression, even for its historic victims.

What's remarkable is not how many failed in the face of discrimination, but ... how many were able to make a way out of no way for those like me who would come after them.... But for all those who scratched and clawed their way to get a piece of the American Dream, there were many who didn't make it.... Even for those blacks who did make it, questions of race, and racism, continue to define their worldview in fundamental ways.... They must always believe that they can write their own destiny.... Not just with words, but with deeds ... by providing this generation with ladders of opportunity that were unavailable for previous generations.[17]

Once in the White House, Obama has done little to uplift the lower class, whether black, white, or any other race. Most of the benefits of his stimulus package have accrued to banks and other corporations. Neoclassicism has become so pervasive that even contemporary Keynesian presidents cannot escape its power. As we have seen, earlier Keynesian presidents like Lyndon Johnson made it the responsibility of the federal government to end poverty and racism. At the time, the amounts he spent for this goal seemed massive. The agency overseeing the Great Society's War on Poverty was called the Office of Economic Opportunity. This implies a goal of giving people who start at the bottom, largely because of their race, a chance to compete and rise. However, in a hierarchical society with class distinctions, there can only be so many slots at the top. Some can start poor and become richer, but others must remain poor. People at the bottom can be black or white. A few blacks, usually already the wealthiest and most educated, can advance, but most will be left behind. Black sociologist William Julius Wilson suggested,

> The removal of racial barriers creates the greatest opportunities for the more trained and educated minority members. People develop resources because of the advantages associated with family background and the resources that the parents passed on to the children, financial means, family stability, and peer groups, so on. All of these things place more advantaged minorities in a position where they can compete with other individuals of society when racial barriers are removed.[18]

Underlying the programs was the assumption that poverty, especially black poverty, was not just a caste problem, but an individual problem, which could be cured largely through job training. However, as we saw in Chapter 11 on education, little can be accomplished by training for jobs that do not exist. Until the 1970s, there were many high-paying manufacturing jobs that only required a high school diploma—no need for advanced education. Their disappearance aborted the growing black middle class. Changes in the economy will have more impact on poverty for people of any race than Keynesian antipoverty programs that help people compete for a limited number of existing jobs rather than increase the total size of the job market. Wilson again said it well.

> The internationalization of economic activity had combined to decrease the demand for low-skilled workers. Therefore, the gap between low-scale and higher scale workers is widening. Because of historic racism, there are a disproportionate number of blacks in the low-scale, poorly educated category, and they are falling further and further behind.
>
> Trained and educated blacks are benefiting from changes in the economy in the same way the trained and educated whites are benefiting. You see it in many ways: take a look at black income today. If you divide black income into quintiles, the top quintile has now secured almost 50 percent of the total black income, which is a record. The top quintile in the white population has secured about 44 percent of the white income, which is also a record.[19]

The Keynesian Great Society endorsed the civil rights movement goal of ending segregated housing, hotels, and restaurants. Blacks were now free to go or eat anywhere they could afford, even in formerly restricted all-white neighborhoods and accommodations, but very few could afford million-dollar mansions or thousand-dollar-a-night hotel suites. What this really did was eliminate a caste barrier to consumption within the capitalist marketplace. Richer blacks were now free to leave the ghettos and move to wealthy white neighborhoods.

We do not want to suggest people of any race should not have the right to live wherever they want. As long as racial caste barriers existed, blacks of any class were deprived of their full rights. The Keynesian Great Society was certainly concerned with class differences and poverty, but there was an underlying assumption that if caste barriers were lifted, economic opportunity would follow. However, as Sowell implied, affirmative action and other Keynesian Great Society remedies had a contradictory impact, unintentionally serving some blacks at the expense of others. William Julius Wilson points out that the upward mobility of privileged blacks, facilitated by affirmative action and capitalist markets, deprived inner-city black communities of their educated members, professionals, entrepreneurs, and civic leaders[20]—what Du Bois had called the "talented tenth," whom Du Bois assumed were essential to uplift the black race.[21] As the talented tenth moved to formerly all-white neighborhoods, many black youth would seldom encounter positive role models on a daily basis. There were more black males of college age in jail than in college.[22] The ghettos became abandoned enclaves, with boarded up buildings, homelessness, crime, and drug addiction. The black population became all the more polarized with a growing middle class and even an upper class, but also an ever-expanding underclass. The different black classes no longer lived together, and the majority of blacks saw their income decline, in the context of Keynesian affirmative action laws that did not address class issues undermining the poor of all races.

Keynesian liberal politicians tended to endorse the aspects of the civil rights movement that called for abolishing caste differences—a goal entirely consistent with capitalism. Although some Keynesian politicians may want to eliminate poverty and can be very critical of the corporate elite, they do not question the core assumptions of capitalism. Keynesian economist and former secretary of labor Robert Reich seems to think class and caste differences can be rectified through education, but capitalism is fundamentally about maintaining class differences. Reich rightfully points out the corporations do not want to spend on education and are willing to export jobs, but there is a conclusion he does not draw. If jobs are not created, educating more people to qualify for them is not going to end poverty. A capitalist society whose very existence is premised on class inequality is not going to end class inequality. Eliminating caste and racial barriers for entering a higher class is going to leave large numbers at the bottom. As Reich observed,

> Over the long term, the only way we're going to raise wages, grow the economy and improve American competitiveness is by investing in our people—especially their educations. . . . Yet we're falling behind. Why have we allowed this to happen? . . . Maybe the answer is that America's biggest corporations don't especially care. They're getting the talent they need all over the world. Many of them now have research and development operations in Europe and China, for example. . . . When big corporations and the wealthy demand tax cuts, and don't particularly care about public education, the inevitable result is that most of America's kids are vulnerable.[23]

There is another problem that some Keynesians may recognize but not easily solve. Class boundaries are hard to determine and then resolve by writing legislation reflecting them. Caste categories seem black and white, literally. In fact, though, as the mixed race population grows, race itself becomes a more ambiguous distinction. Class definitions are more arbitrary. It is harder to draw the lines. How much more wealth or income do you need in order to be placed in one class or another? Accordingly, fair employment, fair housing, antidiscrimination, and affirmative action laws tended to emphasize caste instead of class. On an application for a job or college, you can check off black, but not poor. As we have seen, most benefits of these policies have gone to the already wealthy, educated, and privileged.

Racial discrimination can end, and by many standards, it has, but the majority can be left poorer. There is a black upper class, even a black president, but also a huge underclass. Many civil rights leaders, including Martin Luther King, recognized this dilemma. Problems that can be solved within a capitalist framework are likely to be, but issues that require challenging capitalism will often be neglected. Arguably, the side of the civil rights movement that emphasized caste ended in victory, but the side that focused on poverty and class has made little headway. The net result may be that the average black is worse off, not better.

Black poverty is at least as much a consequence of class as caste. Class distinctions are at the core of capitalism. Because Keynesians accept capitalism, they cannot develop adequate strategies to end class inequality and may end up making the problem even worse.

Capitalism is not going to end any time soon. As long as it exists, caste-based affirmative action will be necessary to give blacks and other minorities their full rights under capitalism. However, it will hardly be sufficient. Keynesians have tried to create programs to eliminate poverty as much as possible within capitalist boundaries. These must continue. William Wilson and Keynesians like Robert Reich have called for rewriting affirmative action laws to take account of class as well as caste discrimination. For the foreseeable future, we urge that their proposals be supported. Abandoning Keynesianism for the neoclassical approach of essentially ignoring the problem by letting the market take care of it has led to the disaster of the last thirty years, a disaster that continues to unfold with even greater suffering for the underclass.

Neo-Marxists

Neo-Marxists debate among themselves how much to focus on race, whether to treat it as a subcategory of class or a caste difference that lends itself to even more exploitation. Although William Julius Wilson does not identify himself as a Marxist, many Marxists agree with him[24] that paying attention to the caste question, without addressing class, can be self-defeating. Self-identified Marxist sociologist Howard Winant proposes that racial caste barriers have declined since the civil rights movement, yet the real impact of racism persists.

> In the post–civil rights era US society has undergone a substantial modification of the previously far more rigid lines of exclusion and segregation, permitting real mobility for more favored sectors (that is, certain class-based segments) of racially defined minority groups.... The racial reaction

has rearticulated the demands for equality and justice made by the black movement and its allies in a conservative discourse of individualism, competition, and laissez-faire.... It has not been possible fully to transform the social, political, economic, and cultural institutions that afford systematic privileges to whites. It has not been possible to alter the displacement of the burdens and problems of the society (such as unemployment, undereducation, poverty, and disease) onto the shoulders of nonwhites.[25]

Wilson's and Winant's propositions are a recent manifestation of an observation Marx made in the 1800s. Capitalism eliminated a fixed caste hierarchy and replaced it with class differences that proved to be even more brutal. Marx proclaimed,

In the earlier epochs of history, we find almost everywhere a complicated arrangement of society into various orders, a manifold gradation of social rank. In ancient Rome we have patricians, knights, plebeians, slaves; in the Middle Ages, feudal lords, vassals, guild-masters, journeymen, apprentices.... The modern bourgeois society that has sprouted from the ruins of feudal society has not done away with class antagonisms. It has but established new classes, new conditions of oppression, new forms of struggle in place of the old ones.[26]

Even if the class issue were completely solved, racial prejudice would still be alive and well. However, it would not produce the misery that stems from rampant poverty. Most Marxists prefer the Keynesian approach, having the state intervene to overcome racism, to the neoclassical solution of letting the capitalist market take care of it. However, unlike both Keynesians and neoclassicists, neo-Marxists see capitalism as the real cause of the problem and inherently incapable of solving it.

Marxists have long worried that the civil rights movement could backfire. As early as 1957, Herbert Marcuse warned that it could create a black middle class and leave the majority behind.[27] Whatever their original intentions, many civil rights advocates have found that leading the movement is a plum ticket into the corporate upper class. Vernon Jordan, a leading African American adviser to several presidents, has sat on the board of American Express, Xerox, J. C. Penney, Revlon, Hillshire, Lazard, and other major corporations.[28] Does it matter to a black whose wages are not high enough to pay her American Express credit card bill, which she amassed to buy Revlon cosmetics she cannot afford at J. C. Penney, if the directors are black, white, civil rights leaders, or Southern segregationists?

By having blacks, especially civil rights leaders, on corporate boards, capitalists can justify their claim that they have indeed built an economy that provides maximum opportunity equally to everyone, regardless of their race or background. The critique that the civil rights movement served the black elite more than ordinary blacks is shared by neoclassicist Sowell and many Marxists. Sowell, himself, was a beneficiary of the equal opportunity carved by the civil rights movement, affirmative action, and the Great Society. Although there are points of agreement between Sowell, Wilson, and some Marxists, Marxists reject Sowell's solution. Leaving the capitalist market alone will not lead to the advancement of blacks and other races. Capitalist profit depends on exploiting the majority and will leave many in the underclass.

Marxists debate among themselves whether capitalism fosters racism. As we have seen, the purer the form of capitalism, the less it needs caste discrimination, but the more it needs class exploitation. Some Marxists believe that prior to the Civil War, America's most valuable commodity may have been slaves, more valuable than all the Northern factories at the time. Slavery may have been the foundation of the great fortunes of the North as well as the South. Without cotton and tobacco, produced by slaves, Northern textiles factories and financial centers could hardly exist.

> The Cotton Gin increased the amount of cotton that a single slave could produce in a day, by fifty-fold! "What this meant was that growing cotton was incredibly, incredibly profitable.".... In the upper South the selling of slaves became more profitable than the growing of tobacco.... Slaves vary widely in value from fifty dollars to two thousand dollars depending on who they are, how old they are, but the valuable ones are very, very valuable.... Cotton became the key crop, the key cash producer in the life of the nation. For a period of time, there are more millionaires along a narrow band of land along the Mississippi River than in the entire rest of the nation combined. This is a terribly profitable crop that we're talking about. By 1840 the value of cotton exports was greater than everything else the nation exported to the world combined! And that made slaves the most valuable thing in the nation beside the land itself.... Cotton generated an extensive textile industry in New England. Insurance companies insured slaves as property (much as they do today, when corporations are allowed to insure their workers). "Many Wall Street firms got their start as middlemen in the cotton trade. Senator Charles Sumner of Massachusetts called it [Wall Street] 'The Lords of the Loom and the Lords of the Lash.'"[29]

Many Marxists, based on the thinking above, feel capitalism and slavery were intertwined, with capitalism supporting or using a caste system to maximize profit. But other Marxists disagree. Marxist historian Eugene Genovese claimed that slavery was less profitable than free labor because planters could not trust blacks with training that would empower them to use the most sophisticated technologies of the period. Well-trained slaves would be more likely to rebel.[30] According to Genovese, Southern planters envisioned themselves more like European aristocrats, who considered profit beneath their dignity, than Northern industrialists. Their goal was to maintain a caste system, not a class system. It was virtually a point of pride to not run the plantations efficiently. As a result, the Northern economy overwhelmed the Southern and when the Civil War came, the Northern industrial productivity brought victory. Essentially, Genovese was suggesting that the Southern racial caste system inhibited it from developing capitalism and reduced the South to an economic vassal, almost at the mercy of the North. When America became independent, the South may have been richer than the North, but after the Civil War, Northern capitalism made the South poorer.

Marxists, like Genovese, feel that after the Civil War, precapitalist attitudes persisted among the Southern upper class. Defeat did not teach them to change their thinking. These Marxists argue that the desire to maintain a caste system and keep blacks ignorant and servile continued, for almost a century, undermined modernization and kept the South an economic backwater compared to the North. Other Marxists disagree and claim that racism made wages exceptionally low in the South, resulting in even greater profits for businesses there. The appeal of low wages and minimal unions, stemming from the racial divide, motivated many corporations to close their factories in the North and move South. It thus contributed to the deindustrialization of the North. Thus, these other Marxists, in opposition to Genovese, insist the capitalist class has a vested interest in maintaining a rigid racial caste hierarchy.

There is one benefit that almost all Marxists agree capitalists receive from racism. The racial divide also divides the working class. It pits white workers against black workers and the black underclass. Hence, the 99 percent fight against each other, blame each other for their problems, and do not turn against the 1 percent. Often, underpaid exploited white workers would still take pride in their whiteness, which allowed them to feel part of a superior race or caste. Their white identity compensated for low wages and gave them a sense of power, making them likely to bond with their boss rather than their black fellow workers. Marxist sociologist Stanley Aronowitz suggested that the more white workers felt economically threatened, the more they would cling to their racial and caste status.

The genetic inferiority of Black people was given as a justification for their inferior position in society and in the labor process.... It was when Black labor was put in direct competition with white labor that it [racism] became a popular creed and established deep roots among the working class as a whole. It expresses, in ideal form, the genuine fears of people in the throes of spatial as well as social transition.[31]

Marx, himself, saw slavery as splitting the oppressed against each other. He saw Southern slave owners as more serious enemies than Northern industrialists, hoped that slave revolts would inspire uprisings among white workers, and feared racism would breed complacency among white laborers. He even sent a letter to Abraham Lincoln, praising him for carrying out the Civil War.

[Counterrevolutionaries] maintained slavery to be "a beneficent institution."... Confederate gentry had given its dismal warning, that the slaveholders' rebellion was to sound the tocsin for a general holy crusade of property against labor, and that for the men of labor, with their hopes for the future, even their past conquests were at stake in that tremendous conflict on the other side of the Atlantic. Everywhere they bore therefore patiently the hardships imposed upon them by the cotton crisis, opposed enthusiastically the proslavery intervention of their betters—and, from most parts of Europe, contributed their quota of blood to the good cause.... While the workingmen, the true political powers of the North, allowed slavery to defile their own republic, while before the Negro, mastered and sold without his concurrence, they boasted it the highest prerogative of the white-skinned laborer to sell himself and choose his own master, they were unable to attain the true freedom of labor, or to support their European brethren in their struggle for emancipation; but this barrier to progress has been swept off by the red sea of civil war.[32]

The more white workers latched onto their alleged privilege of skin color, the less likely they were to understand who was their true enemy and true ally. Du Bois believed the white working class embraced racism to their detriment. "The plight of the white working class throughout the world today is directly traceable to Negro slavery in America, on which modern commerce and industry was founded, and which persisted to threaten free labor.... The resulting color caste founded and retained by capitalism was adopted ... and approved by white labor."[33]

In more recent times, corporations may not care if their employees are white or black, but affirmative action sacrifices white jobs for black jobs. The same is true for slots in selective schools. Whites with low-paying jobs are taxed to pay for blacks on welfare. They are apt to resent welfare recipients more than the corporate elite who underpay them. Some poor whites may feel racial caste solidarity with white elites against blacks. As long as the lower classes are split along racial lines, they are less likely to unite in ways that threaten the corporations. Although hardly a Marxist, Obama recognized this and even suggested that the corporate elite may be the real source of the declining standard of living for both blacks and whites.

Most working- and middle-class white Americans don't feel that they have been particularly privileged by their race. Their experience is the immigrant experience—as far as they're concerned, no one's handed them anything, they've built it from scratch. They've worked hard all their lives, many times only to see their jobs shipped overseas or their pension dumped after a lifetime of labor. They are anxious about their futures, and feel their dreams slipping away; in an era of stagnant wages and global competition, opportunity comes to be seen as a zero sum game, in which your dreams come at my expense. So when they are told to bus their children to a school across town; when they hear that an African American is getting an advantage in landing a good job or a spot in a good college because of an injustice that they themselves never committed ... resentment builds. ... Anger over welfare and affirmative action helped forge the Reagan Coalition. ... These white resentments distracted attention from the real culprits of the middle class squeeze—a corporate culture rife with inside dealing, questionable accounting practices, and short-term greed; a Washington dominated by lobbyists and special interests; economic policies that favor the few over the many.[34]

As we pointed out, some blacks are now among the favored few, but that has hardly improved the condition of most blacks. Almost no one can dispute that Keynesian policies have helped create a black middle class and even a black upper class. However, the emphasis on caste instead of class has intensified the gap in wealth between the average white and the average black. "The median wealth of white households is 20 times that of black households." The most recent recession had a heavier toll on blacks than whites. From 2005 to 2009 median black wealth fell by 53 percent per household, but median white wealth only fell by 16 percent per household.[35] The racial caste problem is solvable within capitalism, but the class problem is not. In fact, the class problem is a synonym for capitalism. For neo-Marxists, it can only be ended by abolishing capitalism. As long as capitalism persists, some blacks can thrive and do as well as any white, but the majority of all races—black, white, or whatever—face alienation, restricted mobility, fear of poverty, and being at the mercy of a 1 percent and a government that will sacrifice the long-term interests of the vast majority to assure the domination and continued wealth of a lucky few. The 99 percent of all races must unite against their common enemies to create a society and an economy that emancipate everyone.

Even if racial caste barriers were eliminated the majority of blacks still have second-class status. For them, racial profiling and police harassment are still routine, as the family of Trayvon Martin learned all too well. Black legal scholar Michelle Alexander proposed that the 2 million blacks in prison constitute a new segregation, perhaps more brutal than the original.[36] If felons are not allowed to vote, this becomes a new mechanism to ensure black disenfranchisement. Despite the appearance that capitalism minimizes caste distinctions, prisons may be a way through which caste and class oppression merge. One may not end if the other persists. Race and class are intimately intertwined. Abolishing both hierarchies is a cause in which the entire 99 percent of all races have a stake.

CHAPTER 13

Gender and Family

In the 2012 election, President Obama and many Democrats ran on the idea that Republicans were waging "a war on women." This went beyond numerous and extreme attacks on contraception, abortion, and discussions of "legitimate rape." Democrats showed that Republicans, using neoclassical economic arguments as justifications, wanted to kill not just Planned Parenthood but social programs such as food stamps that helped support low-wage working and poor people—the majority of whom are women. Austerity overwhelmingly hurt women, especially single moms—and its neoclassical assaults on welfare programs were not-so-veiled attacks on women.

The Democrats were responding to these kinds of ideas from prominent Republicans:

Senate candidate Richard Mourdock (endorsed by Mitt Romney): "I think that even when life begins in that horrible situation of rape, that it is something that God intended to happen."

State senator Glenn Grothman: "Women make less because 'money is more important for men.'"

Grover Norquist: "Bipartisanship is another name for date rape."

Gubernatorial candidate Clayton Williams: "If [rape]'s inevitable, just relax and enjoy it."

Former senator Rick Santorum: "Radical feminists have been making the pitch that justice demands that men and women be given an equal opportunity to make it to the top in the workplace."

State representative Alan Dick: "If I thought that the man's signature was required ... required, in order for a woman to have an abortion, I'd have a little more peace about it."

Congressman Todd Akin on pregnancy resulting from rape: "It seems to be, first of all, from what I understand from doctors, it's really rare. If it's a legitimate rape, the female body has ways to try to shut the whole thing down."

Rush Limbaugh: "If we are going to pay for your contraceptives, and thus pay for you to have sex, we want you to post the videos online so we can all watch."[1]

Democrats argued that these Republicans embrace an effort to push women back into a 1950s housewife role, out of the workplace, which Republicans still believe belongs to men. Social conservatives felt that society rested on maintaining traditional families, and lack of control over their bodies would keep women, in the vernacular, "barefoot and pregnant." Affirmative action—hiring a woman rather than a man if all else was equal—was pushing men out of the workplace when jobs were getting scarce. It was also likely to hurt rather than help women, who would benefit more from market-based approaches. Democrats pointed out that most families could not get by on one wage, as wages have stagnated over recent decades. Most women and families had no choice but to have wives or single women working—a "second shift" as sociologist Arlie Russell Hochschild called it.[2] And they argued that denying women work or paying them less was blatant sexism, not good economics.

Women seemed to agree about the idea of a Republican war on women, voting overwhelmingly for Obama and Democrats. The gender gap in recent decades is one of the most decisive factors determining the outcome of elections.[3]

But how much truth is there to the war on women argument? The role of women turns out to be a fiercely contentious economic and political issue—not just a social one. Should women work? Is affirmative action based on gender economically and morally right? Do welfare programs benefiting women actually help those women? How do we explain differences in the pay of men and women doing the same job—and does Equal Pay for Equal Work legislation help reduce these differences? Is there a glass ceiling? Should women play a different role in the economy and family than men? Is the war on women a policy approach aimed at disadvantaging women, keeping them home and subordinate to men?

Each of our three paradigms offers different answers, based on distinctive views of women's role in capitalist economies and each has its own take on the war on women. Deciphering the differences helps make clear how the three schools think about gender and the family in the context of capitalism and the US economy.

Neoclassicists

The most prominent neoclassical economist on issues of women and the family is Nobelist Gary Becker at the University of Chicago. In his pioneering work, *A Treatise on the Family*, Becker argued that family decisions were simply another arena of market behavior. There is a "marriage market" that operates on the same principles as all other markets, leading Becker to controversial arguments about the benefits of polygamy. The same market logic is used to analyze choices to have and raise children—with Becker known for his arguments on the merits of considering children as commodities consumed or traded on the market by parents or employers. The role of government in promoting women's role in the economy is treated within the broader context of neoclassical views of efficient markets and inefficient government. Government interventions—such as welfare or anti-discrimination laws—to aid those considered to be subject to discrimination are viewed as typically hurting rather than helping women and minorities, related to the general neoclassical principle that government action distorts market rationality and hurts individuals in the name of group or collective interests.[4]

Becker views gender and family within the broader neoclassical lens of individuals; he sees gender and family as ultimately shaped by choices of rational individuals seeking to maximize personal utility. Not surprisingly, Becker looks at the role and decisions of women not in terms of historical and social contexts, but in terms of the decision of individual women to maximize their own preferences. If many women end up in lower-wage or low-skill secretarial or other "pink collar" jobs, Becker argued, this reflects preferences by individual women to invest less in their education or human capital than individual men, since their priority is to spend more time with their children than men do.[5]

In a 2013 interview, when asked about persisting limits to women rising to the top in business, with only fourteen women CEOs in the Fortune 500 companies, Becker said that any historical artificial market barriers based on gender could not be viewed as glass ceilings: "A lot of barriers [to women and blacks] have been broken down. That's all for the good. It's much less clear what we see today is the result of such artificial barriers. Going home to take care of the kids when the man doesn't: Is that a waste of a woman's time? There's no evidence that it is."[6]

Using neoclassical logic, Becker is essentially arguing that discrimination against women has largely eroded—one of the great accomplishments of capitalist societies—and that the situation of women who earn less or do not get promoted reflects personal decisions of the women themselves. Becker's neoclassical argument is partly embraced by Cheryl Sandberg, the Facebook executive and bestselling author of *Lean In*, who argues that women are somewhat to blame and must change their personal behavior.[7] As journalist David Wessel wrote, "The Sandberg recipe for women who want to change is: 1) Sit at the table. You're as good as anyone else there. 2) Don't curtail your career aspirations in anticipation of having children. As she puts it, 'Don't leave before you leave.' And 3) find a mate who wants for you what you want, as Ms. Sandberg did on her second try."[8] Sandberg does not exonerate society but is suggesting that women's own decisions explain their failure to get all the way to the top. She is partially echoing the neoclassical view that individual choice explains female limitations.

In his own analysis, Becker is reflecting the general neoclassical view that the market is a meritocracy, rewarding talent and motivation and indifferent to gender identity. While women in earlier times may have faced discrimination based on precapitalist societies, capitalist markets operate to ensure that all individuals, whether men or women, have the same rights and responsibilities in the workplace. They also have the same opportunities. Those who want to work and have what it takes to succeed can be the big winners—and increasingly are. The market equalizes women's opportunities and creates a level playing field between men and women. The market is now color blind and also gender blind, and thus any differences in outcomes between women and men reflect purely individual abilities and motivations, with neoclassicists such as Becker emphasizing especially individual choices about education and investment in human capital. This is, of course, entirely consistent with the neoclassical fundamentals, which define the market as individual behavior driven by individual free choice, with group identification a distorting factor frequently introduced by government and harming both men and women together.[9]

No economic system has been better for women, say neoclassicists, than American capitalism. That is not because it gives women unfair advantages but because it deprives men of advantages (as it does whites) they may have had historically and still have in many societies.[10] At the same time, the focus on individuals and rational choice leads neoclassicists to argue that traditional gender roles often reflected women's preferences. Many middle-class women in the 1950s did not want to work and chose a life built around family. Some women today have the same priorities. Neoclassicists see past gender differences as reflecting not just discrimination but completely acceptable and valued choices by women who chose not to work—or to work at less skilled jobs than men, an argument that Cheryl Sandberg, as just noted, reflected in her huge bestseller, *Lean In*.[11]

Neoclassicists often minimize but do not deny historical discrimination based on gender or race. The virtue of capitalism, they argue, is that it historically eliminates discrimination fostered by all other past and current systems, something that, Milton Friedman argued, minorities and women, the great beneficiaries, fail to grasp:

> It is a striking historical fact that the development of capitalism has been accompanied by a major reduction in the extent to which particular religious, racial or social groups have operated under special handicaps in respect of their economic activities; have, as the saying goes been discriminated against.... [Women and minorities] have tended to attribute to capitalism the residual restrictions they experience rather than to recognize that the free market has been the major factor enabling these restrictions to be as small as they are.[12]

Many neoclassical economists do not see their role as making social value judgments but often agree with the economic merits of the social conservative agenda to prioritize women's roles in the family. The family is the ultimate source of social stability, the precondition of the very existence and success of the market and capitalist society. And women who are good mothers provide the socialization necessary to create disciplined, responsible workers who are educated and increase the pool of vital human capital in a high-tech age. This convergence between neoclassical economics and social conservatism underlies the coalition currently at the base of the Republican Party.[13]

Neoclassicists tend to oppose affirmative action or Equal Pay for Equal Work legislation for women today. It represents government intervention that distorts and undercuts the efficient market. With gender discrimination of the past largely overcome, affirmative action is unfair to men and leads to labor market choices that are inefficient, creating political pressures to hire or promote individuals because of their gender rather than their merit. It is feminist "political correctness," deeply unfair and economically harmful to market rationality and economic growth, and ultimately harmful to women themselves, since it will stigmatize them and lead to less jobs for both women and men by decreasing market efficiency and growth, the same argument that Milton Friedman, Gary Becker, and other neoclassicists made in rejecting affirmative action and equal pay laws for blacks or Hispanics or other minorities.[14]

What about the idea that neoclassical arguments for austerity are part of a war on women, since they disproportionately cut programs on which women, especially poor women and single moms, depend? Neoclassicists argue that austerity shrinks government, eliminates deficits, and expands growth in the private sector, thus creating growth and more employment opportunities for both women and men. This argument has been reinforced by many moderate economists, such as Carmen Reinhart and Kenneth Rogoff, two of the most influential American economists, blending neoclassical central themes with some Keynesian arguments. Their article, "Growth in a Time of Debt," showed that high debts killed growth and debt-reduction fueled growth over many different historical eras and countries. It was a major legitimation for the severe austerity pursued by European central banks and the International Monetary Fund (IMF) in Europe and by the Republican deficit-hawks in the United States after the 2008 financial meltdown. Reinhart's and Rogoff's work, severely compromised in 2013 after significant mistakes in their data analysis were revealed, is evidence of how neoclassical arguments can drive major policies creating disastrous effects on minorities and women—and labor more broadly—all in the name of helping these minority populations.[15]

Cutting social welfare programs inevitably impacts women—and single moms—the most. But such cuts, in the neoclassical view, are not intended to target women, who are, in a sense, collateral damage in a necessary effort to reduce deficits and end government distortions of the market. The short-term adverse effects on women will be balanced by long-term benefits associated with economic growth that will bring low-income women many more job opportunities. Neoclassicists emphasize that a war on women suggests a deliberate effort to harm women, while their policies are intended to expand women's long-term hopes and prospects. Neoclassicists promote endless policy papers—in conservative think tanks such as the American Enterprise Institute—showing how women are hurt by Keynesian-inspired government antidiscrimination policies, which undercut female employment and wages and ultimately the dignity of women themselves, who are compromised as victims and denied the benefits the free market would provide more efficiently and permanently.

Austerity is also likely to strengthen families, who will depend on each other more financially and will need to find ways to work out family or marital difficulties. Single parents face great challenges. If economic incentives based on welfare cuts increase prospects of parents staying together, this will be a social and economic gain for both parents and children. Neoclassical economists advocate such incentives even when there is no need for austerity, because welfare programs enable free riders, undermine the work ethic, and subvert the personal responsibility and intact family on which capitalism is founded.

Neoclassicists ridicule the idea that they are waging a war on women. They argue that their policies are most likely to benefit all low-income groups, including single mothers and working women. Since the market is a meritocracy, neoclassical economics ensures that women with talent and hard work will rise to the top.

Keynesians

The first bill that President Obama signed into law was the Lilly Ledbetter Fair Pay act, guaranteeing women equal pay for equal work. Running for reelection against Mitt Romney, Obama trumpeted this as one of his finest hours:

> When young women graduate, they should get equal pay for equal work. That should be a simple question to answer. When Governor Romney was asked about it, his campaign said, "We'll get back to you." That shouldn't be a complicated question: equal pay for equal work. I want my daughters paid just like somebody else's sons are paid for the same job. That's straightforward.
>
> Now, I've got to say, last night, Governor Romney's top advisor finally admitted, no, the Governor didn't really support that bill. You don't have to wait for an answer from me. The Lilly Ledbetter Fair Pay Act was the first bill I signed into law as President—the first bill.[16]

Women seemed to believe that Obama was advocating gender equality, and putting the force of government behind it. Twice, they voted overwhelmingly for Obama, giving him his margin of victory. Women's support for equal pay legislation, affirmative action, and social welfare—all benefiting women and requiring substantial government intervention in the economy—is part of broader support by women for progressive politics and "feminized values," embodied in the New Deal and ever since in liberal programs such as LBJ's Great Society and in the Democratic Party's continuing government agenda to ensure equal opportunity for all.[17]

Democrats could not win without women—and women's feminized values, as documented by polls. Democrats promote government-sponsored intervention in all aspects of the economy and society to ensure nondiscrimination, jobs for all, a living wage, and social welfare for the poor, aged, and minorities, as well as women themselves. This agenda should sound familiar to anyone literate in Keynesian thinking, since it seems to echo the core vision of Keynesianism itself. Feminized values, broadly conceived, are baked centrally into the Keynesian framework, at least as interpreted by mainstream Keynesians and Democrats.[18]

Keynes, it is true, did not focus in his writing on the economics of gender. But Keynes was part of the Bloomsbury circle, a group of famous British intellectuals, artists, and politicians that included many prominent feminists, including the novelist Virginia Woolf. He was sympathetic to feminism and, being bisexual, also recognized the importance of gender issues more broadly in the economy and society. Although a wealthy stockbroker, who traveled in the most elite British circles, Keynes was a free thinker and progressive on social issues, such as women and the family.[19]

Supporting women's rights and equal opportunity is consistent with—in fact, integral to—Keynes's basic economic outlook. Ending discrimination of all forms was central to Keynesian social philosophy, and making the market a level playing field and a true meritocracy was an idea that Keynes shared with neoclassicists. But recognizing the role of power in capitalist markets and government policy, Keynes was much more likely than the neoclassicists to see the long history of discrimination against women, in the economy and larger society. He was also far more sympathetic to government intervention in the markets to promote both economic and social equality, something that contemporary Keynesians such as Paul Krugman, Joseph Stiglitz, Robert Kuttner, and Robert Reich have brought to the center of Keynesian thinking today.[20]

Keynesians support strong government regulation and see affirmative action as essential to counter past and continuing discrimination against women. Affirmative action is not only justified by social justice but also plays an important economic role. At the heart of Keynesian theory is the idea that full employment is the most important measure of a healthy economy and the good society.[21] If more than half the population—women—are denied full access to jobs, Keynesian economics has failed. Without women working, Keynesians see the economy limping, failing to utilize vast pools of talented and motivated labor essential to boost productivity and growth.[22]

Keynes sees full employment as essential to maintaining high demand and boosting economic growth. Women bring human capital and buying power into the economy. To waste their skills or shrink their capacity to purchase goods and services is a recipe for lower growth and potentially recession or depression. Full employment for women who want to work is inseparable from the larger Keynesian ideal of a well-managed economy.

In the Great Depression, the collapse in demand and the ensuing poverty and unemployment hit women particularly hard. To help save capitalism, Keynes supported New Deal public investment, direct government job creation, and Social Security and social welfare measures that benefited the poor and their families and gave women a better shot at a good life. The welfare state that Keynes supported was the only way both to stimulate and rejuvenate capitalist economies in crises and to ensure women and families a true "new deal." Without major government intervention, women and children were destined to live a depressed life in a depressed economy.

Robert Kuttner, a leading Keynesian, has made this argument a central part of the contemporary Keynesian strategy for how to end the 2008 Great Recession. In his 2008 work, *Obama's Challenge*, Kuttner argued that one of the most important things that Obama could do to save the economy was to professionalize social service work, giving it the dignity that primarily female service workers deserved, recognizing the importance of their work, and enabling a structural increase in their pay that could help catapult the economy out of the doldrums. Kuttner wrote that we had moved from a manufacturing to a service economy, and that creating good-wage jobs for human service workers was central to both economic recovery and social justice:

> As a signature initiative, Obama could use government's broader regulatory and spending power to transform the thirty-year trend toward bad and insecure jobs. During the same three decades, the service sector has exploded as a source of employment.... Suppose the new administration announced a national policy goal of converting every human-service job to a good job that pays a living wage with good benefits and includes adequate training, professional status and the prospect of advancement—a career rather than casual labor. These, after all are jobs caring for our parents, our children and ourselves. Transforming all human-service work into good jobs ... would vastly improve the quality of care delivered to the elderly at home or in institutions; to young children in pre-kindergartens or day-care facilities and to sick people whether in hospitals, hospices, outpatient settings, or other jobs.[23]

While Kuttner does not explicitly discuss this as job-creation and wage-lifting for women, he understands that the majority of human service workers are women, and the majority of them—nurses' aides, kindergarten teachers, nursing home assistants—are poor and economically insecure. Despite the social importance of their work, they are treated as unskilled workers lacking job security, good wages and benefits, and any control over their work. Kuttner's proposal is thus a classic Keynesian strategy for simultaneously aiding the economy and helping women.

This Keynesian approach directly contradicts the neoclassical one, which argues that government involvement exacerbates both capitalist crises and the problems of low-income women or minorities. But neoclassical austerity supported by laissez-faire Republican presidents such as Calvin Coolidge and Herbert Hoover—and their followers who attacked the New Deal in the

1930s—only exacerbated the desperate situation of women after the Depression hit. Neoclassicists today lionize Coolidge as an early and great president of austerity, a tradition largely embraced by President Hoover after the 1929 crash.[24] Keynesians view Coolidge and Hoover as failing to enact the government spending and investment that could bring the economy out of the Depression and employ both women and men. Keynesians also say neoclassicists failed to enact the social welfare that ensured women the prospect of raising a family, working in a well-paid job, and staying out of poverty.

Keynesians such as Paul Krugman today see neoclassicists blindly repeating the catastrophic errors of Coolidge and Hoover. The austerity agenda of Paul Ryan, the Republican House budget leader and vice presidential running mate of Mitt Romney in 2012, is viewed by Krugman, Stiglitz, Kuttner, Reich, and other Keynesians today as a Republican, neoclassical blueprint of the war on women. It cuts social welfare programs on which poor women and single moms depend. It also prevents government stimulus and public investment that could put these women to work. In the longer run, it cuts Social Security and privatizes Medicare while turning Medicaid into state grants that are likely to shrink and disproportionately hurt women, who live longer and at every stage depend more on social service programs. This brazen assault on the core New Deal Social Security and welfare programs is the heart of what Keynesians now see as the war on women.[25]

Keynesians view the war on women as the tip of the spear in the war on the general populace. The Ryan budget plan targets programs on which minorities and poor and working women most depend. But its long-term effect, as Keynesians see it, is to undermine the economic prospects of much of the population, creating a vast surplus population of both women and men. Protecting women is part and parcel of the Keynesian strategy for protecting the public and saving capitalism. Saving women is integral to saving capitalism, a notion viewed by more radical critics of capitalism as upside down, since it would take women helping lead a struggle for a totally different economy ultimately to help women and save society itself.

Neo-Marxists

Marx was married to an aristocratic woman named Jenny Von Westphalen and named four of his daughters Jenny. All the Jennys were feminists and influenced Marx. He regarded the struggle for women's rights one of the great liberation causes of humanity.[26]

In his 1844 manuscripts, his most important early writing defining alienation, he conceived the relation of men and women as the barometer of the development of civilization, the extent to which people have become fully human: "The direct, natural, and necessary relation of person to person is the relation of man to woman. In this natural relationship of the sexes man's relation to nature is immediately his relation to man.... From this relationship one can therefore judge man's whole level of development.... It therefore reveals the extent to which man's natural behaviour has become human."[27]

Marx thus championed all his life the fundamental need to liberate women, arguing that it was the most important measure of progress in civilization: "The change in a historical epoch can always be determined by the progress of women toward freedom, because in the relation of woman to man, of the weak to the strong, the victory of human nature over brutality is most evident. The degree of emancipation of woman is the natural measure of general emancipation."[28] Marx saw women as a form of property in early capitalism, writing about such gender slavery as a terrible disgrace. Men literally had ownership rights of their wives, and women had no legal standing on their own. Marx regarded the bourgeois family as a corrupt institution, giving men the right to sexually abuse wives, engage in affairs without any accountability, and dominate everyday life. He wrote, "The bourgeoisie sees in his wife a mere instrument of production.... Our bourgeois, not content with having the wives and daughters of their proletarians at their disposal, not to speak of common prostitutes, take the greatest pleasure in seducing each other's wives."[29]

While he had deep love for his own wife, he wrote in *The Communist Manifesto* that the family was a capitalist deformation, since it enshrined the wife as the property of her husband—literally in capitalism wives being the collective property of the bourgeoisie males—and had to be transformed.[30]

Marx wrote that the family was the original soil from which the concept of private property emerged: "The nucleus, the first form of [property] lies in the family, where wife and children are slaves of the husband. This latent slavery in the family, though still very crude, is the first property."[31]

Shortly after Marx's death, Engels published a famous book, *On the Origins of the Family, Private Property, and the State*, which Marx had helped conceptualize and had intended to write before he died.[32] The book looked at the lost history of the family and argued that the capitalist family emerged from precapitalist forms as one of the first social institutions to enshrine a type of male dominance that would become the model of dominance relations in all later economic and social systems: "Thus, in the monogamian family, in those cases that faithfully reflect its historical origin and that clearly bring out the sharp conflict between man and woman resulting from the exclusive domination of the male, we have a picture in miniature of the very antagonisms and contradictions in which society, split up into classes since the commencement of civilisation, moves, without being able to resolve and overcome them."[33]

Marx and Engels saw the relation of men to women in the patriarchal family as a seedbed of more generalized property rights and class power, not unlike the relation between the capitalist and worker in the factory. Men monopolized the legal property rights related to all family members, and women, like workers, were disenfranchised, with no legal rights of their own.

> The wife became the first domestic servant, pushed out of participation in social production.... Today [1884], in the great majority of cases, the man has to be the earner, the bread-winner of the family, at least among the propertied classes, and this gives him a dominating position which requires no special legal privileges. In the family, he is the bourgeois; the wife represents the proletariat.[34]

Engels argued that ownership of women and their progeny allowed capitalists to pass their property on exclusively to their heirs and prevented any broader claims of society to the capitalist's wealth after his death.[35]

The capitalist family, then, is both a reflection of class relations and a model of how to create it. The family is not just a cultural reflection of property relations but a building block integral to the creation of property itself. The family helps create the property system on which capitalism stands.

Within the economy itself, working women and their children were the most exploited sector of the labor force, a theme that Marx returns to repeatedly in *Capital*. They were subjected to the most demeaning and unskilled work, paid less, fired first, and subject to sexual harassment. Marx writes that turning of the worker into "the living appendage of the machine," where "each man is bound hand and foot for life to a single detail-operation," is made possible through employment of family labor:[36] "by the general introduction of the labour of women and children ... in the frightful fact that a great part of the children employed in modern factories and manufactures, are from their earliest years riveted to the most simple manipulations for years, without being taught the single sort of work that would afterwards make them of use in the same manufactory or factory."[37]

Working men who themselves endured exploitation from capitalist employers gained a measure of compensation by enjoying a higher status and security than their fellow women workers or their children. Women were also an important part of the reserve army of the unemployed. The larger the pool of the unemployed, the more power capitalists enjoyed to extract more labor from male workers at lower wages. Women expanded the reserve army, creating the conditions in which working men could be subject to intensified exploitation.

Women's plight illustrates the relation between caste and class in Marx's thinking. Marx focused on class, but recognized that caste—based on gender or race—was an integral part of class relations. Class exploitation could be legitimated and class warfare controlled through caste exploitation. Owner-ship of one caste by another provided a justification and model for broader ownership of property. Caste divided class by gender and became part of a divide and conquer strategy. The exploitation of women helped capitalists sustain the exploitation of their male workers, raising the question of whether capitalism could endure without patriarchy.[38]

This is a theme taken up by modern twentieth-century "second wave" feminists in the 1960s and 1970s. Many feminist theorists, such as Germaine Greer, Ellen Willis, Angela Davis, and Clara Fraser, argued that patriarchy and capitalism were interdependent and mutually reinforcing. Just as male control of women—patriarchy—supported capitalists to maintain social stability and power over male workers, capitalist exploitation of men fueled the male need to sustain their patriarchal power over women.[39]

Other second wave feminists saw the relation between capitalism and patriarchy in different ways. Many feminists, typically from professional or upper-class backgrounds, and represented in mainstream organizations like NOW, did not address the relation at all, viewing patriarchy as a central and autonomous set of power relations within capitalist and noncapitalist societ-ies. They chose not to challenge capitalism. Engels vigorously critiqued this form of "bourgeois feminism," cropping up in his own era:

> The English women who championed the formal rights of members of their sex to permit themselves to be as thoroughly exploited by the capitalists as the men are mostly, directly or indirectly, interested in the capitalist exploitation of both sexes.... It is my conviction that real equal-ity of women and men can come true only when exploitation of either by capital has been abolished and private housework has been transformed into a public industry.[40]

Marxist or socialist feminists, as well as another group of "separatist" radical feminists, rejected bourgeois feminism and moved in different more radi-cal directions. Separatist radical feminists, such as Mary Daly and Andrea Dworkin, believed that patriarchy was the original and more fundamental system of power, from which capitalism derived some of its own ideas and stratification. They devoted their energy to critiques of patriarchy and ways of building new communities of liberated and autonomous women.

Socialist feminists, such as Ellen Willis, Germaine Greer, Angela Davis, and Clara Fraser, saw capitalism as a root evil and patriarchy as partly deriva-tive from capitalist models of ownership and power. While patriarchal power was a partially autonomous and deeply exploitative driving force, it derived much of its strength from its role in helping consolidate capitalist power.

The goal of socialist feminists is to challenge capitalism, as the only way to liberate women and society:

> Socialist feminism (which can also be termed Marxist feminism or materialist feminism) traces the oppression of women to inequalities that developed in connection with the class system of private property. Socialist feminists view gender inequalities as intrinsic to the capitalist system, which makes vast profits off women's unpaid labor in the home and underpaid labor in the workforce.[41]

Socialist feminists increasingly see women at the leading edge of both women's movements and the workers' movements in the twenty-first century. Women constitute more than half the labor force and are represented disproportionately in the most exploited and organized labor sectors, including teachers, social workers, waitresses, nurses' aides, and other service workers, where capitalist exploitation is most brutal, requiring that women lead intertwined feminist and socialist movements.

> Like racism, homophobia and other forms of bigotry, sexism divides the working class and thereby allows the capitalists to make super-profits. Because these different forms of oppression have a common source, they also have a common solution: socialism. Socialist feminists seek to eliminate the capitalist system and replace it with socialism, which collectively shares the wealth created by human labor and has no economic stake in maintaining exploitation.[42]

As austerity hits public sector workers the hardest, it draws much blood from both women welfare workers and their women clients. Since women lead many public sector unions, as sociologist Sharon Kurtz has argued, they are now in a position to take leadership of a mobilized labor movement seeking to save the labor movement itself and commit to a broader vision of social welfare and justice for all.[43]

Since the second wave feminists of the 1960s and 1970s, new socialist feminists have reframed these issues, calling for a more encompassing intertwined analysis and activism of women, workers, and minority groups. Sociologist bell hooks has been a crucial and inspiring contemporary theorist linking oppression of women to capitalism, as well as to racism and other social oppressions. Hooks, along with the influential sociologists Patricia Hill Collins and Audre Lorde, developed the idea of "intersectionality" to highlight the structural and cultural intersections of class, race, and gender. Hooks has helped to mentor a new generation of socialist feminists and feminist sociologists who seek to closely integrate research and social movements simultaneously challenging patriarchy, capitalism, and racism. Hooks's work, which is deeply humanistic and seeks to address problems of all humanity, including those of men, stresses the need to confront systems of domination in all areas of society, that constrain men as well as women, and shape society as a whole. Challenging the structure of that domination—in the culture, the economy, and the family, and in our own personal relationships, love life, and psyches—is central to her work:

> Dominator culture teaches all of us that the core of our identity is defined by the will to dominate and control others. We are taught that this will to dominate is more biologically hardwired in males than in females. In actuality, dominator culture teaches us that we are all natural-born killers but that males are more able to realize the predator role. In the dominator model the pursuit of external power, the ability to manipulate and control others, is what matters most. When culture is based on a dominator model, not only will it be violent but it will frame all relationships as power struggles.[44]

Hooks's emphasis on intersectionality and the inseparable relation of struggles against domination in all economic and social spheres is developed in her famous book *Feminist Theory: From Margin to Center*: "Since all forms of oppression in our society are linked in our society because they are supported by similar institutional and social structures, one system cannot be eradicated while the others remain intact."[45] And she talked about the problem of trying to end one oppression while ignoring all others:

> Significantly, struggle to end sexist oppression that focuses on destroying the cultural basis for such domination strengthens other liberation struggles. Individuals who fight for the eradication of sexism without supporting struggles to end racism or classism undermine their own efforts. Individuals who fight for the eradication of racism or classism while supporting sexist oppression are helping to maintain the cultural basis of all forms of group oppression. While they may initiate successful reforms, their efforts will not lead to revolutionary change. Their ambivalent relationship to oppression in general is a contradiction that must be resolved, or they will daily undermine their own radical work.[46]

Hooks argued that feminists who ignore class, race, or other intertwined forms of domination will only deepen their own repression—and that of all others.

All forms of oppression are important, and one shouldn't be viewed as dominant or more fundamental than others, according to hooks. This is also the position taken by other feminist theorists of "intersectionality" such as

Patricia Hill Collins and Audre Lorde. But, in this, all these theorists do not depart entirely from Marx, who, as shown above, saw the oppression of women as historically of the greatest importance—crucially important in the perpetuation and sustaining of capitalist oppression. In her book, *Where We Stand: Class Matters*, hooks expands on her view of the relation between gender and class oppression in capitalism and recognizes that the connection between the women's movement and the labor movement is of the utmost importance.[47] Capitalism is threatening the basic interests of workers, and women are the most vulnerable workers. Contraception, abortion, and women's rights in society are also under attack, by social and evangelical conservatives who are the base of the Republican Party and the most ardent supporters of capitalist austerity. Since the social and economic perpetrators of the war on women are politically aligned, so too must women and workers come together to contest the elites who sponsor both the social and economic elements of the war on women.

The stakes are high during periods of capitalist crisis. In 1920s Germany, when the economy went into a complete tailspin, rightist groups—including the Nazis—blamed communists and feminists for the crisis.[48] Capitalist crises and culture wars have been historically intertwined. When capitalist systems go into depression, the response from the Right and capitalists themselves has often been to blame women who are destabilizing the family and the basic values of the social order.[49] We see this in the Tea Party today and the corporate billionaires such as the Koch brothers who fund both their assaults on workers and on women.

Women and workers have no choice under these conditions but to ally to fight their common enemy. Since the labor movement has itself often been sexist, as has been the Left, this is not as easy or comfortable an alliance as it might appear. Historical divisions between men and women continue to complicate prospects for a cooperative and egalitarian alliance. Nonetheless, failure to succeed will set back both movements and could lead to Far Right austerity and antifeminist politics that could create a neofascist regime even more dangerous than capitalism.

PART IV

Conclusion

CHAPTER 14

The Sociological Imagination, the New Economics, and Saving the World

In the twenty-first century, the world is approaching the brink. At least three existential crises threaten social survival. One is climate change. A second is war with weapons of mass destruction. A third is sociopathic global capitalism producing unacceptable poverty and inequality—and destruction of democracy and community.

All three of these crises are intertwined, with a hegemonic capitalist system the root cause of both climate change and militarism. In that sense, they are the core subject of political economy, making it arguably the most important field of intellectual work in the world.

But we shall argue in this chapter that while neoclassicists, Keynesians, and neo-Marxists all have something to contribute, each school has serious limits. We need a new synthesis and, ultimately, a bold, new paradigm if we are to survive.

We have already discussed the strengths and limits of the three paradigms, especially in relation to great social topics including climate change and war and democracy. Our purpose here is to outline where we might go from here, both as intellectuals and citizens concerned with survival.

Ideally, we would offer a new paradigm of political economy—and there are elements of such a new school that is being discussed especially among Keynesians and neo-Marxists that we will review here. But nobody yet has framed a new paradigm that is up to the challenge. In this chapter, we want to highlight the implicit argument in our book about why this crisis in intellectual political economy exists and what we can do about it.

In the first chapter, we argued that economists have created a professional discipline that makes it impossible to understand the economy. In the second chapter, we argued that the best sociology offers a form of imagination that might help remedy that limitation. Sociologists—along with other social scientists such as economists, political scientists, and historians embracing the interdisciplinary sociological imagination—have to play a major role in creating the twenty-first-century political economy that we now desperately need.

Why are sociologists involved (along with all the other social sciences)? The answer is simple: because the economy is a part, or sector, of society. It is the part of society that engages people in the exchange of goods and services with each other, and economic behavior is nothing other than social behavior dealing with production and consumption. Society's elites and institutions prescribe and enforce this behavior in the name of social values such as freedom, efficiency, and prosperity.

When we look at the economy, then, we are looking simply at one element of the larger society. Contrary to the impression created by economists, the economy is not a separate or distinct system governed by its own laws. It is totally embedded in—a creation of—the larger society and those who rule it. The roots or causes of economic behavior and their outcomes are determined by the society itself.

While this may seem obvious, it challenges, as discussed in Chapter 2, the reigning views in the university and in academic disciplines. These tend to view each discipline as having its own autonomy. This view has been institutionalized in the construction of the university itself, conceived as a set of autonomous and separate departments. The implicit theory is that the subject material can be disentangled from any other or broader discipline: that it has an autonomous core rooted in its own universal logic.

Economists have been particularly forceful in making this argument. As shown in Chapter 1, economists have argued that the economy is a system governed by laws independent of any particular society. The aim of economics is to discover those universal laws. To do so requires no understanding of the society in which economies are embedded since the laws are universal and invariant, grounded in nature much like the laws of physics.[1]

Economists have been the most successful social scientists in making this argument, partly because they have turned economic laws into mathematical formulations resembling the laws of physics. For this reason, economists have defined economics as the only true social science, since no other social discipline has created such rigorous mathematical logic, although most are busy trying to do so.

But as economic commentator Robert Kuttner has noted, there may be as much emotion as analytical rigor at work here. Kuttner has written that economists are afraid—perhaps only vaguely or subconsciously—of being "outed" as sociologists. Kuttner notes that Charles L. Schultze, a former president of the American Economics Association, wrote, "You dig deep, economists are deathly afraid of being sociologists."[2] Kuttner based his broader critique of economics less on what economists say but on the argument we are making here: that the economy is inherently and inevitably a part of and product of history and society rather than a natural system or law of nature. To examine economics is to examine society, and the nature and outcomes of the economy reflect the values, power structures, and rules of the society itself.

Might it be that economists are sociologists afraid to "come out of the closet"? We think yes.

But we also think sociologists have been complicit in this "cover-up." They have increasingly conceded economics to the economists themselves. The same dynamic has occurred in political science and all social sciences, each carving out its own "scientific" specialty to legitimate itself in the university and in capitalism itself.

Solving this problem requires remaking both sociology and economics, as well as all political science and other social sciences. We need to reconstruct a political economy that integrates both economics and sociology, as well as history, political science, cultural studies, and other fields. What this means for sociology is we need to return sociology (along with all the social sciences) to the original interdisciplinary focus on economy, politics, and society—and on the capitalist system in all its economic, political, and cultural aspects—as its fundamental object of study.

But for such change to take place will require a larger change in the intellectual world and the university. Western intellectual life has become organized around sovereign disciplines. For sociologists, economists, and social scientists to make the necessary changes will require a large shift in our way of thinking.

Great intellectual explosions of the kind we need typically arise out of great societal explosions. The great social crises of our times are going to require going back to the basics of our thinking about society itself, and we hope enough people will recognize this and act accordingly. They must lead a recalcitrant professionalized university and academic professors and researchers into a paradigm shift about their own forms of thinking.[3]

As noted at the beginning of the book, we have to go back to the founding of the social sciences in the nineteenth century, when industrial capitalism was transforming and disrupting all life in Europe, to find the great social theorists—such as Karl Marx and Max Weber—who knitted together the now distinct academic disciplines. They viewed themselves as economists, historians, political scientists, cultural theorists, and sociologists, all combined. They integrated all of these disciplines in the field of political economy because it was the only way to understand the explosive birth of industrial capitalism that rocked European societies to their core.

The great early social science pioneers, such as Marx and Weber, have come to be identified today primarily as the founders of sociology. This is because politics, culture, and economics are all part of society. If you separate economics from society, you make it a mathematical parody of the flesh and blood social world creating it (the same is true of political science). If you separate sociology from the study of politics and economics and culture, you blind yourself to the foundations of the society itself.

The New Twenty-First-Century Sociological Imagination

Our argument can be boiled down to the idea that we need to renew the sociological imagination that C. Wright Mills called for in the mid-twentieth century. But in the second decade of the twenty-first century, this requires new ideas.

Let us summarize the core arguments that we think are central to the new sociological imagination that is required.

First, twenty-first-century societies are facing new crises of survival: climate change and wars of weapons of mass destruction, all driven by a more fully globalized corporate capitalism eroding worldwide equality and democracy.

Second, these crises arise out of the sociopathic foundations of both developed Western capitalist societies themselves and less developed nations around the world as they are more deeply integrated into—and shaped by—global corporate capitalism.[4]

Third, the aim of the new sociological imagination is to analyze the reigning global capitalist system and its increasingly financialized power elite. Its mission is not just to analyze but help guide social change toward a more democratic, egalitarian, and sustainable world.

Fourth, since the great current crises are rooted in the economic and political foundations of globalized capitalist society, the sociological imagination must create a new political economy, conceptualizing alternative sustainable economies and a new politics that can avert the looming crises as well as spark the social forces and movements that can make them a reality.

Fifth, all social sciences must embrace the sociological imagination and rebuild their disciplines to create an interdisciplinary political economy with a focus on the economics, politics, culture, and sociology of capitalism.

Beyond these five basic principles, the new sociological imagination—and the new political economy that it seeks to create—must include the following assumptions:

1. Economy exists to serve society, not the reverse. By "serve society" we mean serve the interests and well-being of the vast majority of ordinary people in society, not its elites.

2. Economic laws are not invariant, universal, or natural; they are always the creation of people, typically those who govern each society. The same is true of "political laws." These laws are usually invented by elites to serve and justify their own power.

3. Society, typically its ruling elites, shapes the economy, but the economy acts back to shape society's elites and masses. The same is true of politics and culture.

4. Economies typically are structured to protect and reinforce the interests of ruling elites. The aim of a new political economy is to conceive of alternative, democratic economies that serve and are accountable to the public and larger society, meaning ordinary citizens, not the rich and powerful—and to imagine the politics that can create these alternatives.

5. The new sociological imagination must understand itself—and the political economy it creates—as a reflection of society and of the interests and values of those creating it. Its economics, politics, and culture are themselves always social constructions and should not be understood as universal, invariant, or free of social influence.

6. The new political economy must critique the elements within the three existing paradigms of political economy that claim to establish universal or socially invariant economic and political laws. One of the great flaws of the three paradigms is that they all accede, in some measure, to the temptation to universalize or naturalize their "laws" of political economy, and particularly of the economy itself. They all, in greater or lesser degree, present their "laws" not as historical and social constructions, but as universal, scientific truth, contradicting the basic "code" of political economy presented in Chapter 1.

The New Political Economy and the Three Existing Schools

In the United States, neoclassicists dominate the political economy conversation and the policy world in the early twenty-first century. Keynesians, who are diverse and often blend neoclassical and Keynesian frameworks, have an important voice but are the loyal opposition without great influence in Washington. Neo-Marxists have no influence inside the Beltway, and not much outside, although if you travel to Asia or Latin America or Africa, the picture changes.

If you have read this far, it won't surprise you that we regard the hierarchy of influence in the United States backward. The most compelling is neo-Marxism, the least neoclassicism, with Keynesianism in the middle.

Neo-Marxists and Keynesians both have important contributions to add to the new political economy we need in the twenty-first century.

Most of the neoclassical arguments—intellectually elegant but wrong-headed and out of touch with the real world—need to be discarded.

The neo-Marxist and Keynesian paradigms have their own serious limits. While a new political economy needs to build on neo-Marxist and Keynesian insights, and especially on certain developments within green or ecologically oriented neo-Marxism, it needs to go well beyond them. This reflects both the inherent limits and contradictions of these two paradigms, as well as the new existential crises now facing the world. Too much is at stake—and time is too short—to stay within the existing paradigms. We need to absorb their best ideas and move beyond, building a new way of thinking.

In earlier chapters, we have already offered our view of the strengths and weaknesses of each paradigm, but we need a brief review to move forward.

Neoclassicists offer one key truth. Concentrating power is always danger-ous. The fusion of dominant political and economic power in one institution, whether a government or corporation, can threaten freedom.

The problems with the neoclassicists begin with their profoundly mis-guided belief that the government is the only locus of concentrated power. In today's world, the corporation has become an even more formidable locus of power, and corporate elites have largely taken over government for their own ends. This is something that Adam Smith, the founder of neoclassi-cism, actually recognized: that large corporations could accumulate great power and destroy the competitive market. But neoclassicists since Smith have, in their greatest failure, abandoned this insight of Smith and focused their attention exclusively on central government power, claiming that the market is competitive and free of corporate dominance.

Neoclassicists live in a world of their own imagination, but their deeply flawed arguments gain influence because they serve the capitalist elites who dominate the United States. We don't—and never have—lived in a world of "free markets." The United States has historically been, and remains, a highly controlled economy managed by a tightly intertwined circle of corporate, political, and military elites.[5] They largely serve the interests of the giant global corporations headquartered in the United States, and they structure and control the markets to ensure that profits trump people.[6] The lives of most people and the conditions of the larger society are in decline, fueled by the class warfare and austerity measures that dominate all the Western capitalist states at this writing.

The basic premises of the neoclassicists are patently false. Free markets do not exist. Irrationality plays a major role in human and financial behavior. The markets are inefficient and laden with externalities. Supply does not always create its own demand. Crises, including demand-side crises, occur frequently, are getting worse, and do not self-correct. The corporate system tends toward monopoly and oligopoly rather than competition. The state—a corporate state—plays a major role in all economic sectors. Corpocracy supplants democracy, and consumerism substitutes for the public interest and democracy. Social welfare for the masses, decimated by austerity policies, declines.[7]

The invisible hand doesn't work for society. It is actually the fist of the wealthy class pounding out profits for itself at the expense of the public interest.

Neoclassicism offers double standards, and it rigs the rules. It advocates global "free trade" while embracing or tolerating protectionism and corporate subsidies in the United States. It promotes bailouts for the global rich and austerity for everyone else. It underwrites socialization of risks for the very wealthy and privatization of risk for everyone else. It advocates corporate welfare for the big corporations and austerity for everyone else.[8]

With such flaws, how has neoclassicism gained hegemony? Neoclassicism is largely an ideology that has gained overwhelming ascendancy in the United States since the Reagan revolution. It survives because it legitimates the power of the powerful. It produces the illusion of freedom in corporate capitalism that is shrinking freedom and prosperity for the majority of the people. It offers the justification for corporate power in a world where such power serves the interests of a tiny oligarchy. In the name of balancing budgets, it advances austerity to cut benefits for the masses while redistributing welfare up to the corporations.[9]

The nightmarish increase of climate change, militarism, and extreme inequality and poverty since the Reagan revolution tells the real story. Neoclassicism does not solve our great twenty-first-century existential crises. It helps produce them and legitimates the corporate capitalism at the root of our terrifying future prospects.

If we abandon neoclassical thinking, most people in the United States would view Keynesianism as the only possible option. But neoclassicists have succeeded in persuading the majority of Americans that Keynesians are simply a liberal stand-in for radical neo-Marxists hovering right behind them and waiting to ensnare the society in "big government" tyranny.

As we have seen, this is nonsense. Keynesians are dedicated capitalists. They believe in markets and reject socialism and communism. Keynesianism was born in the Great Depression to save capitalism. The whole paradigm is, in fact, dedicated to preserving capitalism from its own contradictions, something that Keynes himself, a wealthy investor, frequently and proudly acknowledged.[10]

Keynesians offer a healthy antidote, nonetheless, to the illusions of the neoclassicists, with Nobelist Paul Krugman being the most brilliant voice skewering the ignorance and dissecting the economic illusions of the neoclassical orthodoxy. Keynesians know that markets are not always efficient and that externalities are real and serious. They see that people often act irrationally. They understand that supply does not create its own demand and that demand-side crises create chronic massive economic crises. They know these crises do not self-correct. They understand that austerity will wreck a depressed economy. They build their paradigm around the set of countervailing forces and government interventions that can correct the crises that will otherwise destroy capitalism itself.[11]

Moreover, Keynesians are not blinded by the view of the invisible hand. They know that capitalism requires a visible hand to protect the public interest against private greed and corruption. Unlike neoclassicists, they understand that giant corporations gain monopolistic powers over both the economy and the political world. They understand that a visible hand of labor, a mobilized public, and an activist government are essential to preserving both capitalism and the public interest. They know that promoting massive public investment—the opposite of austerity—is the only way to save capitalism in its current crisis.[12]

There are critical truths, if also serious flaws, in these Keynesian arguments. Keynesianism sees economics as part of an effort to build a good society. It believes in the public interest and rejects the idea that unleashing private interests ensures the public good. It seeks a regulated capitalism dedicated to prosperity for all. It pursues full employment, greater equality, social welfare, and more democracy. It rejects austerity during downturns. It seeks public investment, regulation in the public interest, and taxation to internalize externalities (that is, build the social or environmental costs not registered by the market today into the cost structure producers and consumers must pay now) and distribute wealth.[13]

Nonetheless, Keynesianism is flawed precisely because of its faith in the power of its own tools. It assures the world that it can make capitalism work for all. In fact, it assumes this is not a difficult project: to use Krugman's metaphor, it's like driving the car to the neighborhood garage and getting a tune-up. The mechanic doesn't have to be brilliant—just a good one with an up-to-date Keynesian tool kit at his side.[14]

This is deeply misleading. First, capitalism is not easy to fix—in fact, there are strong reasons to believe that its flaws cannot be remedied. Keynesians underestimate the structural capitalist problems and overestimate their own powers to fix them. In the process, they legitimate a system that cannot solve the great crises threatening humanity in the twenty-first century and are part of the problem rather than the solution.

Keynesians view well-regulated markets as efficient and democratic. But if governments in capitalist societies are run by capitalists, this faith in regulation is like faith in the fox guarding the henhouse. And why would capitalist elites permit massive public investment in jobs and the environment that might suggest public spending is more effective than corporate investment? History tells us that the corporate elites and their political allies will never permit the government to invest or regulate or tax at a level that would ensure protection of the public good over private property and profit. This was the lesson of the Great Recession, where a moderate liberal Keynesian, Barack Obama, struggled to implement mild Keynesian tools that would protect the public. Instead, he bailed out the banks and companies that drove us into a ditch, ensuring that Wall Street is making money again hand over fist.[15]

Keynesians such as Nobelist Joseph Stiglitz have offered profoundly important reformist critiques,[16] but most Keynesians have supported an American globalization and world order largely serving corporate interests and US power. They have not been able to prevent a global economy that increases inequality in nearly every country and allows global corporate elites to enrich themselves at the expense of the global poor. Nor have they tried to stop US hegemonic wars that secure resources, markets, and cheap labor for US companies at the expense of the world's poorest nations and US workers at home.

Keynesians assume that public investment can save the US economy as it globalizes. But it never anticipated that corporate elites might choose to abandon the United States and disinvest in the US infrastructure because of cheaper opportunities abroad.[17] Without corporate elites committed to US infrastructure, Keynesian tools for reviving the US economy and creating full employment fall apart.

The bottom line is that Keynesians lack a realistic analysis of power in capitalist societies and in the world system, and often they themselves work directly with elites to help them preserve their power, usually by recommending "soft" tactics (although the most progressive and brilliant Keynesians, such as Stiglitz, have resigned their positions—in his case, chief economist of the World Bank—when he realized the constraints of power operating in the Bank and the larger global economy). The economy reflects the power and interests of elites, who can mobilize their enormous wealth to prevent Keynesian reforms. Moreover, Keynesians fail to see how power constructs a market system and social order ultimately designed to fail, falling on its own sword of labor too cheap and environmental destruction too drastic to permit Keynesian or any other reforms to succeed.

In the end, most Keynesians see themselves as economists—technicians or mechanics of the economy—rather than stewards of society as a whole. They, too, have fallen for the economic illusion that the economy is a problem for economists rather than sociologists and the larger public.

Neo-Marxists are less likely to fall prey to most of these illusions. They do not think about tinkering with technical flaws in the car. They know a car built to fail when they see it. And they aren't about to bet the ranch on modest reforms when only wholesale change to the system will offer us a chance for surviving the coming century.[18]

Neo-Marxists shout out vital truths denied by both neoclassicists and Keynesians. One is that US corporate capitalism is on a collision path with a civilized future. It is not an impediment to the solution. *It is the problem.* Its abolition is a prerequisite to any solution. Neo-Marxists have no illusions about the gravity of our existential crises, nor do they doubt that climate change, militarism, global poverty, and austerity are rooted in corporate capitalism. It will take a change in our basic socioeconomic order to survive the twenty-first century.[19]

Second, neo-Marxists understand that the economy and society are totally intertwined. There is no separation of economy and society. If you want a democratic society, you need economic democracy. If you want a democratic economy, you need a genuinely democratic social order. A transformation in the economy must arise from society and revolutionize it. We need a truly socialized economy emerging from social movements and reflecting principles enshrined in the society and its people.[20]

Third, neo-Marxists see the reality of power at the heart of both the capitalist economy and society. They have no illusion about the prospects of reforms that can save the system. They see Keynesian tinkering as politically naïve and economically insufficient. It will take deeper change arising out of mass movements and a new wave of popular revolutionary power to create the transformative change we need.[21]

Fourth, neo-Marxists see the disastrous threat of austerity and the inability of Keynesian policies to catalyze public investment at the scale required. It will take public ownership in the worlds of finance and energy and major public investment in the social, physical, and environmental infrastructure to protect the well-being and very survival of people all over the world. Yet the corporate elites have selected austerity because they are addicted to the short-term profits that arise from disinvesting in US and other Western infrastructure as they relocate production abroad.[22]

Neo-Marxists also understand that change must be global because capitalism is. Neo-Marxist critique is leveled not just at the United States—although it is the hegemonic power—but at the organization of the world system. Right from the beginning, Marx saw capitalism as a global system that could only be overcome through an international revolution. Neo-Marxism understands that the change we need must come from deep popular passion and movements coming together from around the world.

Why not, then, simply embrace neo-Marxism as the answer for the twenty-first century? Its critique will certainly inform the new paradigm we need—and we are not proposing abandoning its core critiques of capitalism and many of its concrete alternative economic models, particularly those developed by ecological neo-Marxists seeking economic democracy and sustainability at both the local and global levels. But neo-Marxism suffers from its own deep flaws and huge hurdles.

The most important is political. The neo-Marxist tradition, despite its contemporary focus on economic democracy, is perceived as a recipe for authoritarianism and centralized power. The brutal twentieth-century examples of Leninism, Stalinism, and Maoism have reinforced this perception in the public. This history is devastating, staining the Marxist tradition with a deep credibility problem, especially as a means for creating a democratic and free society. And there is a legitimate worry: How do we implement Marxism, particularly with its traditional focus on concentrating political and economic power in the state, without succumbing to authoritarianism?[23]

The problem does not arise simply because of the misperceptions of Stalinism and Maoism as "authentic" Marxism. True, Marx himself said he was no "Marxist," in a sense washing his hands of the twentieth-century authoritarian regimes ruling in his name decades after his death. But Marx bears responsibility, as discussed earlier, for the fact that his ideas can be used to justify centralized power and even dictatorship. After all, he used the phrase "dictatorship of the proletariat." And he made strong arguments that state power would have to be centralized and harsh in beating back capitalist counterreactions after revolutionary socialist changes.[24]

The problem is deeper in "structural Marxism" than in "critical Marxism."[25] Contemporary neo-Marxists tend to intensely focus on economic and participatory democracy. Nonetheless, in both traditions, there are too many forms of political correctness and too much focus on central power—both in the history of most Left movements and the practice of regimes defining themselves as communist—for those seeking participatory democracy to feel entirely comfortable with the entire Marxist tradition.[26]

There are other important Marxist flaws. Structural Marxism has its own version of the economists' fallacy: the idea that the economy operates according to universal and deterministic laws independent of the social context. Marx's own philosophy of historical materialism can be viewed as subordinating society to scientific laws of the economy, while failing to recognize that the social order evolves in unpredictable ways, much as the economy does, and is not totally determined by economic laws resembling those of physics. Society and economy mutually affect each other, and neither is determined by natural law but rather by unpredictable and constantly changing constellations of power and ruling ideas.

We are suggesting that core elements of Marxism share with neoclassicism and Keynesianism the economists' fallacy discussed in Chapter 1. When we understand the necessity of the sociological imagination for surviving the twenty-first century, we realize that we cannot be satisfied with any paradigm that does not recognize society itself as the necessary central focus of analysis—with economic analysis integral to that inquiry—and the making of a new democratic, just, and sustainable society as the primary aim.

The "New Economics" and Political Economy for the Twenty-First Century

While we can safely discard most neoclassical theory, the flaws of Keynesianism and neo-Marxism do not suggest throwing out the baby with the bathwater. Both traditions have major insights that are important in building a new twenty-first-century way of thinking that we desperately need.

The best of Keynesian thinking looks toward a Green New Deal that would create an ecologically oriented, socially regulated, social welfare capitalism ensuring more equality, employment, and social justice.[27] We could do worse. Such Keynesianism would promote carbon taxes, international financial exchange taxes, financial regulation, and public investment that could point us in a new and promising direction. It will seek countervailing power to limit corporate power and end austerity and corporate globalization. It will create a greener and more egalitarian capitalism with a higher quality of life, something like we see in Denmark or Sweden. It will begin to end sociopathic austerity—one nightmarish manifestation of sociocide, the death of society[28]—but it will not solve our existential crises of climate change and militarized capitalism. It is a beginning of a new path that points beyond its own analysis.

The best of neo-Marxism would lead us further in the struggle against sociocide: toward a more socialized economy that puts power in the hands of worker cooperatives, local communities, and publicly owned banks and energy companies. It would break up corporations too big to fail and it would redistribute wealth dramatically to ensure a decent living standard for all. It would reverse austerity and promote massive public investment in all forms of social and environmental infrastructure, funded by new taxes on wealth, corporations, and carbon. It would charter businesses as creations of the public to serve the public and be accountable to it. It would create public financing of elections, eliminate the idea of corporations as persons with constitutional rights, and reconstruct the world around collective security and international governance based on the UN Universal Declaration of Human Rights rather than US hegemony. It would promote a concept of freedom based on positive rights to a socially dignified life rather than the negative rights to be left alone of the US Constitution and capitalist principles.[29]

In a 2013 book, *What Is to Be Done?* historian and political economist Gar Alperovitz has argued for a new society based on many of these principles and policies.[30] Alperovitz, along with the neo-Marxist sociologist and environmental economist Juliet Schor, and political economist and environmentalist David Korten, are part of a loosely affiliated group of political economists, who identify their work with a simple label: the "new economics." Their primary focus is on a new economic framework that can solve the environmental crisis and democratize the economy and society.

Beyond this self-identified group, there are many other innovative political economists, sociologists, journalists, and activists with much the same focus, including James Speth, John Bellamy Foster, Bill McKibben, Barbara Ehrenreich, Van Jones, Naomi Klein, Michael Lerner, Cornel West, Michael Albert, Walden Bello, Robert McChesney, Michael Moore, Erik Olin Wright, Michael Burawoy, Chuck Collins, Noam Chomsky, and us, to name just a few. While most of these writers and activists seek alternatives to capitalism in the long term, there is a wide range of vision and political strategy among them, with some focusing on local alternatives that might scale up to macro change over time, and others arguing for global change that will "scale down" to the community.

The "new economics" is a search for a twenty-first-century political economy. It is interdisciplinary and radical in vision, centered on the unprecedented existential crisis of the environment and the frightening sociopathy of hegemonic capitalism, yet pragmatic in many of its solutions. It recognizes that corporate capitalism—and the Wall Street ruling plutocracy—are at the heart of the environmental crisis and that solving climate change and other environmental problems means building a new economy based on democracy, on a reconstructed financial and energy system, and on social and environmental justice.

The approach of the self-identified "new economists"—such as Alperovitz, Schor, and Korten—is deeply critical of the capitalist macro-system but focuses more strongly than traditional neo-Marxists on solutions that start at the community level. Localism has its limits, but reflects a keen understanding of the social foundations of the crisis in the breakdown of community. It correctly sees the need to build new diverse and democratic local "living economies" that connect and support an atomized population with visceral needs for solidarity and security in new communities. The localists advancing new economics look at community agriculture, community banking, community ownership, and community production, from food to crafts to clothes, as well as worker-owned companies and consumer co-ops based at the community level.

Alperovitz argues that these community-based and worker-owned cooperatives are already spreading rapidly:

> Indeed, if you look closely, there are some 13 million people involved in one form or another of worker-owned companies, a form that changes who owns; there are 130 million people involved in credit unions and co-ops, another democratized form of ownership; there are 4,000 or 5,000 neighborhood corporations devoted to neighborhood development; there are 2,000 utilities that are owned by cities. People don't realize that. A quarter of the American electricity supply is essentially socialized in a radically decentralized way, utilities and co-ops, city-owned utilities. And it's been growing. There's a whole quiet building up of a different model that has a very American tone to it but goes at the central question of who owns capital, who owns the wealth. That I think is a critical basis for possible longer-term change.[31]

Alperovitz sees this as an embryo of a new democratic community-based economy, with special historical resonance in the United States:

> Unlike France, for instance, or Russia or the former Soviet Union, we have a very decentralized tradition, localism and states and kind of participatory American idea that comes from the agricultural frontier days. So there is something in the culture that can go many different ways: it can go far to the right, to individualism, but it also has community spirit and a kind of you-can-do-it, roll-up-your-sleeves, we-can-try-something-here.
>
> The models that are interesting—and I think of this as a long historical development—are very much at the local, neighborhood, workplace level of democratizing. I see that, one, as a precondition of how you could actually develop a system which was not state-dominated but also change who owned the productive capital. That's a precondition, building up that kind of an experienced culture and also a vision, models of what could be.[32]

Alperovitz recognizes that the power of Wall Street and the big corporations will not be undermined by this approach in the short term. In fact, it is Wall Street and the global capitalist class's overwhelming current power that leads him to prepare the ground now with these smaller-scale experiments, building the foundation for the larger assault on the centers of power:

> The struggle for real triumph over the systemic issues is a many-decade struggle. So if you say now is the fight, tomorrow, it's obvious that the deck is stacked. If that's where the confrontation comes, that's not going to happen. On the other hand, if you take—I wear a hat as a political

economist and historian, but if you stand back and ask, how does historical change really take place, what you're looking at is decades of developmental struggle.[33]

Alperovitz is looking ultimately for new a postcapitalist economy with limited forms of federal government ownership, a departure from the focus on nationalization in traditional Marxism. David Korten has the same approach, advocating an explicitly localist approach that ultimately replaces large-scale state and corporate power with a self-governing community approach:

> Communities are best able to set their own economic priorities and achieve economic security when most of their basic needs are met by local businesses that employ local labor and use local resources to meet the needs of local residents for employment, goods and services. Local owners have a far greater natural interest than absentee owners in managing environmental resources responsibly and sustainably because their own long term well-being depends on it.[34]

This localist approach is driven heavily by its ecological power, its strongest virtue. With Alperovitz, Juliet Schor made the argument that community-based initiatives are already proliferating rapidly and are our best hope for building a sustainable twenty-first-century economic model, most obviously in agriculture and food:

> Urban and suburban gardening are burgeoning. Individuals are planting vegetable plots, community gardens are sprouting and in a number of major cities, efforts to grow healthy organic food for inner-city residents are thriving. Detroit, Milwaukee and Chicago all have large-scale organizations that are reshaping residents' food habits. Farmers' markets, community-supported agriculture, local sourcing by restaurants, Slow Food chapters, school-yard gardens and related initiatives are on the rise. Practices are expanding from simple vegetable plots to urban homesteading.... New ways of living are proliferating in the United States and around the world, both at the household level and, more important, as people come together in community. These centers, or eco-villages, are pioneering earth-friendly ways of growing food, harvesting water, getting energy, healing the body and making products as well as democratic and collaborative methods for human interaction.[35]

Schor argued that there are national policies that can accelerate this shift, ranging from state policy favoring the choice of shorter work hours, the "share economy" used with bicycles and Zipcars, and economic incentives for local community-based start-ups in production and service sectors that will produce more sustainably. Won't large corporations buy these out if they become successful? Schor argued, "If starting an economic revolution from individuals and small scale activities sounds unrealistic, it's worth remembering that the first industrial revolution in Britain developed in just this manner. What became the powerhouse companies in textiles, potteries, shoes and other manufactures began from individual craftspeople working on a small scale."[36]

Korten advocates for an assault on the centers of global financial power, arguing for movements that seek not to reform Wall Street but abolish it and replace it with community-based banking and credit systems: "Efforts to fix Wall Street miss an important point. It can't be fixed. It is corrupt beyond repair, and we cannot afford it. Moreover, because the essential functions it does perform are served better in less costly ways, we do not need it."[37]

Korten, Schor, and Alperovitz all suggest that a combination of anticorporate and anti–Wall Street social movements, such as Occupy, changing consumer and lifestyle choices, and economic efficiencies will lead to a crumbling of central financial and corporate power over the long term. Their vision of a localist alternative is especially attractive on ecological grounds, but it is also controversial, breaking with other neo-Marxists and environmentalists who believe that the urgency of the crises and the key long-term solutions require substantial public ownership at the highest level of the economy, that is, national as well as community and worker ownership. In his book, *Greed to Green*, for example, Derber argued that the environmental crisis can only be resolved by nationalization of the largest banks and energy companies, suggesting that the president enact emergency measures to halt ecological ecocide as carbon dioxide (as measured in parts per million) rises above 400, a clear red zone for the planet. President Obama should address the nation and say,

> I call for a temporary nationalization of the biggest Wall Street and financial institutions that are systemically critical and require government aid to survive. Nationalization means that the government will buy ownership of a majority of common voting shares in these firms. Most other financial companies will remain in the private sector and will compete with the public ones. The aim of nationalization will be to stabilize the economy and prevent depression while moving rapidly toward a new sustainable and clean energy foundation that can not only help our economy but also the survival prospects of the entire human species.[38]

Obama enacted temporary nationalization in the auto industry, when he bailed out and took over GM and Chrysler. The president could present nationalization of the biggest banks and oil companies in the same spirit. Americans will likely welcome social or public ownership more with each passing year, as the nightmarish dimensions of the climate change crisis become clearer and the predatory casino behavior of Wall Street and Big Oil continue unabated. Derber paired this presidential proposal for public ownership with broader arguments focusing on a sweeping restructuring of the macro-corporate regime:

> Democracy and sustainability require that corporate control over the state be ended. The president must act not just to create lobbying limitations but also to build a new systemic firewall protecting the government against overweening corporate power. Both require that the president propose total public financing of elections, drastic limitation of corporate ownership of mass media and schools, reversal of the trend to permit commercial speech as protected under the First Amendment, criminalization of threats of corporations to influence the vote of employees, and rescinding of "investor rights" clauses that allow corporations to sue governments for passing laws protecting labor and the environment.[39]

Derber argued that movements such as Occupy must push these measures relentlessly on the national level. Nonetheless, visions of the macroeconomic alternative remain controversial, and there is no single or even clearly developed macro alternative vision. What is clear is that new principles will have to guide a sustainable and democratic national and global new system to prevent global sociocide.

At minimum, it is clear that the new political economy paradigm must look to anticapitalist policies going beyond traditional Marxist analysis. The most important macro principle of the new economics is the rejection of growth as the goal of the economy, linked to the rejection of consumerism as a philosophy of life. These challenge almost all the traditional political economy models, including the materialist assumptions built into both traditional Keynesianism and some traditions within neo-Marxism. Finding alternatives to growth and mass consumerism is one of the greatest challenges in the time we have left. Both elite interests and popular gratifications create formidable obstacles, but the new economics is beginning to find a path beyond them.

James Speth, an eminent Yale environmental scientist and political economist, has made the case forcefully that the reigning vision of unfettered economic growth is taking us like lemmings off the cliff:

> To sum up, we live in a world where economic growth is generally seen as both beneficent and necessary—the more the better; where past growth has brought us to a perilous state environmentally; where we are poised

for unprecedented increments in growth; where this growth is proceeding with wildly wrong market signs, including prices that do not incorporate environmental costs ... right now, one can only conclude that growth is the enemy of environment. Economy and environment remain in collision.[40]

The concern, of course, is that limiting growth and moving toward a steady-state economy will trap millions, especially in poor countries, into permanent poverty. But Juliet Schor shows, counterintuitively, that this can be avoided:

> A simple cessation of growth is a disaster, as unemployment and poverty soar, and income per person falls.... But with a modest amount of policy tinkering, much better outcomes emerge. If working hours fall, unemployment declines and free time rises. Poverty can even be reduced if the government transfers some income to the poor ... [and] income per head can improve without expansion of the overall size of the economy, through higher investment. This in turn raises productivity and well-being.[41]

As noted earlier, Schor has also offered persuasive arguments about the prospects of moving beyond mass consumerism, replaced with self-provisioning or household production, shorter work time and greater community and civic involvement, and "slow spending," that replaces quantity of consumption with quality. These are part of a shift away from our current mode of consumption toward a more meaningful way of life that is also sustainable and might just avoid ecological suicide.[42]

All of this leads less to a definitive vision than to a recognition of the need for a new political economy that breaks from all three political economy schools, in order to deal with the new existential crises that threaten capitalist-driven sociocide. The neo-Marxist approach offers powerful guides but needs to be restructured to deal with twenty-first-century crises that are new and merciless regarding their urgent threat to survival of societies and species.

The Sociological Imagination, Political Economy, and Survival

Hope for survival lies in the sociological imagination and intellectuals and social movements who act in its spirit. The hope lies in people recognizing that the greatest human fulfillment lies not in accumulating more and more stuff at the mall—or more and more money in the bank. It is in meaningful and loving social relations, and being seen and embraced as a person worthy of respect in a community. Given the challenges that we face, that respect can only be achieved by participation in creative work contributing toward transformations that prevent sociocide and build a sustainable and just world.

The sociological imagination provides a fundamental truth: human beings are a social species and need one another. Most people's intuition and life experience lead them to recognize this truth but we live in a society that inhibits the ability to organize a life based on this reality. As a result, we pursue the life channels offered by the existing order, even if they make us unhappy and preclude our pursuing the life that we know will fulfill us and help preserve life and the human community.

A political economy will be built in the twenty-first century based on this truth. It is the intellectual foundation of society's survival and personal well-being.

It will also ultimately help catalyze the real forces on the ground that can bring this truth to life. The Occupy movement was a reminder of that hope for social transformation. It made clear that political movements of the most unexpected form would arise at the most unexpected times and places, although, like Occupy, many may weaken and fizzle out, as they are always repressed by the state and rejected by elites as well as much of an indoctrinated population. But as our existential crises grow more severe, the rise of such movements will spread and grow, as they have in movements such as the Arab Spring, the indigenous rights movements, the global environmental coalitions for a sustainable world, the women's and peace global movements, and many more popular movements seeking to press beyond the existing capitalist order.

We also have to face another sobering truth: we lack a fully credible alternative model and vision—or new paradigm of political economy—though we have many concrete ideas about what such a system must incorporate. This is not the worst possible fate. New societies may be inspired by blueprints imagined by thinkers but are worked out in thousands of experiments over decades.

The best we can do at this point is to suggest guiding principles and be prepared ourselves to act on them and walk our talk. Let us highlight one last time the principles—with a focus on newly urgent priorities of preventing sociocide—that should guide a twenty-first-century political economy.

1. Environmental protection—and solving the climate change crisis—is the greatest challenge facing us. The new political economy paradigm must thus pass the most stringent standards of sustainability and help advance a society, values, and an economy that put environmental health at the heart of our new sociological imagination.

2. The environmental crisis arises from the sociopathic drives of elites to gain more profit and wealth through endless growth at the expense of people and the commons. The new political economy thinking must target this tragedy of the commons and end the privatization of resources, replacing economic growth with sufficiency as the aim of a postcapitalist economy and limit consumption to the carrying capacity of the earth.

3. The same argument applies to wars, militarism, and the possibility of sociocide based on use of weapons of mass destruction. Creating peace, like ending climate change, is part of a movement for social justice, since it requires transformation of hegemonic capitalism.

4. The new political economy paradigm must highlight the sociopathic economics of global corporate capitalism, governed by a globally knit financial plutocracy centered on Wall Street. It generates unacceptable levels of extreme inequality, poverty, surplus mass populations, and austerity, threatening basic social needs and the very survival of billions of people throughout the world. The new political economy must demonstrate that disinvestment from entire societies through the globalization process is creating possibilities of sociocide in both rich and poor nations.

5. All these arguments point to the need for a political economy paradigm that can help educate and mobilize the population to support social movements to prevent capitalist sociocide. It must theorize and help create a society committed to ending the tragedy of the commons, limiting privatization of natural and social resources, ending the concentration of money in a Wall Street plutocracy at the center of global power, walling off corporate wealth from politics, and ensuring creation of public goods and a social welfare state that can supplant the empty and ecologically violent culture of mass consumerism. A movement against austerity, war, Wall Street, *Citizens United*, big money in politics, and Big Oil and Big Coal's agenda of environmental degradation is only the first step. Failure to scale up these movements to challenge corporate power and sociopathic capitalism will end civilized society as we know it.

The twenty-first century has moved beyond traditional struggles around justice. We are now approaching the ultimate challenge: the prospect of saving civilized society from extinction. Time is short, and current policy—embodied in neoclassical ideas of private property, free markets, free trade, austerity, corporate globalization, and the invisible hand—now threatens not just justice but human survival.

The new sociological imagination is thus facing greater odds, shorter time frames, and the ultimate stakes. We have a corporate capitalism that generates a sociopathic society and ultimately sociocide.[43] We need a vision of a society affirming life—the life of both the creative individual and a sustainable and just society rather than the barbaric specter of societal destruction looming in front of us.

Time is very short. Moving from a political economy of death toward one sustaining life is a huge challenge. We have no option but to create the ideas and action that can create a new tipping point. It is not only our personal future but that of all future generations that is at stake.

Notes

Chapter 1

1. Fred Ebb, *Cabaret*, Warner Bros., 1972.
2. John Maynard Keynes, *The General Theory of Employment, Interest, and Money* (New York: Harcourt, Brace and World, 1965), book 5, chapter 21, section 3, p. 298.
3. Lawrence Summers, quoted in "The Committee to Change the World," *Time*, February 15, 1999.
4. Paul Samuelson, "Sunrise—Or False Dawn," *Washington Post*, April 28, 1999.
5. John K. Galbraith, "Power and the Useful Economist," *Annals of an Abiding Liberal* (Boston: Houghton Mifflin, 1979).
6. Kurt Vonnegut, *God Bless You, Mr. Rosewater* (New York: Dial, 1998).
7. *The American Heritage Dictionary of the English Language*, 4th ed. (Boston: Houghton Mifflin Company, 2009).
8. *Collins English Dictionary: Complete and Unabridged* (New York: HarperCollins, 2003).
9. John Stuart Mill, *Principles of Political Economy*, edited by Jonathan Riley (New York: Oxford University Press Classics, 2008).
10. Alfred Marshall, *Principles of Economics*, 8th ed. (Rome: Cosimo Classics, 2009).
11. William Stanley Jevons, *The Theory of Political Economy*, 2nd ed. (Charleston, SC: BiblioBazaar, 2009), p. xiv.
12. Mark Hannah, "Money and the Financing of Campaigns," CivilPolitics.org, quote made in 1895, www.civilpolitics.org/content/money-and-financing-campaigns.
13. Alice Walker, quoted in Fernanda Sayao, "Capitalism" (Rio De Janeiro: Animal Farm Research, 2012).
14. Charles Derber, *Sociopathic Society: A People's Sociology of the United States* (Boulder, CO: Paradigm Publishers, 2013).

Chapter 2

1. David Brown, "Free Radical: Review of *Radical Ambition: C. Wright Mills, the Left, and American Social Thought*, by Daniel Geary," *The Magazine of Columbia Unversity* (Summer 2009).

2. Alvin Gouldner, *The Coming Crisis of Western Sociology* (New York: Avon, 1971).

3. Ibid.

4. C. Wright Mills, *The Sociological Imagination* (New York: Oxford University Press, 1959).

5. Karl Marx, *Capital: An Abridged Edition* (New York: Oxford University Press, 2008); Max Weber, *Economy and Society*, 4th ed. (Berkeley: University of California Press, 1978).

6. Weber, *Economy and Society*, chapter 2.

7. Randall Collins, *Weberian Sociological Theory* (New York: Cambridge University Press, 1986), p. 21.

8. Karl Marx and Friedrich Engels, *The Communist Manifesto*, in Robert C. Tucker (ed.), *The Marx-Engels Reader* (New York: Norton, 1972), p. 338.

9. C. Wright Mills, *The Sociological Imagination* (Harmondsworth: Penguin, 1971 [1959]), p. 12.

10. Ibid.

11. C. Wright Mills, *The Power Elite* (New York: Oxford University Press, 1959), p. 4.

12. Ibid., p. 361.

13. Ibid.

14. Gertrud Lenzer, *Auguste Comte and Positivism: The Essential Writings* (New York: Transaction, 1997); Herbert Spencer and Jonathan Turner, *The Principles of Sociology* (New York: Transaction, 2002).

15. Emile Durkheim, *The Rules of Sociological Method* (New York: Free Press, 1982).

16. Galbraith, quoted in Clive Cook, "John Kenneth Galbraith, Revisited," *Atlantic Monthly*, May 15, 2006.

17. Phil Ochs, "I'm Gonna Say It Now," Elektra Records, 1966.

18. Ronald Reagan, *Los Angeles Times*, April 7, 1970.

19. Mills, *The Power Elite*.

Chapter 3

1. Cited in Edmund L. Andrews, "Greenspan Concedes Error on Regulation," *New York Times*, October 23, 2008, www.nytimes.com/2008/10/24/business/economy/24panel.html?_r=0.

2. Ibid.

3. Cited in Judy Woodruff, "Transcript, Greenspan Admits Flaw to Congress, Predicts More Economic Problems," PBS NewsHour, October 23, 2008, www.pbs.org/newshour/bb/business/july-dec08/crisishearing_10-23.html.

4. Ibid.

5. In an online poll, the UK *Guardian* surveyed readers asking who was most responsible for the meltdown. Greenspan was selected by 32 percent of respondents, by far the largest number. "Who Led Us Down the Road to Ruin?" *Guardian*, January 26, 2009, www.guardian.co.uk/business/poll/2009/jan/26/road-to-ruin-recession.

6. Derber has made this argument in his book, *Hidden Power* (San Francisco: Berrett-Koehler Publishers, 2005).

7. All quotes from Reagan cited at http://thinkexist.com/quotes.

8. Adam Smith, *The Wealth of Nations*, reprint ed. (New York: Bantam Classics, 2003).

9. The neoclassical code, as we conceive it, is most clearly articulated in the works of Milton Friedman, including especially Milton Friedman and Rose Friedman, *Free to Choose* (New York: Harvest, 1990); and Milton Friedman, *Capitalism and Freedom*, 40th anniversary ed. (Chicago: University of Chicago Press, 2002).

10. Friedman quote cited at www.brainyquote.com/quotes/quotes/m/miltonfrie173377.html#ySGFO3TeCSCLMfw2.99.

11. Friedman quote cited at www.brainyquote.com/quotes/authors/m/milton_friedman.html#P5B8EfHAbPSvIP8Q.99.

12. Smith, *Wealth of Nations*.

13. Tom Friedman, *The Lexus and the Olive Tree* (New York: Anchor, 2000), p. 113.

14. This is most clearly argued in Milton Friedman, *Capitalism and Freedom*, chapter 1.

15. Ibid.

16. Friedman and Friedman, *Free to Choose*, chapter 1, pp. 13ff.

17. Smith, cited in Robert Heilbroner, *The Worldly Philosophers*, 6th ed. (New York: Simon and Schuster, 1986), p. 55.

18. Smith, *Wealth of Nations*, cited in Friedman and Friedman, *Free to Choose*, p. 2.

19. Friedman and Friedman, *Free to Choose*, p. 13.

20. Milton Friedman, *Capitalism and Freedom*, chapter 3.

21. This has become the orthodoxy not only of advocates of the neoclassical paradigm but their political allies today, in both parties but especially the Republican Party.

22. Milton Friedman quote cited at www.brainyquote.com/quotes/authors/m/milton_friedman.html#Zveg8fkRiGcml1bt.99.

23. This has become the orthodoxy of the Republican Party and the neoclassical school, explained and critiqued most clearly by the Keynesian economist, Paul Krugman, in his *New York Times* columns and his book, *End This Depression Now!* (New York: Norton, 2012).

24. Romney quote cited at www.brainyquote.com/quotes/keywords/small_government.html#CkODfXPIUUsbB4IL.99.

25. Casey Mulligan, quoted in Paul Krugman, "How Did Economists Get It So Wrong?" *New York Times*, September 6, 2009.

26. Again, Milton Friedman is the contemporary prophet of this neoclassical orthodoxy, with the argument against interventionist or "big government" made with great force in *Capitalism and Freedom* (chapter 2) and *Free to Choose* (chapter 4). The

other most influential mid-twentieth-century economic thinker beyond Friedman, who equated the rise of "big government" with tyranny both in Europe and the United States was Frederick Hayek, *The Road to Serfdom* (Chicago: University of Chicago Press, 1944). Friedman's and Hayek's philosophical manifestos became the mantra of the Reagan revolution and intellectually help shape and legitimate the "small government" orthodoxy of the contemporary Republican Party and its libertarian wing, the Tea Party.

27. Milton Friedman quote cited at www.brainyquote.com/quotes/quotes/m/miltonfrie153357.html.

28. Milton Friedman quote cited at http://appalachianconservative.wordpress.com/2009/08/01/milton-friedman-quotes.

29. Ibid.

30. Gary Becker, *A Treatise on the Family* (Cambridge, MA: Harvard University Press, 1993).

31. Charles Derber, *Corporation Nation* (New York: St. Martin's Press, 2000).

32. See Lori Wallach, *Whose Trade Organization*, 2nd ed. (New York: New Press, 2004).

33. See Charles Derber, *Greed to Green* (Boulder, CO: Paradigm Publishers, 2010).

34. Derber, *Corporation Nation*, chapter 8.

35. Obama quote cited at www.quoteauthors.com/quotes/barack-obama-quotes.html#rjrFW7JMHPrulb7c.99.

36. Derber, *Hidden Power*, chapters 1–3.

37. Norquist cited in Chris Cillizza, "Who Is Grover Norquist?" *Washington Post*, November 26, 2012, www.washingtonpost.com/blogs/the-fix/wp/2012/11/26/who-is-grover-norquist/.

38. Friedman and Friedman, *Free to Choose*, chapter 1.

39. Milton Friedman, *Capitalism and Freedom*, chapter 2, p. 25.

40. Ibid., p. 27.

41. Derber, *Corporation Nation*, especially chapters 2, 8. See also Charles Derber, *People before Profit* (New York: Picador, 2003), especially chapters 2, 3.

42. Smith, *Wealth of Nations*.

43. Heilbroner, *The Worldly Philosophers*, p. 71.

44. Adam Smith, *A Theory of Moral Sentiments* (New York: Empire Books, 2011).

45. Heilbroner, *The Worldly Philosophers*.

46. David Ricardo, *The Principles of Political Economy and Taxation* (New York: Dover, 2004).

47. Heilbroner, *The Worldly Philosophers*, pp. 95ff.

48. Chadwick, secretary to the Royal Commission, cited in George R. Boyer, *An Economic History of the English Poor Law, 1750–1850* (Cambridge, UK: Cambridge University Press, 1990), quoting *Parliamentary Papers*, 1834, p. 228.

49. Auguste Comte, *Introduction to Positive Philosophy*, reprint ed. (New York: Hackett, 1988).

50. Alfred Marshall, *Principles of Economics*, reprint ed. (New York: Prometheus Books, 1997).

51. Heilbroner, *The Worldly Philosophers*, pp. 209ff.

52. Andrew Carnegie, *Gospel of Wealth*, reprint ed. (New York: Applewood Books, 1998).

53. Frederick Hayek, *The Road to Serfdom* (Chicago: University of Chicago, 2007 [1944]), p. 110.

54. Ibid.; see introduction by Bruce Caldwell.

55. Ibid., chapter 2.

56. Ibid.

57. Charles Derber and Yale Magrass, *Morality Wars* (Boulder, CO: Paradigm Publishers, 2010), part III.

58. Ayn Rand, *The Fountainhead*, centennial ed. (New York: Plume, 1994); Ayn Rand, *Atlas Shrugged*, reprint ed. (New York: Plume, 1999).

59. Ayn Rand, *Capitalism: The Unknown Ideal* (New York: Signet, 1967), p. 45.

60. Ibid., p. 61.

61. Ibid.

62. Milton Friedman, *Capitalism and Freedom*; Friedman and Friedman, *Free to Choose*.

63. Milton Friedman, *Capitalism and Freedom*, p. 15.

64. Tom Friedman, *The Lexus and the Olive Tree*, p. 104.

Chapter 4

1. Warren Buffet, "A Minimum Tax for the Wealthy," *New York Times*, November 25, 2012.

2. Edward Filene, *Speaking of Change* (Washington, DC: National Home Library Foundation, 1939), p. 270; emphasis in original.

3. Mitt Romney, "Economic Freedom," Chicago, March 19, 2012.

4. John Maynard Keynes, quoted in John M. Blum, *Years of Crisis* (Boston: Houghton Mifflin, 1959), p. 408.

5. John Maynard Keynes, *The Applied Theory of Money* (London: Macmillan, 1930), pp. 148–149.

6. John Maynard Keynes, *Collected Writing* (Cambridge, UK: Cambridge University, 2012), vol. 9, p. 106.

7. John Maynard Keynes, *The General Theory of Employment Interest and Money* (Whitefield, MT: Kessinger, 2010), p. 245.

8. John Maynard Keynes, *The Means to Prosperity* (London: Macmillan, 1933), p. 16.

9. David Jarmul, "By 1920, America Had Become World's Top Economic Power," *The Making of a Nation* (Washington, DC: VOA, 2006).

10. John Maynard Keynes, *The Economic Consequences of the Peace* (Philadelphia: Empire, 2013), pp. 226–228.

11. "Great Depression," *Encyclopedia of North American History* (Terrytown, NY: Marshall Cavendish, 1999).

12. John T. Landry, "Time for a New Five Dollar Day," *Harvard Business Review*, November 8, 2010.

13. Tom Raum, "Intervention in Banks Not without Precedents," *USA Today*, October 15, 2008.

14. Richard W. Stewart, *The United States Army in a Global Era, 1917–2003* (Washington, DC: Center of Military History, United States Army, 2005), p. 54.

15. Burton Fulsom, *The Myth of the Robber Barons* (Herndon, VA: Young America's Foundation, 1991).

16. Calvin Coolidge, "Address to the American Society of Newspaper Editors," Washington, DC, January 17, 1925.

17. Calvin Coolidge, quoted in Robert Sobel, "Coolidge and American Business," Coolidge Memorial Foundation, 1988.

18. Calvin Coolidge, "Coolidge Explains Cause of Progress," *New York Times*, November 20, 1920.

19. Calvin Coolidge, quoted in Ted Abram, "Personal Freedom and Taxation 104," Freedom Works, December 26, 2012, www.freedomworks.org.

20. Calvin Coolidge, quoted in Mikhail Kryzhanovsky, *White House Special Handbook: How to Rule the World in the 21st Century* (New York: Algora, 2007), p. 225.

21. Calvin Coolidge, quoted in Kassandra Lee, *Calvin Coolidge* (St. Petersburg, FL, 2012).

22. John Maynard Keynes, *The General Theory of Employment, Interest, and Money* (New York: Harcourt, Brace and World, 1965).

23. Robert Skidelsky, *John Maynard Keynes* (New York: Penguin, 2003), pp. 520–521.

24. John Maynard Keynes, quoted in Edgar Hardcastle, "Keynes and the Russian Revolution," *Socialist Standard*, May 1967.

25. Franklin D. Roosevelt, radio address, White House, Washington, DC, April 14, 1938.

26. Paul Krugman, *End This Depression Now!* (New York: Norton, 2012), p. 24.

27. Frances Fox Piven and Richard Cloward, *Regulating the Poor* (New York: Random House, 1971), p. 123.

28. Arthur Schlesinger, *The Coming of the New Deal* (Boston: Houghton Mifflin, 1958), p. 338.

29. Ibid., p. 486.

30. Piven and Cloward, *Regulating the Poor*, p. 115.

31. Quoted in Krugman, *End This Depression Now!* p. 56.

32. Robert Lekachman, *The Age of Keynes* (New York: Random House, 1966), p. 151.

33. "Chart of US Gross Domestic Product, 1929–2004," Bureau of Economic Analysis, http://economics-charts.com/gdp/gdp-1929-2004.html.

34. Victor Zarnowitz, *Business Cycles* (Chicago: University of Chicago Press, 1966), p. 229.

35. Glenn C. Altschuler, *The GI Bill* (New York: Oxford University Press, 2006).

36. Herbert Gans, *The Urban Villagers* (New York: Free Press, 1982).

37. Charles Siegel, *The Politics of Simple Living* (Berkeley: Preservation Institute, 2008).

38. *Taken for a Ride*, directed by Jim Klein and Martha Olson, New Day Films, 1996. Excerpts cited at Culture Change, www.culturechange.org/issue10/taken-for -a-ride.htm.

39. Stephen Ambrose, *Eisenhower: Soldier and President* (New York: Simon and Schuster, 1990), p. 573.

40. Paul McMorrow, "A Ticking Clock for Cities," *Boston Globe*, August 26, 2012.

41. Paul Samuelson, *Economics* (New York: McGraw-Hill, 1964), pp. 3–4.

42. John Kenneth Galbraith, *The Affluent Society* (Boston: Mariner, 1998); John Kenneth Galbraith, *The New Industrial State* (Princeton, NJ: Princeton University Press, 2007).

43. Galbraith, *The New Industrial State*, chapter 1.

44. Vance Packard, *The Waste Makers* (New York: Simon and Schuster, 1978).

45. Chris Paine, *Who Killed the Electric Car?* Sony Pictures, 2006.

46. Paul Baran and Paul Sweezy, *Monopoly Capital* (New York: Monthly Review Press, 1966).

47. Seymour Melman, *Our Depleted Society* (Concord, CA: Delta Books, 1966).

48. Paul Samuelson, "Unemployment Ahead: (II.) The Coming Economic Crisis," *New Republic*, September 18, 1944, p. 333.

49. Lyndon Johnson, address to Congress, March 16, 1964.

50. Lyndon Johnson, television speech, March 31, 1968.

51. *New York Times*, January 4, 1971.

52. Jeremy Rifkin, *The European Dream* (New York: Tarcher, 2005).

53. "The 'First' 9/11, the 1973 Overthrow of Salvador Allende in Chile," *The History They Didn't Teach You in School*, vi.uh.edu/pages/buzzmat/htdtisallende.html.

54. Krugman, *End This Depression Now!* p. 102.

55. Quoted in Bonnie Kavoussi, "11 Things the Republicans Don't Want You to Know about the Deficit," *Huffington Post*, September 5, 2012.

56. Bentsen-Quayle debate, Omaha, Nebraska, October 5, 1988.

57. CBS Moneywatch, February 28, 2011.

58. Krugman, *End This Depression Now!*

59. Paul Krugman, "How the Case for Austerity Has Crumbled," *New York Review of Books*, June 6, 2013, pp. 8–73.

60. Tom Friedman, "Average Is Over," *New York Times*, January 25, 2012, p. 25.

61. Arianna Huffington, *Third World America* (New York: Crown, 2011).

Chapter 5

1. Karl Marx, "Theories of Surplus Values," in Robert Freedman, *Marx on Economics* (New York: Penguin, 1962), p. 213.

2. Friedrich Engels, *The Condition of the Working Class in England* (Oxford, UK: Oxford University Press, 2009).

3. Friedrich Engels, Letter to Marx, January 20, 1945.

4. Martin Daunton, "London's 'Great Stink' and Victorian Urban Planning," BBC History Trail, London, 2004.

5. Karl Marx, *Economic and Philosophic Manuscripts of 1844* (Ranford, VA: Wilder, 2011).

6. Karl Marx, *Capital* (New York: Penguin, 1992), vol. 1, chapter 1.

7. Karl Marx and Friedrich Engels, *The Communist Manifesto*, in Lawrence Simon (ed.), *Karl Marx: Selected Writings* (New York: Hackett, 1994).

8. Ibid.

9. Alvin Gouldner, *The Two Marxisms* (New York: Oxford University Press, 1982). We understand the paradigm somewhat differently from Gouldner. For example, he places Lenin in the critical camp and we identify him as structural/scientific.

10. Marx and Engels, *The Communist Manifesto*, p. 159.

11. Ibid., p. 161.

12. John Bellamy Foster and Fred Magdoff, *The Great Financial Crisis* (New York: Monthly Review Press, 2009), pp. 120, 121.

13. Ibid., pp. 101–102.

14. Marx and Engels, *The Communist Manifesto*, p. 169.

15. Karl Marx, *Capital*, vol. 1, reprinted in Robert C. Tucker, *The Marx-Engels Reader* (New York: Norton, 1972), p. 259.

16. Ibid.

17. Ibid., p. 287.

18. Ibid., pp. 286, 287.

19. Marx and Engels, *The Communist Manifesto*, chapter 1.

20. Vladimir Lenin, *State and Revolution* (New York: Penguin, 1993).

21. V. I. Lenin, *The Proletarian Revolution and the Renegade Kautsky, Collected Works*, vol. 28, p. 235.

22. Rosa Luxemburg, *The Russian Revolution and Leninism or Marxism?* (Ann Arbor, MI: Ann Arbor Paperbacks, 1981).

23. Ibid.

24. Emma Goldman, *Living My Life* (Claremont, CA: Anarchy Archives, 2011).

25. Marx, *Economic and Philosophic Manuscripts of 1844*.

26. Karl Marx, "Estranged Labor," *Economic and Philosophic Manuscripts of 1844*.

27. This is actually the title of a book Lenin wrote. Vladimir Lenin, *What Is to Be Done?* (New York: International, 1969).

28. Gouldner, *The Two Marxisms*, p. 35.

29. Ibid.

30. Ibid.

31. Mike Davis, *Be Realistic: Demand the Impossible* (Chicago: Haymarket, 2012).

32. Antonio Gramsci, *Selections from "The Prison Notebooks"* (London: Elecbook, 1999).

33. Martin Jay, *The Dialectical Imagination: A History of the Frankfurt School* (Berkeley: University of California Press, 1996).

34. Herbert Marcuse, *One-Dimensional Man* (Boston: Beacon, 1968).

35. Ibid., chapter 1.

36. Bernard J. Brommel, *Eugene V. Debs: Spokesman for Labor and Socialism* (Chicago: Charles H. Kerr Publishing Co., 1978).

37. Eugene Debs, Canton, Ohio, June 16, 1918.

38. David Kennedy, *The American Pageant* (Boston: Houghton Mifflin, 2006), p. 716.

39. Robert K. Murray, *Red Scare: A Study in National Hysteria, 1919–1920* (Minneapolis: University of Minnesota Press, 1955).

40. Sharon Smith, "The 1930s: Turning Point for US Labor," *International Socialist Review* 25 (September–October 2002).

41. Yale Magrass, *Thus Spake the Moguls* (Cambridge, MA: Schenkman, 1981).

42. Edward Filene, *The Way Out* (London: Routledge, 1925), p. 164.

43. Edward Filene, *Speaking of Change* (Washington, DC: National Home Library Foundation, 1939), p. 245.

44. Paul Sweezy, *The Present as History* (New York: Monthly Review Press, 1953).

45. Ellen Schrecker, *The Age of McCarthyism* (Boston: St. Martin's Press, 1994).

46. William Keach, "Rehabilitating McCarthyism," *International Socialist Review* 12 (June–July 2000).

47. John Meroney, "Left in the Past," *Los Angeles Times*, February 2012.

48. Daniel Bell, *The End of Ideology* (Cambridge, MA: Harvard University Press, 2000).

49. Ibid., chapter 13.

50. Michael Harrington, *The Other America* (New York: Scribner, 1997).

51. Ibid.

52. W. E. B. Du Bois, "Marxism and the Negro Problem," *The Crisis*, May 1933, pp. 103–104.

53. A. Philip Randolph Institute, Washington, DC, 2013.

54. Angela Davis, *Angela Davis: An Autobiography* (New York: Random House, 1974).

55. Angela Davis, *Women, Race and Class* (London: Women's Press, 1981), chapter 13.

56. Vladimir Lenin, *Imperialism: The Highest Stage of Capitalism* (London: Pluto, 1996).

57. Immanuel Wallerstein, *World-Systems Analysis: An Introduction* (Durham, NC: Duke University Press, 2004).

58. Charles Derber and Yale Magrass, *The Surplus American* (Boulder, CO: Paradigm Publishers, 2012).

59. Charles Derber, William Schwartz, and Yale Magrass, *Power in the Highest Degree* (New York: Oxford University Press, 1990), p. 182.

60. Jerry Rubin, *Do It!* (New York: Simon and Schuster, 1970).

61. Jack Weinberg, *Berkeley Daily Planet*, April 6, 2000.

62. Marcuse, *One-Dimensional Man*.

63. Paul Baran and Paul Sweezy, *Monopoly Capital* (New York: Monthly Review, 1966).

64. Ibid., pp. 1–3.

65. Paul Goodman, *Growing Up Absurd* (New York: New York Book Review Classics, 2012).

66. C. Wright Mills, *White Collar* (New York: Oxford University Press, 2002).

67. Sloan Wilson, *The Man in the Gray Flannel Suit* (Cambridge, MA: De Capo, 2002).

68. Mario Savio, "The Berkeley Student Rebellion of 1964," Free Speech Movement Archives.

69. Ibid.

70. Noam Chomsky, *American Power and the New Mandarins* (New York: New Press, 2002).

71. Howard Zinn, *You Can't Be Neutral on a Moving Train* (Boston: Beacon, 2002).

72. *New York Times*, May 9, 1970.

73. W. Lunch and P. Sperlich, "American Public Opinion and the War in Vietnam," *Western Political Quarterly* 32, no. 1 (1979): 21–44.

74. Tom Friedman, "Average Is Over," *New York Times*, January 25, 2012, p. 25.

75. Barry Bluestone and Bennett Harrison, *The Deindustrialization of America* (New York: Basic Books, 1984).

76. Harry Braverman, *Labor and Monopoly Capital* (New York: Monthly Review Press, 1974).

77. Stanley Aronowitz, *False Promises: The Shaping of American Working Class Consciousness* (Durham, NC: Duke University Press, 1991).

78. Michael Burawoy, *Manufacturing Consent* (Chicago: University of Chicago, 1979).

79. Erik Olin Wright, *Class Counts* (Cambridge, UK: Cambridge University Press, 1996).

80. *St. Louis Post-Dispatch*, December 5, 1960.

81. Lawrence Mishel, "CEO-to-Worker Pay Imbalance Grows," *Economic Policy Institute*, June 21, 2006.

82. Jennifer Liberto, *CNN Money*, April 20, 2011.

83. Tami Luhby, *CNN Money*, September 11, 2012.

84. Charles Riley, *CNN Money*, June 12, 2012.

85. "Dow Jones Industrial Average History," *FedPrimeRate*, 2013.

86. Chrystia Freeland, "Jobless Recovery Leaves Middle Class Behind," *New York Times*, April 12, 2012.

87. Mohandas Gandhi, 1913, vol. 13, chapter 153, p. 241.

Chapter 6

1. Data are cited in Chuck Collins, *99 to 1* (San Francisco: Berrett-Koehler, 2012), pp. 21, 23.

2. Farhad Ebrahimi, "Occupy Boston," cited in Collins, *99 to 1*, p. 83.

3. Warren Buffet, cited on Eric Beam, "Elites Pushing Class Warfare Is Just Another False Paradigm," Infowars, January 25, 2012.

4. Plutarch cited in Collins, *99 to 1*, p. 7.

5. Matthew 19:24.

6. John Calvin, quoted in Gene Taylor, *Calvinism III* (Tallahassee, FL: Centerville Road Church of Christ, 2011).

7. Max Weber, *The Protestant Ethic and the Spirit of Capitalism* (New York: Oxford University Press, 2010).

8. Paul Ryan, "60 Percent of Americans Are Takers—Not Makers," 2010 video, on www.huffingtonpost.com/2012/10/05/paul-ryan-60-percent-of-a_n_1943073.html.

9. Adam Smith, *The Wealth of Nations* (New York: Bantam, 2003).

10. Ibid.

11. Weber, *The Protestant Ethic and the Spirit of Capitalism*.

12. Kingsley Davis and Wilbert E. Moore, "Some Principles of Stratification," *American Sociological Review* 10, no. 2 (1970 [1945]): 242–249.

13. Ayn Rand, "What Is Capitalism?" in *Capitalism: The Unknown Ideal* (New York: Signet, 1967), pp. 18–19.

14. Ibid.

15. Ibid., p. 21.

16. Ibid., p. 23.

17. Paul Ryan, cited in Hunter Stuart and Saki Knafu, "Paul Ryan Looks at Poor, Sees 'Takers,'" *Huffington Post*, October 26, 2012, www.huffingtonpost.com/2012/10/25/paul-ryan-poverty_n_2019092.html.

18. Ibid.

19. Robert Lekachman, *The Age of Keynes* (New York: Random House, 1966), p. 120.

20. Joseph Stiglitz, "Inequality Is Holding Back Our Recovery," *New York Times*, January 19, 2013, http://opinionator.blogs.nytimes.com/2013/01/19/inequality-is-holding-back-the-recovery/.

21. Ibid.

22. Ibid.

23. Robert Reich, *Aftershock* (New York: Vintage, 2011), p. 75.

24. Ibid., p. 127.

25. Paul Krugman, *End This Depression Now!* (New York: Norton, 2012).

26. Charles Derber, *Regime Change Begins at Home* (San Francisco: Berrett-Koehler, 2004), chapter 1.

27. Lekachman, *The Age of Keynes*, p. 121.

28. Ibid.

29. Krugman, *End This Depression Now!*

30. Joseph Stiglitz, *The Price of Inequality* (New York: Norton, 2013).

31. Ibid.

32. Stiglitz, "Inequality Is Holding Back Our Recovery."

33. Ibid.

34. J. K. Galbraith, *American Capitalism: The Concept of Countervailing Power* (New York: Transaction Press, 1993).

35. Galbraith's two most important works in this area are *The Affluent Society* (Boston: Mariner, 1998), and *The New Industrial State* (Princeton, NJ: Princeton University Press, 2007).

36. J. K. Galbraith, quoted in Robert Fuller, *All Rise* (San Francisco: Berrett-Koehler, 2006), p. 57.

37. J. K. Galbraith, *The Great Crash of 1929* (Boston: Mariner, 2009).

38. Galbraith, *The Affluent Society*.

39. Lyndon B. Johnson, "Special Message to the Congress Proposing a Nationwide War on the Sources of Poverty," March 16, 1964.

40. Charles Derber and Yale Magrass, *The Surplus American* (Boulder, CO: Paradigm Publishers, 2012).

41. Karl Marx and Friedrich Engels, *The Communist Manifesto,* in Robert Tucker (ed.), *The Marx-Engels Reader* (New York: Norton, 1978), p. 336.

42. Barbara Ehrenreich, *Nickel and Dimed* (New York: Picador, 2011).

43. Marx and Engels, *The Communist Manifesto*, pp. 341–342.

44. Paul Baran and Paul Sweezy, *Monopoly Capital* (New York: Monthly Review Press, 1966), pp. 51, 52–53.

45. Marx and Engels, *The Communist Manifesto*, p. 345.

46. Charles Derber, *Sociopathic Society: A People's Sociology of the United States* (Boulder, CO: Paradigm Publishers, 2013).

47. Karl Marx, *Theories of Surplus Value* (Moscow, USSR: Progress, 1969), pp. 237, 239.

48. Karl Marx, *Capital*, vol. 1 (New York: Penguin, 1992), p. 179.

49. Derber and Magrass, *The Surplus American*.

50. Marx and Engels, *The Communist Manifesto*, p. 337.

51. G. William Domhoff, *Who Rules America?* 6th ed. (New York: McGraw-Hill, 2009).

52. Thomas Ferguson, *The Golden Rule* (Chicago: University of Chicago Press, 1995).

53. Charles Derber, *Hidden Power* (San Francisco: Berrett-Koehler Publishers, 2005), chapter 2.

54. Collins, *99 to 1*, p. 34.

55. Ibid., p. 35.

56. Ibid.

57. Ibid., p. 51.

58. Ibid., p. 39.

59. Ibid., chapter 9.

60. Milton Friedman, *Capitalism and Freedom*, 40th anniversary ed. (Chicago: University of Chicago Press, 2002), chapter 2.

61. Charles Derber, *Marx's Ghost* (Boulder, CO: Paradigm Publishers, 2011).

62. Gabriel Kolko, *The Triumph of Conservatism* (New York: Free Press, 1977).

63. Derber, *Marx's Ghost*.

64. Derber, *Sociopathic Society*.

65. Baran and Sweezy, *Monopoly Capital*.

66. Antonio Gramsci, *The Prison Notebooks* (New York: International Publisher, 1971). See also Tom Frank, *What's the Matter with Kansas* (New York: Holt, 2005).

Chapter 7

1. Sarah Palin quoted in Susan Sherwood Parr, *Sarah Palin: Faith, Family, Country* (Alachua, FL: Bridge-Logos, 2008).

2. Milton Friedman and Rose Friedman, *Free to Choose* (New York: Harvest, 1990), pp. 2–3.

3. Abraham Lincoln, "Letter to Col. William F. Elkins," November 21, 1864.

4. Louis Brandeis, quoted in Michael Parenti, "Capital's Self-Inflicted Apocalypse," 2009, Political Archive, michaelparenti.org.

5. Noam Chomsky, "One Man's View," *Business Today*, May 1973, pp. 13–15.

6. Fran Lebowitz, Jewish Comedians (website), May 5, 2012.

7. Ayn Rand, *Atlas Shrugged*, reprint ed. (New York: Plume, 1999). See also Ayn Rand, *The Fountainhead*, centennial ed. (New York: Plume, 1994).

8. Milton Friedman, *Capitalism and Freedom*, 40th anniversary ed. (Chicago: University of Chicago Press, 2002), pp. 34–35. See also Friedman and Friedman, *Free to Choose*, chapter 1.

9. Friedman, *Capitalism and Freedom*.

10. Friedman and Friedman, *Free to Choose*, chapter 1.

11. Ibid. See also F. A. Hayek, *The Road to Serfdom* (Chicago: University of Chicago Press, 1944), for a philosophical manifesto dedicated entirely to this theme of government economic power as what Hayek calls "slavery."

12. While Friedman refers to Coolidge, the modern neoclassical ode to Coolidge is by Amity Shlaes, *Coolidge* (New York: Harper, 2013). The quote from Coolidge is cited in Ed Driscoll, "Interview: Amity Shlaes Discusses Coolidge," posted on http://pjmedia.com/eddriscoll/2013/02/11/amity-shlaes-coolidge-interview/.

13. Friedman and Friedman, *Free to Choose*, chapter 1.

14. Milton Friedman, *Capitalism and Freedom*, p. 9

15. Ibid., p. 15.

16. Ibid., p. 9.

17. Ibid., p. 8.

18. Newt Gingrich, cited in FoxNews, Newt Gingrich, "The 'Food Stamp President' vs the 'Paycheck President,'" August 12, 2012, posted on http://nation.foxnews.com/newt-gingrich/2012/08/12/newt-pay-check-president-vs-food-stamp-president#ixzz2R3ByOGaG.

19. Max Weber, *Economy and Society*, 4th ed. (Berkeley: University of California Press, 1978).

20. Hayek, *The Road to Serfdom*, p. 67.

21. Charles Derber, *Corporation Nation* (New York: St. Martin's Press, 2000).

22. David Korten, *When Corporations Rule the World* (San Fransisco: Berrett-Koehler, 1997).

23. The concept of corpocracy is developed by Derber in *Corporation Nation*, which argues that corporate power has reduced electoral democracy into ritual procedures that offer no serious power to ordinary citizens.

24. Milton Friedman, *Capitalism and Freedom*, chapter 2.

25. Derber, *Corporation Nation*, chapter 8.

26. Paul Krugman, "Depression and Democracy," *New York Times*, December 11, 2011.

27. Ibid.

28. Paul Krugman, *End This Depression Now!* (New York: Norton, 2012).

29. Ibid. See also Robert Kuttner, *Everything for Sale* (Chicago: University of Chicago Press, 1999); Joseph Stiglitz, *Globalization and Its Discontents* (New York: Norton, 2003); Robert Reich, *Beyond Outrage* (New York: Vintage, 2012).

30. John Kenneth Galbraith, *American Capitalism: The Concept of Countervailing Power* (New York: Transaction Press, 1993).

31. John K. Galbraith, quoted in Ronald Dworkin, "The Moral Reading and the Majoritarian Premise," in Harold Hongju and Ronald Slye (eds.), *Deliberative Democracy and Human Rights* (New Haven, CT: Yale University Press, 1999), p. 101.

32. Galbraith, *American Capitalism*.

33. A. Philip Randolph, "Why We Should March," *Survey Graphic*, November 1942, p. 488.

34. Galbraith, *American Capitalism*.

35. Robert Kuttner, *The Squandering of America* (New York: Vintage, 2008); Robert Reich, *Aftershock* (New York: Vintage, 2011).

36. Robert Reich, "How Capitalism Is Killing Democracy," *Foreign Policy*, September 5, 2007, posted on http://economistsview.typepad.com/economistsview/2007/09/robert-reich-ho.html.

37. John Kenneth Galbraith, *The New Industrial State* (Princeton, NJ: Princeton University Press, 2007). See also Galbraith, *The Affluent Society*, 40th anniversary ed. (Boston: Mariner Press, 1998).

38. Reich, *Aftershock*; Krugman, *End This Depression Now!*

39. Kuttner, *The Squandering of America*.

40. Robert Kuttner, *Obama's Challenge* (White River Junction, VT: Chelsea Green, 2008), chapter 4.

41. Robert Kuttner, *A Presidency in Peril* (White River Junction, VT: Chelsea Green, 2010).

42. Ibid., p. 337.

43. Karl Marx, quoted by Nicholas Latorre, History Hall of Fame (website), June 9, 2011.

44. Friedrich Engels, "On the Origins of the State," in Robert C. Tucker (ed.), *The Marx-Engels Reader* (New York: Norton, 1972), p. 654.

45. Friedrich Engels, private letter in 1892, cited in Doug Henwood, LBO News from Doug Henwood, "Engels, in 1892, Explains USA 120 Years Later,"

January 8, 2012. Posted on http://lbo-news.com/2012/01/18/engels-in-1892-explains -usa-120-years-later/.

46. Derber, *Corporation Nation*. See also Charles Derber, *Marx's Ghost* (Boulder, CO: Paradigm Publishers, 2011).

47. Derber, *Marx's Ghost*.

48. Karl Marx and Friedrich Engels, *The Communist Manifesto*, in Robert C. Tucker (ed.), *The Marx-Engels Reader* (New York: Norton, 1972) p. 337.

49. Ibid.

50. Ibid., pp. 337ff.

51. C. Wright Mills, *The Power Elite* (New York: Oxford University Press, 1959).

52. G. William Domhoff, *Who Rules America?* 6th ed. (New York: McGraw-Hill, 2009); G. William Domhoff, *The Higher Circles* (New York: Vintage, 1971).

53. This is drawn from recent commentary by Domhoff himself on his arguments in *Who Rules America?* See Domhoff, "The Class Domination Theory of Power," April 2005, posted on www2.ucsc.edu/whorulesamerica/power/class_domination.html.

54. Ibid.

55. Stanley Aronowitz, *False Promises*, rev. ed. (Durham, NC: Duke University Press, 1991).

56. Domhoff, "The Class Domination Theory of Power."

57. Ibid.

58. Thomas Ferguson, *The Golden Rule* (Chicago: University of Chicago Press, 1995).

59. Ibid., p. 206.

60. Ibid.

61. Charles Derber, *People before Profit* (New York: Picador, 2003), p. 52.

62. Charles Derber, *Hidden Power* (San Francisco: Berrett-Koehler, 2005).

63. Ibid. See also Charles Derber, *Regime Change Begins at Home* (San Francisco: Berrett-Koehler, 2004).

64. Derber, *Hidden Power*, p. 19.

65. Karl Marx, "Marginal Notes on Bakunin's Statism and Anarchy," in Lawrence Simon, *Karl Marx: Selected Writings* (Indianapolis: Hackett, 1944), p. 334.

66. Marx and Engels, *The Communist Manifesto*, p. 345.

67. Derber, *Marx's Ghost*.

68. Ibid., pp. 113ff.

Chapter 8

1. Milton Friedman, *Capitalism and Freedom*, 40th anniversary ed. (Chicago: University of Chicago Press, 2002), p. 12.

2. Ibid., pp. 8ff.

3. Ibid., p. 8.

4. Ibid.

5. Ibid.

6. Adam Smith, *The Wealth of Nations*, cited in Milton Friedman and Rose Friedman, "Introduction," *Free to Choose* (New York: Harvest, 1990), p. 2.

7. Friedman and Friedman, *Free to Choose*, p. 2.

8. Charles Derber, *Hidden Power* (San Francisco: Berrett-Koehler, 2005), chapter 2.

9. Paul Krugman has launched from his *New York Times* column an unrelenting Keynesian attack on the Reagan revolution and its evolution into the austerity programs and war on government in the Republican Party of Paul Ryan, John Boehner, and others. See Paul Krugman, *End This Depression Now!* (New York: Norton, 2012).

10. Derber, *Hidden Power*.

11. Alan Wolfe, *Whose Keeper? Social Science and Moral Obligation* (Berkeley: University of California Press, 1991).

12. Friedman, *Capitalism and Freedom*, chapters 1, 2. See also Friedman and Friedman, *Free to Choose*, introduction and chapter 1.

13. Friedman, *Capitalism and Freedom*, p. 13.

14. Ibid., p. 10.

15. John Locke, *Second Treatise* (Cambridge, MA: Hackett, 1980), chapter 2.

16. Max Lerner, "John Marshall and the Campaign of History," in Leonard W. Levy (ed.), *American Constitutional Law: Historical Essays* (New York: Harper, 1996), pp. 47–90.

17. Adam Smith, cited in Friedman, *Capitalism and Freedom*, p. 6.

18. Friedman and Friedman, *Free to Choose*, p. 6.

19. Ibid. Regarding Smith on moral sentiments, see Wolfe, *Whose Keeper?* See also Adam Smith, *The Theory of Moral Sentiments* (New York: Empire Books, 2011).

20. Charles Derber, *Marx's Ghost* (Boulder, CO: Paradigm Publishers, 2011). See also Derber, *Hidden Power*.

21. Frederick Hayek, *The Road to Serfdom* (Chicago: University of Chicago Press, 1944).

22. Krugman, *End This Depression Now!*

23. Charles Derber, *Regime Change Begins at Home* (San Francisco: Berrett-Keoehler, 2004).

24. John Maynard Keynes, quoted in Michael Albert, *Moving Forward: Programme for a Participatory Economy* (Oakland, CA: AK Press, 2000), p. 128.

25. John M. Keynes, *The General Theory of Employment, Interest and Money* (Whitefield, MT: Kessinger, 2010).

26. Robert Heilbroner, *The Worldly Philosophers* (New York: Touchstone, 1986).

27. First draft of the "Declaration of Policy" in the Employment Act of 1946, cited in Robert Lekachman, *The Age of Keynes* (New York: Random House, 1966), p. 171.

28. John Kenneth Galbraith, *The Affluent Society* (Boston: Mariner, 1998).

29. John Kenneth Galbraith, *The Great Crash of 1929* (Boston: Mariner, 2009).

30. John K. Galbraith, *The Affluent Society* (Boston: Houghton Mifflin, 1958), pp. 251–253, 329–333.

31. John Kenneth Galbraith, *The Age of Uncertainty* (Boston: Houghton Mifflin, 1977).

32. Ibid.

33. Lekachman, *The Age of Keynes.*

34. Krugman, *End This Depression Now!*

35. Mitt Romney, fundraiser, May 2012.

36. Paul Krugman, "The 1 Percent's Solution," *New York Times*, April 26, 2013.

37. Derber, *Marx's Ghost.*

38. Karl Marx and Friedrich Engels, *The Communist Manifesto*, in Robert Tucker (ed.), *The Marx-Engels Reader* (New York: Norton, 1978), p. 352.

39. Karl Marx, "Marginal Notes on Bakunins's Statism and Anarchy," in Simons, *Karl Marx: Selected Writings* (Cambridge, MA: Hackett, 1994), p. 333.

40. Karl Marx, "Private Property and Communism," *Economic and Philosophic Manuscripts of 1844*, www.marxists.org/archive/marx/works/1844/manuscripts/comm .htm#44CC5; emphasis in original.

41. Karl Marx, cited on www.brainyquote.com/quotes/authors/k/karl_marx_2 .html#LMUq5TUlCgU9etwG.99.

42. Karl Marx, "Letter to Weydemeyer," 1852, posted on www.marxists.org /archive/marx/works/subject/quotes/index.htm.

43. Harry Braverman, *Labor and Monopoly Capital* (New York: Monthly Review Press, 1974).

44. Karl Marx, *Capital*, vol. 1 (New York: Penguin Classics, 1992), p. 286.

45. Karl Marx, *The Grundrisse*, November 1857 (New York: Penguin, 1993); "Capital," Notebook II.

46. Karl Marx, cited in Derber, *Marx's Ghost*, p. 13.

47. Marx and Engels, *The Communist Manifesto*, p. 337.

48. Charles Derber, *Sociopathic Society: A People's Sociology of the United States* (Boulder, CO: Paradigm Publishers, 2013), p. 203.

49. Ibid., p. 350.

50. Charles Derber, *The Wilding of America*, 5th ed. (New York: Worth Publishers, 2009).

51. Ibid., p. 19.

52. Ibid.

53. Derber, *Sociopathic Society.*

54. Ibid.

55. Ibid.

56. Derber, *Marx's Ghost.*

Chapter 9

1. Immanuel Wallerstein, *The Modern World-System I* (New York: Academic, 1997). See also Charles Derber, People before Profit (New York: Picador, 2003), chapter 2.

2. Thomas Friedman, *The Lexus and the Olive Tree* (New York: Anchor, 2000).

3. Ibid., pp. xxi–xxii.

4. Jeremy Brecher and Tim Costello, *Global Village or Global Pillage?* (Cambridge, MA: South End Press, 1999).

5. Jeremy Brecher and Tim Costello, *Globalization from Below* (Cambridge, MA: South End Press, 2000), p. 5.

6. Cited in Derber, *People before Profit*, p. 36.

7. Adam Smith, *The Wealth of Nations*, Vol. 1, reprint ed. (New York: Bantam Classics, 2003), pp. 422, 458.

8. David Ricardo, *On the Principles of Political Economy and Taxation* (London: John Murray, 1817).

9. Friedman, *The Lexus and the Olive Tree*, chapter 7.

10. Ibid., pp. 112ff.

11. Ibid., p. 104.

12. Ibid., pp. 104–106, 112–114.

13. Milton Friedman and Rose Friedman, *Free to Choose* (New York: Harvest, 1990), pp. 50–51.

14. Ibid.

15. Ibid., p. 39.

16. Cited in Derber, *People before Profit*, p. 24.

17. Friedman, *The Lexus and the Olive Tree*, p. 112.

18. Joseph Stiglitz, *Globalization and Its Discontents* (New York: Norton, 2003); Stiglitz, *Making Globalization Work* (New York: Norton, 2007); Stiglitz, *Freefall* (New York: Norton, 2010).

19. Robert Lekachman, *The Age of Keynes* (New York: Vintage, 1968), pp. 180ff.

20. Stiglitz has written several important books arguing for reforming globalization to permit many of the original Keynesian ideals of preserving full employment and ending poverty. See Stiglitz, *Globalization and Its Discontents*; Stiglitz, *Making Globalization Work*.

21. Stiglitz, *Globalization and Its Discontents*, pp. 12ff.

22. Kevin Danaher, *Ten Reasons to Abolish the IMF and the World Bank* (New York: Seven Stories Press, 2001), p. 11.

23. Barry Bluestone and Ben Harrison, *The Deindustrialization of America* (New York: Basic Books, 1983).

24. Charles Derber and Yale Magrass, *The Surplus American* (Boulder, CO: Paradigm Publishers, 2012).

25. Stiglitz, *Globalization and Its Discontents*; Stiglitz, *Making Globalization Work*; Stiglitz, *Freefall*.

26. Stiglitz, *Globalization and Its Discontents*, pp. 214–216.

27. Stiglitz, *Globalization and Its Discontents*; Stiglitz, *Making Globalization Work*; Stiglitz, *Freefall*.

28. Stiglitz, *Globalization and Its Discontents*.

29. Ibid., p. 214.

30. Ibid., p. 215.

31. Benn Steil, *The Battle for Bretton Woods* (Princeton, NJ: Princeton University Press, 2013).

32. Stiglitz, *Globalization and Its Discontents*, p. 221.

33. Karl Marx and Friedrich Engels, *The Communist Manifesto*, in Robert C. Tucker (ed.), *The Marx-Engels Reader* (New York: Norton, 1972), p. 338.

34. Ibid., p. 339.

35. Ibid., p. 337.

36. Ibid., p. 350.

37. Charles Derber, *Marx's Ghost* (Boulder, CO: Paradigm Publishers, 2011), chapter 34.

38. Ibid., part VI.

39. Marx and Engels, *The Communist Manifesto*, p. 336.

40. Wallerstein, *The Modern World-System I.*

41. Christopher Chase-Dunn and Thomas H. Hall, *Core/Periphery Relations in the Pre-Capitalist Worlds* (Boulder, CO: Westview Press, 1991).

42. Derber, *People before Profit*, p. 42.

43. Ibid., pp. 52ff.

44. Ibid.

45. Derber and Magrass, *The Surplus American.*

46. Ibid.

47. Ibid.

48. Lori Wallach and Michelle Sforza, *The WTO* (New York: Seven Stories Press, 1999), p. 13.

49. Friedman, *The Lexus and the Olive Tree*, p. 112.

50. Wallach and Sforza, *The WTO.*

51. Derber, *People before Profit*, chapter 4.

52. Wallach and Sforza, *The WTO.*

53. Derber, *People before Profit*, chapter 6.

54. Ibid.

55. Ibid. See also Charles Derber, *Greed to Green* (Boulder, CO: Paradigm Publishers, 2009).

Chapter 10

1. The climate scientists making this assessment are Charles H. Greene, Cornell professor of earth and atmospheric sciences and director of Cornell's Ocean Resources and Ecosystems program; Jennifer A. Francis of Rutgers University's Institute of Marine and Coastal Sciences; and Bruce C. Monger, Cornell senior research associate, earth and atmospheric sciences. They coauthored a study published in the journal *Oceanography* (March 2013). C. H. Greene, J. A. Francis, and B. C. Monger, "Superstorm Sandy: A Series of Unfortunate Events?" *Oceanography* 26(1): 8–9, http://dx.doi.org/10.5670/oceanog.2013.11. For a summary online, see Friedlander Blaine, "Arctic

Ice Loss Amplified Superstorm Sandy Violence," March 4, 2013, www.news.cornell
.edu/stories/2013/03/arctic-ice-loss-amplified-superstorm-sandy-violence.

2. These data are reported in Justin Gillis, "Not Even Close: 2012 Was Hottest
Ever in US," *New York Times*, January 9, 2013, www.nytimes.com/2013/01/09/science
/earth/2012-was-hottest-year-ever-in-us.html?_r=0.

3. Maureen Raymo, cited in Justin Gillis, "Heat-Trapping Gas Passes Milestone,
Raising Fears," *New York Times*, May 11, 2013, p. A1.

4. Gillis, "Heat-Trapping Gas Passes Milestone," p. A1.

5. Charles Derber, *Greed to Green* (Boulder, CO: Paradigm Publishers, 2009).

6. Ibid., chapter 7.

7. Barack Obama, Second Inaugural Address, January 21, 2013, http://
articles.washingtonpost.com/2013-01-21/politics/36473487_1_president-obama
-vice-president-biden-free-market.

8. Milton Friedman and Rose Friedman, *Free to Choose* (New York: Harvest,
1990), p. 27.

9. Jacqueline Medalye, "Neoclassical, Institutional and Marxist Approaches to the
Environment-Economics Relationship," *Encyclopedia of the Earth*, November 1, 2010,
www.eoearth.org/article/Neoclassical,_institutional,_and_marxist_approaches_to
_the_environment-economic_relationship.

10. Ibid.

11. Tom Friedman, *Hot, Flat, and Crowded* (New York: Farrar, Straus and Giroux,
2008), pp. 243–244.

12. Ibid., p. 244.

13. Ibid.

14. Ibid.

15. Cited in Friedman, *Hot, Flat, and Crowded*, p. 259.

16. A leading economist writing on the need to limit consumption to save the
environment and create a better society is Juliet Schor, *Plenitude* (New York: Penguin,
2010).

17. Robert Kuttner, "Notes from a Manifesto," *Huffington Post*, November 4,
2012.

18. Ibid.

19. Ibid.

20. Joseph Stiglitz, "A New Agenda for Global Warming," *Economists' Voice*, Bepress
.com/Ev, July 2006. See the more developed argument in Stiglitz, *Making Globalization
Work* (New York: Norton, 2007).

21. Stiglitz, *Making Globalization Work*.

22. Paul Krugman, *End This Depression Now!* (New York: Norton, 2012).

23. Robert Kuttner, *Obama's Challenge* (White River Junction, VT: Chelsea Green,
2008), chapter 4.

24. Ibid.

25. Derber, *Greed to Green*.

26. Barack Obama, cited in Kuttner, *Obama's Challenge*, pp. 123–124.

27. Derber, *Greed to Green*.

28. The limits of growth are crucial for consideration in any environmental solution. The issue is highlighted in the pioneering book by Herman Daly, *Beyond Growth: The Economics of Sustainable Development* (Boston: Beacon, 1997).

29. Schor, *Plenitude*.

30. Friedrich Engels, *The Dialectic of Nature* (New York: International, 1979), chapter 9.

31. Karl Marx, *Capital*, vol. 1, edited by Ernest Mandel (New York: Penguin, 1992), p. 638.

32. Ibid.

33. Charles Derber, *Marx's Ghost* (Boulder, CO: Paradigm Publishers, 2011).

34. See John Bellamy Foster, *The Ecological Rift* (New York: Monthly Review Press, 2011); John Bellamy Foster, *Marx's Ecology: Materialism and Nature* (New York: Monthly Review Press, 2000); David Harvey, *Rebel Cities* (London: Verso, 2012); Derber, *Greed to Green*, chapters 9, 10.

35. Friedrich Engels, quoted in Derber, *Marx's Ghost*, p. 96.

36. John Mackey, *Conscious Capitalism* (Cambridge, MA: Harvard University Press, 2012).

37. John Bellamy Foster, "Occupy Denialism: Toward Ecological and Social Revolution," Znet, November 12, 2011, www.zcommunications.org/occupy-denialism -toward-ecological-and-social-revolution-by-john-bellamy-foster.

38. Ibid.

39. Ibid.

40. Ibid.

41. Juliet Schor, *Born to Buy* (New York: Scribner, 2005).

42. Derber, *Greed to Green*.

43. Marx, *Capital*, vol. 1, chapter 1.

44. Juliet Schor, *True Wealth* (New York: Penguin, 2011), pp. 128–129.

45. Ibid., p. 26.

46. Ibid., chapter 3.

47. Ibid., p. 130.

48. Derber, *Greed to Green*, chapters 9, 10.

Chapter 11

1. Milton Friedman, *Capitalism and Freedom*, 40th anniversary ed. (Chicago: University of Chicago Press, 2002), p. 96.

2. Kingsley Davis and Wilbert Moore, "Some Principles of Stratification," *American Sociological Review* 10, no. 2 (1944): 244.

3. Quoted in Shawn Lawrence Otto, "America's Science Problem," *Scientific American* (November 2012): 71.

4. Lynne Cheney, *Telling the Truth* (New York: Touchstone, 1996).

5. Matt Cohen, "The Myth of 'Throwing Money at the Problem,'" *Huffington Post*, May 4, 2011.

6. "No Child Left Behind," *Education Week*, September 19, 2011.

7. Michelle Rhee, "Poverty Must Be Tackled but Never Used as an Excuse," *Huffington Post*, September 5, 2012.

8. Jacques Steinberg and Diana B. Henriques, "Complex Calculations on Academics," *New York Times*, July 16, 2002.

9. Tamar Lewin, "Senate Committee Report on For-Profit Colleges Condemns Costs and Practices," *New York Times*, July 29, 2012.

10. Ibid.

11. Aaron Maslow, Matt Bernard, and Jonathan Katz, *Boston Busing Crisis*, documentary film, 2013.

12. Lyndon Johnson, "Great Society Speech," Ann Arbor, Michigan, May 22, 1964.

13. Robert Reich, *The Work of Nations* (New York: Vintage, 1992), p. 230.

14. National Association of Student Financial Aid Administrators, www.nasfaa.org.

15. Thomas G. Mortenson, "State Funding: A Race to the Bottom," *American Council on Education* (Winter 2012).

16. Melissa Block, "Student Loan Debt Exceeds One Trillion Dollars," NPR, April 24, 2012.

17. Josh Mitchell and May Jackson-Randall, "Student-Loan Debt Tops $1 Trillion," *Wall Street Journal*, March 22, 2012.

18. Robert Reich, "The Problem Isn't Outsourcing," *Huffington Post*, July 19, 2012.

19. Ibid.

20. Barack Obama, State of the Union Address, February 12, 2013.

21. Ibid.

22. Ibid.

23. Samuel Bowles and Herbert Gintis, *Schooling in Capitalist America* (New York: Harper, 1977).

24. John Dewey quoted in ibid., p. 22.

25. Bowles and Gintis, *Schooling in Capitalist America*, p. 131.

26. Jody Fester, "Military Recruit Provisions under the No Child Left Behind Act," *Congressional Research Service Report to Congress*, January 8, 2008.

27. Paul Willis, *Learning to Labor* (New York: Columbia, 1977), pp. 149–150.

28. Richard Sennett and Jonathan Cobb, *The Hidden Injuries of Class* (New York: Norton, 1993).

29. Ibid., pp. 158, 159.

30. Bowles and Gintis, *Schooling in Capitalist America*, pp. 42, 43.

31. Stanley Aronowitz, preface to Willis, *Learning to Labor*, p. x.

Chapter 12

1. Martin Luther King Jr., "I Have a Dream Speech," Washington, DC, August 28, 1963.

2. Martin Luther King Jr., Speech on Vietnam, New York, April 4, 1967.

3. Cheryl Bentsen, "Henry Louis Gates Jr.: Head Negro in Charge," *Boston Magazine*, April 1998.

4. Jonathan Marshall, "William Graham Sumner: Critic of Progressive Liberalism," *Journal of Libertarian Studies* (2004).

5. Arthur Jensen, "How Much Can We Boost IQ and Scholastic Achievement?" *Harvard Education Review* 39 (1969): 1–123.

6. Richard Herrnstein and Charles Murray, *The Bell Curve* (New York: Free Press, 1994).

7. Milton Friedman, *Capitalism and Freedom*, 40th anniversary ed. (Chicago: University of Chicago Press, 2002), p. 109.

8. Thom Hartmann and Sam Sacks, "Reagan's 'Welfare Queen' FOUND!" Truth-out, December 3, 2012.

9. Dick Williams, *Newt!* (New Orleans: Longstreet, 1995), pp. 3–4.

10. Ibid., pp. 33–34.

11. Thomas Sowell, "Affirmative Action: A World-Wide Disaster," *Commentary*, December 1989, p. 28.

12. Ibid., p. 35.

13. Ibid., pp. 34, 35.

14. Ibid., p. 26.

15. Barack Obama, Acceptance Speech, Democratic Convention, Denver, Colorado, August 27, 2008.

16. Barack Obama, Speech on Race, Philadelphia, March 18, 2008.

17. Ibid.

18. William Julius Wilson and Henry Louis Gates, "The Two Nations of Black America," *Frontline*, February 10, 1998.

19. Ibid.

20. William Julius Wilson, *The Truly Disadvantaged* (Chicago: University of Chicago Press, 1990); William Julius Wilson, *The Declining Significance of Race* (Chicago: University of Chicago Press, 2012).

21. W. E. B. Du Bois, "The Talented Tenth," Teaching History Document Library, September 1903.

22. "More Black Men in Jail Than in College," Justice Policy Institute, Washington, DC, August 30, 2002.

23. Robert Reich, "The Stealth Attack on American Education," January 9, 2011, http://robertreich.org/post/2420649887.

24. Satyananda Gabriel, "Continuing Significance of Race," *Rethinking Marxism* 3, no. 3–4 (Fall–Winter 1990).

25. Howard Winant, "Racism Today: Continuity and Change in the Post–Civil Rights Era," *Ethnic and Racial Studies* 21, no. 4 (1998).

26. Karl Marx and Friedrich Engels, *The Communist Manifesto* (New York: Norton, 2012).

27. Wilson and Gates, "The Two Nations of Black America."

28. "Vernon Jordan," *Forbes*, www.forbes.com/profile/vernon-jordan-1/.

29. Jim Kirwan, *Slavery Transformed America*, http://rense.com/general88/slavery.htm, November 25, 2009.

30. Eugene Genovese, *The Political Economy of Slavery* (Middleton, CT: Wesleyan, 1988); Eugene Genovese and Frances Fox-Genovese, *The Mind of the Master Class* (Cambridge, UK: Cambridge University Press, 2005).

31. Stanley Aronowitz, *False Promises* (New York: McGraw-Hill, 1973), p. 198.

32. Karl Marx, "Letter to Abraham Lincoln," January 28, 1865.

33. W. E. B. Du Bois, *Black Reconstruction in America* (Piscataway, NJ: Transaction, 2013), p. 30.

34. Obama, Speech on Race.

35. Rakesh Kochhar, Richard Fry, and Paul Taylor, "Wealth Gaps Rise to Record Highs between Whites, Blacks, Hispanics," *Pew Social Trends*, July 2011.

36. Michelle Alexander, *The New Jim Crow* (New York: New Press, 2012).

Chapter 13

1. All above quotes cited in post by Alex Leo, "Quotes from the War on Women," August 30, 2012, posted on http://alexleo.tumblr.com/post/30553490224 /quotes-from-the-war-on-women.

2. Arlie Russell Hochschild, *The Second Shift* (New York: Avon Books, 1990).

3. Katherine Adam and Charles Derber, *The New Feminized Majority* (Boulder, CO: Paradigm Publishers, 2009).

4. Gary Becker, *A Treatise on the Family*, expanded ed. (Cambridge, MA: Harvard University Press, 1993).

5. Ibid.

6. David Wesson, "The Economics of Learning," *Wall Street Journal*, April 3, 2013, retrieved April 4, 2013, and posted on http://en.wikipedia.org/wiki/Gary_Becker.

7. Cheryl Sandberg, *Lean In* (New York: Knopf, 2013).

8. David Wessel, "The Positive Economics of 'Leaning In,'" *Wall Street Journal*, April 13, 2013, http://online.wsj.com/article/SB1000142412788732391630457840 0192414995044.h.

9. Becker, *Treatise on the Family*.

10. Milton Friedman, *Capitalism and Freedom*, 40th anniversary ed. (Chicago: University of Chicago Press, 2002), pp. 108–109.

11. Sandberg, *Lean In*.

12. Ibid.

13. Charles Derber and Yale Magrass, *Morality Wars* (Boulder, CO: Paradigm Publishers, 2010), chapter 9.

14. Milton Friedman, *Capitalism and Freedom*; Becker, *Treatise on the Family*.

15. Carmen Reinhart and Kenneth Rogoff, "Growth in a Time of Debt," *American Economic Review: Papers and Proceedings* 100 (May 2010): 573–578. See also Carmen Reinhart and Kenneth Rogoff, *This Time Is Different* (Princeton, NJ: Princeton University Press, 2011).

16. Barack Obama, October 19, 2012, posted on www.politicalruminations.com /equal-pay/.

17. Adam and Derber, *The New Feminized Majority*.

18. Ibid.

19. Robert Heilbroner, *The Worldly Philosophers* (New York: Touchstone, 1986).

20. Paul Krugman, *Conscience of a Liberal* (New York: Norton, 2007).

21. Robert Lekachman, *The Age of Keynes* (New York: Random House, 1966); Heilbroner, *The Worldly Philosophers*.

22. Robert Reich, *Beyond Outrage* (New York: Vintage, 2012); Joseph Stiglitz, *The Price of Inequality* (New York: Norton, 2012).

23. Robert Kuttner, *Obama's Challenge* (White River Junction, VT: Chelsea Green, 2008), pp. 146–147.

24. Amity Shlaes, *Coolidge* (New York: Harper, 2013).

25. Paul Krugman, *End This Depression Now!* (New York: Norton, 2012); Stiglitz, *The Price of Inequality*; Reich, *Beyond Outrage*.

26. In this section on Marx and Engels writings on women and the family, I have found most useful, beyond their own writings, the synthesis offered by Hal Draper. See Draper, "Marx and Lenin on Women's Liberation," July 1979, www.marxists.org /archive/draper/1970/07/women.htm.

27. Karl Marx, *Economic and Philosophic Manuscripts of 1844* (Moscow: Foreign Languages Publishing House, 1961), p. 101; emphasis in the original.

28. Ibid.

29. Karl Marx and Friedrich Engels, *The Communist Manifesto*, in Lawrence Simon (ed.), *Karl Marx: Selected Writings* (New York: Hackett, 1994), p. 350.

30. Ibid.

31. Marx, "Abstract of Morgan's *Ancient Society*," quoted by Engels in *On the Origins of the Family, Private Property, and the State*. Cited in Marx and Engels, *Selected Works* (Moscow: Foreign Languages Publishing House, 1955), p. 217.

32. Engels, *On the Origins of the Family*.

33. Ibid., p. 226.

34. Ibid., p. 232.

35. Ibid.

36. Karl Marx, *Capital*, vol. 1, reprinted in Robert C. Tucker (ed.), *The Marx-Engels Reader* (New York: Norton, 1972), pp. 300–301.

37. Ibid.

38. Charles Derber, *Marx's Ghost* (Boulder, CO: Paradigm Publishers, 2011).

39. The analysis of different feminisms—bourgeois, socialist, and separatist—is developed succinctly in "Feminism 101," Red Letter Press, www.redletterpress .org/feminism101.html. See also Janet Sutherland, "Clara Fraser: Quintessential Feminist and Revolutionary," *Freedom Socialist*, April 1998, http://socialism.com /drupal-6.8/?q=node/1293.

40. Letter, Engels to G. Guillaume-Schack, July 5, 1885, in Karl Marx and Friedrich Engels, *Selected Correspondence* (Moscow: Foreign Languages Publishing House, 1956), pp. 461–462, corrected after Karl Marx and Friedrich Engels, *Werke* (Berlin: Dietz, 1961–1968), vol. 36, p. 341.

41. Red Letter Press, "Feminism 101."

42. Ibid.

43. Sharon Kurtz, *Workplace Justice: Organizing Multi-Identity Movements* (Minneapolis: University of Minnesota Press, 2002).

44. bell hooks, cited on www.goodreads.com/author/quotes/10697.bell_hooks ?page=2.

45. bell hooks, *Feminist Theory: From Margin to Center* (Boston: South End Press, 2000), p. 36.

46. Ibid., p. 75.

47. bell hooks, *Where We Stand: Class Matters* (New York: Routledge, 2000).

48. Derber and Magrass, *Morality Wars*.

49. Ibid.

Chapter 14

1. As noted in Chapter 1, we are hardly the first to make these arguments. Among the most forceful twentieth-century advocates of this view have been economists themselves, such as John Kenneth Galbraith, who built a career challenging the orthodoxy of his own profession. See his *History of Economics* (New York: Penguin, 1998), which makes clear that economic ideas always reflect social context rather than universal laws; and his autobiography, *A Life in Our Times* (New York: Ballantine, 1982). The astute economics commentator and journalist, Robert Kuttner, has also made persuasive arguments to this effect, most colorfully in "The Poverty of Economics," *Atlantic Magazine*, February 1985. Other less known but cogent and recent critics who have made these arguments include sociologist Frans Doorman, "Crisis, Economics, and the Emperor's Clothes," www.new-economics.info /CrisisEconomicsandtheEmperorsClothes.pdf, 2012. See also economist Paul Ormerod, *The Death of Economics* (New York: St. Martin's Press, 1995); and economist Deirdre N. McCloskey, *The Vices of Economics—and the Virtues of the Bourgeoisie* (Amsterdam: Amsterdam University Press, 1997).

2. Robert Kuttner, "The Poverty of Economics," pp. 74, 76.

3. In the 1960s, students and young professionals formed organizations to do exactly this, including groups such as Science for the People and Sociologists for the People. Such groups sought to turn their professions into value-based, interdisciplinary scholarship that aligned scholarship with advocacy, precisely what is needed on a larger scale today.

4. See Charles Derber, *Sociopathic Society: A People's Sociology of the United States* (Boulder, CO: Paradigm Publishers, 2013).

5. For early, profound, US sociological analysis of this, see C. Wright Mills, *The Power Elite* (New York: Oxford University Press, 1959).

6. Charles Derber, *Marx's Ghost* (Boulder, CO: Paradigm Publishers, 2011). See also Charles Derber, *Corporation Nation* (New York: St. Martin's Press, 2000); and Charles Derber, *People before Profit* (New York: Picador, 2003).

7. Derber, *Marx's Ghost*; Derber, *Corporation Nation*.

8. Derber, *Marx's Ghost*.

9. These critiques are made by Keynesians such as Paul Krugman, *End This Depression Now!* (New York: Norton, 2012), and neo-Marxists, such as Derber, *Marx's Ghost*.

10. Robert Lekachman, *The Age of Keynes* (New York: Vintage, 1968).

11. The three most influential and incisive Keynesians making these arguments are John Kenneth Galbraith, *The New Industrial State* (Princeton, NJ: Princeton University Press, 2007); Paul Krugman, *End This Depression Now!*; Joseph Stiglitz, *The Price of Inequality* (New York: Norton, 2013).

12. Krugman, *End This Depression Now!*; Stiglitz, *The Price of Inequality*.

13. Robert Reich, *Beyond Outrage* (New York: Vintage, 2012); Robert Kuttner, *A Presidency in Peril* (White River Junction, VT: Chelsea Green, 2010).

14. This is the argument and metaphor repeated frequently by Krugman, *End This Depression Now!*

15. Keynesians often seem to regulate these constraints but nonetheless cling to the public investment strategies well within the capitalist system. See Kuttner, *A Presidency in Peril*. See also Reich, *Beyond Outrage*.

16. See three important critical works of Joseph Stiglitz: *Globalization and Its Discontents* (New York: Norton, 2003); *Making Globalization Work* (New York: Norton, 2007); *Freefall* (New York: Norton, 2010).

17. Charles Derber and Yale Magrass, *The Surplus American* (Boulder, CO: Paradigm Publishers, 2012).

18. Derber, *Sociopathic Society*. See also Derber, *Marx's Ghost*.

19. Derber, *Marx's Ghost*.

20. Derber, *Marx's Ghost*; Derber, *Sociopathic Society*.

21. Ibid.

22. Ibid.

23. Derber, *Marx's Ghost*. See also Charles Derber and Yale Magrass, *Morality Wars* (Boulder, CO: Paradigm Publishers, 2010).

24. Derber, *Marx's Ghost*; Derber and Magrass, *Morality Wars*, part IV.

25. Alvin Gouldner, *The Two Marxisms* (New York: Oxford University Press, 1982).

26. Derber, *Marx's Ghost*; Derber and Magrass, *Morality Wars*, part IV.

27. Robert Kuttner, *Obama's Challenge* (White River Junction, VT: Chelsea Green, 2008); Van Jones, *The Green Collar Economy* (New York: HarperOne, 2009).

28. Derber, *Sociopathic Society*.

29. Ibid. See also Derber, *Marx's Ghost*.

30. Gar Alperovitz, *What Is to Be Done?* (White River Junction, VT: Chelsea Green Publishers, 2013).

31. Gar Alperovitz and David Barsimian, "A New Economic Paradigm: An Interview with Gar Alperovitz," May 15, 2012, Truth-out, http://truth-out.org/news/item/9144-a-new-economic-paradigm-an-interview-with-gar-alperowitz.

32. Ibid.

33. Ibid.

34. David Korten, *Agenda for a New Economy* (San Francisco: Berrett-Koehler Publishers, 2009), pp. 128–129.

35. Juliet Schor, *True Wealth* (New York: Penguin, 2011), pp. 180–181.

36. Ibid., p. 157.

37. Korten, *Agenda for a New Economy*, p. 45.

38. Charles Derber, *Greed to Green* (Boulder, CO: Paradigm Publishers, 2010), p. 125.

39. Ibid., p. 133.

40. James Speth, *The Bridge at the End of the World* (New Haven, CT: Yale University Press, 2008), p. 57.

41. Schor, *True Wealth*, p. 174.

42. Ibid., pp. 127ff.

43. Derber, *Sociopathic Society*.

Index

About the Authors

Charles Derber, Professor of Sociology at Boston College, has written seventeen books, translated into six languages. A noted public intellectual, he has published columns in the *New York Times*, the *Boston Globe*, the *Christian Science Monitor*, *Truthout*, *Newsday*, and many other media. His most recent book is *Sociopathic Society: A People's Sociology of the United States* (Paradigm Publishers 2013).

Yale R. Magrass is a Chancellor Professor of Sociology at the University of Massachusetts–Dartmouth, where he teaches social theory, political sociology, social movements, the social impact of science and technology, and a seminar on millennials versus baby boomers. He is the author of four other books and more than fifty articles, including encyclopedia entries and international public media, has served on the board of six journals, has been a recipient of several grants, and has participated in numerous international forums.